BASIC CONSTITUTIONAL CASES

Basic

CONSTITUTIONAL

Cases

EDITED WITH INTRODUCTORY NOTES BY

C. Gordon POST · Frances P. DeLANCY · Fredryc R. DARBY

DEPARTMENT OF POLITICAL SCIENCE, VASSAR COLLEGE

NEW YORK

OXFORD UNIVERSITY PRESS

1948

PRINTED IN THE UNITED STATES OF AMERICA

Preface

This collection of cases is intended primarily for use in the introductory course in American government and is designed to supplement the standard texts. Its object is to introduce the student to a study of cases, and to give him a deeper understanding and appreciation of the significance of courts and case-law in the American system of government. It is not the editors' intention to cover or even to touch upon, however briefly, the entire field of constitutional law, or to include the last word of the Supreme Court on any particular constitutional question.

In 1946 Vassar College published *Twenty Cases on the Constitution,* a small collection of Supreme Court opinions edited by the present collaborators. This volume was used for two years in our course in American national government and is now out of print. The present book is in no sense a reissue of *Twenty Cases on the Constitution,* for it not only includes thirty-one cases instead of twenty, but also the organization of the material has been changed so completely as to make of this a virtually new presentation.

The editors gratefully acknowledge their indebtedness to Edward S. Corwin of Princeton University, Carl Brent Swisher of the Johns Hopkins University, Harold Zink of DePauw University, and Harlow J. Heneman, formerly of the University of Michigan and now of the Department of State, all of whom, by their helpful criticism and friendly advice, greatly improved this book. The editors also are happy to express their appreciation for the able and courteous assistance given them by William M. Oman of the Oxford University Press.

C. Gordon Post
Frances P. DeLancy
Fredryc R. Darby

January 1948
Vassar College

Contents

vii

Introduction

The Supreme Court of the United States, the most powerful judicial tribunal in the world, meets in Washington on the first Monday of each October. It remains in intermittent session until the following June, recessing from time to time for considerable periods so that the nine justices may concentrate on the reading of briefs, passing upon petitions, and on the writing of opinions in cases which have been considered.

Most cases come before the Supreme Court on appeal from lower courts. After the appeal has been allowed, counsel for each side provides the Court with briefs in advance of oral argument. The Supreme Court *Rules* prescribe the contents of the brief. It must contain, for example, a statement of the facts, an assignment of errors, the legal question involved, the argument, and a conclusion. These briefs are printed at the expense of the parties.[1]

Formal argument takes place after the briefs are submitted at the convenience of Court and calendar. In the early days, when cases were few, there was no time-limit upon counsels' argument. Mr. Justice Story, who was on the Court from 1811 to 1845, declared that the mode 'of arguing causes in the Supreme Court is excessively prolix and tedious.'[2] In a case that came before the Court shortly after Story's appointment, the printed brief consisted of 230 pages and the argument lasted five days.[3] With an increase in the number of cases coming before the Court, it was necessary to limit argument for each side to two hours, and then later to one hour. No witnesses appear before the Court. During argument, the justices are free to address questions to counsel for either side in the case.

The next step in the process of deciding a case is the conference. Here the justices discuss the case. The Chief Justice states his opinion first, the latest appointee states his last. Then a vote is taken, the Chief Justice voting last. If all the justices are agreed in regard to the decision, the Chief Justice assigns the writing of the opinion. If the Court is divided and the Chief Justice is with the majority, he allots the writing of the opinion to one of the majority. Should the Chief Justice side with the minority, then the assignment of the Court's opinion falls upon the senior Associate Justice with the majority. Whichever side the Chief Justice supports, he may at his discretion undertake to write the opinion for that side.

---

[1] Any citizen unable to meet the cost of a suit or action in a United States court, including the printing of briefs in appellate proceedings, has recourse to a fund provided by the government. 28 U.S.C.A. §§ 832-6.

[2] Quoted in Warren, Charles, *The Supreme Court in United States History*, Boston, 1935, I, p. 423.

[3] Ibid. p. 424.

The opinion of the majority is spoken of as the majority opinion or the opinion of the Court. If a justice agrees with the majority in regard to the decision but differs regarding the reasons for the decision, he will more than likely write what is called a concurring opinion. If a justice disagrees with the decision of the majority he is at liberty to set forth the reasons for his disagreement in a dissenting opinion.[4]

THE JUSTICES OF THE SUPREME COURT

Though the Constitution does not require that the justices of the Supreme Court shall be lawyers, all of them, in fact, have been members of the legal profession. Some of the justices have come to the Court with little judicial background; most of them have been practicing attorneys; others have had large political or administrative experience; approximately half have come to the Court with judicial experience behind them.

Once appointed to the Supreme Court, a justice is supposed to drop the trappings of political partisanship. Unlike Congress or the Executive, where a man who is not a loyal party adherent is suspect, the Supreme Court is alleged to be free of partisanship; in fact, partisanship is frowned upon.

A Supreme Court justice does not have to be partisan. He cannot be removed except by impeachment. President Theodore Roosevelt appointed Oliver Wendell Holmes, Jr., to the Supreme Court after much thought and after convincing himself that Holmes would decide cases 'properly.' As Holmes wrote later, Roosevelt 'looked on my dissent to the *Northern Securities case* as a political departure (or, I suspect, more truly, couldn't forgive anyone who stood in his way) . . . if he had not been restrained by his friends, I am told that he would have made a fool of himself and would have excluded me from the White House. . .'[5] A President will always choose men whose opinions in his judgment will be 'right.' Once a justice is appointed to the Supreme Court, however, tenure and the absence of a need for partisanship provide him with conditions conducive to independent judgment, so necessary in a democracy.

ORIGINAL JURISDICTION

The Supreme Court has both original and appellate jurisdiction. By original jurisdiction is meant the power of the Court, conferred by Article III of the Constitution, to entertain a case or controversy as a court of first instance. It means that instead of being heard originally in a lower court, the case is taken

---

[4] All opinions of the Court are found in the Supreme Court *Reports.* The *Reports* prior to 1875 are cited by name of the court reporter who prepared them for publication: Dallas, 4 vols., 1790-1800; Cranch, 9 vols., 1801-15; Wheaton, 12 vols., 1816-27; Peters, 16 vols., 1828-42; Howard, 24 vols., 1843-60; Black, 2 vols., 1861-2; Wallace, 23 vols., 1863-74. Beginning with the 1875 volume, which is cited as 91 U.S., the volumes are numbered consecutively. There are two unofficial publications of Supreme Court decisions: *United States Supreme Court Reporter,* cited as S.Ct., beginning with the opinions found in 106 U.S.; and *United States Supreme Court Reports, Lawyers' Edition,* cited as L.Ed.

[5] *Holmes-Pollock Letters,* ed. by Howe, Mark DeWolfe, Cambridge, 1941, II, pp. 63-4.

directly to the Supreme Court. This power extends to all cases 'affecting ambassadors,[6] other public ministers, and consuls, and those in which a State shall be a party. . .' If one state desires to prevent the negligent deposit by another state, in an interstate stream, of drainage containing typhoid germs, because dangerous to the health of the inhabitants of the former, it may take the issue directly to the Supreme Court.

APPELLATE JURISDICTION

In all other cases within the purview of Federal judicial power, the Supreme Court hears and decides cases that have already been decided or are in process of being decided in the lower courts. This is called appellate jurisdiction. The appellate jurisdiction of the Supreme Court is exercised 'with such exceptions and under such regulations as the Congress shall make.'[7]

THE JUDICIAL CODE

Federal statutes governing the judiciary were revised, amended, and codified in what is called the Judicial Code. This code became effective 1 January 1912, and has been amended many times. The Judicial Code with its amendments and revisions is part of the United States Code, a compilation of the laws of the United States of a general and permanent character in force 3 January 1941. Since the issuance of the 1940 edition there have been several Supplements containing revisions and amendments.

Title 28 of the United States Code is entitled 'Judicial Code and the Judiciary.' In conformity with Article III of the Constitution, Title 28, as amended, governs the organization, jurisdiction, and procedure of the Federal judicial system. It regulates the appellate jurisdiction of the Supreme Court.

METHODS OF REVIEW

The Judicial Code provides for three methods whereby cases are appealed to the Supreme Court: (a) by appeal; (b) by certificate; and (c) by writ of certiorari.

(a) In general, the term 'appeal' applies to any method whatsoever by which a case is carried from a lower court to a higher court for review. This is not the meaning of the term as it is used here.

The term 'appeal' in a narrower and more technical sense means an appeal as of right, involving no discretion on the part of the higher court whether it will entertain the cause, and depending solely upon the wishes of one of the parties to the suit in the lower court.

(b) The term 'certificate' relates to a method of appeal whereby a lower court 'certifies' to a higher court certain questions of law the answers to which

---

[6] Under international law, diplomatic officers are not subject to our courts. See Hackworth, Green Haywood, *Digest of International Law*, Washington, 1942, IV, pp. 513-604.

[7] Art. III.

are important in a case pending in the lower court. Unlike the 'appeal,' this method of review is not within the control of the litigants or parties to the suit, but of the lower court.

(c) 'Certiorari,' which means 'to be informed more fully,' is also within the control of the court, but this time the higher court. The party adversely affected by the decision of the lower court petitions the higher court for a writ of certiorari. If the petition is granted, the higher court then issues the writ to the lower court, which is then required to send up the entire record of the case for review. But it is within the discretion of the higher court whether the writ will issue.

COURTS TO WHICH THE SUPREME COURT'S APPELLATE JURISDICTION APPLIES

The appellate jurisdiction of the Supreme Court applies to the following courts: the Federal District Courts, the Circuit Courts of Appeals, the Court of Appeals of the District of Columbia,[8] and certain courts of the forty-eight states.

Federal District Courts. The Judicial Code provides for direct review by the Supreme Court, on *appeal,* of a final judgment or decree of a Federal District Court in the following cases only:

(a) in suits brought by the United States to enforce the anti-trust and inter-state commerce laws;

(b) under the Criminal Appeals Act where the District Court has decided against the United States;

(c) in suits to enjoin the operation and enforcement of state statutes or the order of a state administrative board;

(d) in suits to enjoin enforcement of the orders of the Interstate Commerce Commission;

(e) in suits to set aside the orders of the Secretary of Agriculture under the Packers and Stockyards Act;

(f) in suits involving the constitutionality of an act of Congress.

In all other cases, decisions of the District Courts may be reviewed by the Circuit Courts of Appeals.

Circuit Courts of Appeals and the *Court of Appeals of the District of Columbia.* In any case, civil or criminal, these courts may *certify* to the Supreme Court any questions of law concerning which instructions are desired for a proper decision of the cause. Also, the Supreme Court, upon petition of one of the parties to the suit, may require by *certiorari* that the cause be *certified* to it for review.

In any case (this applies to the Circuit Courts of Appeals only) where a

---

[8] These are all 'constitutional courts,' established by Congress by virtue of Article III of the Constitution. We have omitted consideration of such courts as the Court of Claims, the Court of Customs and Patent Appeals, and the territorial courts. These are called 'legislative courts' and they have been created by Congress on the basis of powers conferred in Article I. They are not part of the 'regular' Federal judicial system.

state statute is alleged to be repugnant to the Constitution, treaties, or laws of the United States, and the decision is against its validity, the party relying upon the state statute may carry the case to the Supreme Court on *appeal*.

State Courts. The Judicial Code confers upon the Supreme Court the power to review certain decisions of the highest state courts in which a decision could be had.[9]

In the following cases the Supreme Court will review the decision of the state court on *appeal*:

(a) where the validity of a treaty or statute of the United States is questioned and the decision is against its validity;

(b) where the validity of a state statute is questioned on the ground that it is repugnant to the Constitution, treaties, or laws of the United States, and the decision upholds its validity.

The Supreme Court may by *certiorari* require that certain cases be *certified* to it for review and determination whether the Federal claim has been sustained or not. These are:

(a) where the validity of a treaty or statute is questioned;

(b) where a state statute is questioned as being repugnant to the Constitution, treaties, or laws of the United States;

(c) or where any title, right, or privilege is claimed by either party to a suit under the Constitution, treaties, or laws of the United States.

[9] In all cases the highest court is not necessarily the court of last resort in the state.

Table of Cases

This is a selected table of cases. The cases printed in italics comprise the main text of this volume. The other cases listed are discussed sufficiently in the Notes or opinions to make reference to them useful.

The Development of the Constitution

NOTE

In *Marbury* v. *Madison* the Supreme Court for the first time declared an Act of Congress unconstitutional. From 1803 to the present, the Court, exercising the power of judicial review, has played the role of arbiter in American constitutional development.

Judicial review was little discussed at the convention of 1787. What discussion there was arose in connection with the veto power. The Virginia plan, for example, provided that 'the Executive and a convenient number of the National Judiciary, ought to compose a council of revision with authority to examine every act of the National Legislature before it shall operate . . . and that the dissent of the said Council shall amount to a rejection. . .'[1] Similar proposals were made at different times during the proceedings, but each was rejected.

Although opposed to a council of revision, a number of convention leaders assumed the power of courts to invalidate legislative acts. Gerry spoke of the power of judges to decide on the constitutionality of laws. Rufus King declared that the judges 'will no doubt stop the operation of such [laws] as shall appear repugnant to the constitution.'[2] And Madison was of the opinion that a 'law violating a constitution established by the people themselves, would be considered by the Judges as null & void.'[3]

By 1787 the states already had a history of judicial review. Gerry, speaking in the convention, asserted that in 'some States the Judges had [actually] set aside laws as being agst. the Constitution. This was done too with general approbation.'[4] Between 1780 and 1787 there had been a number of decisions or dicta in the state courts to the effect that an unconstitutional legislative act might be disregarded by the courts.[5]

There had developed in the colonies and later in the states the notion of a fundamental law or basic constitution as a source of governmental power and individual liberty. 'From the day in 1639,' says Benjamin Wright, 'when the settlers in Connecticut gave to the modern world its first constitution[6] adopted by popular authority, it gradually became increasingly clear that in this country the theory and practice of written constitutions was to occupy a position of importance. . .'[7] Again and again in the struggle with Britain the colonists

---

[1] *The Records of the Federal Convention of* 1787, ed. by Max Farrand, New Haven, 1937, I, p. 21.
[2] Ibid. p. 109.
[3] Ibid. II, p. 93.
[4] Ibid. I, p. 97.
[5] See Thayer, James Bradley, *Cases on Constitutional Law,* Cambridge, 1895, I, pp. 55-80.
[6] The Fundamental Orders of Connecticut.
[7] *The Growth of American Constitutional Law,* New York, 1942, p. 11.

asserted the existence of a fundamental law superior to Parliament and the executive. 'There are, my Lord,' so ran a letter from the Massachusetts House to the Earl of Shelburne in protest against the Townshend Acts of 1767, 'fundamental rules of the constitution, which it is humbly presumed, neither the supreme legislative nor the supreme executive can alter. In all free states, the constitution is fixed; it is from thence, that the legislative derives its authority; therefore it cannot change the constitution without destroying its own foundation.' [8] A Massachusetts circular letter written by Sam Adams contained the proposition that 'the constitution ascertains & limits both Sovereignty and allegiance, &, therefore, his Majesty's American subjects, who acknowledge themselves bound by the Ties of Allegiance, have an equitable Claim to the full enjoyment of the fundamental Rules of the British Constitution. . .' [9] The Pennsylvania Resolutions of 1774, protesting against the closing of the port of Boston, set forth a hope for the re-establishment of 'peace and harmony between Great Britain and these colonies, on a constitutional foundation.' [10] The framers of the Constitution might well have assumed that the document they were building, if adopted, would be the source of governmental power and the guarantor of liberty, and that it would be superior to the legislature, the executive, and the judiciary; and some of the framers were of the opinion that if the legislature enacted laws contrary to the basic instrument, the courts would declare them null and void. But such power was not expressly given the federal judiciary.

The Supreme Court under the chief-justiceship of John Marshall laid the foundation of judicial review in the American constitutional system. This was in the case of *Marbury* v. *Madison,* decided in 1803. In accordance with an act of Congress, William Marbury and forty-one others were appointed by President Adams justices of the peace for the District of Columbia. The commissions were signed and the seal of the United States affixed to them by the Secretary of State, John Marshall. The commissions, however, were not delivered; and when Jefferson became President he ordered his Secretary of State, James Madison, to issue commissions to twenty-five of the justices but to withhold the remaining seventeen. Of the latter, four, including Marbury, instituted an original mandamus proceeding in the Supreme Court on the basis of section 13 of the Judiciary Act of 1789. This section authorized the Supreme Court to issue 'writs of mandamus [11] in cases warranted by the principles and usages of law, to any courts appointed, or persons holding office, under authority of the United States.' The plaintiffs moved for a rule to Secretary of State Madison to show cause why a mandamus should not issue commanding the delivery of the commissions to the applicants.

[8] *Documents of American History,* ed. by Henry Steele Commager, New York, 1935, p. 65.
[9] Ibid. p. 66.
[10] Ibid. p. 76.
[11] A prerogative writ issued by a court requiring the person (in this case a public officer) to whom it is addressed to do some act of a non-discretionary nature therein specified.

MARBURY v. MADISON
1 Cranch 137 (1803)

At the last term, viz., December term 1801, William Marbury, Dennis Ramsay, Robert Townsend Hooe and William Harper, by their counsel, Charles Lee, Esq., late attorney-general of the United States, severally moved the court for a rule on James Madison, secretary of state of the United States, to show cause why a *mandamus* should not issue, commanding him to cause to be delivered to them, respectively, their several commissions as justices of the peace in the district of Columbia.

This motion was supported by affidavits of the following facts; that notice of this motion had been given to Mr. Madison; that Mr. Adams, the late president of the United States, nominated the applicants to the senate, for their advice and consent, to be appointed justices of the peace of the district of Columbia; that the senate advised and consented to the appointments; that commissions in due form were signed by the said president, appointing them justices, &c., and that the seal of the United States was in due form affixed to the said commissions, by the secretary of state; that the applicants have requested Mr. Madison to deliver them their said commissions, who has not complied with that request; and that their said commissions are withheld from them; that the applicants have made application to Mr. Madison, as secretary of state of the United States, at his office, for information whether the commissions were signed and sealed as aforesaid; that explicit and satisfactory explanation has not been given, in answer to that inquiry, either by the secretary of state, or any officer in the department of state; that application has been made to the secretary of the senate, for a certificate of the nomination of the applicants, and of the advice and consent of the senate, who has de-

clined giving such a certificate. Whereupon, a rule was laid, to show cause on the fourth day of this term. . .

Afterwards, on the 24th February, the following opinion of the court was delivered by the Chief Justice:

OPINION OF THE COURT.—At the last term, on the affidavits then read and filed with the clerk, a rule was granted in this case, requiring the secretary of state to show cause why a *mandamus* should not issue, directing him to deliver to William Marbury his commission as a justice of the peace for the county of Washington, in the district of Columbia.

No cause has been shown, and the present motion is for a *mandamus*. The peculiar delicacy of this case, the novelty of some of its circumstances, and the real difficulty attending the points which occur in it, require a complete exposition of the principles on which the opinion to be given by the court is founded. These principles have been, on the side of the applicant, very ably argued at the bar. In rendering the opinion of the court, there will be some departure in form, though not in substance, from the points stated in that argument.

In the order in which the court has viewed this subject, the following questions have been considered and decided: 1st. Has the applicant a right to the commission he demands? 2d. If he has a right, and that right has been violated, do the laws of his country afford him a remedy? 3d. If they do afford him a remedy, is it a *mandamus* issuing from this court?

The first object of inquiry is—Has the applicant a right to the commission he demands? . . .

Mr. Marbury, then, since his commission was signed by the president, and sealed by the secretary of state, was appointed; and as the law creating the office, gave the officer a right to hold for five years, independent of the executive, the appointment was not revocable, but vested in the officer legal rights, which are protected by the laws of his country. To withhold his commission, therefore, is an act deemed by the court not warranted by law, but violative of a vested legal right.

2. This brings us to the second inquiry; which is: If he has a right, and that right has been violated, do the laws of his country afford him a remedy? . . .

It is, then, the opinion of the Court: 1st. That by signing the commission of Mr. Marbury, the President of the United States appointed him a justice of peace for the county of Washington, in the district of Columbia; and that the seal of the United States, affixed thereto by the secretary of state, is conclusive testimony of the verity of the signature, and of the completion of the appointment; and that the appointment conferred on him a legal right to the office for the space of five years. 2d. That, having this legal title to the office, he has a consequent right to the commission; a refusal to deliver which is a plain violation of that right, for which the laws of his country afford him a remedy.

3. It remains to be inquired whether he is entitled to the remedy for which he applies? This depends on—1st. The nature of the writ applied for; and 2d. The power of this court.

1st. The nature of the writ. . .

This, then, is a plain case for a *mandamus,* either to deliver the commission, or a copy of it from the record; and it only remains to be inquired, whether it can issue from this court? . . .

[The Court then decided that power to issue mandamus in this case was not within the original jurisdiction of the Supreme Court under Art. III, § 2, of the Constitution.]

It has been stated at the bar, that the appellate jurisdiction may be exercised in a variety of forms, and that if it be the will of the legislature that a *mandamus* should be used for that purpose, that will must be obeyed. This is true, yet the jurisdiction must be appellate, not original. It is the essential criterion of appellate jurisdiction, that it revises and corrects the proceedings in a cause already instituted, and does not create that cause. Although, therefore, a *mandamus* may be directed to courts, yet to issue such a writ to an officer, for the delivery of a paper, is, in effect, the same as to sustain an original action for that paper, and therefore, seems not to belong to appellate, but to original jurisdiction. Neither is it necessary in such a case as this, to enable the court to exercise its appellate jurisdiction. The authority, therefore, given to the supreme court by the act establishing the judicial courts of the United States, to issue writs of *mandamus* to public officers, appears not to be warranted by the constitution; and it becomes necessary to inquire, whether a jurisdiction so conferred can be exercised.

The question, whether an act, repugnant to the constitution, can become the law of the land, is a question deeply interesting to the United States; but, happily, not of an intricacy proportioned to its interest. It seems only necessary to recognize certain principles, supposed to have been long and well established, to decide it. That the people have an original right to establish, for their future government, such principles as, in their opinion, shall most conduce to their own happiness, is the basis on which the whole American fabric has been erected. The exercise of this original right is a very great exertion; nor can it, nor ought it, to be frequently repeated. The principles, therefore, so established, are deemed fundamental; and as the authority from which they proceed is supreme, and can seldom act, they are designed to be permanent.

This original and supreme will organizes the government, and assigns to different departments their respective powers. It may either stop here, or establish certain limits not to be transcended by those departments. The government of the United States is of the latter description. The powers of the legislature are defined and limited; and that those limits may not be mistaken or forgotten, the constitution is written. To what purpose are powers limited, and to what purpose is that limitation committed to writing, if these limits may, at any time, be passed by those intended to be restrained? The distinction between a government with limited and unlimited powers is abolished, if those limits do not confine the persons on whom they are imposed, and if acts prohibited and acts allowed, are of equal obligation. It is a proposition too plain to be contested, that the constitution controls any legislative act repugnant to it; or that the legislature may alter the constitution by an ordinary act.

Between these alternatives, there is no middle ground. The constitution is either a superior paramount law, unchangeable by ordinary means, or it is on a level with ordinary legislative acts, and, like other acts, is alterable when the legislature shall please to alter it. If the former part of the alternative be true, then a legislative act, contrary to the constitution, is not law; if the latter part be true, then written constitutions are absurd attempts, on the part of the people, to limit a power, in its own nature, illimitable.

Certainly, all those who have framed written constitutions contemplate them as forming the fundamental and paramount law of the nation, and consequently, the theory of every such government must be, that an act of the legislature, repugnant to the constitution, is void. This theory is essentially attached to a written constitution, and is, consequently, to be considered, by this court, as one of the fundamental principles of our society. It is not, therefore, to be lost sight of, in the further consideration of this subject.

If an act of the legislature, repugnant to the constitution, is void, does it, notwithstanding its invalidity, bind the courts, and oblige them to give it effect? Or, in other words, though it be not law, does it constitute a rule as operative as if it was a law? This would be to overthrow, in fact, what was established in theory; and would seem, at first view, an absurdity too gross to be insisted on. It shall, however, receive a more attentive consideration.

It is, emphatically, the province and duty of the judicial department, to say what the law is. Those who apply the rule to particular cases, must of necessity expound and interpret that rule. If two laws conflict with each other, the courts must decide on the operation of each. So, if a law be in opposition to the constitution; if both the law and the constitution apply to a particular case, so that the court must either decide that case, conformable to the law, disregarding the constitution; or conformable to the constitution, disregarding the law; the court must determine which of these conflicting rules governs the case; this is of the very essence of judicial duty. If then, the courts are to regard the constitution, and the constitution is superior to any ordinary act of the legislature, the constitution, and not such ordinary act, must govern the case to which they both apply.

Those, then, who controvert the principle, that the constitution is to be considered, in court, as a paramount law, are reduced to the necessity of maintaining that courts must close their eyes on the constitution, and see only the law. This doctrine would subvert the very foundation of all written constitutions. It would declare that an act which, according to the principles and theory of our government, is entirely void, is yet, in practice, completely obligatory. It would declare, that if the legislature shall do what is expressly forbidden, such act, notwithstanding the express prohibition, is in reality effectual. It would be giving to the legislature a practical and real omnipotence, with the same breath which professes to restrict their powers within narrow limits. It is prescribing limits, and declaring that those limits may be passed at pleasure. That it thus reduces to nothing, what we have deemed the greatest improvement on political institutions, a written constitution, would, of itself, be sufficient, in America, where written constitutions have been viewed with so much reverence, for rejecting the construction. But the peculiar expressions of the constitution of the United States furnish additional arguments in favor of its rejection. The judicial power of the United States is extended to all cases arising under the constitution. Could it be the intention of those who gave this power, to say, that in using it, the constitution should not be looked into? That a case arising under the constitution should be decided, without examining the instrument under which it arises? This is too extravagant to be maintained. In some cases, then, the constitution must be looked into by the judges. And if they can open it at all, what part of it are they forbidden to read or to obey?

There are many other parts of the constitution which serve to illustrate this subject. It is declared, that 'no tax or duty shall be laid on articles exported from any state.' Suppose, a duty on the export of cotton, of tobacco or of flour; and a suit instituted to recover it. Ought judgment to be rendered in such a case? ought the judges to close their eyes on the constitution, and only see the law?

The constitution declares 'that no bill of attainder or *ex post facto* law shall be passed.' If, however, such a bill should be passed, and a person should be prosecuted under it; must the court condemn to death those victims whom the constitution endeavors to preserve?

'No person,' says the constitution, 'shall be convicted of treason, unless on the testimony of two witnesses to the same *overt* act, or on confession in open court.' Here, the language of the constitution is addressed especially to the courts. It prescribes, directly for them, a rule of evidence not to be departed from. If the legislature should change that rule, and declare one witness, or a confession out of court, sufficient for conviction, must the constitutional principle yield to the legislative act?

From these, and many other selections which might be made, it is apparent, that the framers of the constitution contemplated that instrument as a rule for the government of courts, as well as of the legislature. Why otherwise does it direct the judges to take an oath to support it? This oath certainly applies in an especial manner, to their conduct in their official character. How immoral to impose it on them, if they were to be used as the instruments, and the knowing instruments, for violating what they swear to support!

The oath of office, too, imposed by the legislature, is completely demonstrative of the legislative opinion on this subject. It is in these words: 'I do solemnly swear, that I will administer justice, without respect to persons, and do equal right to the poor and to the rich; and that I will faithfully and impartially discharge all the duties incumbent on me as ――, according to the best of my abilities and understanding, agreeably to the constitution and laws of the United States.' Why does a judge swear to discharge his duties agreeably to the constitution of the United States, if that constitution forms no rule for his government? if it is closed upon him, and cannot be inspected by him? If such be the real state of things, this is worse than solemn mockery. To prescribe, or to take this oath, becomes equally a crime.

It is also not entirely unworthy of observation, that in declaring what shall be the supreme law of the land, the constitution itself is first mentioned; and not the laws of the United States, generally, but those only which shall be made in pursuance of the constitution, have that rank.

Thus, the particular phraseology of the constitution of the United States confirms and strengthens the principle, supposed to be essential to all written constitutions, that a law repugnant to the constitution is void; and that courts, as well as other departments, are bound by that instrument.

The rule must be discharged.

NOTE

Whether the referendum provisions of the state constitutions and statutes are applicable in the adoption or rejection of amendments to the federal Constitution was the question before the Supreme Court in *Hawke* v. *Smith*.

Aware that the instrument of government they were building would contain defects, and that, whatever its nature, it would have to meet the needs of succeeding generations, the framers of the Constitution accepted unanimously the principle 'That provision ought to be made for the amendment of the articles of union, whensoever it shall seem necessary.'[1] This would seem an obvious principle to adopt, but several members of the convention at first did not appreciate the need of an amending clause.

The method of amendment had yet to be decided. Originally, the delegates approved a plan whereby the national legislature, on application of the legislatures of two-thirds of the states, would call a convention for the purpose of amending the Constitution. The initiative was to rest with the states alone. Dissatisfaction with the method proposed led to its reconsideration.

It was Madison who proposed that 'The Legislature of the U—S—whenever two thirds of both Houses shall deem necessary, or on the application of two thirds of the Legislatures of the several States, shall propose amendments to this Constitution, which shall be valid to all intents and purposes as part thereof, when the same shall have been ratified by three fourths at least of the Legislatures of the several States, or by Conventions in three fourths thereof, as one or the other mode of ratification may be proposed by the Legislature of the U.S.'[2]

Rutledge of South Carolina approved Madison's proposal in general but 'he never could agree to give a power by which the articles relating to slaves might be altered by the States not interested in that property. . .'[3] To meet this objection the following proviso was added to Madison's proposition: 'provided that no amendments which may be made prior to the year 1808. shall in any manner affect the 4 & 5 sections of the VII article.'[4] With this change, Madison's proposal was approved.

[1] *The Records of the Federal Convention of* 1787, ed. by Max Farrand, New Haven, 1937, II, p. 84.
[2] Ibid. p. 559.
[3] Ibid.
[4] Ibid. The seventh article of a draft of the Constitution prepared by the Committee of Detail and reported to the convention, 6 August 1787. See *The Records of the Federal Convention of* 1787, op. cit. II, pp. 177-89. Section 4 provided that 'No tax or duty shall be laid by the Legislature on articles exported from any State; nor on the migration or importation of such persons as the several States shall think proper to admit; nor shall such migration or importation be prohibited.' Section 5 provided that 'No capitation tax shall be laid, unless in proportion to the Census hereinbefore directed to be taken.' Ibid. p. 183.

Two days previous to the final adjournment of the convention the amending article was reconsidered and two provisions added. In addition to the power of Congress to propose amendments, Congress was to call a convention for the purpose of proposing amendments when called upon to do so by two-thirds of the state legislatures. As an added safeguard to the states it was provided 'that no State, without its consent shall be deprived of its equal suffrage in the Senate.'[5] Thus, Madison's proposition as amended became Article v.

Formal amendment of the Constitution has been deemed by some writers to be slow and cumbersome. One scholar holds that the Constitution 'was purposely made most difficult to amend.'[6] Be this as it may, the procedure adopted in 1787 was a step forward. Though the Articles of Confederation did provide for formal change, amendment could be accomplished only by the unanimous approval of Congress and confirmation by the legislatures of all the states. Some of the state constitutions, for example, those of Virginia, New Jersey, and New York, provided no means of amendment whatsoever.[7]

The people of the colonies had had little or no experience with amending processes.[8] Of all the colonial charters only Pennsylvania's *Frame of Government* incorporated a means of amendment. *The Frame of Government* of 1682-3 required that the charter was not to be changed, altered, or diminished in form or effect, 'without the consent of the Governor, his heirs, or assigns, and six parts of seven of the said freemen in provincial Council and General Assembly.'[9] This would seem to be the first instance of a definite amending procedure in American government.

The framers of the Constitution were seeking stability in government; as Madison declared in the *Federalist,* they provided a mode of amendment that would guard 'equally against that extreme facility, which would render the Constitution too mutable'; at the same time, they wished to avoid that extreme difficulty of amendment 'which might perpetuate its discovered faults.'

The Supreme Court considered the validity of the Eleventh Amendment in the early case of *Hollingsworth* v. *Virginia.*[10] Mr. Justice Chase declared without argument that a proposed amendment need not be submitted to the President for approval. In the *National Prohibition Cases*[11] the Court interpreted the two-thirds of both Houses requirement in proposing amendments to mean two-thirds of the members present, assuming the presence of a quorum. In *Dillon* v. *Gloss*[12] it was decided that Congress could impose a time-limit upon ratification. In *United States* v. *Sprague*[13] the Court held that Congress alone decided the

---

[5] Ibid. p. 631.

[6] Finer, Herman, *The Theory and Practice of Modern Government*, New York, 1934, pp. 118-19.

[7] Dodd, Walter Fairleigh, *The Revision and Amendment of State Constitutions*, Baltimore, 1910, p. 27.

[8] Jameson, John Alexander, *A Treatise on Constitutional Conventions: Their History, Powers, and Modes of Proceeding*, Chicago, 1887, pp. 547-8.

[9] Thorpe, Francis Newton, *The Federal and State Constitutions, Colonial Charters, and Other Organic Laws*, Washington, 1909, p. 3059.

[10] 3 Dall. 378 (1798).

[11] 253 U.S. 350 (1920).

[12] 256 U.S. 368 (1921).

[13] 282 U.S. 716 (1931).

mode of ratification. In *Leser* v. *Garnett*[14] it was contended that the amending power did not extend to the subject-matter of the Nineteenth Amendment. The argument was that the Nineteenth Amendment, which was not ratified by the State of Maryland, so greatly added to the electorate as to destroy the political autonomy of the state. The Court rejected this contention. How long a proposed amendment shall be subject to ratification was held in *Coleman* v. *Miller*[15] to be a political question and thus for Congress to decide.

An amendment to the Ohio Constitution adopted in 1918 provided that 'The people also reserve to themselves the legislative power of the referendum on the action of the General Assembly ratifying any proposed amendment to the Constitution of the United States.' The Eighteenth Amendment was proposed by Congress in December 1917, and the General Assembly of Ohio ratified the proposed amendment in January 1919. The Secretary of State of the United States proclaimed the adoption of the amendment on 29 January 1919, naming Ohio as one of the thirty-six ratifying States.

The plaintiff in error (plaintiff in the lower court), Hawke, sought an injunction to enjoin the Secretary of State of Ohio, Smith, from spending public money in printing ballots for submission of a referendum to the voters of the state on the action of the General Assembly in ratifying the Eighteenth Amendment. A demurrer to the petition was sustained in the Court of Common Pleas. Its judgment was affirmed by the Court of Appeals of Franklin County. The Supreme Court of Ohio affirmed the judgment of the lower court. Appeal was then made to the Supreme Court of the United States.

HAWKE v. SMITH
253 U.S. 221 (1920)

Mr. Justice Day delivered the opinion of the court. . .

The question for our consideration is: Whether the provision of the Ohio constitution, adopted at the general election, November, 1918, extending the referendum to the ratification by the General Assembly of proposed amendments to the Federal Constitution is in conflict with Article v of the Constitution of the United States. . .

The Fifth Article is a grant of authority by the people to Congress. The determination of the method of ratification is the exercise of a national power specifically granted by the Constitution; that power is conferred upon Congress, and is limited

to two methods, by action of the legislatures of three-fourths of the States, or conventions in a like number of States. *Dodge* v. *Woolsey,* 18 How. 331, 348. The framers of the Constitution might have adopted a different method. Ratification might have been left to a vote of the people, or to some authority of government other than that selected. The language of the article is plain, and admits of no doubt in its interpretation. It is not the function of courts or legislative bodies, national or state, to alter the method which the Constitution has fixed.

All of the amendments to the Constitution have been submitted with a requirement for legislative ratification; by

[14] 258 U.S. 130 (1922).
[15] 307 U.S. 433 (1939).

this method all of them have been adopted.

The only question really for determination is: What did the framers of the Constitution mean in requiring ratification by 'Legislatures'? That was not a term of uncertain meaning when incorporated into the Constitution. What it meant when adopted it still means for the purpose of interpretation. A Legislature was then the representative body which made the laws of the people. The term is often used in the Constitution with this evident meaning. Article 1, § 2, prescribes the qualifications of electors of congressmen as those 'requisite for electors of the most numerous branch of the state legislature.' Article 1, § 3, provided that senators shall be chosen in each State by the legislature thereof, and this was the method of choosing senators until the adoption of the Seventeenth Amendment which made provision for the election of senators by vote of the people, the electors to have the qualifications requisite for electors of the most numerous branch of the state legislature. That Congress and the States understood that this election by the people was entirely distinct from legislative action is shown by the provision of the amendment giving the legislature of any State the power to authorize the Executive to make temporary appointments until the people shall fill the vacancies by election. It was never suggested, so far as we are aware, that the purpose of making the office of Senator elective by the people could be accomplished by a referendum vote. The necessity of the amendment to accomplish the purpose of popular election is shown in the adoption of the amendment. In Article IV the United States is required to protect every State against domestic violence upon application of the legislature, or of the Executive when the legislature cannot be convened. Article VI requires the members of the several legislatures to be bound by oath, or affirmation, to support the Constitution of the United States. By Article 1, § 8, Congress

is given exclusive jurisdiction over all places purchased by the consent of the legislature of the State in which the same shall be. Article IV, § 3, provides that no new States shall be carved out of old States without the consent of the legislatures of the States concerned.

There can be no question that the framers of the Constitution clearly understood and carefully used the terms in which that instrument referred to the action of the legislatures of the States. When they intended that direct action by the people should be had they were no less accurate in the use of apt phraseology to carry out such purpose. The members of the House of Representatives were required to be chosen by the people of the several States. Article 1, § 2.

The constitution of Ohio in its present form, although making provision for a referendum, vests the legislative power primarily in a General Assembly consisting of a Senate and House of Representatives. Article II, § 1, provides:

'The legislative power of the state shall be vested in a general assembly consisting of a senate and house of representatives, but the people shall reserve to themselves the power to propose to the general assembly laws and amendments to the constitution, and to adopt or reject the same at the polls on a referendum vote as hereinafter provided.'

The argument to support the power of the State to require the approval by the people of the State of the ratification of amendments to the Federal Constitution through the medium of a referendum rests upon the proposition that the Federal Constitution requires ratification by the legislative action of the States through the medium provided at the time of the proposed approval of an amendment. This argument is fallacious in this—ratification by a State of a constitutional amendment is not an act of legislation within the proper sense of the word. It is but the expression of the assent of the State to a proposed amendment.

At an early day this court settled that the submission of a constitutional amendment did not require the action of the President. The question arose over the adoption of the Eleventh Amendment. *Hollingsworth* v. *Virginia,* 3 Dall. 378. In that case it was contended that the amendment had not been proposed in the manner provided in the Constitution as an inspection of the original roll showed that it had never been submitted to the President for his approval in accordance with Article 1, § 7, of the Constitution. The Attorney General answered that the case of amendments is a substantive act, unconnected with the ordinary business of legislation, and not within the policy or terms of the Constitution investing the President with a qualified negative on the acts and resolutions of Congress. In a foot-note to this argument of the Attorney General, Justice Chase said: 'There can, surely, be no necessity to answer that argument. The negative of the president applies only to the ordinary cases of legislation: He has nothing to do with the proposition or adoption of amendments to the constitution.' The court by a unanimous judgment held that the amendment was constitutionally adopted.

It is true that the power to legislate in the enactment of the laws of a State is derived from the people of the State. But the power to ratify a proposed amendment to the Federal Constitution has its source in the Federal Constitution. The act of ratification by the State derives its authority from the Federal Constitution to which the State and its people have alike assented.

This view of the provision for amendment is confirmed in the history of its adoption found in 2 Watson on the Con-

stitution, 1301 *et seq.* Any other view might lead to endless confusion in the manner of ratification of federal amendments. The choice of means of ratification was wisely withheld from conflicting action in the several States.

But it is said this view runs counter to the decision of this court in *Davis* v. *Hildebrant,* 241 U.S. 565. But that case is inapposite. It dealt with Article 1, § 4, of the Constitution, which provides that the times, places and manners of holding elections for Senators and Representatives in each State shall be determined by the respective legislatures thereof, but that Congress may at any time make or alter such regulations, except as to the place for choosing Senators. As shown in the opinion in that case, Congress had itself recognized the referendum as part of the legislative authority of the State for the purpose stated. It was held, affirming the judgment of the Supreme Court of Ohio, that the referendum provision of the state constitution when applied to a law redistricting the State with a view to representation in Congress was not unconstitutional. Article 1, § 4, plainly gives authority to the State to legislate within the limitations therein named. Such legislative action is entirely different from the requirement of the Constitution as to the expression of assent or dissent to a proposed amendment to the Constitution. In such expression no legislative action is authorized or required.

It follows that the court erred in holding that the State had authority to require the submission of the ratification to a referendum under the state constitution, and its judgment is reversed and the cause remanded for further proceedings not inconsistent with this opinion.

Reversed.

II

National Supremacy and the Implied Powers

NOTE

In *McCulloch* v. *Maryland* the Supreme Court set forth with fullness and clarity the doctrine of implied powers, and for the first time grappled with the connecting problems of two powerful economic instrumentalities, namely, the Bank of the United States and the tax power of the states. The Court also affirmed the doctrine of national supremacy.

The first Bank of the United States was chartered by Congress in 1791. This was in accord with a proposal of the Secretary of the Treasury, Alexander Hamilton, who, in company with other Federalists, desired commercial and financial stability, and who considered a national bank as one means among several of realizing that stability.

Hamilton wanted a sound circulating medium, a reliable depository for the public funds, and an agency for the collection and disbursement of the revenues. He wished to increase the amount of fluid capital in the country, to restrain state bank issues, to aid the government in arranging loans, and to provide businessmen with opportunity for safe investment; in general, he wished to improve the national credit.

Both Jefferson and the erstwhile Federalist, James Madison, opposed the establishment of such an institution, the chief argument being that the Constitution did not empower Congress to charter a bank. Hamilton's arguments, however, prevailed, and the Bank was incorporated for a period of twenty years with a capital of ten million dollars. The Federal government was to subscribe two million dollars while private investors were to subscribe eight million. The Bank's notes were to be receivable as taxes as long as they were redeemable in specie.

Though the first Bank of the United States was efficiently managed and salutary in its effects upon the commercial and financial interests of the country, it was not a popular institution. Monopolies were not popular and the Bank was a virtual monopoly; Englishmen were not popular among the followers of Jefferson, and most of the Bank stock was held by Englishmen; the popularity of the Federalists, which had never been great, was declining, and the Bank was directed by Federalists; a great part of the people favored states' rights and localism, and the Bank was a powerful agency of a central government; finally, because the Bank laid a restraining hand upon the activities of state banks and thus denied them much lucrative business, these institutions hated the Bank. As a consequence, when the Bank's charter expired in 1811, during the administration of James Madison, it was not renewed. George Clinton, president of the Senate, cast his deciding vote against the bill which would have extended the life of the first Bank. '[T]he power to create corporations,' he said, 'is not expressly granted [in the Constitution]; it is a high attribute of sovereignty, and in its nature not accessorial or derivative by implication. . .' [1]

Thus, at the commencement of the War of 1812 the Federal government was without an adequate fiscal agent; and foreign holders of the Bank's stock withdrew a great quantity of specie which was sorely needed in this country. Within five years the number of state banks increased from 88 to 246; and the amount of money in circulation rose from forty-five million to about one hundred million dollars. In his opening address to the New York legislature in 1812, Governor Tompkins declared: 'It has already been announced, that petitions for new banks, to the amount of eighteen and a half millions of capital, will be presented during the present session. . . [O]ur existing bank capital . . . amounts to nearly thirteen millions of dollars. The debts which may now be legally contracted upon that capital, are thirty-nine millions; and if eighteen millions and a half of additional capital should be granted, the banks of this state alone, will then be enabled to contract debts, or in other words to issue their paper to the enormous sum of ninety-four millions of dollars, a sum at least sixteen times greater than the whole specie capital of the state. A failure to discharge such a debt will produce universal bankruptcy and ruin.' [2]

Governor Tompkins spoke of 'the difficulty experienced by enterprising farmers, manufacturers and mechanics to raise money at lawful interest upon the best security; and hence it follows, that the necessity of temporary pecuniary relief, frequently drives them into the embraces of unprincipled, avaricious usurers, who fertilize upon the wants and distresses of the needy and unfortunate.' [3] Albert J. Beveridge, the biographer of John Marshall, declares that during this period, 'local banking began a course that ended in a mad carnival of roguery, to the ruin of legitimate business and the impoverishment and bankruptcy of hundreds of thousands of the general public.' [4]

In his seventh annual message to Congress, 5 December 1815, President Madison proposed the establishment of a second national bank in order that 'the benefits of an uniform national currency should be restored to the community.' And in 1816, the second Bank of the United States was incorporated. Despite the need for such an institution, it was bitterly opposed. At the instigation of the state banks, state legislatures enacted laws which, had they been enforced, would have sharply curtailed the activities of the second Bank and thus destroyed its usefulness. The means employed was taxation.

The constitutions of Indiana, 1816, and Illinois, 1818, restricted the business of banking to those banks chartered by the state. Georgia, Tennessee, North Carolina, Kentucky, Ohio, and Maryland placed special taxes upon branches of the Bank of the United States. [5] The Maryland law provided for the payment of a $15,000 tax only if the bank not chartered by the legislature issued 'notes, in

---

[1] Quoted in Adams, Henry, *History of the United States of America During the Administration of James Madison*, New York, 1930, Book v, p. 337.

[2] Lincoln, Charles Z., *Messages and Papers from the Governors*, Albany, 1909, ii, p. 696.

[3] Ibid. p. 698.

[4] *The Life of John Marshall*, Boston, 1929, iv, p. 177.

[5] See Swisher, Carl Brent, *American Constitutional Development*, Boston, 1943, pp. 173-4.

any manner . . . except upon stamped paper (supplied by the state) of the following denominations: that is to say, every five dollar note shall be upon a stamp of ten cents; every ten dollar note, upon a stamp of twenty cents; every twenty dollar note upon a stamp of thirty cents . . . ,' and so on, up to 'every thousand dollar note, upon a stamp of twenty dollars.' [6]

McCulloch v. *Maryland* had its beginnings in an action of debt brought by John James, who sued as an informer in behalf of himself and the State of Maryland to recover a penalty of $100 from James McCulloch, cashier of the Baltimore branch of the Bank of the United States, for circulating an unstamped banknote in violation of the state taxing statute. In the court of original jurisdiction, the Baltimore County Court, the decision was in favor of the State. The tax law was again upheld by the Maryland Court of Appeals, and an appeal on a writ of error carried the case to the United States Supreme Court.

McCULLOCH v. MARYLAND
4 Wheaton 316 (1819)

MARSHALL, C. J., delivered the opinion of the Court.

In the case now to be determined, the defendant, a sovereign state, denies the obligation of a law enacted by the legislature of the Union, and the plaintiff, on his part, contests the validity of an act which has been passed by the legislature of that state. The constitution of our country, in its most interesting and vital parts, is to be considered; the conflicting powers of the government of the Union and of its members, as marked in that constitution, are to be discussed; and an opinion given, which may essentially influence the great operations of the government. No tribunal can approach such a question without a deep sense of its importance, and of the awful responsibility involved in its decision. But it must be decided peacefully, or remain a source of hostile legislation, perhaps of hostility of a still more serious nature; and if it is to be so decided, by this tribunal alone can the decision be made. On the supreme court of the United States has the constitution of our country devolved this important duty.

The first question made in the cause is—has congress power to incorporate a bank?

It has been truly said, that this can scarcely be considered as an open question, entirely unprejudiced by the former proceedings of the nation respecting it. The principle now contested was introduced at a very early period of our history, has been recognized by many successive legislatures, and has been acted upon by the judicial department, in cases of peculiar delicacy, as a law of undoubted obligation.

It will not be denied that a bold and daring usurpation might be resisted, after an acquiescence still longer and more complete than this. But it is conceived that a doubtful question, one on which human reason may pause, and the human judgment be suspended, in the decision of which the great principles of liberty are not concerned, but the respective powers of those who are equally the representatives of the people, are to be adjusted; if not put at rest by the practice of the government, ought to receive a considerable impression from that practice. An exposi-

[6] *McCulloch* v. *Maryland,* 4 Wheat. 316, 321.

tion of the constitution, deliberately established by legislative acts, on the faith of which an immense property has been advanced, ought not to be lightly disregarded.

The power now contested was exercised by the first congress elected under the present constitution. The bill for incorporating the Bank of the United States did not steal upon an unsuspecting legislature, and pass unobserved. Its principle was completely understood, and was opposed with equal zeal and ability. After being resisted, first in the fair and open field of debate, and afterwards in the executive cabinet, with as much persevering talent as any measure has ever experienced, and being supported by arguments which convinced minds as pure and as intelligent as this country can boast, it became a law. The original act was permitted to expire; but a short experience of the embarrassments to which the refusal to revive it exposed the government, convinced those who were most prejudiced against the measure of its necessity and induced the passage of the present law. It would require no ordinary share of intrepidity to assert that a measure adopted under these circumstances was a bold and plain usurpation to which the constitution gave no countenance. These observations belong to the cause; but they are not made under the impression that, were the question entirely new, the law would be found irreconcilable with the constitution.

In discussing this question, the counsel for the state of Maryland have deemed it of some importance, in the construction of the constitution, to consider that instrument not as emanating from the people, but as the act of sovereign and independent states. The powers of the general government, it has been said, are delegated by the states, who alone are truly sovereign; and must be exercised in subordination to the states, who alone possess supreme dominion. It would be difficult to sustain this proposition. The conven-

tion which framed the constitution was indeed elected by the state legislatures. But the instrument, when it came from their hands, was a mere proposal, without obligation, or pretensions to it. It was reported to the then existing congress of the United States, with a request that it might 'be submitted to a convention of delegates, chosen in each state by the people thereof, under the recommendation of its legislature, for their assent and ratification.' This mode of proceeding was adopted; and by the convention, by congress, and by the state legislatures, the instrument was submitted to the people. They acted upon it in the only manner in which they can act safely, effectively, and wisely, on such a subject, by assembling in convention. It is true, they assembled in their several states—and where else should they have assembled? No political dreamer was ever wild enough to think of breaking down the lines which separate the states, and of compounding the American people into one common mass. Of consequence, when they act, they act in their states. But the measures they adopt do not, on that account, cease to be the measures of the people themselves, or become the measures of the state governments.

From these conventions the constitution derives its whole authority. The government proceeds directly from the people; is 'ordained and established' in the name of the people; and is declared to be ordained, 'in order to form a more perfect union, establish justice, insure domestic tranquillity, and secure the blessings of liberty to themselves and to their posterity.' The assent of the states, in their sovereign capacity, is implied in calling a convention, and thus submitting that instrument to the people. But the people were at perfect liberty to accept or reject it; and their act was final. It required not the affirmance, and could not be negatived, by the state governments. The constitution, when thus adopted, was of complete obligation, and bound the state sovereignties. . .

The government of the Union then (whatever may be the influence of this fact on the case), is, emphatically and truly, a government of the people. In form, and in substance, it emanates from them. Its powers are granted by them, and are to be exercised directly on them, and for their benefit.

This government is acknowledged by all to be one of enumerated powers. The principle, that it can exercise only the powers granted to it, would seem too apparent to have required to be enforced by all those arguments which its enlightened friends, while it was depending before the people, found it necessary to urge; that principle is now universally admitted. But the question respecting the extent of the powers actually granted, is perpetually arising, and will probably continue to arise, so long as our system shall exist. In discussing these questions, the conflicting powers of the general and state governments must be brought into view, and the supremacy of their respective laws, when they are in opposition, must be settled.

If any one proposition could command the universal assent of mankind, we might expect it would be this—that the government of the Union, though limited in its powers, is supreme within its sphere of action. This would seem to result necessarily from its nature. It is the government of all; its powers are delegated by all; it represents all, and acts for all. Though any one state may be willing to control its operations, no state is willing to allow others to control them. The nation, on those subjects on which it can act, must necessarily bind its component parts. But this question is not left to mere reason; the people have, in express terms, decided it by saying, 'this constitution, and the laws of the United States, which shall be made in pursuance thereof,' 'shall be the supreme law of the land,' and by requir-

ing that the members of the state legislatures, and the officers of the executive and judicial departments of the states shall take the oath of fidelity to it.

The government of the United States, then, though limited in its powers, is supreme; and its laws, when made in pursuance of the constitution, form the supreme law of the land, 'anything in the constitution or laws of any state to the contrary notwithstanding.'

Among the enumerated powers, we do not find that of establishing a bank or creating a corporation. But there is no phrase in the instrument which, like the articles of confederation, excludes incidental or implied powers; and which requires that everything granted shall be expressly and minutely described. Even the 10th amendment, which was framed for the purpose of quieting the excessive jealousies which had been excited, omits the word 'expressly,' and declares only that the powers 'not delegated to the United States, nor prohibited to the states, are reserved to the states or to the people'; thus leaving the question whether the particular power which may become the subject of contest has been delegated to the one government, or prohibited to the other, to depend on a fair construction of the whole instrument. The men who drew and adopted this amendment had experienced the embarrassments resulting from the insertion of this word in the articles of confederation, and probably omitted it to avoid those embarrassments. A constitution, to contain an accurate detail of all the subdivisions of which its great powers will admit, and of all the means by which they may be carried into execution, would partake of the prolixity of a legal code, and could scarcely be embraced by the human mind. It would, probably, never be understood by the public. Its nature, therefore, requires, that only its great outlines should be marked, its important objects designated, and the minor ingredients which compose those objects be deduced from the nature of the objects themselves. . .

Although, among the enumerated powers of government, we do not find the word 'bank' or 'incorporation,' we find the great powers, to lay and collect taxes; to borrow money; to regulate commerce; to declare and conduct a war; and to raise and support armies and navies. The sword and the purse, all the external relations, and no inconsiderable portion of the industry of the nation, are entrusted to its government. It can never be pretended that these vast powers draw after them others of inferior importance, merely because they are inferior. Such an idea can never be advanced. But it may with great reason be contended, that a government, entrusted with such ample powers, on the due execution of which the happiness and prosperity of the nation so vitally depends, must also be entrusted with ample means for their execution. The power being given, it is the interest of the nation to facilitate its execution. It can never be their interest, and cannot be presumed to have been their intention, to clog and embarrass its execution, by withholding the most appropriate means. . . But it is denied that the government has its choice of means; or, that it may employ the most convenient means, if, to employ them, it be necessary to erect a corporation.

On what foundation does this argument rest? On this alone: the power of creating a corporation, is one appertaining to sovereignty, and is not expressly conferred on congress. This is true. But all legislative powers appertain to sovereignty. The original power of giving the law on any subject whatever, is a sovereign power; and if the government of the Union is restrained from creating a corporation, as a means for performing its functions, on the single reason that the creation of a corporation is an act of sovereignty; if the sufficiency of this reason be acknowledged, there would be some difficulty in sustaining the authority of congress to pass other laws for the accomplishment of the same objects.

The government which has a right to do an act, and has imposed on it the duty of performing that act, must, according to the dictates of reason, be allowed to select the means; and those who contend that it may not select any appropriate means, that one particular mode of effecting the object is excepted, take upon themselves the burden of establishing that exception. . . The power of creating a corporation, though appertaining to sovereignty, is not, like the power of making war, or levying taxes, or of regulating commerce, a great substantive and independent power, which cannot be implied as incidental to other powers, or used as a means of executing them. It is never the end for which other powers are exercised, but a means by which other objects are accomplished. No contributions are made to charity for the sake of an incorporation, but a corporation is created to administer the charity; no seminary of learning is instituted in order to be incorporated, but the corporate character is conferred to subserve the purposes of education. No city was ever built with the sole object of being incorporated, but is incorporated as affording the best means of being well governed. The power of creating a corporation is never used for its own sake, but for the purpose of effecting something else. No sufficient reason is, therefore, perceived, why it may not pass as incidental to those powers which are expressly given, if it be a direct mode of executing them.

But the constitution of the United States has not left the right of congress to employ the necessary means, for the execution of the powers conferred on the government, to general reasoning. To its enumeration of powers is added that of making 'all laws which shall be necessary and proper, for carrying into execution the foregoing powers, and all other powers vested by this constitution, in the government of the United States, or in any department thereof.'

The counsel for the state of Maryland have urged various arguments, to prove that this clause, though, in terms a grant of power, is not so, in effect; but is really restrictive of the general right, which might otherwise be implied, of selecting means for executing the enumerated powers. In support of this proposition, they have found it necessary to contend, that this clause was inserted for the purpose of conferring on congress the power of making laws. That, without it, doubts might be entertained whether congress could exercise its powers in the form of legislation.

But could this be the object for which it was inserted? A government is created by the people, having legislative, executive, and judicial powers. Its legislative powers are vested in a congress, which is to consist of a senate and house of representatives. . . That a legislature, endowed with legislative powers, can legislate, is a proposition too self-evident to have been questioned.

But the argument on which most reliance is placed, is drawn from that peculiar language of this clause. Congress is not empowered by it to make all laws, which may have relation to the powers conferred on the government, but such only as may be *'necessary and proper'* for carrying them into execution. The word *'necessary'* is considered as controlling the whole sentence, and as limiting the right to pass laws for the execution of the granted powers, to such as are indispensable, and without which the power would be nugatory. That it excludes the choice of means, and leaves to congress, in each case, that only which is most direct and simple.

Is it true, that this is the sense in which the word 'necessary' is always used? Does it always import an absolute physical necessity, so strong, that one thing to which another may be termed necessary,

cannot exist without that other? We think it does not. If reference be had to its use, in the common affairs of the world, or in approved authors, we find that it frequently imports no more than that one thing is convenient, or useful, or essential to another. To employ the means necessary to an end, is generally understood as employing any means calculated to produce the end, and not as being confined to those single means, without which the end would be entirely unattainable. Such is the character of human language, that no word conveys to the mind, in all situations, one single definite idea; and nothing is more common than to use words in a figurative sense. Almost all compositions contain words, which, taken in their rigorous sense, would convey a meaning different from that which is obviously intended. It is essential to just construction, that many words which import something excessive should be understood in a more mitigated sense—in that sense which common usage justifies. The word 'necessary' is of this description. It has not a fixed character peculiar to itself. It admits of all degrees of comparison; and is often connected with other words, which increase or diminish the impression the mind receives of the urgency it imports. A thing may be necessary, very necessary, absolutely or indispensably necessary. To no mind would the same idea be conveyed by these several phrases. The comment on the word is well illustrated by the passage cited at the bar, from the 10th section of the 1st article of the constitution. It is, we think, impossible to compare the sentence which prohibits a state from laying 'imposts or duties on imports or exports, except what may be *absolutely* necessary for executing its inspection laws,' with that which authorizes congress 'to make all laws which shall be necessary and proper for carrying into execution' the powers of the general government, without feeling a conviction that the convention understood itself to change materially the meaning of the word 'necessary,' by prefixing the word 'absolutely.' This word, then, like others, is used in various senses; and, in its construction, the subject, the context, the intention of the person using them, are all to be taken into view.

Let this be done in the case under consideration. The subject is the execution of those great powers on which the welfare of a nation essentially depends. It must have been the intention of those who gave these powers, to insure, so far as human prudence could insure, their beneficial execution. This could not be done by confiding the choice of means to such narrow limits as not to leave it in the power of congress to adopt any which might be appropriate, and which were conducive to the end. This provision is made in a constitution intended to endure for ages to come, and, consequently, to be adapted to the various *crises* of human affairs. . . The powers vested in congress may certainly be carried into execution, without prescribing an oath of office. The power to exact this security for the faithful performance of duty, is not given, nor is it indispensably necessary. The different departments may be established; taxes may be imposed and collected; armies and navies may be raised and maintained; and money may be borrowed, without requiring an oath of office. It might be argued, with as much plausibility as other incidental powers have been assailed, that the convention was not unmindful of this subject. The oath which might be exacted —that of fidelity to the constitution—is prescribed, and no other can be required. Yet, he would be charged with insanity, who should contend, that the legislature might not superadd, to the oath directed by the constitution, such other oath of office as its wisdom might suggest.

So, with respect to the whole penal code of the United States: whence arises the power to punish in cases not prescribed by the constitution? All admit that the government may, legitimately, punish any violation of its laws; and yet, this is not among the enumerated powers of congress. The right to enforce the observance of law, by punishing its infraction, might be denied with the more plausibility because it is expressly given in some cases. Congress is empowered 'to provide for the punishment of counterfeiting the securities and current coin of the United States,' and 'to define and punish piracies and felonies committed on the high seas, and offenses against the law of nations.' The several powers of congress may exist, in a very imperfect state, to be sure, but they may exist and be carried into execution, although no punishment should be inflicted, in cases where the right to punish is not expressly given.

Take, for example, the power 'to establish post-offices and post-roads.' This power is executed, by the single act of making the establishment. But, from this has been inferred the power and duty of carrying the mail along the post-road, from one post-office to another. And, from this implied power, has again been inferred the right to punish those who steal letters from the post-office, or rob the mail. It may be said, with some plausibility, that the right to carry the mail, and to punish those who rob it, is not indispensably necessary to the establishment of a post-office and post-road. This right is indeed essential to the beneficial exercise of the power, but not indispensably necessary to its existence. . .

If this limited construction of the word 'necessary' must be abandoned in order to punish, whence is derived the rule which would reinstate it, when the government would carry its powers into execution by means not vindictive in their nature? If the word 'necessary' means 'needful,' 'requisite,' 'essential,' 'conducive to,' in order to let in the power of punishment for the infraction of law; why is it not equally comprehensive when required to authorize the use of means which facilitate the execution of the powers of government, without the infliction of punishment?

In ascertaining the sense in which the word 'necessary' is used in this clause of the constitution, we may derive some aid from that with which it is associated. Congress shall have power 'to make all laws which shall be necessary and proper to carry into execution' the powers of the government. If the word 'necessary' was used in that strict and rigorous sense for which the counsel for the state of Maryland contend, it would be an extraordinary departure from the usual course of the human mind, as exhibited in composition, to add a word, the only possible effect of which is, to qualify that strict and rigorous meaning; to present to the mind the idea of some choice of means of legislation, not strained and compressed within the narrow limits for which gentlemen contend.

But the argument which most conclusively demonstrates the error of the construction contended for by the counsel for the state of Maryland, is founded on the intention of the convention, as manifested in the whole clause. To waste time and argument in proving that without it congress might carry its powers into execution, would be not much less idle than to hold a lighted taper to the sun. As little can it be required to prove, that in the absence of this clause, congress would have some choice of means. That it might employ those which, in its judgment, would most advantageously effect the object to be accomplished. That any means adapted to the end, any means which tended directly to the execution of the constitutional powers of the government, were in themselves constitutional. This clause, as construed by the state of Maryland, would abridge, and almost annihilate, this useful and necessary right of the legislature to select its means. That this could not be intended, is, we should think, had it not been already controverted, too apparent for controversy. We think so for the following reasons:

1st. The clause is placed among the powers of congress, not among the limitations on those powers. 2d. Its terms purport to enlarge, not to diminish the powers vested in the government. It purports to be an additional power, not a restriction on those already granted. No reason has been, or can be assigned, for thus concealing an intention to narrow the discretion of the national legislature, under words which purport to enlarge it. The framers of the constitution wished its adoption, and well knew that it would be endangered by its strength, not by its weakness. . . Had the intention been to make this clause restrictive, it would unquestionably have been so in form as well as in effect.

The result of the most careful and attentive consideration bestowed upon this clause is, that if it does not enlarge, it cannot be construed to restrain the powers of congress, or to impair the right of the legislature to exercise its best judgment in the selection of measures to carry into execution the constitutional powers of the government. If no other motive for its insertion can be suggested, a sufficient one is found in the desire to remove all doubts respecting the right to legislate on that vast mass of incidental powers which must be involved in the constitution, if that instrument be not a splendid bauble.

We admit, as all must admit, that the powers of the government are limited, and that its limits are not to be transcended. But we think the sound construction of the constitution must allow to the national legislature that discretion, with respect to the means by which the powers it confers are to be carried into execution, which will enable that body to perform the high duties assigned to it, in the manner most beneficial to the people. Let the end be legitimate, let it be within the scope of the constitution, and all means which are appropriate, which are plainly adapted to that end, which are not prohibited, but consist with the letter and spirit of the constitution, are constitutional.

That a corporation must be considered as a means not less usual, not of higher dignity, not more requiring a particular specification than other means, has been sufficiently proved. If we look to the origin of corporations, to the manner in which they have been framed in that government from which we have derived most of our legal principles and ideas, or to the uses to which they have been applied, we find no reason to suppose that a constitution, omitting, and wisely omitting, to enumerate all the means for carrying into execution the great powers vested in government, ought to have specified this. Had it been intended to grant this power, as one which should be distinct and independent, to be exercised in any case whatever, it would have found a place among the enumerated powers of the government. But being considered merely as a means, to be employed only for the purpose of carrying into execution the given powers, there could be no motive for particularly mentioning it. . .

If a corporation may be employed indiscriminately with other means to carry into execution the powers of the government, no particular reason can be assigned for excluding the use of a bank, if required for its fiscal operations. To use one, must be within the discretion of congress, if it be an appropriate mode of executing the powers of government. That it is a convenient, a useful, and essential instrument in the prosecution of its fiscal operations, is not now a subject of controversy. All those who have been concerned in the administration of our finances, have concurred in representing its importance and necessity; and so strongly have they been felt, that statesmen of the first class, whose previous opinions against it had been confirmed by every circumstance which can fix the human judgment, have yielded those opinions to the exigencies of the nation. . .

But were its necessity less apparent, none can deny its being an appropriate measure; and if it is, the degree of its necessity, as has been very justly observed, is to be discussed in another place. Should congress, in the execution of its powers, adopt measures which are prohibited by the constitution; or should congress, under the pretext of executing its powers, pass laws for the accomplishment of objects not intrusted to the government, it would become the painful duty of this tribunal, should a case requiring such a decision come before it, to say, that such an act was not the law of the land. But where the law is not prohibited, and is really calculated to effect any of the objects intrusted to the government, to undertake here to inquire into the degree of its necessity, would be to pass the line which circumscribes the judicial department, and to tread on legislative ground. This court disclaims all pretensions to such a power.

After this declaration, it can scarcely be necessary to say that the existence of state banks can have no possible influence on the question. No trace is to be found in the constitution, of an intention to create a dependence of the government of the Union on those of the states, for the execution of the great powers assigned to it. Its means are adequate to its ends; and on those means alone was it expected to rely for the accomplishment of its ends. To impose on it the necessity of resorting to means which it cannot control, which another government may furnish or withhold, would render its course precarious; the result of its measures uncertain, and create a dependence on other governments, which might disappoint its most important designs, and is incompatible with the language of the constitution. But were it otherwise, the choice of means implies a right to choose a national bank in preference to state banks, and congress alone can make the election.

After the most deliberate consideration, it is the unanimous and decided opinion of this court, that the act to incorporate the Bank of the United States is a law made in pursuance of the constitution, and is a part of the supreme law of the land.

The branches, proceeding from the same stock, and being conducive to the complete accomplishment of the object, are equally constitutional. . .

It being the opinion of the court, that the act incorporating the bank is constitutional; and that the power of establishing a branch in the state of Maryland might be properly exercised by the bank itself, we proceed to inquire—

2. Whether the state of Maryland may, without violating the constitution, tax that branch? That the power of taxation is one of vital importance; that it is retained by the states; that it is not abridged by the grant of a similar power to the government of the Union; that it is to be concurrently exercised by the two governments—are truths which have never been denied. But such is the paramount character of the constitution, that its capacity to withdraw any subject from the action of even this power, is admitted. The states are expressly forbidden to lay any duties on imports or exports, except what may be absolutely necessary for executing their inspection laws. If the obligation of this prohibition must be conceded—if it may restrain a state from the exercise of its taxing power on imports and exports—the same paramount character would seem to restrain, as it certainly may restrain, a state from such other exercise of this power, as is in its nature incompatible with, and repugnant to, the constitutional laws of the Union. A law, absolutely repugnant to another, as entirely repeals that other as if express terms of repeal were used.

On this ground, the counsel for the bank place its claim to be exempted from the power of a state to tax its operations. There is no express provision for the case, but the claim has been sustained on a principle which so entirely pervades the constitution, is so intermixed with the materials which compose it, so interwoven with its web, so blended with its texture, as to be incapable of being separated from it without rendering it into shreds. This great principle is, that the constitution and the laws made in pursuance thereof are supreme; that they control the constitution and laws of the respective states, and cannot be controlled by them. From this, which may be almost termed an axiom, other propositions are deduced as corollaries, on the truth or error of which, and on their application to this case, the cause has been supposed to depend. These are, 1st. That a power to create implies a power to preserve: 2d. That a power to destroy, if wielded by a different hand, is hostile to, and incompatible with these powers to create and to preserve: 3d. That where this repugnancy exists, that authority which is supreme must control, not yield to that over which it is supreme. . .

The argument on the part of the state of Maryland, is, not that the states may directly resist a law of congress, but that they may exercise their acknowledged powers upon it, and that the constitution leaves them this right, in the confidence that they will not abuse it.

Before we proceed to examine this argument, and to subject it to the test of the constitution, we must be permitted to bestow a few considerations on the nature and extent of this original right of taxation, which is acknowledged to remain with the states. It is admitted that the power of taxing the people and their property is essential to the very existence of government, and may be legitimately exercised on the objects to which it is applicable, to the utmost extent to which the government may choose to carry it. The only security against the abuse of this power, is found in the structure of the government itself. In imposing a tax, the legislature acts upon its constituents. This is in general, a sufficient security against erroneous and oppressive taxation.

The people of a state, therefore, give to their government a right of taxing themselves and their property, and as the exigencies of government cannot be limited, they prescribe no limits to the exercise of this right, resting confidently on the interest of the legislator, and on the influence of the constituents over their representative, to guard them against its abuse. But the means employed by the government of the Union have no such security, nor is the right of a state to tax them sustained by the same theory. Those means are not given by the people of a particular state, not given by the constituents of the legislature, which claim the right to tax them, but by the people of all the states. They are given by all, for the benefit of all—and upon theory, should be subjected to that government only which belongs to all.

It may be objected to this definition, that the power of taxation is not confined to the people and property of a state. It may be exercised upon every object brought within its jurisdiction. This is true. But to what source do we trace this right? It is obvious, that it is an incident of sovereignty, and is co-extensive with that to which it is an incident. All subjects over which the sovereign power of a state extends, are objects of taxation; but those over which it does not extend, are, upon the soundest principles, exempt from taxation. This proposition may almost be pronounced self-evident.

The sovereignty of a state extends to everything which exists by its own authority, or is introduced by its permission; but does it extend to those means which are employed by congress to carry into execution powers conferred on that body by the people of the United States? We think it demonstrable, that it does not. Those powers are not given by the people of a single state. They are given by the people of the United States, to a govern-

ment whose laws, made in pursuance of the constitution, are declared to be supreme. Consequently, the people of a single state cannot confer a sovereignty which will extend over them.

If we measure the power of taxation residing in a state, by the extent of sovereignty which the people of a single state possess, and can confer on its government, we have an intelligible standard, applicable to every case to which the power may be applied. We have a principle which leaves the power of taxing the people and property of a state unimpaired; which leaves to a state the command of all its resources, and which places beyond its reach, all those powers which are conferred by the people of the United States on the government of the Union, and all those means which are given for the purpose of carrying those powers into execution. We have a principle which is safe for the states, and safe for the Union. We are relieved, as we ought to be, from clashing sovereignty; from interfering powers; from a repugnancy between a right in one government to pull down, what there is an acknowledged right in another to build up; from the incompatibility of a right in one government to destroy, what there is a right in another to preserve. We are not driven to the perplexing inquiry, so unfit for the judicial department, what degree of taxation is the legitimate use, and what degree may amount to the abuse of the power. The attempt to use it on the means employed by the government of the Union, in pursuance of the constitution, is itself an abuse, because it is the usurpation of a power which the people of a single state cannot give.

We find, then, on just theory, a total failure of this original right to tax the means employed by the government of the Union, for the execution of its powers. The right never existed, and the question whether it has been surrendered, cannot arise.

But, waiving this theory for the present, let us resume the inquiry, whether this power can be exercised by the respective states, consistently with a fair construction of the constitution? That the power to tax involves the power to destroy; that the power to destroy may defeat and render useless the power to create; that there is a plain repugnance in conferring on one government a power to control the constitutional measures of another, which other, with respect to those very measures, is declared to be supreme over that which exerts the control, are propositions not to be denied. But all inconsistencies are to be reconciled by the magic of the word *confidence*. Taxation, it is said, does not necessarily and unavoidably destroy. To carry it to the excess of destruction, would be an abuse, to presume which, would banish that confidence which is essential to all government.

But is this a case of confidence? Would the people of any one state trust those of another with a power to control the most insignificant operations of their state government? We know they would not. Why, then, should we suppose that the people of any one state should be willing to trust those of another with a power to control the operations of a government to which they have confided their most important and most valuable interests? In the legislature of the Union alone, are all represented. The legislature of the Union alone, therefore, can be trusted by the people with the power of controlling measures which concern all, in the confidence that it will not be abused. This, then, is not a case of confidence, and we must consider it as it really is. . . If the controlling power of the states be established; if their supremacy as to taxation be acknowledged; what is to restrain their exercising control in any shape they may please to give it? Their sovereignty is not confined to taxation. That is not the only mode in which it might be displayed. The question is, in truth, a question of

supremacy; and if the right of the states to tax the means employed by the general government be conceded, the declaration that the constitution, and the laws made in pursuance thereof, shall be the supreme law of the land, is empty and unmeaning declamation. . . .

It has also been insisted, that, as the power of taxation in the general and state governments is acknowledged to be concurrent, every argument which would sustain the right of the general government to tax banks chartered by the states, will equally sustain the right of the states to tax banks chartered by the general government. But the two cases are not on the same reason. The people of all the states have created the general government, and have conferred upon it the general power of taxation. The people of all the states, and the states themselves, are represented in congress, and, by their representatives, exercise this power. When they tax the chartered institutions of the states, they tax their constituents; and these taxes must be uniform. But when a state taxes the operations of the government of the United States, it acts upon institutions created, not by their own constituents, but by people over whom they claim no control. It acts upon the measures of a government created by others as well as themselves, for the benefit of others in common with themselves. The difference is that which always exists, and always must exist, between the action of the whole on a part, and the action of a part on the whole—between the laws of a government declared to be supreme, and those of a government which, when in opposition to those laws, is not supreme.

But if the full application of this argument could be admitted, it might bring into question the right of congress to tax the state banks, and could not prove the right of the states to tax the Bank of the United States.

The court has bestowed on this subject

its most deliberate consideration. The result is a conviction that the states have no power, by taxation or otherwise, to retard, impede, burden, or in any manner control the operations of the constitutional laws enacted by congress to carry into execution the powers vested in the general government. This is, we think, the unavoidable consequence of that supremacy which the constitution has declared.

We are unanimously of opinion that the law passed by the legislature of Maryland, imposing a tax on the Bank of the United States, is unconstitutional and void.

This opinion does not deprive the states of any resources which they originally possessed. It does not extend to a tax paid by the real property of the bank, in common with the other real property within the state, nor to a tax imposed on the interest which the citizens of Maryland may hold in this institution, in common with other property of the same description throughout the state. But this is a tax on the operations of the bank, and is, consequently, a tax on the operation of an instrument employed by the government of the Union to carry its powers into execution. Such a tax must be unconstitutional.

III

The Constitutional Position of the States

NOTE

The subject of *The Proprietors of the Charles River Bridge* v. *The Proprietors of the Warren Bridge* is the contract clause of the Constitution. It was decided in 1837 after John Marshall's death. Roger Taney was Chief Justice.

Article 1, § 10, of the Constitution in part provides that 'No state shall . . . pass any . . . law impairing the obligation of contracts.' Debate on this clause, both in the convention of 1787 and in the ratifying conventions, was not extensive. It is clear that the clause was intended to protect those property rights based upon and guaranteed by contract.

The first important statement of the United States Supreme Court on the meaning of the contract clause was made in *Fletcher* v. *Peck*,[1] decided in 1810. In 1795, the legislature of Georgia sold some thirty-five million acres of public land to four speculating land companies. The sale was not in itself evil. What irritated the people was the general legislative corruption attending the sale and the fact that the recent invention of the cotton gin had enhanced the value of cotton-bearing soil. As a consequence, the succeeding legislature annulled the grant. The state courts were forbidden 'to receive any evidence of title of any kind whatever to lands from the grantees under the "usurped act." '[2] Under the Eleventh Amendment it was impossible for a disgruntled investor to sue the state in a federal court.

John Peck of Boston had dealt heavily in Georgia lands. In 1803 he sold fifteen thousand acres of his holdings to Robert Fletcher of New Hampshire for three thousand dollars. On the basis of diversity of citizenship, Fletcher then sued Peck in a federal court for the recovery of the purchase money. The case finally reached the Supreme Court where it was decided that the original grant was a contract and that the grant had been impaired by the rescinding statute. This was a broad interpretation of the contract clause, since it would seem that the framers of the Constitution intended the clause to apply to private contracts, that is, to contracts between private parties and not to agreements to which the state was a party.

The second important contract clause decision of the Supreme Court came in *Trustees of Dartmouth College* v. *Woodward*.[3] Dartmouth College was established in 1769. Its charter, granted by the Crown, provided for a board of trustees which was empowered to elect a president and to fill vacancies in its membership. In 1816, the New Hampshire legislature amended the charter so

[1] 6 Cranch 87.
[2] See Beveridge, Albert J., *The Life of John Marshall*, Boston, 1929, III, p. 564.
[3] 4 Wheat. 518 (1819).

as to place the institution under state control and changed its name to Dartmouth University. The trustees under the original charter refused to recognize the validity of the 1816 enactment, but the Court of Appeals of New Hampshire decided against them. The court declared that the contract clause was 'intended to protect private rights only,'[4] and not to limit the power of the states over their own civil institutions. The college was a public organization and thus subject to control by the legislature. Appeal to the United States Supreme Court brought a reversal. Chief Justice Marshall, speaking for the Court, held the college to be a private institution. What was more important, the Court decided for the first time that a charter of incorporation was a contract.

In *Fletcher* v. *Peck* and the Dartmouth College Case the Supreme Court construed broadly the scope of the contract clause. Both opinions contain good Federalist doctrine, namely, the sanctity of private property or the irrevocable nature of contract.

In 1785 Thomas Russell and others petitioned the Massachusetts legislature for a charter of incorporation in order that a bridge might be built across the Charles river, connecting Charlestown and Boston. The petition set forth 'the inconvenience of the transportation by ferries, over Charles river, and the public advantages that would result from a bridge.'[5] The charter was granted, a bridge was to be built and tolls exacted for forty years, at the expiration of which time the bridge would become the property of the state.

The Charles River Bridge was a successful business venture. 'Shares,' says Swisher, 'which had a par value of $333.33 sold in 1805 at $1,650 and in 1814 at $2,080.' He adds that '[w]hereas the original capitalization had been $50,000, the bridge company in 1823 claimed that the value of its property was $280,000.'[6]

In the meantime, Boston was growing. In 1792, the legislature granted a charter to another bridge company over the protests of the proprietors of the Charles River Bridge. Apparently, to mollify the proprietors the legislature extended the life of their charter to seventy years from the date of the opening of the bridge, 17 June 1786.

Then in 1828 the legislature incorporated 'The Proprietors of the Warren Bridge' for the purpose of building another bridge across the Charles. On the Boston side, the Charles and Warren Bridges were 825 feet apart, while on the Charlestown side the distance between them was only 264 feet. The Warren Bridge 'was to be surrendered to the state, as soon as the expenses of the proprietors in building and supporting it should be reimbursed; but this period was not in any event to exceed six years from the time the company commenced receiving toll.'[7] Thenceforth it was to be a free bridge.

The Charles River Bridge Company thereupon filed a bill in the Supreme Judicial Court of Massachusetts against the proprietors of the Warren Bridge, first for an injunction to prevent the erection of the bridge, and after the bridge

---

[4] Quoted in Wright, Benjamin F., *The Contract Clause of the Constitution*, Cambridge, 1938, p. 41.
[5] 11 Pet. 420, 536.
[6] Swisher, Carl Brent, *Roger B. Taney*, New York, 1935, p. 362.
[7] 11 Pet. 420, 427.

was built, for general relief, contending that the legislature in authorizing the Warren Bridge violated the contract clause of the Constitution. The Massachusetts Court dismissed the bill. The Charles River Bridge Company then appealed on a writ of error to the United States Supreme Court under the twenty-fifth section of the Judiciary Act of 1789.

PROPRIETORS OF THE CHARLES RIVER BRIDGE v. PROPRIETORS OF THE WARREN BRIDGE
11 Peters 420 (1837)

MR. CHIEF JUSTICE TANEY . . .

This brings us to the act of the legislature of Massachusetts, of 1785, by which the plaintiffs were incorporated by the name of 'The Proprietors of the Charles River Bridge'; and it is here, and in the law of 1792, prolonging their charter, that we must look for the extent and nature of the franchise conferred upon the plaintiffs.

Much has been said in the argument of the principles of construction by which this law is to be expounded, and what undertakings, on the part of the state, may be implied. The court think there can be no serious difficulty on that head. It is the grant of certain franchises by the public to a private corporation, and in a matter where the public interest is concerned. The rule of construction in such cases is well settled, both in England and by the decisions of our own tribunals. In 2 Barn. & Adol. 793, in the case of the Proprietors of the Stourbridge Canal against Wheely and others, the court say, 'the canal having been made under an act of parliament, the rights of the plaintiffs are derived entirely from that act. This, like many other cases, is a bargain between a company of adventurers and the public, the terms of which are expressed in the statute; and the rule of construction, in all such cases, is now fully established to be this; that any ambiguity in the terms of the contract, must operate against the adventurers, and in favor of the public, and the plaintiffs can claim nothing that is not clearly given them by the act.' And

the doctrine thus laid down is abundantly sustained by the authorities referred to in this decision. The case itself was as strong a one, as could well be imagined, for giving to the canal company, by implication, a right to the tolls they demanded. Their canal had been used by the defendants, to a very considerable extent, in transporting large quantities of coal. The rights of all persons to navigate the canal, were expressly secured by the act of parliament; so that the company could not prevent them from using it, and the toll demanded was admitted to be reasonable. Yet, as they only used one of the levels of the canal, and did not pass through the locks; and the statute, in giving the right to exact toll, had given it for articles which passed '*through any one or more of the locks*,' and had said nothing as to toll for navigating one of the levels; the court held that the right to demand toll, in the latter case, could not be implied, and that the company were not entitled to recover it. This was a fair case for an equitable construction of the act of incorporation, and for an implied grant; if such a rule of construction could ever be permitted in a law of that description. For the canal had been made at the expense of the company; the defendants had availed themselves of the fruits of their labours, and used the canal freely and extensively for their own profit. Still the right to exact toll could not be implied, because such a privilege was not found in the charter.

Borrowing, as we have done, our system

of jurisprudence from the English law; and having adopted, in every other case, civil and criminal, its rules for the construction of statutes; is there any thing in our local situation, or in the nature of our political institutions, which should lead us to depart from the principle where corporations are concerned? Are we to apply to acts of incorporation, a rule of construction differing from that of the English law, and, by implication, make the terms of a charter in one of the states, more unfavourable to the public, than upon an act of parliament, framed in the same words, would be sanctioned in an English court? Can any good reason be assigned for excepting this particular class of cases from the operation of the general principle; and for introducing a new and adverse rule of construction in favour of corporations, while we adopt and adhere to the rules of construction known to the English common law, in every other case, without exception? We think not; and it would present a singular spectacle, if, while the courts in England are restraining, within the strictest limits, the spirit of monopoly, and exclusive privileges in nature of monopolies, and confining corporations to the privileges plainly given to them in their charter; the courts of this country should be found enlarging these privileges by implication; and construing a statute more unfavourably to the public, and to the rights of the community, than would be done in a like case in an English court of justice. . . [Here follows a brief discussion of several cases, the chief of which, *Providence Bank* v. *Billings,* 4 Pet. 514, 7 L. Ed. 939 (1830), decided that a charter incorporating a bank with the usual powers carried with it no exemption from state taxation upon the banking business.]

The case now before the court is, in principle, precisely the same. It is a charter from a state. The act of incorporation is silent in relation to the contested power. The argument in favour of the Proprietors

of the Charles river bridge is the same, almost in words, with that used by the Providence Bank; that is, that the power claimed by the state, if it exists, may be so used as to destroy the value of the franchise they have granted to the corporation. The argument must receive the same answer; and the fact that the power has been already exercised so as to destroy the value of the franchise, cannot in any degree affect the principle. The existence of the power does not, and cannot, depend upon the circumstance of its having been [exercised] or not.

It may, perhaps, be said, that in the case of the Providence Bank, this court were speaking of the taxing power; which is of vital importance to the very existence of every government. But the object and end of all government is to promote the happiness and prosperity of the community by which it is established; and it can never be assumed, that the government intended to diminish its power of accomplishing the end for which it was created. And in a country like ours, free, active, and enterprising, continually advancing in numbers and wealth; new channels of communication are daily found necessary, both for travel and trade; and are essential to the comfort, convenience, and prosperity of the people. A state ought never to be presumed to surrender this power, because, like the taxing power, the whole community have an interest in preserving it undiminished. And when a corporation alleges, that a state has surrendered for seventy years, its power of improvement and public accommodation, in a great and important line of travel, along which a vast number of its citizens must daily pass; the community have a right to insist, in the language of this court above quoted, 'that its abandonment ought not to be presumed, in a case, in which the deliberate purpose of the state to abandon it does not appear.' The continued existence of a government would be of no great value, if, by implications and presumptions, it was disarmed of the powers necessary to accomplish the ends of its creation; and the functions it was designed to perform, transferred to the hands of privileged corporations. The rule of construction announced by the court, was not confined to the taxing power; nor is it so limited in the opinion delivered. On the contrary, it was distinctly placed on the ground that the interests of the community were concerned in preserving, undiminished, the power then in question; and whenever any power of the state is said to be surrendered or diminished, whether it be the taxing power or any other affecting the public interest, the same principle applies, and the rule of construction must be the same. No one will question that the interests of the great body of the people of the state, would, in this instance, be affected by the surrender of this great line of travel to a single corporation, with the right to exact toll, and exclude competition for seventy years. While the rights of private property are sacredly guarded, we must not forget that the community also have rights, and that the happiness and well being of every citizen depends on their faithful preservation.

Adopting the rule of construction above stated as the settled one, we proceed to apply it to the charter of 1785, to the proprietors of the Charles river bridge. . .

The relative position of the Warren bridge has already been described. It does not interrupt the passage over the Charles river bridge, nor make the way to it or from it less convenient. None of the faculties or franchises granted to that corporation have been revoked by the legislature; and its right to take the tolls granted by the charter remains unaltered. In short, all the franchises and rights of property enumerated in the charter, and there mentioned to have been granted to it, remain unimpaired. But its income is destroyed by the Warren bridge; which, being free, draws off the passengers and property which

would have gone over it, and renders their franchise of no value. This is the gist of the complaint. For it is not pretended that the erection of the Warren bridge would have done them any injury, or in any degree affected their right of property; if it had not diminished the amount of their tolls. In order then to entitle themselves to relief, it is necessary to show, that the legislature contracted not to do the act of which they complain; and that they impaired, or in other words, violated that contract by the erection of the Warren bridge.

The inquiry then is, does the charter contain such a contract on the part of the state? Is there any such stipulation to be found in that instrument? It must be admitted on all hands, that there is none—no words that even relate to another bridge, or to the diminution of their tolls, or to the line of travel. If a contract on that subject can be gathered from the charter, it must be by implication; and cannot be found in the words used. Can such an agreement be implied? The rule of construction before stated is an answer to the question. In charters of this description, no rights are taken from the public, or given to the corporation, beyond those which the words of the charter, by their natural and proper construction, purport to convey. There are no words which import such a contract as the plaintiffs in error contend for, and none can be implied; and the same answer must be given to them that was given by this court to the Providence Bank. The whole community are interested in this inquiry, and they have a right to require that the power of promoting their comfort and convenience, and of advancing the public prosperity, by providing safe, convenient, and cheap ways for the transportation of produce, and the purposes of travel, shall not be construed to have been surrendered or diminished by the state; unless it shall appear by plain words, that it was intended to be done. . .

[The court then discussed the act of 1792 which extended the term to 70 years and said that, by establishing another bridge at that time and by the terms of the act itself, the legislature asserted power to authorize improvements diminishing the profits of the Charles river bridge; the proprietors of that bridge could therefore not claim privileges in conflict with the law from which they derived their corporate existence, the original grant having expired in 1826.]

Indeed, the practice and usage of almost every state in the Union, old enough to have commenced the work of internal improvement, is opposed to the doctrine contended for on the part of the plaintiffs in error. Turnpike roads have been made in succession, on the same line of travel; the later ones interfering materially with the profits of the first. These corporations have, in some instances, been utterly ruined by the introduction of newer and better modes of transportation, and traveling. In some cases, rail roads have rendered the turnpike roads on the same line of travel so entirely useless, that the franchise of the turnpike corporation is not worth preserving. Yet in none of these cases have the corporation supposed that their privileges were invaded, or any contract violated on the part of the state. Amid the multitude of cases which have occurred, and have been daily occurring for the last forty or fifty years, this is the first instance in which such an implied contract has been contended for, and this court called upon to infer it from an ordinary act of incorporation, containing nothing more than the usual stipulations and provisions to be found in every such law. The absence of any such controversy, when there must have been so many occasions to give rise to it, proves that neither states, nor individuals, nor corporations, ever imagined that such a contract could be implied from such charters. It shows that the men who voted for these laws, never imagined that they were forming such a

contract; and if we maintain that they have made it, we must create it by a legal fiction, in opposition to the truth of the fact, and the obvious intention of the party. We cannot deal thus with the rights reserved to the states; and by legal intendments and mere technical reasoning, take away from them any portion of that power over their own internal police and improvement, which is so necessary to their well being and prosperity.

And what would be the fruits of this doctrine of implied contracts on the part of the states, and of property in a line of travel by a corporation, if it should now be sanctioned by this court? To what results would it lead us? If it is to be found in the charter to this bridge, the same process of reasoning must discover it, in the various acts which have been passed, within the last forty years, for turnpike companies. And what is to be the extent of the privileges of exclusion on the different sides of the road? The counsel who have so ably argued this case, have not attempted to define it by any certain boundaries. How far must the new improvement be distant from the old one? How near may you approach without invading its rights in the privileged line? If this court should establish the principles now contended for, what is to become of the numerous rail roads established on the same line of travel with turnpike companies; and which have rendered the franchises of the turnpike corporations of no value? Let it once be understood that such charters carry with them these implied contracts, and give this unknown and undefined property in a line of travelling; and you will soon find the old turnpike corporations awakening from their sleep, and calling upon this court to put down the improvements which have taken their place. The millions of property which have been invested in rail roads and canals, upon lines of travel which had been before occupied by turnpike corporations, will be put in jeopardy. We shall be thrown back to the improvements of the last century, and obliged to stand still, until the claims of the old turnpike corporations shall be satisfied; and they shall consent to permit these states to avail themselves of the lights of modern science, and to partake of the benefit of those improvements which are now adding to the wealth and prosperity, and the convenience and comfort, of every other part of the civilized world. Nor is this all. This court will find itself compelled to fix, by some arbitrary rule, the width of this new kind of property in a line of travel; for if such a right of property exists, we have no lights to guide us in marking out its extent, unless, indeed, we resort to the old feudal grants, and to the exclusive rights of ferries, by prescription, between towns; and are prepared to decide that when a turnpike road from one town to another, had been made, no rail road or canal, between these two points, could afterwards be established. This court are not prepared to sanction principles which must lead to such results. . .

[Judgment affirmed.]

NOTE

In *Pacific States Telephone and Telegraph Co.* v. *State of Oregon* (1912) it was contended that by the adoption of the initiative and referendum Oregon's government was divested of its republican character, contrary to Article IV, section 4, of the Constitution. The Court dismissed the case for want of jurisdiction on the ground that whether or not the state's government was republican in form was a political question.[1]

In reaching decisions the courts of the United States are, upon occasion, presented with questions the answers to which are found in the actions or words of the political departments, namely, the Congress or the executive. Such questions are called political questions. The development of political questions has been the work of the courts and affords a clear manifestation of judicial restraint, self-imposed chiefly on grounds of expediency.

The Supreme Court has declared the following to be political questions: Does a state of war exist? When did a war begin and end? Does the jurisdiction of the United States extend to an island in the high seas? What is the status of a gentleman who claims to be a representative of a foreign power? Has the government of a foreign nation been recognized by the United States? Has the United States recognized the existence of a foreign state? Has a treaty been violated or terminated? Has a treaty been properly negotiated? Has a proposed amendment to the Constitution been ratified by a given state legislature? This list is not complete, but it serves to indicate that the doctrine of political questions relates largely to questions affecting the foreign relations of the United States.

In 1867, Russia ceded to the United States the territory of Alaska, the western limit of the cession being a line running midway through the Bering Sea in a north-south direction. In 1868, Congress by law provided that 'the laws of the United States relating to customs, commerce, and navigation be . . . extended to and over all the mainland, islands, and waters of the territory ceded to the United States' by Russia. The act provided further that 'it shall be unlawful for any person or persons to kill any otter, mink, marten, sable, or fur seal, or other fur-bearing animal, within the limits of said territory, or in the waters thereof. . .'

A British schooner owned by one Cooper was captured by a United States revenue cutter fifty-nine miles off the coast of Alaska. Cooper was charged with having hunted and killed seals in violation of the act of Congress. The vessel

---

[1] The leading case on the subject, *Luther* v. *Borden*, 7 How. 1 (1849), is discussed in the opinion of the Court which follows. A recent case relating to political questions is *Colegrove* v. *Green*, 328 U.S. 549 (1946). See also *Cook* v. *Fortson*, 67 S.Ct. 21 (1946).

was libelled in the district court at Sitka and condemned. Cooper then made application to the Supreme Court of the United States for a writ of prohibition [2] to restrain the enforcement of a sentence of forfeiture and condemnation on the ground that the United States did not have jurisdiction at the point of capture.[3]

The Supreme Court in *In re Cooper* [4] considered itself bound by the position assumed by the political departments in claiming jurisdiction over half the Bering Sea and thus held that the district court did have jurisdiction over the case and so denied the writ of prohibition.

In the meantime, the British government had protested against the claims of the United States. Adjustment of differences through diplomatic channels failed. The dispute was finally submitted to arbitration; this was in 1892, and over a year later an award was made unfavorable to the claims of the United States. In the midst of this controversy, it is hardly probable that a court of the United States would have handed down a decision undermining the position of its own government. Had the Supreme Court done so we should have had the anomalous situation of the judiciary pitted against the executive and legislative departments in a matter affecting international relations.

The doctrine of the separation of powers has been offered as the theoretical basis of political questions. A more valid basis would seem to be expedience. The practicality of the Court's decision in the Cooper case is obvious. 'The national will,' said District Judge Dietrick with reference to the recognition of Russia, 'must be expressed through a single political organization; two conflicting "governments" cannot function at the same time. By the same token, discordant voices cannot express the sovereign will of the American nation.' [5] As Justice McLean has said: 'if this were not the rule, cases might often arise in which, on the most important questions of foreign jurisdiction, *there would be an irreconcilable difference between the executive and judicial departments.* By one of these departments, a foreign island or country might be considered as at peace with the United States, whilst the other would consider it in a state of war. No well regulated government has ever sanctioned a principle so unwise, and so destructive of national character.' [6] And as Chief Justice Taney declared in connection with the negotiation of treaties, 'it would be impossible for the Executive Department of the government to conduct our foreign relations with any advantage to the country, and fulfill the duties which the Constitution has imposed upon it, if every court in the country was authorized to inquire and decide whether the person who ratified the treaty on behalf of a foreign nation had the power, by its Constitution and laws, to make the engagements into which he entered. . .' [7]

[2] A common law writ which lies to an inferior court when that court is acting in excess of its jurisdiction.
[3] Territorial waters ordinarily extend to a line three miles from the low-water mark.
[4] 143 U.S. 472 (1892).
[5] The *Rogdai*, 278 Fed. 294 (1920).
[6] *Williams* v. *Suffolk Insurance Co.*, 13 Pet. 415, 420 (1839). Italics ours.
[7] *Doe* v. *Braden*, 16 How. 635, 657 (1853).

The courts, however, will assume jurisdiction over a controversy where private justiciable rights are involved, in spite of the presence of questions of extreme political significance. The Supreme Court held itself bound by the decisions of the political departments in the case of *In re Cooper,* yet as Chief Justice Fuller remarked: 'We are not to be understood, however, as underrating the weight of the argument that in a case involving private rights, the court may be obliged, if those rights are dependent upon the construction of acts of Congress or of a treaty, and the case turns upon a question, public in its nature, which has not been determined by the political departments in the form of a law specifically settling it, or authorizing the executive to do so, to render judgment, since we have no more right to decline the jurisdiction which is given than to usurp that which is not given.' [8]

PACIFIC STATES TELEPHONE & TELEGRAPH CO. v. STATE OF OREGON
223 U.S. 118 (1912)

In error to the Supreme Court of the State of Oregon to review a judgment which affirmed a judgment of the Circuit Court for Multnomah County, in that state, enforcing a tax on the gross revenue of a domestic corporation.

MR. CHIEF JUSTICE WHITE delivered the opinion of the court.

We premise by saying that while the controversy which this record presents is of much importance, it is not novel. It is important, since it calls upon us to decide whether it is the duty of the courts or the province of Congress to determine when a state has ceased to be republican in form and to enforce the guaranty of the Constitution on that subject. It is not novel, as that question has long since been determined by this court conformably to the practice of the Government from the beginning to be political in character, and therefore not cognizable by the judicial power, but solely committed by the Constitution to the judgment of Congress.

The case is this: In 1902 Oregon amended its constitution. This amendment while retaining an existing clause vesting the exclusive legislative power in a

General Assembly consisting of a senate and a house of representatives added to that provision the following: 'But the people reserve to themselves power to propose laws and amendments to the constitution and to enact or reject the same at the polls, independent of the legislative assembly, and also reserve power at their own option to approve or reject at the polls any act of the legislative assembly.' Specific means for the exercise of the power thus reserved was contained in further clauses authorizing both the amendment of the constitution and the enactment of laws to be accomplished by the method known as the initiative and that commonly referred to as the referendum. As to the first, the initiative, it suffices to say that a stated number of voters were given the right at any time to secure a submission to popular vote for approval of any matter which it was desired to have enacted into law, and providing that the proposition thus submitted, when approved by popular vote, should become the law of the State. The second, the referendum, provided for a reference to a popular vote, for approval or disapproval, of any law passed by the legislature, such

[8] 143 U.S. 472, 503 (1892).

reference to take place either as the result of the action of the legislature itself or of a petition filed for that purpose by a specified number of voters. . .

In 1903 . . . detailed provisions for the carrying into effect of this amendment were enacted by the legislature.

By resort to the initiative in 1906 a law taxing certain classes of corporations was submitted, voted on, and promulgated by the governor in 1906 . . . as having been duly adopted. By this law telephone and telegraph companies were taxed, by what was qualified as an annual license, 2 per centum upon their gross revenue derived from business done within the State. Penalties were provided for non-payment, and methods were created for enforcing payment in case of delinquency.

The Pacific States Telephone & Telegraph Company, an Oregon corporation engaged in business in that State, made a return of its gross receipts, as required by the statute, and was accordingly assessed 2 per cent. upon the amount of such return. The suit which is now before us was commenced by the State to enforce payment of this assessment and the statutory penalties for delinquency. The petition alleged the passage of the taxing law by resort to the initiative, the return made by the corporation, the assessment, the duty to pay, and the failure to make such payment.

The answer of the corporation contained twenty-nine paragraphs. Four of these challenged the validity of the tax because of defects inhering in the nature or operation of the tax. The defenses stated in these four paragraphs, however, may be put out of view, as the defendant corporation, on its own motion, was allowed by the court to strike these propositions from its answer. We may also put out of view the defenses raised by the remaining paragraphs based upon the operation and effect of the state constitution, as they are concluded by the judgment of the state court. Coming to consider these para-

graphs of the answer thus disembarrassed, it is true to say that they all, in so far as they relied upon the Constitution of the United States, rested exclusively upon an alleged infirmity of the powers of government of the State, begotten by the incorporation into the state constitution of the amendment concerning the initiative and the referendum.

The answer was demurred to as stating no defense. The demurrer was sustained, and the defendant electing not to plead further, judgment went against it, and that judgment was affirmed by the Supreme Court of Oregon. . . The court sustained the conclusion by it reached, not only for the reasons expressed in its opinion but by reference to the opinion in a prior case (*Kadderly* v. *Portland,* 44 Oregon 118, 146), where a like controversy had been determined.

The assignments of error filed on the allowance of the writ of error are numerous. The entire matters covered by each and all of them in the argument, however, are reduced to six propositions, which really amount to but one, since they are all based upon the single contention that the creation by a State of the power to legislate by the initiative and referendum causes the prior lawful state government to be bereft of its lawful character as the result of the provisions of § 4 of Art. IV of the Constitution, that 'The United States shall guarantee to every State in this Union, a Republican Form of Government, and shall protect each of them against Invasion; and on Application of the Legislature, or of the Executive (when the Legislature cannot be convened), against domestic Violence.' This being the basis of all the contentions, the case comes to the single issue whether the enforcement of that provision, because of its political character, is exclusively committed to Congress or is judicial in its character. . .

In other words, the propositions each and all proceed alone upon the theory that the adoption of the initiative and referendum destroyed all government republican in form in Oregon. This being so, the contention, if held to be sound, would necessarily affect the validity, not only of the particular statute which is before us, but of every other statute passed in Oregon since the adoption of the initiative and referendum. And indeed, the propositions go further than this, since in their essence they assert that there is no governmental function, legislative or judicial, in Oregon, because it cannot be assumed, if the proposition be well founded, that there is, at one and the same time, one and the same government, which is republican in form and not of that character.

Before immediately considering the text of § 4 of Art. iv, in order to uncover and give emphasis to the anomalous and destructive effects upon both the state and national governments which the adoption of the proposition implies, as illustrated by what we have just said, let us briefly fix the inconceivable expansion of the judicial power and the ruinous destruction of legislative authority in matters purely political which would necessarily be occasioned by giving sanction to the doctrine which underlies and would be necessarily involved in sustaining the propositions contended for. First. That however perfect and absolute may be the establishment and dominion in fact of a state government, however complete may be its participation in and enjoyment of all its powers and rights as a member of the national Government, and however all the departments of that Government may recognize such state government, nevertheless every citizen of such State, or person subject to taxation therein, or owing any duty to the established government, may be heard, for the purpose of defeating the payment of such taxes or avoiding the discharge of such duty, to assail in a court of justice the rightful existence of the State. Second. As a result, it becomes the duty of the courts of the United States, where such a claim is made, to examine as a justiciable issue the contention as to the illegal existence of a State and if such contention be thought well founded, to disregard the existence in fact of the State, of its recognition by all of the departments of the Federal Government, and practically award a decree absolving from all obligation to contribute to the support of or obey the laws of such established state government. And as a consequence of the existence of such judicial authority a power in the judiciary must be implied, unless it be that anarchy is to ensue, to build by judicial action upon the ruins of the previously established government a new one, a right which by its very terms also implies the power to control the legislative department of the Government of the United States in the recognition of such new government and the admission of representatives therefrom, as well as to strip the executive department of that government of its otherwise lawful and discretionary authority.

Do the provisions of § 4, Art. iv, bring about these strange, far-reaching, and injurious results? That is to say, do the provisions of that Article obliterate the division between judicial authority and legislative power upon which the Constitution rests? In other words, do they authorize the judiciary to substitute its judgment as to a matter purely political for the judgment of Congress on a subject committed to it and thus overthrow the Constitution upon the ground that thereby the guarantee to the States of a government republican in form may be secured, a conception which after all rests upon the assumption that the States are to be guaranteed a government republican in form by destroying the very existence of a government republican in form in the Nation.

We shall not stop to consider the text to point out how absolutely barren it is of support for the contentions sought to be based upon it, since the repugnancy of those contentions to the letter and spirit of that text is so conclusively established by prior decisions of this court as to cause the matter to be absolutely foreclosed.

In view of the importance of the subject, the apparent misapprehension on one side and seeming misconception on the other suggested by the argument as to the full significance of the previous doctrine, we do not content ourselves with a mere citation of the cases, but state more at length than we otherwise would the issues and the doctrine expounded in the leading and absolutely controlling case—*Luther* v. *Borden,* 7 How. 1.

The case came from a Circuit Court of the United States. It was an action of damages for trespass. The case grew out of what is commonly known as the Dorr Rebellion in Rhode Island and the conflict which was brought about by the effort of the adherents of that alleged government, sometimes described as 'the government established by a voluntary convention,' to overthrow the established charter government. The defendants justified on the ground that the acts done by them charged as a trespass were done under the authority of the charter government during the prevalence of martial law and for the purpose of aiding in the suppression of an armed revolt by the supporters of the insurrectionary government. The plaintiffs, on the contrary, asserted the validity of the voluntary government and denied the legality of the charter government. In the course of the trial the plaintiffs, to support the contention of the illegality of the charter government and the legality of the voluntary government, 'although that government never was able to exercise any authority in the State, nor to command obedience to its laws or to its officers,' offered certain evidence tending to show that nevertheless it was 'the lawful and established government,' upon the ground that its powers to govern have been ratified by a large majority of the male people of the State of the age of 21 years and upwards and also by a large

majority of those who were entitled to vote for general officers cast in favor of a constitution which was submitted as the result of a voluntarily assembled convention of what was alleged to be the people of the State of Rhode Island. The Circuit Court rejected this evidence and instructed the jury that, as the charter government was the established state government at the time the trespass occurred, the defendants were justified in acting under the authority of that government. This court, coming to review this ruling, at the outset pointed out 'the novelty and serious nature' of the question which it was called upon to decide. Attention also was at the inception directed to the far-reaching effect and gravity of the consequences which would be produced by sustaining the right of the plaintiff to assail and set aside the established government by recovering damages from the defendants for acts done by them under the authority of and for the purpose of sustaining such established government. On this subject it was said (p. 38):

'For, if this court is authorized to enter upon this inquiry as proposed by the plaintiff, and it should be decided that the charter government had no legal existence during the period of time above mentioned, if it had been annulled by the adoption of the opposing government, then the laws passed by its legislature during that time were nullities; its taxes wrongfully collected; its salaries and compensation to its officers illegally paid; its public accounts improperly settled; and the judgments and sentences of its courts in civil and criminal cases null and void, and the officers who carried their decisions into operation, answerable as trespassers, if not in some cases as criminals.'

Coming to review the question, attention was directed to the fact that the courts of Rhode Island had recognized the complete dominancy in fact of the charter government, and had refused to investigate the legality of the voluntary government for the purpose of decreeing the established government to be illegal, on the ground (p. 39) 'that the inquiry proposed to be made belonged to the political power and not to the judicial; that it rested with the political power to decide whether the charter government had been displaced or not; and when that decision was made, the judicial department would be bound to take notice of it as the paramount law of the State, without the aid of oral evidence or the examination of witnesses, et cetera.' It was further remarked:

'This doctrine is clearly and forcibly stated in the opinion of the supreme court of the State in the trial of Thomas W. Dorr, who was the governor elected under the opposing constitution, and headed the armed force which endeavored to maintain its authority.'

Reviewing the grounds upon which these doctrines proceeded, their cogency was pointed out and the disastrous effect of any other view was emphasized, and from a point of view of the state law the conclusive effect of the judgments of the courts of Rhode Island was referred to. The court then came to consider the correctness of the principle applied by the Rhode Island courts, in the light of § 4 of Art. iv of the Constitution of the United States. The contention of the plaintiff in error concerning that Article was, in substantial effect, thus pressed in argument: The ultimate power of sovereignty is in the people, and they in the nature of things, if the government is a free one, must have a right to change their constitution. Where, in the ordinary course, no other means exists of doing so, that right of necessity embraces the power to resort to revolution. As, however, no such right, it was urged, could exist under the Constitution, because of the provision of § 4 of Art. iv, protecting each State, on application of the legislature, or of the executive, when the legislature cannot be convened, against domestic violence, it followed that the guarantee of a government

republican in form was the means provided by the Constitution to secure the people in their right to change their government, and made the question whether such change was rightfully accomplished a judicial question determinable by the courts of the United States. To make the physical power of the United States available, at the demand of an existing state government, to suppress all resistance to its authority, and yet to afford no method of testing the rightful character of the state government, would be to render people of a particular State hopeless in case of a wrongful government. It was pointed out in the argument that the decision of the courts of Rhode Island in favor of the charter government illustrated the force of these contentions, since they proceeded solely on the established character of that government, and not upon whether the people had rightfully overthrown it by voluntarily drawing and submitting for approval a new constitution. It is thus seen that the propositions relied upon in this case were presented for decision in the most complete and most direct way. The court, in disposing of them, while virtually recognizing the cogency of the argument in so far as it emphasized the restraint upon armed resistance to an existing state government, arising from the provision of § 4 of Art. iv, and the resultant necessity for the existence somewhere in the Constitution of a tribunal, upon which the people of a State could rely, to protect them from the wrongful continuance against their will of a government not republican in form, proceeded to inquire whether a tribunal existed and its character. In doing this it pointed out that, owing to the inherent political character of such a question, its decision was not by the Constitution vested in the judicial department of the Government, but was on the contrary exclusively committed to the legislative department by whose action on such subject the judiciary were absolutely controlled. The court said (p. 42):

'Moreover, the constitution of the United States, as far as it has provided for an emergency of this kind and authorized the general government to interfere in the domestic concerns of a State, has treated the subject as political in its nature, and placed the power in the hands of that department.

'The fourth section of the fourth article of the constitution of the United States provides that the United States shall guarantee to every State in the Union a republican form of government, and shall protect each of them against invasion; and on the application of the legislature or of the executive (when the legislature cannot be convened) against domestic violence.

'Under this article of the constitution it rests with congress to decide what government is the established one in a State. For, as the United States guarantee to each State a republican government, congress must necessarily decide what government is established in the State before it can determine whether it is republican or not. And when the senators and representatives of a State are admitted into the councils of the Union, the authority of the government under which they are appointed, as well as its republican character, is recognized by the proper constitutional authority. And its decision is binding on every other department of the government, and could not be questioned in a judicial tribunal. It is true that the contest in this case did not last long enough to bring the matter to this issue; and as no senators or representatives were elected under the authority of the government of which Mr. Dorr was the head, Congress was not called upon to decide the controversy. Yet the right to decide is placed there, and not in the courts.'

Pointing out that Congress, by the act of February 28, 1795 (1 Stat. 424, c. 36), had recognized the obligation resting upon it to protect from domestic violence by conferring authority upon the President of the United States, on the application of the legislature of a State or of the Governor, to call out the militia of any other State or States to suppress such insurrection, it was suggested that if the question of what was the rightful government within the intendment of § 4 of Art. IV was a judicial one, the duty to afford protection from invasion and to suppress domestic violence would be also judicial, since those duties were inseparably related to the determination of whether there was a rightful government. If this view were correct, it was intimated, it would follow that the delegation of authority made to the President by the act of 1795 would be void as a usurpation of judicial authority, and hence it would be the duty of the courts, if they differed with the judgment of the President as to the manner of discharging this great responsibility, to interfere and set at naught his action; and the pertinent statement was made (p. 43): 'If the judicial power extends so far, the guarantee contained in the constitution of the United States is a guarantee of anarchy, and not of order.'

The fundamental doctrines thus so lucidly and cogently announced by the court, speaking through Mr. Chief Justice Taney in the case which we have thus reviewed, have never been doubted or questioned since, and have afforded the light guiding the orderly development of our constitutional system from the day of the deliverance of that decision up to the present time. We do not stop to cite other cases which indirectly or incidentally refer to the subject, but conclude by directing attention to the statement by the court, speaking through Mr. Chief Justice Fuller, in *Taylor* v. *Beckham, No. 1*, 178 U.S. 548, where, after disposing of a contention made concerning the Fourteenth Amendment and coming to consider a proposition which was necessary to be decided concerning the nature and effect of the guarantee of § 4 of Art. IV, it was said (p. 578):

'But it is said that the Fourteenth Amendment must be read with § 4 of Art. IV, of the Constitution, providing that: "the United States shall guarantee to every State in this Union a republican form of government, and shall protect each of them against invasion; and on application of the legislature, or of the executive (when the legislature cannot be convened), against domestic violence." It is argued that when the State of Kentucky entered the Union, the people "surrendered their right of forcible revolution in state affairs," and received in lieu thereof a distinct pledge to the people of the State of the guarantee of a republican form of government, and of protection against invasion, and against domestic violence; that the distinguishing feature of that form of government is the right of the people to choose their own officers for governmental administration; that this was denied by the action of the General Assembly in this instance; and, in effect, that this court has jurisdiction to enforce that guarantee, albeit the judiciary of Kentucky was unable to do so because of the division of the powers of government. And yet the writ before us was granted under § 709 of the Revised Statutes to revise the judgment of the state court on the ground that a constitutional right was decided against by that court.

'It was long ago settled that the enforcement of this guarantee belonged to the political department. *Luther* v. *Borden,* 7 How. 1. In that case it was held that the question, which of the two opposing governments of Rhode Island, namely, the charter government or the government established by a voluntary convention, was the legitimate one, was a question for the determination of the political department; and when that department had decided, the courts were bound to take notice of the decision and follow it. . .'

It is indeed a singular misconception

of the nature and character of our constitutional system of government to suggest that the settled distinction which the doctrine just stated points out between judicial authority over justiciable controversies and legislative power as to purely political questions tends to destroy the duty of the judiciary in proper cases to enforce the Constitution. The suggestion but results from failing to distinguish between things which are widely different, that is, the legislative duty to determine the political questions involved in deciding whether a state government republican in form exists, and the judicial power and everpresent duty whenever it becomes necessary, in a controversy properly submitted, to enforce and uphold the applicable provisions of the Constitution as to each and every exercise of governmental power.

How better can the broad lines which distinguish these two subjects be pointed out than by considering the character of the defense in this very case? The defendant company does not contend here that it could not have been required to pay a license tax. It does not assert that it was denied an opportunity to be heard as to the amount for which it was taxed, or that there was anything inhering in the tax or involved intrinsically in the law which violated any of its constitutional rights. If such questions had been raised they would have been justiciable, and therefore would have required the calling into operation of judicial power. Instead, however, of doing any of these things, the attack on the statute here made is of a wholly different character. Its essentially political nature is at once made manifest by understanding that the assault which the contention here advanced makes is not on the tax as a tax, but on the State as a State. It is addressed to the framework and political character of the government by which the statute levying the tax was passed. It is the government, the political entity, which (reducing the case to its essence) is called to the bar of this court, not for the purpose of testing judicially some exercise of power, assailed on the ground that its exertion has injuriously affected the rights of an individual because of repugnancy to some constitutional limitation, but to demand of the State that it establish its right to exist as a State, republican in form.

As the issues presented, in their very essence, are, and have long since by this court been, definitely determined to be political and governmental, and embraced within the scope of the powers conferred upon Congress, and not, therefore, within the reach of judicial power, it follows that the case presented is not within our jurisdiction, and the writ of error must therefore be, and it is, dismissed for want of jurisdiction.

Dismissed for want of jurisdiction.

NOTE

In *Williams* v. *North Carolina*[1] the Supreme Court was faced squarely with the question whether North Carolina had power to refuse full faith and credit to a Nevada divorce decree because, contrary to the findings of a Nevada court, North Carolina found that no bona fide domicile had been acquired in Nevada.

The Constitution requires each state to give full faith and credit to the public acts, records, and judicial proceedings of every other state, and provides that 'Congress may by general laws prescribe the manner in which such acts, records, and proceedings shall be proved, and the effect thereof.' By virtue of this authority, Congress has acted twice, in 1790 and again in 1804. These two acts, says Robert H. Jackson, 'constitute the entire contribution of Congress to the evolution of our law of faith and credit.'[2]

The act of 1790 provides that 'the acts of the legislatures of the several states shall be authenticated by having the seal of their respective states affixed thereto: That the records and the judicial proceedings of the courts of any state, shall be proved or admitted in any other court within the United States, by the attestation of the clerk, and the seal of the court annexed, if there be a seal, together with a certificate of the judge, chief justice, or presiding magistrate, as the case may be, that the said attestation is in due form. And the said records and judicial proceedings authenticated as aforesaid, shall have such faith and credit given to them in every court within the United States, as they have by law or usage in the courts of the state from whence the said records are or shall be taken.' The second act relates to the exemplification of non-judicial records and prescribes their effect in terms similar to the first act.

The 'acts, records, and judicial proceedings' to which full faith and credit is accorded relate to legislative acts, ordinances, records of deeds, wills, births, marriages, contracts, and the decisions, decrees, and judgments of state courts in civil cases. Faith and credit does not require one state to enforce the criminal laws of another state.[3]

The 'acts, records, and judicial proceedings' of one state do not, by virtue of full faith and credit, operate of their own force in another state. The seller of furniture sues to collect his money from A and gets a judgment against him. Before the judgment can be executed, A moves to a neighboring state taking the furniture with him. The seller follows A with an authenticated copy of the judgment against A, but it is necessary for the seller to bring suit against A in a court where the authenticated judgment will be accepted *as evidence* and thus

[1] 325 U.S. 226 (1945).
[2] *Full Faith and Credit, The Lawyer's Clause of the Constitution*, New York, 1945, p. 9.
[3] *Wisconsin* v. *Pelican Insurance Co.*, 127 U.S. 265 (1888).

avoid the necessity of going into the merits of the case a second time. A may claim that the court in the first state had no jurisdiction or that the procedure was faulty; but if these defenses fail, the court of the second state will enforce the judgment. Full faith and credit declared Chief Justice Fuller, 'did not make the judgments of the states domestic judgments to all intents and purposes, but only gave a general validity, faith and credit to them as evidence. No execution can be issued upon such judgments without a new suit in the tribunals of other states. . .'[4]

If the court of the original proceeding had no jurisdiction to entertain the case, then any judgment it might render would not be given full faith and credit by the courts of other states.[5] The question of jurisdiction has brought complications, particularly in connection with divorce.

The courts of each state decide for themselves the question of such jurisdiction, and the United States Supreme Court 'keeps them within proper bounds.'[6]

In the first Williams case[7] the Supreme Court held that a divorce granted by Nevada, on a finding that one spouse was domiciled in Nevada, must be respected in North Carolina, *where Nevada's finding of domicile was not questioned* though the other spouse had neither appeared nor been served with process in Nevada and though recognition of such a divorce offended the policy of North Carolina.

In the second Williams case which follows, Nevada's finding of domicile *was* questioned.

WILLIAMS ET AL. v. NORTH CAROLINA
325 U.S. 226 (1945)

Mr. Justice Frankfurter delivered the opinion of the Court.

This case is here to review judgments of the Supreme Court of North Carolina, affirming convictions for bigamous cohabitation, assailed on the ground that full faith and credit, as required by the Constitution of the United States, was not accorded divorces decreed by one of the courts of Nevada. . .

The implications of the Full Faith and Credit Clause, Article IV, § 1 of the Constitution, first received the sharp analysis of this Court in *Thompson* v. *Whitman*, 18 Wall. 457. Theretofore, uncritical notions about the scope of that Clause had

been expressed in the early case of *Mills* v. *Duryee*, 7 Cranch 481. The 'doctrine' of that case, as restated in another early case, was that 'the judgment of a state court should have the same credit, validity, and effect, in every other court in the United States, which it had in the state where it was pronounced.' *Hampton* v. *M'Connel*, 3 Wheat. 234, 235. This utterance, when put to the test, as it was in *Thompson* v. *Whitman, supra,* was found to be too loose. *Thompson* v. *Whitman* made it clear that the doctrine of *Mills* v. *Duryee* comes into operation only when, in the language of Kent, 'the jurisdiction of the court in another state is not im-

---

[4] *Atchison, T. & S. F. R. Co.* v. *Sowers,* 213 U.S. 55 (1909).

[5] For a discussion of the power of a state court to inquire into the jurisdiction of the court of another state, see *Thompson* v. *Whitman,* 18 Wall. 457 (1874).

[6] Dodd, Walter F., 1945 *Supplement: Cases on Constitutional Law,* St. Paul, 1945, p. 34.

[7] *Williams* v. *North Carolina,* 317 U.S. 287 (1942).

peached, either as to the subject matter or the person.' Only then is 'the record of the judgment . . . entitled to full faith and credit.' 1 Kent, Commentaries (2d ed., 1832) * 261 n.b. The essence of the matter was thus put in what *Thompson* v. *Whitman* adopted from Story: ' "The Constitution did not mean to confer [upon the States] a new power or jurisdiction, but simply to regulate the effect of the acknowledged jurisdiction over persons and things within their territory." ' 18 Wall. 457, 462. In short, the Full Faith and Credit Clause puts the Constitution behind a judgment instead of the too fluid, ill-defined concept of 'comity.'

But the Clause does not make a sister-State judgment a judgment in another State. The proposal to do so was rejected by the Philadelphia Convention. 2 Farrand, The Records of the Federal Convention of 1787, 447-8. 'To give it the force of a judgment in another state, it must be made a judgment there.' *M'Elmoyle* v. *Cohen,* 13 Pet. 312, 325. It can be made a judgment there only if the court purporting to render the original judgment had power to render such a judgment. A judgment in one State is conclusive upon the merits in every other State, but only if the court of the first State had power to pass on the merits— had jurisdiction, that is, to render the judgment.

'It is too late now to deny the right collaterally to impeach a decree of divorce made in another State, by proof that the court had no jurisdiction, even when the record purports to show jurisdiction. . .' It was 'too late' more than forty years ago. *German Savings Society* v. *Dormitzer,* 192 U.S. 125, 128.

Under our system of law, judicial power to grant a divorce—jurisdiction, strictly speaking—is founded on domicil. *Bell* v. *Bell,* 181 U.S. 175; *Andrews* v. *Andrews,* 188 U.S. 14. The framers of the Constitution were familiar with this jurisdictional prerequisite, and since 1789 neither this

Court nor any other court in the English-speaking world has questioned it. Domicil implies a nexus between person and place of such permanence as to control the creation of legal relations and responsibilities of the utmost significance. The domicil of one spouse within a State gives power to that State, we have held, to dissolve a marriage wheresoever contracted. In view of *Williams* v. *North Carolina,* [317 U.S. 287] *supra,* the jurisdictional requirement of domicil is freed from confusing refinements about 'matrimonial domicil,' see *Davis* v. *Davis,* 305 U.S. 32, 41, and the like. Divorce, like marriage, is of concern not merely to the immediate parties. It affects personal rights of the deepest significance. It also touches basic interests of society. Since divorce, like marriage, creates a new status, every consideration of policy makes it desirable that the effect should be the same wherever the question arises.

It is one thing to reopen an issue that has been settled after appropriate opportunity to present their contentions has been afforded to all who had an interest in its adjudication. This applies also to jurisdictional questions. After a contest these cannot be relitigated as between the parties. . . But those not parties to a litigation ought not to be foreclosed by the interested actions of others; especially not a State which is concerned with the vindication of its own social policy and has no means, certainly no effective means, to protect that interest against the selfish action of those outside its borders. The State of domiciliary origin should not be bound by an unfounded, even if not collusive, recital in the record of a court of another State. As to the truth or existence of a fact, like that of domicil, upon which depends the power to exert judicial authority, a State not a party to the exertion of such judicial authority in another State but seriously affected by it has a right, when asserting its own unquestioned authority, to ascertain the truth or existence of that crucial fact.

These considerations of policy are equally applicable whether power was assumed by the court of the first State or claimed after inquiry. This may lead, no doubt, to conflicting determinations of what judicial power is founded upon. Such conflict is inherent in the practical application of the concept of domicil in the context of our federal system. See *Worcester County Co.* v. *Riley,* 302 U.S. 292. . . What was said in *Worcester County Co.* v. *Riley, supra,* is pertinent here. 'Neither the Fourteenth Amendment nor the full faith and credit clause requires uniformity in the decisions of the courts of different states as to the place of domicil, where the exertion of state power is dependent upon domicil within its boundaries.' 302 U.S. 292, 299. If a finding by the court of one State that domicil in another State has been abandoned were conclusive upon the old domiciliary State, the policy of each State in matters of most intimate concern could be subverted by the policy of every other State. This Court has long ago denied the existence of such destructive power. The issue has a far reach. For domicil is the foundation of probate jurisdiction precisely as it is that of divorce. The ruling in *Tilt* v. *Kelsey,* 207 U.S. 43, regarding the probate of a will, is equally applicable to a sister-State divorce decree: 'the full faith and credit due to the proceedings of the New Jersey court do not require that the courts of New York shall be bound by its adjudication on the question of domicil. On the contrary, it is open to the courts of any State in the trial of a collateral issue to determine upon the evidence produced the true domicil of the deceased.' 207 U.S. 43, 53.

Although it is now settled that a suit for divorce is not an ordinary adversary proceeding, it does not promote analysis, as was recently pointed out, to label divorce proceedings as actions *in rem. Williams* v. *North Carolina, supra,* at 297.

But insofar as a divorce decree partakes of some of the characteristics of a decree *in rem,* it is misleading to say that all the world is party to a proceeding *in rem.* . . All the world is not party to a divorce proceeding. What is true is that all the world need not be present before a court granting the decree and yet it must be respected by the other forty-seven States provided—and it is a big proviso—the conditions for the exercise of power by the divorce-decreeing court are validly established whenever that judgment is elsewhere called into question. In short, the decree of divorce is a conclusive adjudication of everything except the jurisdictional facts upon which it is founded, and domicil is a jurisdictional fact. To permit the necessary finding of domicil by one State to foreclose all States in the protection of their social institutions would be intolerable.

But to endow each State with controlling authority to nullify the power of a sister State to grant a divorce based upon a finding that one spouse had acquired a new domicil within the divorcing State would, in the proper functioning of our federal system, be equally indefensible. No State court can assume comprehensive attention to the various and potentially conflicting interests that several States may have in the institutional aspects of marriage. The necessary accommodation between the right of one State to safeguard its interest in the family relation of its own people and the power of another State to grant divorces can be left to neither State.

The problem is to reconcile the reciprocal respect to be accorded by the members of the Union to their adjudications with due regard for another most important aspect of our federalism whereby 'the domestic relations of husband and wife . . . were matters reserved to the States,' *Popovici* v. *Agler,* 280 U.S. 379, 383-4, and do not belong to the United States. . . The rights that belong to all the States and the obligations which membership in the Union imposes upon all, are made effective because this Court is open to consider claims, such as this case presents, that the courts of one State have not given the full faith and credit to the judgment of a sister State that is required by Art. IV, § I of the Constitution.

But the discharge of this duty does not make of this Court a court of probate and divorce. Neither a rational system of law nor hard practicality calls for our independent determination, in reviewing the judgment of a State court, of that rather elusive relation between person and place which establishes domicil. 'It is not for us to retry the facts,' as was held in a case in which, like the present, the jurisdiction underlying a sister-State judgment was dependent on domicil. *Burbank* v. *Ernst,* 232 U.S. 162, 164. The challenged judgment must, however, satisfy our scrutiny that the reciprocal duty of respect owed by the States to one another's adjudications has been fairly discharged, and has not been evaded under the guise of finding an absence of domicil and therefore a want of power in the court rendering the judgment.

What is immediately before us is the judgment of the Supreme Court of North Carolina. We have authority to upset it only if there is want of foundation for the conclusion that that Court reached. The conclusion it reached turns on its finding that the spouses who obtained the Nevada decrees were not domiciled there. The fact that the Nevada court found that they were domiciled there is entitled to respect, and more. The burden of undermining the verity which the Nevada decrees import rests heavily upon the assailant. But simply because the Nevada court found that it had power to award a divorce decree cannot, we have seen, foreclose reexamination by another State. Otherwise, as was pointed out long ago, a court's record would establish its power and the power would be proved by the record. Such circular reasoning would give

one State a control over all the other States which the Full Faith and Credit Clause certainly did not confer. *Thompson* v. *Whitman, supra.* If this Court finds that proper weight was accorded to the claims of power by the court of one State in rendering a judgment the validity of which is pleaded in defense in another State, that the burden of overcoming such respect by disproof of the substratum of fact—here domicil—on which such power alone can rest was properly charged against the party challenging the legitimacy of the judgment, that such issue of fact was left for fair determination by appropriate procedure, and that a finding adverse to the necessary foundation for any valid sister-State judgment was amply supported in evidence, we cannot upset the judgment before us. And we cannot do so even if we also found in the record of the court of original judgment warrant for its finding that it had jurisdiction. If it is a matter turning on local law, great deference is owed by the courts of one State to what a court of another State has done. . . But when we are dealing as here with an historic notion common to all English-speaking courts, that of domicil, we should not find a want of deference to a sister State on the part of a court of another State which finds an absence of domicil where such a conclusion is warranted by the record.

When this case was first here, North Carolina did not challenge the finding of the Nevada court that petitioners had acquired domicils in Nevada. For her challenge of the Nevada decrees, North Carolina rested on *Haddock* v. *Haddock,* 201 U.S. 562. Upon retrial, however, the existence of domicil in Nevada became the decisive issue. The judgments of conviction now under review bring before us a record which may be fairly summarized by saying that the petitioners left North Carolina for the purpose of getting divorces from their respective spouses in Nevada and as soon as each had done so and married one another they left Nevada and returned to North Carolina to live there together as man and wife. Against the charge of bigamous cohabitation under § 14-183 of the North Carolina General Statutes, petitioners stood on their Nevada divorces and offered exemplified copies of the Nevada proceedings. The trial judge charged that the State had the burden of proving beyond a reasonable doubt that (1) each petitioner was lawfully married to one person; (2) thereafter each petitioner contracted a second marriage with another person outside North Carolina; (3) the spouses of petitioners were living at the time of this second marriage; (4) petitioners cohabited with one another in North Carolina after the second marriage. The burden, it was charged, then devolved upon petitioners 'to satisfy the trial jury, not beyond a reasonable doubt nor by the greater weight of the evidence, but simply to satisfy' the jury from all the evidence, that petitioners were domiciled in Nevada at the time they obtained their divorces. The court further charged that 'the recitation' of *bona fide* domicil in the Nevada decree was 'prima facie evidence' sufficient to warrant a finding of domicil in Nevada but not compelling 'such an inference.' If the jury found, as they were told, that petitioners had domicils in North Carolina and went to Nevada 'simply and solely for the purpose of obtaining' divorces, intending to return to North Carolina on obtaining them, they never lost their North Carolina domicils nor acquired new domicils in Nevada. Domicil, the jury was instructed, was that place where a person 'has voluntarily fixed his abode . . . not for a mere special or temporary purpose, but with a present intention of making it his home, either permanently or for an indefinite or unlimited length of time.'

The scales of justice must not be unfairly weighted by a State when full faith and credit is claimed for a sister-State judgment. But North Carolina has not so dealt with the Nevada decrees. She has not raised unfair barriers to their recognition. North Carolina did not fail in appreciation or application of federal standards of full faith and credit. Appropriate weight was given to the finding of domicil in the Nevada decrees, and that finding was allowed to be overturned only by relevant standards of proof. There is nothing to suggest that the issue was not fairly submitted to the jury and that it was not fairly assessed on cogent evidence.

State courts cannot avoid review by this Court of their disposition of a constitutional claim by casting it in the form of an unreviewable finding of fact. *Norris* v. *Alabama,* 294 U.S. 587, 590. This record is barren of such attempted evasion. What it shows is that petitioners, long-time residents of North Carolina, came to Nevada, where they stayed in an auto-court for transients, filed suits for divorce as soon as the Nevada law permitted, married one another as soon as the divorces were obtained, and promptly returned to North Carolina to live. It cannot reasonably be claimed that one set of inferences rather than another regarding the acquisition by petitioners of new domicils in Nevada could not be drawn from the circumstances attending their Nevada divorces. It would be highly unreasonable to assert that a jury could not reasonably find that the evidence demonstrated that petitioners went to Nevada solely for the purpose of obtaining a divorce and intended all along to return to North Carolina. Such an intention, the trial court properly charged, would preclude acquisition of domicils in Nevada. . . And so we cannot say that North Carolina was not entitled to draw the inference that petitioners never abandoned their domicils in North Carolina, particularly since we could not conscientiously prefer, were it our business to do so, the contrary finding of the Nevada court.

If a State cannot foreclose, on review here, all the other States by its finding that one spouse is domiciled within its bounds, persons may, no doubt, place themselves in situations that create unhappy consequences for them. This is merely one of those untoward results inevitable in a federal system in which regulation of domestic relations has been left with the States and not given to the national authority. But the occasional disregard by any one State of the reciprocal obligations of the forty-eight States to respect the constitutional power of each to deal with domestic relations of those domiciled within its borders is hardly an argument for allowing one State to deprive the other forty-seven States of their constitutional rights. Relevant statistics happily do not justify lurid forebodings that parents without number will disregard the fate of their offspring by being unmindful of the status of dignity to which they are entitled. But, in any event, to the extent that some one State may, for considerations of its own, improperly intrude into domestic relations subject to the authority of the other States, it suffices to suggest that any such indifference by a State to the bond of the Union should be discouraged, not encouraged.

In seeking a decree of divorce outside the State in which he has theretofore maintained his marriage, a person is necessarily involved in the legal situation created by our federal system whereby one State can grant a divorce of validity in other States only if the applicant has a *bona fide* domicil in the State of the court purporting to dissolve a prior legal marriage. The petitioners therefore assumed the risk that this Court would find that North Carolina justifiably concluded that they had not been domiciled in Nevada. Since the divorces which they sought and received in Nevada had no legal validity in North Carolina and their North Carolina spouses were still alive, they subjected themselves to prosecution for bigamous cohabitation under North Carolina

law. The legitimate finding of the North Carolina Supreme Court that the petitioners were not in truth domiciled in Nevada was not a contingency against which the petitioners were protected by anything in the Constitution of the United States. A man's fate often depends, as for instance in the enforcement of the Sherman Law, on far greater risks that he will estimate 'rightly, that is, as the jury subsequently estimates it, some matter of degree. If his judgment is wrong, not only may he incur a fine or a short imprisonment, as here; he may incur the penalty of death.' *Nash* v. *United States,* 229 U.S. 373, 377. The objection that punishment of a person for an act as a crime when ignorant of the facts making it so, involves a denial of due process of law has more than once been overruled. In vindicating its public policy and particularly one so important as that bearing upon the integrity of family life, a State in punishing particular acts may provide that 'he who shall do them shall do them at his peril and will not be heard to plead in defense good faith or ignorance.' *United States* v. *Balint,* 258 U.S. 250, 252, quoting *Shevlin-Carpenter Co.* v. *Minnesota,* 218 U.S. 57, 69-70. Mistaken notions about one's legal rights are not sufficient to bar prosecution for crime.

We conclude that North Carolina was not required to yield her State policy because a Nevada court found that petitioners were domiciled in Nevada when it granted them decrees of divorce. North Carolina was entitled to find, as she did, that they did not acquire domicils in Nevada and that the Nevada court was therefore without power to liberate the petitioners from amenability to the laws of North Carolina governing domestic relations. And, as was said in connection with another aspect of the Full Faith and Credit Clause, our conclusion 'is not a matter to arouse the susceptibilities of the States, all of which are equally concerned

in the question and equally on both sides.'
Fauntleroy v. *Lum,* 210 U.S. 230, 238. . . .
Affirmed.

[Dissenting opinions were presented by Mr. Justice Rutledge and Mr. Justice Black, Mr. Justice Douglas joining in the dissent of Mr. Justice Black. Chief Justice Stone and Mr. Justice Jackson joined in a concurring opinion by Mr. Justice Murphy.]

Federal-State Relations

NOTE

The Supreme Court in *Coyle* v. *Smith,* decided in 1911, affirmed the principle that Congress in admitting a state to the Union cannot impose conditions which deprive the new state of equality with other states.

It was proposed at the convention of 1787 that new states should be admitted 'on the same terms with the original States.' [1] Gouverneur Morris moved the deletion of this provision because he did not wish 'to throw the power' into the hands of future western states. This was seconded by Langdon of New Hampshire, who declared that 'he did not know but circumstances might arise which would render it inconvenient to admit new States on terms of equality.' [2] The motion was carried. As adopted, the Constitution provides simply that Congress shall admit new states into the Union. [3]

The policy of Congress has been to admit new states on a basis of equality with the old. Vermont and Kentucky were admitted as 'new and entire' members of the United States, while Tennessee was declared 'to be one of the United States of America, on an equal footing with the original states, in all respects whatever. . .'

One circumstance led to the imposition of conditions. The United States early acquired a large public domain. After the Revolution such states as Virginia, Massachusetts, Connecticut, South Carolina, and Georgia claimed lands as far west as the Mississippi. These claims were challenged by New Jersey, Delaware, and Rhode Island; and Maryland refused to ratify the Articles of Confederation until the great land-owning states should relinquish their claims. Between 1780 and 1802, the states mentioned above, and North Carolina, ceded their western lands to Congress either under the Articles or the Constitution. [4] Thus the public domain originated. By conquest, annexation, and purchase, this domain was enlarged, and that part of the lands over which the United States acquired dominion and which was not in private ownership at the time of acquisition became the property of the United States. [5] Public lands made possible a policy of land-grants to new states.

There were conditions attached to the land-grants. Ordinarily they were to be used or sold by the state for certain purposes—the use of schools, the support

[1] *The Records of the Federal Convention of* 1787, ed. by Max Farrand, New Haven, 1937, II, p. 454.
[2] Ibid.
[3] There is a qualifying clause: no new state may be created within the jurisdiction of another state, nor may a state be created by the junction of two or more states or parts of states, without the consent of Congress and the state legislatures concerned.
[4] Georgia did not cede her western territory until 1802.
[5] However, title to unappropriated lands in Texas was retained by the state. 5 Stat. 797 (1845).

of universities, public buildings, and capitol grounds. These grants, however, were part of a bargain. In return for the land, the state agreed that each and every tract of land sold by Congress should be exempt from any tax laid by authority of the state for a period of years. This policy was in part due to the early efforts of the Federal government to reduce its war debt. To the Secretary of the Treasury, Albert Gallatin, it was 'a matter of considerable importance to make certain that no new state created in the Northwest Territory should be in a position to impose burdens upon the federal lands within its borders that would render them unsalable or diminish their value.' [6]

Such agreements relative to exemption from state taxation of lands sold by Congress have been upheld by the Supreme Court. In *Stearns* v. *Minnesota* [7] a provision in the act admitting Minnesota to the Union which limited its legislative power over Federal public lands was upheld, Mr. Justice Brewer saying 'that a State admitted into the Union enters therein in full equality with all the others, and such equality may forbid any agreement or compact limiting or qualifying political rights and obligations; whereas, on the other hand, a mere agreement in reference to property involves no question of equality of status, but only of the power of a State to deal with the nation or with any other State in reference to such property. The case before us is one involving simply an agreement as to property between a State and the nation.' [8]

Congress has imposed upon new states conditions other than those relating to the sale of public lands. Louisiana entered the Union upon condition 'that the river Mississippi, and the navigable rivers and waters leading into the same, and into the Gulf of Mexico, shall be common highways, and forever free.' [9] Missouri was admitted on condition that a certain clause of the constitution submitted 'shall never be construed to authorize the passage of any law . . . by which any citizen, of either of the states in this Union, shall be excluded from the enjoyment of any of the privileges and immunities to which such citizen is entitled under the constitution of the United States. . .' [10] Utah was admitted on condition that polygamy would be forever banned, although the regulation of marriage is among the reserved powers of the states. Arizona entered the Union only after a clause providing for the recall of judges was removed from her constitution. [11]

The enabling act of 1906, under which Oklahoma was admitted to the Union, provided that 'The capital [sic] of said State shall temporarily be at the city of Guthrie, and shall not be changed therefrom previous to' the year 1913. The

---

[6] Orfield, Matthias Nordberg, *Federal Land Grants to the States with Special Reference to Minnesota*, Minneapolis, 1915, pp. 84-5.

[7] 179 U.S. 223 (1900).

[8] Ibid. 245.

[9] A somewhat similar condition was imposed upon Alabama. This was upheld by the Supreme Court, not on the basis of compact, but as a regulation of commerce. *Pollard's Lessee* v. *Hagan,* 3 How. 212 (1845).

[10] This precaution was constitutionally unnecessary, such privileges and immunities being already safeguarded by the Federal Constitution.

[11] That Arizona after admission amended her constitution to provide for the recall of judges was acting within her constitutional rights is unquestioned.

act required 'That the constitutional convention provided for herein shall, by ordinance irrevocable, accept the terms and conditions of this act.' The Oklahoma constitutional convention accepted, and the people ratified, the terms and conditions of the enabling act. In 1910 the state legislature by law removed the capitol from Guthrie to Oklahoma City. Coyle, a property-owner in Guthrie, commenced an action against Smith, Secretary of State of Oklahoma, to test the validity of the removal. The removal act was upheld by the state supreme court. Coyle appealed to the Supreme Court of the United States.

COYLE v. SMITH
221 U.S. 559 (1911)

MR. JUSTICE LURTON delivered the opinion of the court. . .

The only question for review by us is whether the provision of the enabling act was a valid limitation upon the power of the State after its admission, which overrides any subsequent state legislation repugnant thereto.

The power to locate its own seat of government and to determine when and how it shall be changed from one place to another, and to appropriate its own public funds for that purpose, are essentially and peculiarly state powers. That one of the original thirteen States could now be shorn of such powers by an act of Congress would not be for a moment entertained. The question then comes to this: Can a State be placed upon a plane of inequality with its sister States in the Union if the Congress chooses to impose conditions which so operate, at the time of its admission? The argument is, that while Congress may not deprive a State of any power which it *possesses,* it may, as a condition to the admission of a new State, constitutionally restrict its authority, to the extent at least, of suspending its powers for a definite time in respect to the location of its seat of government. This contention is predicated upon the constitutional power of admitting new States to this Union, and the constitutional duty of guaranteeing to 'every State in this Union a republican form of gov-

ernment.' The position of counsel for the appellants is substantially this: That the power of Congress to admit new States and to determine whether or not its fundamental law is republican in form, are political powers, and as such, uncontrollable by the courts. That Congress may in the exercise of such power impose terms and conditions upon the admission of the proposed new State, which, if accepted, will be obligatory, although they operate to deprive the State of powers which it would otherwise possess, and, therefore, not admitted upon 'an equal footing with the original States.'

The power of Congress in respect to the admission of new States is found in the third section of the fourth Article of the Constitution. . .

But what is this power? It is not to admit political organizations which are less or greater, or different in dignity or power, from those political entities which constitute the Union. It is, as strongly put by counsel, a 'power to admit States.'

The definition of 'a State' is found in the powers possessed by the original States which adopted the Constitution, a definition emphasized by the terms employed in all subsequent acts of Congress admitting new States into the Union. . .

The power is to admit 'new States into *this* Union.'

'This Union' was and is a union of States, equal in power, dignity and authority, each competent to exert that residuum of sovereignty not delegated to the United States by the Constitution itself. To maintain otherwise would be to say that the Union, through the power of Congress to admit new States, might come to be a union of States unequal in power, as including States whose powers were restricted only by the Constitution, with others whose powers had been further restricted by an act of Congress accepted as a condition of admission. Thus it would result, first, that the powers of Congress would not be defined by the Constitution alone, but in respect to new States, enlarged or restricted by the conditions imposed upon new States by its own legislation admitting them into the Union; and, second, that such new States might not exercise all of the powers which had not been delegated by the Constitution, but only such as had not been further bargained away as conditions of admission.

The argument that Congress derives from the duty of 'guaranteeing to each State in this Union a republican form of government,' power to impose restrictions upon a new State which deprives it of equality with other members of the Union, has no merit. It may imply the duty of such new State to provide itself with such state government, and impose upon Congress the duty of seeing that such form is not changed to one anti-republican,—*Minor* v. *Happersett,* 21 Wall. 162, 174, 175,—but it obviously does not confer power to admit a new State which shall be any less a State than those which compose the Union.

We come now to the question as to whether there is anything in the decisions of this court which sanctions the claim that Congress may by the imposition of conditions in an enabling act deprive a new State of any of those attributes essential to its equality in dignity and power with other States. In considering the decisions of this court bearing upon the question, we must distinguish, first, between provisions which are fulfilled by the admission of the State; second, between compacts or affirmative legislation intended to operate *in futuro,* which are within the scope of the conceded powers of Congress over the subject; and third, compacts or affirmative legislation which operate to restrict the powers of such new States in respect of matters which would otherwise be exclusively within the sphere of state power.

As to requirements in such enabling acts as relate only to the contents of the constitution for the proposed new State, little need to be said. The constitutional provision concerning the admission of new States is not a mandate, but a power to be exercised with discretion. From this alone it would follow that Congress may require, under penalty of denying admission, that the organic laws of a new State at the time of admission shall be such as to meet its approval. A constitution thus supervised by Congress would, after all, be a constitution of a State, and as such subject to alteration and amendment by the State after admission. Its force would be that of a state constitution, and not that of an act of Congress. . .

It may well happen that Congress should embrace in an enactment introducing a new State into the Union legislation intended as a regulation of commerce among the States, or with Indian tribes situated within the limits of such new State, or regulations touching the sole care and disposition of the public lands or reservations therein, which might be upheld as legislation within the sphere of the plain power of Congress. But in every such case such legislation would derive its force not from any agreement or compact with the proposed new State, nor by reason of its acceptance of such enactment as a term of admission, but solely because the power of Congress extended to the subject, and, therefore, would not operate to restrict the State's legislative power in respect of any matter which was not plainly within the regulating power of Congress. . .

No such question is presented here. The legislation in the Oklahoma enabling act relating to the location of the capital of the State, if construed as forbidding a removal by the State after its admission as a State, is referable to no power granted to Congress over the subject, and if it is to be upheld at all, it must be implied from the power to admit new States. If power to impose such a restriction upon the general and undelegated power of a State be conceded as implied from the power to admit a new State, where is the line to be drawn against restrictions imposed upon new States. The insistence finds no support in the decisions of this court. . .

In *Escanaba Co.* v. *Chicago,* cited above [107 U.S. 678], it was contended that the control of the State of Illinois over its internal waters had been restricted by the ordinance of 1787, and by the reference to that ordinance in the act of Congress admitting the State. Concerning this insistence, this court, speaking by Mr. Justice Field, said:

'Whatever the limitation upon her powers as a government whilst in a territorial condition, whether from the ordinance of 1787 or the legislation of Congress, it ceased to have any operative force, except as voluntarily adopted by her, after she became a State of the Union. On her admission she at once became entitled to and possessed of all the rights of dominion and sovereignty which belonged to the original States. She was admitted, and could be admitted, only on the same footing with them. The language of the resolution admitting her is "on an equal footing with the original States in all respects whatever." 3 Stat. 536. Equality of constitutional right and power is the condition of all the States of the Union, old and new. Illinois, therefore, as was well observed by counsel, could afterwards exercise the same power over rivers within her

limits that Delaware exercised over Black Bird Creek, and Pennsylvania over the Schuylkill River. . .'

We are unable to find in any of the decisions of this court cited by counsel for the appellants anything which contravenes the view we have expressed. *Green* v. *Biddle,* 8 Wheat. 1, involved the question as to whether a compact between two States, assented to by Congress, by which private land titles in Kentucky, derived from Virginia before the separation of Kentucky from Virginia, 'should remain valid and secure under the laws of the proposed State of Kentucky, and should be determined by the laws now existing in this (Virginia) State.' By subsequent legislation of the State of Kentucky these titles were adversely affected. This court held that this legislation impaired the obligation of a valid contract within that clause of the Constitution forbidding such impairment. Neither does *Virginia* v. *West Virginia,* 11 Wall. 39, have any bearing here. The question there was one of compact between the two States, assented to by Congress, concerning the boundary between them. Both the cases last referred to concerned compacts between States, authorized by the Constitution when assented to by Congress. They were therefore compacts and agreements sanctioned by the Constitution, while the one here sought to be enforced is one having no sanction in that instrument.

Beecher v. *Wetherby,* 95 U.S. 517, involved the validity of the grant of every sixteenth section in each township for school purposes. The grant was made by the act providing for the organization of a state government for the Territory of Wisconsin, and purported to be upon condition that the proposed State should never interfere with the primary disposal of the public lands of the United States, nor subject them to taxation. The grant was held to operate as a grant taking effect so soon as the necessary surveys were made. The conditions assented to by the State were obviously such as obtained no force from the assent of the State, since they might have been exacted as an exertion of the proper power of Congress to make rules and regulations as to the disposition of the public lands. . .

The case of the *Kansas Indians,* 5 Wall. 737, involved the power of the State of Kansas to tax lands held by the individual Indians in that State under patents from the United States. The act providing for the admission of Kansas into the Union provided that nothing contained in the constitution of the State should be construed to 'impair the rights of persons or property pertaining to the Indians of said territory, so long as such rights shall remain unextinguished by treaty with such Indians.' It was held that so long as the tribal organization of such Indians was recognized as still existing, such lands were not subject to taxation by the State. The result might be well upheld either as an exertion of the power of Congress over Indian tribes, with whom the United States had treaty relations, or as a contract by which the State had agreed to forego taxation of Indian lands, a contract quite within the power of a State to make, whether made with the United States for the benefit of its Indian wards, or with a private corporation for the supposed advantages resulting. Certainly the case has no bearing upon a compact by which the general legislative power of the State is to be impaired with reference to a matter pertaining purely to the internal policy of the State. See *Stearns* v. *Minnesota,* 179 U.S. 223. . .

If anything was needed to complete the argument against the assertion that Oklahoma has not been admitted to the Union upon an equality of power, dignity and sovereignty with Massachusetts or Virginia, it is afforded by the express provision of the act of admission, by which it is declared that when the people of the proposed new State have complied with

the terms of the act that it shall be the duty of the President to issue his proclamation, and that 'thereupon the proposed State of Oklahoma shall be deemed admitted by Congress into the Union under and by virtue of this act, *on an equal footing with the original States.'* The proclamation has been issued and the Senators and Representatives from the State admitted to their seats in the Congress.

Has Oklahoma been admitted upon an equal footing with the original States? If she has, she by virtue of her jurisdictional sovereignty as such a State may determine for her own people the proper location of the local seat of government. She is not equal in power to them if she cannot.

In *Texas* v. *White,* 7 Wall. 700, 725, Chief Justice Chase said in strong and memorable language that, 'the Constitution, in all of its provisions looks to an indestructible Union, composed of indestructible States.'

In *Lane County* v. *Oregon,* 7 Wall. 76, he said:

'The people of the United States constitute one nation, under one government, and this government, within the scope of the powers with which it is invested, is supreme. On the other hand, the people of each State compose a State, having its own government, and endowed with all the functions essential to separate and independent existence. The States disunited might continue to exist. Without the States in union there could be no such political body as the United States.'

To this we may add that the constitutional equality of the States is essential to the harmonious operation of the scheme upon which the Republic was organized. When that equality disappears we may remain a free people, but the Union will not be the Union of the Constitution.

Judgment affirmed.

Mr. Justice McKenna and Mr. Justice Holmes dissent.

V

Citizenship and Aliens

NOTE

The Supreme Court in *Girouard* v. *United States,* decided in 1946, held that citizenship was not to be denied an alien who approved the principles of American government and could defend and support it even though religious convictions prevented him from bearing arms.

It has not always been possible legally for a person to renounce allegiance to king or country. An English court in 1571 condemned to death as a traitor a prisoner of war who had been born in England but who had renounced allegiance to Queen Elizabeth in becoming a subject of King Philip of Spain.[1] Early in the 17th century Sir Edward Coke in the first part of the *Institutes of the Laws of England* set forth as part of the common law the rule *nemo potest exuere patriam:* no man may disclaim his native land, nor abjure the bond of allegiance. Blackstone in his *Commentaries* declared that 'An Englishman who removes to France, or to China, owes the same allegiance to the king of England there as at home, and twenty years hence as well as now. For it is a principle of universal law, that the natural-born subject of one prince cannot by any act of his own, no, not by swearing allegiance to another, put off or discharge his natural allegiance to the former. . .'

The doctrine of perpetual allegiance met with little opposition until the latter part of the 18th century when the American colonies established their independence. The Virginia legislature in 1779 passed an act in which expatriation was declared to be a 'natural right which all men have of relinquishing the country in which birth or other accident may have thrown them. . .'[2]

In the exercise of its power to establish a uniform rule of naturalization, the first Congress enacted a naturalization statute.

The Federal courts espoused the common law doctrine of perpetual allegiance. As Chief Justice Ellsworth said: 'The common law of this country remains the same as it was before the Revolution. . . When a foreigner presents himself here . . .,' and fulfills the requirements of the naturalization law, 'we grant him the privilege of a citizen . . . but this implies no consent of the government, that our own citizens should expatriate themselves.'[3] 'In countries so crowded with inhabitants,' said Ellsworth, 'that the means of subsistence are difficult to be obtained, it is reason and policy to permit emigration. But our policy is dif-

---

[1] *Story's Case.* See Tsiang, I-Mien, *The Question of Expatriation in America Prior to 1907,* Baltimore, 1942, p. 12.

[2] Hening's *Statutes,* Richmond, 1822, x, p. 129.

[3] The Chief Justice was sitting in the Circuit Court, District of Connecticut. *United States* v. *Isaac Williams* (1799) in Scott, James Brown, *Cases on International Law,* St. Paul, 1922, pp. 158, 159, 160.

ferent; for our country is but sparsely settled, and we have no inhabitants to spare.'[4]

For long after the American Revolution Great Britain held to the doctrine of perpetual allegiance, and this led to sharp conflict with the United States particularly as regards impressment. The Ministry, October 16, 1807, issued a proclamation 'For Recalling and Prohibiting British Seamen from Serving Foreign Princes and States,' part of which warned that naturalization would not be regarded as divesting British subjects of their duties to England. Such naturalized persons would be pardoned if they at once returned to their proper allegiance, otherwise they would be guilty of high treason.[5]

The question of expatriation assumed acute form and great indignation was aroused in the United States when a British court in 1867 convicted several naturalized Americans of Irish origin of treason for participation in the Fenian movement.[6] At the trial of Warren and Costello, the defendants demanded as American citizens a jury *de medietate linguae,* which was allowed under British law to aliens. This demand was denied on the ground of their original British allegiance.[7] 'According to the law of this country,' said the court, 'he who is born under the allegiance to the British Crown, cannot, by any act of his own, or by any act of any foreign country or government, be absolved from that allegiance.'[8]

In 1868, Congress by joint resolution declared the right of expatriation to be 'a natural and inherent right of all people.' In 1870, Parliament enacted a law which provided in part that 'Any British subject who has at any time before, or may at any time after the passing of the Act, . . . voluntarily become naturalized in such foreign state, shall, from and after the time of his so having become naturalized in such foreign state, be deemed to have ceased to be a British subject and be regarded as an alien. . .'[9] The expatriation controversy between the United States and Great Britain came to an end with the Anglo-American treaty of August, 1870.[10]

The Federal government provides the rules to be followed when an alien desires to become a citizen of the United States.[11] One of the requirements is that the petitioner must take an oath of allegiance, part of which reads as follows: '. . . I will support and defend the Constitution and laws of the United States of America against all enemies, foreign and domestic. . .' The Supreme Court has construed this to mean the bearing of arms if necessary. 'That it is

[4] Ibid. pp. 159-60.

[5] *American State Papers,* III, pp. 25-6.

[6] A secret society active in Ireland and the United States devoted to the separation of Ireland and England.

[7] See Moore, John Bassett, *A Digest of International Law,* Washington, 1906, III, pp. 579-80.

[8] Quoted in Tsiang, op. cit. p. 86.

[9] 33 Vict. c. 14.

[10] Haswell, John H., *Treaties and Conventions Concluded between the United States and Other Powers,* Washington, 1889, pp. 470-72. Problems of expatriation involved countries other than Great Britain. See Moore, op. cit. III, pp. 552-735; and Hackworth, Green Haywood, *Digest of International Law,* Washington, 1942, III, pp. 161-279.

[11] This power is vested exclusively in Congress. *Chirac* v. *Chirac,* 2 Wheat. 259 (1817).

the duty of citizens,' said Mr. Justice Butler speaking for the Court in *United States* v. *Schwimmer*,[12] 'by force of arms to defend our government against all enemies whenever necessity arises is a fundamental principle of the Constitution.'[13] Rozika Schwimmer was 'an uncompromising pacifist with no sense of nationalism but only a cosmic sense of belonging to the human family. . .'[14] Her application was denied because she was unwilling to bear arms in defense of the United States.

In *United States* v. *Macintosh*,[15] the application of a Canadian, a member of the theological faculty of Yale University, was rejected on the ground that 'he was not willing "to promise beforehand" to take up arms, "without knowing the cause for which (his) country may go to war. . ."'[16] He was not unwilling to bear arms in a war to which the United States was a party, but he would '"have to believe that the war was morally justified."'[17] *United States* v. *Bland*[18] was decided on the same day as the Macintosh case. The applicant in this case was a woman, also a Canadian, who 'refused to take the oath of allegiance prescribed by the statute to defend the Constitution and laws of the United States against all enemies, etc., except with the written interpolation of the words, "as far as my conscience as a Christian will allow."'[19] Her application was denied.

GIROUARD v. UNITED STATES
328 U.S. 61 (1946)

MR. JUSTICE DOUGLAS delivered the opinion of the Court.

In 1943 petitioner, a native of Canada, filed his petition for naturalization in the District Court of Massachusetts. He stated in his application that he understood the principles of the government of the United States, believed in its form of government, and was willing to take the oath of allegiance (54 Stat. 1157, 8 U.S.C. § 735(b)) which reads as follows:

'I hereby declare, on oath, that I absolutely and entirely renounce and abjure all allegiance and fidelity to any foreign prince, potentate, state, or sovereignty of whom or which I have heretofore been a subject or citizen; that I will support and defend the Constitution and laws of the United States of America against all enemies, foreign and domestic; that I will bear true faith and allegiance to the same; and that I take this obligation freely without any mental reservation or purpose of evasion: So help me God.'

To the question in the application 'If necessary, are you willing to take up arms in defense of this country?' he replied, 'No (Non-combatant) Seventh Day Adventist.' He explained that answer before the examiner by saying 'it is a purely religious matter with me, I have no political or personal reasons other than that.' He did not claim before his Selective Service board exemption from all military service, but only from combatant military duty. At the hearing in the District Court petitioner testified that he was a member of the Seventh Day Adventist denomination, of whom approximately 10,000 were then serving in the armed forces of the United States as non-combatants, especially in the medical corps; and that he was willing to serve in the army but would not bear arms. The District Court admitted him to

[12] 279 U.S. 644 (1929).
[13] Ibid. 650.
[14] Ibid. 651-2.

[15] 283 U.S. 605 (1931).
[16] Ibid. 629.
[17] Ibid.

[18] 283 U.S. 636 (1931).
[19] Ibid.

citizenship. The Circuit Court of Appeals reversed, one judge dissenting. 149 F. 2d 760. It took that action on the authority of *United States* v. *Schwimmer,* 279 U.S. 644; *United States* v. *Macintosh,* 282 U.S. 605, and *United States* v. *Bland,* 283 U.S. 636, saying that the facts of the present case brought it squarely within the principles of those cases. The case is here on a petition for a writ of *certiorari* which we granted so that those authorities might be re-examined.

The *Schwimmer, Macintosh* and *Bland* cases involved, as does the present one, a question of statutory construction. At the time of those cases, Congress required an alien, before admission to citizenship, to declare on oath in open court that 'he will support and defend the Constitution and laws of the United States against all enemies, foreign and domestic, and bear true faith and allegiance to the same.' It also required the court to be satisfied that the alien had during the five-year period immediately preceding the date of his application 'behaved as a man of good moral character, attached to the principles of the Constitution of the United States, and well disposed to the good order and happiness of the same.' Those provisions were reenacted into the present law in substantially the same form.

While there are some factual distinctions between this case and the *Schwimmer* and *Macintosh* cases, the *Bland* case on its facts is indistinguishable. But the principle emerging from the three cases obliterates any factual distinction among them. As we recognized in *In re Summers,* 325 U.S. 561, 572, 577, they stand for the same general rule—that an alien who refuses to bear arms will not be admitted to citizenship. As an original proposition, we could not agree with that rule. The fallacies underlying it were, we think, demonstrated in the dissents of Mr. Justice Holmes in the *Schwimmer* case and of Mr. Chief Justice Hughes in the *Macintosh* case.

The oath required of aliens does not in terms require that they promise to bear arms. Nor has Congress expressly made any such finding a prerequisite to citizenship. To hold that it is required is to read it into the Act by implication. But we could not assume that Congress intended to make such an abrupt and radical departure from our traditions unless it spoke in unequivocal terms.

The bearing of arms, important as it is, is not the only way in which our institutions may be supported and defended, even in times of great peril. Total war in its modern form dramatizes as never before the great cooperative effort necessary for victory. The nuclear physicists who developed the atomic bomb, the worker at his lathe, the seaman on cargo vessels, construction battalions, nurses, engineers, litter bearers, doctors, chaplains—these, too, made essential contributions. And many of them made the supreme sacrifice. Mr. Justice Holmes stated in the *Schwimmer* case (279 U.S. p. 655) that 'the Quakers have done their share to make the country what it is.' And the annals of the recent war show that many whose religious scruples prevented them from bearing arms, nevertheless were unselfish participants in the war effort. Refusal to bear arms is not necessarily a sign of disloyalty or a lack of attachment to our institutions. One may serve his country faithfully and devotedly, though his religious scruples make it impossible for him to shoulder a rifle. Devotion to one's country can be as real and as enduring among non-combatants as among combatants. One may adhere to what he deems to be his obligation to God and yet assume all military risks to secure victory. The effort of war is indivisible; and those whose religious scruples prevent them from killing are no less patriots than those whose special traits or handicaps result in their assignment to duties far behind the fighting front. Each is making the utmost contribution according to his capacity. The fact that his role may be limited by religious convictions rather than by physical characteristics has no necessary bearing on his attachment to his country or on his willingness to support and defend it to his utmost.

Petitioner's religious scruples would not disqualify him from becoming a member of Congress or holding other public offices. While Article VI, Clause 3 of the Constitution provides that such officials, both of the United States and the several States, 'shall be bound by Oath or Affirmation, to support this Constitution,' it significantly adds that 'no religious Test shall ever be required as a Qualification to any Office or public Trust under the United States.' The oath required is in no material respect different from that prescribed for aliens under the Nationality Act. It has long contained the provision 'that I will support and defend the Constitution of the United States against all enemies, foreign and domestic; that I will bear true faith and allegiance to the same; that I take this obligation freely, without any mental reservation or purpose of evasion.' R.S. § 1757, 5 U.S.C. § 16. As Mr. Chief Justice Hughes stated in his dissent in the *Macintosh* case (283 U.S. p. 631), 'the history of the struggle for religious liberty, the large number of citizens of our country, from the very beginning, who have been unwilling to sacrifice their religious convictions, and in particular, those who have been conscientiously opposed to war and who would not yield what they sincerely believed to be their allegiance to the will of God'—these considerations make it impossible to conclude 'that such persons are to be deemed disqualified for public office in this country because of the requirement of the oath which must be taken before they enter upon their duties.'

There is not the slightest suggestion that Congress set a stricter standard for aliens seeking admission to citizenship than it did for officials who make and enforce the laws of the nation and administer its af-

fairs. It is hard to believe that one need forsake his religious scruples to become a citizen but not to sit in the high councils of state.

As Mr. Chief Justice Hughes pointed out (*United States* v. *Macintosh, supra,* p. 633) religious scruples against bearing arms have been recognized by Congress in the various draft laws. This is true of the Selective Training and Service Act of 1940 (54 Stat. 889, 50 U.S.C. App. § 305(g)) as it was of earlier acts. He who is inducted into the armed services takes an oath which includes the provision 'that I will bear true faith and allegiance to the United States of America; that I will serve them honestly and faithfully against all their enemies whomsoever.' 41 Stat. 809, 10 U.S.C. § 1581. Congress has thus recognized that one may adequately discharge his obligations as a citizen by rendering non-combatant as well as combatant services. This respect by Congress over the years for the conscience of those having religious scruples against bearing arms is cogent evidence of the meaning of the oath. It is recognition by Congress that even in time of war one may truly support and defend our institutions though he stops short of using weapons of war.

That construction of the naturalization oath received new support in 1942. In the Second War Powers Act, 56 Stat. 176, 182, 8 U.S.C., Supp. IV, § 1001, Congress relaxed certain of the requirements for aliens who served honorably in the armed forces of the United States during World War II and provided machinery to expedite their naturalization. Residence requirements were relaxed, educational tests were eliminated, and no fees were required. But no change in the oath was made; nor was any change made in the requirement that the alien be attached to the principles of the Constitution. Yet it is clear that these new provisions cover non-combatants as well as combatants. If petitioner had served as a non-combatant (as he was willing to do), he could have been admitted to citizenship by taking the identical oath which he is willing to take. Can it be that the oath means one thing to one who has served to the extent permitted by his religious scruples and another thing to one equally willing to serve but who has not had the opportunity? It is not enough to say that petitioner is not entitled to the benefits of the new Act since he did not serve in the armed forces. He is not seeking the benefits of the expedited procedure and the relaxed requirements. The oath which he must take is identical with the oath which both non-combatants and combatants must take. It would, indeed, be a strange construction to say that 'support and defend the Constitution and laws of the United States of America against all enemies, foreign and domestic' demands something more from some than it does from others. That oath can hardly be adequate for one who is unwilling to bear arms because of religious scruples and yet exact from another a promise to bear arms despite religious scruples.

Mr. Justice Holmes stated in the *Schwimmer* case (279 U.S. pp. 654-55): 'if there is any principle of the Constitution that more imperatively calls for attachment than any other it is the principle of free thought—not free thought for those who agree with us but freedom for the thought that we hate. I think that we should adhere to that principle with regard to admission into, as well as to life within this country.' The struggle for religious liberty has through the centuries been an effort to accommodate the demands of the State to the conscience of the individual. The victory for freedom of thought recorded in our Bill of Rights recognizes that in the domain of conscience there is a moral power higher than the State. Throughout the ages men have suffered death rather than subordinate their allegiance to God to the authority of the State. Freedom of religion guaranteed by the First Amendment is the product of that struggle. As we recently stated in *United States* v. *Ballard*, 322 U.S. 78, 86, 'Freedom of thought, which includes freedom of religious belief, is basic in a society of free men. *Board of Education* v. *Barnette*, 319 U.S. 624.' The test oath is abhorrent to our tradition. Over the years Congress has meticulously respected that tradition and even in time of war has sought to accommodate the military requirements to the religious scruples of the individual. We do not believe that Congress intended to reverse that policy when it came to draft the naturalization oath. Such an abrupt and radical departure from our traditions should not be implied. See *Schneiderman* v. *United States*, 320 U.S. 118, 132. Cogent evidence would be necessary to convince us that Congress took that course.

We conclude that the *Schwimmer, Macintosh* and *Bland* cases do not state the correct rule of law.

We are met, however, with the argument that even though those cases were wrongly decided, Congress has adopted the rule which they announced. The argument runs as follows: Many efforts were made to amend the law so as to change the rule announced by those cases; but in every instance the bill died in committee. Moreover, when the Nationality Act of 1940 was passed, Congress reenacted the oath in its pre-existing form, though at the same time it made extensive changes in the requirements and procedure for naturalization. From this it is argued that Congress adopted and reenacted the rule of the *Schwimmer, Macintosh,* and *Bland* cases. . .

We stated in *Helvering* v. *Hallock,* 309 U.S. 106, 119, that 'It would require very persuasive circumstances enveloping Congressional silence to debar this Court from reexamining its own doctrines.' It is at best treacherous to find in Congressional silence alone the adoption of a controlling rule of law. We do not think under the circumstances of this legislative history that we can properly place on the shoulders of Congress the burden of the Court's own error. The history of the 1940 Act is at most equivocal. It contains no affirmative recognition of the rule of the *Schwimmer, Macintosh* and *Bland* cases. The silence of Congress and its inaction are as consistent with a desire to leave the problem fluid as they are with an adoption by silence of the rule of those cases. But for us, it is enough to say that since the date of those cases Congress never acted affirmatively on this question but once and that was in 1942. At that time, as we have noted, Congress specifically granted naturalization privileges to non-combatants who like petitioner were prevented from bearing arms by their religious scruples. That was affirmative recognition that one could be attached to the principles of our government and could support and defend it even though his religious convictions prevented him from bearing arms. And, as we have said, we cannot believe that the oath was designed to exact something more from one person than from another. Thus the affirmative action taken by Congress in 1942 negatives any inference that otherwise might be drawn from its silence when it reenacted the oath in 1940.

Reversed.

Mr. Justice Jackson took no part in the consideration or decision of this case.

Mr. Chief Justice Stone dissenting.

I think the judgment should be affirmed, for the reason that the court below, in applying the controlling provisions of the naturalization statutes, correctly applied them as earlier construed by this Court, whose construction Congress has adopted and confirmed.

In three cases decided more than fifteen years ago, this Court denied citizenship to applicants for naturalization who had announced that they proposed to take the prescribed oath of allegiance with the reservation or qualification that they would not, as naturalized citizens, assist in the defense of this country by force of arms or give their moral support to the government in any war which they did not believe to be morally justified or in the best interests of the country. See *United States* v. *Schwimmer,* 279 U.S. 644; *United States* v. *Macintosh,* 283 U.S. 605; *United States* v. *Bland,* 283 U.S. 636.

In each of these cases this Court held that the applicant had failed to meet the conditions which Congress had made prerequisite to naturalization by § 4 of the Naturalization Act of June 29, 1906, c. 3592, 34 Stat. 596, the provisions of which, here relevant, were enacted in the Nationality Act of October 14, 1940. See c. 876, 54 Stat. 1137, as amended by the Act of March 27, 1942, c. 199, 56 Stat. 176, 182-183, and by the Act of December 7, 1942, c. 690, 56 Stat. 1041, 8 U.S.C. §§ 707, 735. Section 4 of the Naturalization Act of 1906, paragraph 'Third,' provided that before the admission to citizenship the applicant should declare on oath in open court that 'he will support and defend the Constitution and laws of the United States against all enemies, foreign and domestic, and bear true faith and allegiance to the same.' And paragraph 'Fourth' required that before admission it be made to appear 'to the satisfaction of the court admitting any alien to citizenship' that at least for a period of five years immediately preceding his application the applicant 'has behaved as a man of good moral character, attached to the principles of the Constitution of the United States, and well disposed to the good order and happiness of the same.' In applying these provisions in the cases mentioned, this Court held only that an applicant who is unable to take the oath of allegiance without the reservations or qualifications insisted upon by the applicants in those cases manifests his want of attachment to the principles of the Constitution and his unwillingness to meet the requirements of the oath, that he will support and defend the Constitution of the United States and bear true faith and allegiance to the same, and so does not comply with the statutory conditions of his naturalization. No question of the constitutional power of Congress to withhold citizenship on these grounds was involved. That power was not doubted. See *Selective Draft Law Cases,* 245 U.S. 366; *Hamilton* v. *Regents,* 293 U.S. 245. The only question was of construction of the statute which Congress at all times has been free to amend if dissatisfied with the construction adopted by the Court.

With three other Justices of the Court I dissented in the *Macintosh* and *Bland* cases, for reasons which the Court now adopts as ground for overruling them. Since this Court in three considered earlier opinions has rejected the construction of the statute for which the dissenting Justices contended, the question, which for me is decisive of the present case, is whether Congress has likewise rejected that construction by its subsequent legislative action, and has adopted and confirmed the Court's earlier construction of the statutes in question. A study of Congressional action taken with respect to proposals for amendment of the naturalization laws since the decision in the *Schwimmer* case, leads me to conclude that Congress has adopted and confirmed this Court's earlier construction of the naturalization laws. For that reason alone I think that the judgment should be affirmed.

The construction of the naturalization statutes, adopted by this Court in the three cases mentioned, immediately became the target of an active, publicized legislative attack in Congress which persisted for a period of eleven years, until the adoption of the Nationality Act in 1940. Two days after the *Schwimmer* case was decided, a bill was introduced in the House, H.R. 3547, 71st Cong., 1st Sess., to give the Naturalization Act a construction contrary to that which had been given to it by this Court and which, if adopted, would have made the applicants rejected by this Court in the *Schwimmer, Macintosh* and *Bland*

cases eligible for citizenship. This effort to establish by Congressional action that the construction which this Court had placed on the Naturalization Act was not one which Congress had adopted or intended, was renewed without success after the decision in the *Macintosh* and *Bland* cases, and was continued for a period of about ten years. All of these measures were of substantially the same pattern as H.R. 297, 72d Cong., 1st Sess., introduced December 8, 1931, at the first session of Congress, after the decision in the *Macintosh* case. It provided that no person otherwise qualified 'shall be debarred from citizenship by reason of his or her religious views or philosophical opinions with respect to the lawfulness of war as a means of settling international disputes, but every alien admitted to citizenship shall be subject to the same obligation as the native-born citizen.' H.R. 3547, 71st Cong., 1st Sess., introduced immediately after the decision in the *Schwimmer* case, had contained a like provision, but with the omission of the last clause beginning 'but every alien.' Hearings were had before the House Committee on Immigration and Naturalization on both bills at which their proponents had stated clearly their purpose to set aside the interpretation placed on the oath of allegiance by the *Schwimmer* and *Macintosh* cases. There was opposition on each occasion. Bills identical with H.R. 297 were introduced in three later Congresses. None of these bills were reported out of Committee. The other proposals, all of which failed of passage . . . had the same purpose and differed only in phraseology.

Thus, for six successive Congresses, over a period of more than a decade, there were continuously pending before Congress in one form or another proposals to overturn the rulings in the three Supreme Court decisions in question. Congress declined to adopt these proposals after full hearings and after speeches on the floor advocating the change. 72 Cong. Rec. 6966-7; 75th Cong. Rec. 15354-7. In the meantime the decisions of this Court had been followed in *Clarke's Case,* 301 Pa. 321; *Beale* v. *United States,* 71 F. 2d 737; *In re Warkentin,* 93 F. 2d 42. In *Beale* v. *United States, supra,* the court pointed out that the proposed amendments affecting the provisions of the statutes relating to admission to citizenship had failed, saying: 'We must conclude, therefore, that these statutory requirements as construed by the Supreme Court have Congressional sanction and approval.'

Any doubts that such were the purpose and will of Congress would seem to have been dissipated by the reenactment by Congress in 1940 of Paragraphs 'Third' and 'Fourth' of § 4 of the Naturalization Act of 1906, and by the incorporation in the Act of 1940 of the very form of oath which had been administratively prescribed for the applicants in the *Schwimmer, Macintosh* and *Bland* cases. See Rule 8(c), Naturalization Regulations of July 1, 1929.

The Nationality Act of 1940 was a comprehensive, slowly matured and carefully considered revision of the naturalization laws. The preparation of this measure was not only delegated to a Congressional Committee, but was considered by a committee of Cabinet members, one of whom was the Attorney General. Both were aware of our decisions in the *Schwimmer* and related cases and that no other question pertinent to the naturalization laws had been as persistently and continuously before Congress in the ten years following the decision in the *Schwimmer* case. The modifications in the provisions of Paragraphs 'Third' and 'Fourth' of § 4 of the 1906 Act show conclusively the careful attention which was given to them.

In the face of this legislative history the 'failure of Congress to alter the Act after it had been judicially construed, and the enactment by Congress of legislation which implicitly recognizes the judicial construction as effective, is persuasive of legislative recognition that the judicial construction is the correct one. This is the more so where, as here, the application of the statute . . . has brought forth sharply conflicting views both on the Court and in Congress, and where after the matter has been fully brought to the attention of the public and the Congress, the latter has not seen fit to change the statute.' *Apex Hosiery Co.* v. *Leader,* 310 U.S. 469, 488-9. . . It is the responsibility of Congress, in reenacting a statute, to make known its purpose in a controversial matter of interpretation of its former language, at least when the matter has, for over a decade, been persistently brought to its attention. In the light of this legislative history, it is abundantly clear that Congress has performed that duty. In any case it is not lightly to be implied that Congress has failed to perform it and has delegated to this Court the responsibility of giving new content to language deliberately readopted after this Court has construed it. For us to make such an assumption is to discourage, if not to deny, legislative responsibility. By thus adopting and confirming this Court's construction of what Congress had enacted in the Naturalization Act of 1906 Congress gave that construction the same legal significance as though it had written the very words into the Act of 1940.

The only remaining question is whether Congress repealed this construction by enactment of the 1942 amendments of the Nationality Act. That Act extended special privileges to applicants for naturalization who were aliens and who have served in the armed forces of the United States in time of war, by dispensing with or modifying existing requirements, relating to declarations of intention, period of residence, education, and fees. It left unchanged the requirements that the applicant's behavior show his attachment to the principles of the Constitution and that he take the oath of allegiance. In adopting the 1942 amendments Congress did not have before it any question of the oath of allegiance with which it had been concerned when it adopted the 1940 Act. In 1942 it was concerned with the grant of special favors to those seeking naturalization who had worn the uniform and rendered military service in time of war and who could satisfy such naturalization requirements as had not been dispensed with by the amendments. In the case of those entitled to avail themselves of these privileges, Congress left it to the naturalization authorities, as in other cases, to determine whether, by their applications and their conduct in the military service, they satisfy the requirements for naturalization which have not been waived.

It is pointed out that one of the 1942 amendments, 8 U.S.C., Supp. IV, § 1004, provided that the provisions of the amendment should not apply to 'any conscientious objector who performed no military duty whatever or refused to wear the uniform.' It is said that the implication of this provision is that conscientious objectors who rendered noncombatant service and wore the uniform were, under the 1942 amendments, to be admitted to citizenship. From this it is argued that since the 1942 amendments apply to those who have been in noncombatant, as well as combatant, military service, the amendment must be taken to include some who have rendered noncombatant service who are also conscientious objectors and who would be admitted to citizenship under the 1942 amendments, even though they made the same reservations as to the oath of allegiance as did the applicants in the *Schwimmer, Macintosh* and *Bland* cases. And it is said that although the 1942 amendments are not applicable to petitioner, who has not been in military service, the oath cannot mean one thing as to him and another as to those who have been in the noncombatant service.

To these suggestions there are two answers. One is that if the 1942 amendment be construed as including noncombatants who are also conscientious objec-

tors, who are unwilling to take the oath without the reservations made by the applicants in the *Schwimmer, Macintosh* and *Bland* cases, the only effect would be to exempt noncombatant conscientious objectors from the requirements of the oath, which had clearly been made applicable to all objectors, including petitioner, by the Nationality Act of 1940, and from which petitioner was not exempted by the 1942 amendments. If such is the construction of the 1942 Act, there is no constitutional or statutory obstacle to Congress' taking such action. Congress if it saw fit could have admitted to citizenship those who had rendered noncombatant service, with a modified oath or without any oath at all. Petitioner has not been so exempted.

Since petitioner was never in the military or naval forces of the United States, we need not decide whether the 1942 amendments authorized any different oath for those who had been in noncombatant service than for others. The amendments have been construed as requiring the same oath, without reservations, from conscientious objectors, as from others. *In re Nielsen,* 60 F. Supp. 240. Not all of those who rendered noncombatant service were conscientious objectors. Few were. There were others in the noncombatant service who had announced their conscientious objections to combatant service, who may have waived or abandoned their objections. Such was the experience in the First World War. See 'Statement Concerning the Treatment of Conscientious Objectors in the Army,' prepared and published by direction of the Secretary of War, June 18, 1919. All such could have taken the oath without the reservations made by the applicants in the *Schwimmer, Macintosh* and *Bland* cases and would have been entitled to the benefits of the 1942 amendments, provided they had performed military duty and had not refused to wear the uniform. The fact that Congress recognized by indirection, in 8 U.S.C., Supp. IV, § 1004, that those who had appeared in the role of conscientious objectors, might become citizens by taking the oath of allegiance and establishing their attachment to the principles of the Constitution, does not show that Congress dispensed with the requirements of the oath as construed by this Court and plainly confirmed by Congress in the Nationality Act of 1940. There is no necessary inconsistency in this respect between the 1940 Act and the 1942 amendments. Without it repeal by implication is not favored. . . The amendments and their legislative history give no hint of any purpose of Congress to relax, at least for persons who had rendered no military service, the requirements of the oath of allegiance and proof of attachment to the Constitution as this Court had interpreted them and as the Nationality Act of 1940 plainly required them to be interpreted. It is not the function of this Court to disregard the will of Congress in the exercise of its constitutional power.

MR. JUSTICE REED and MR. JUSTICE FRANKFURTER join in this opinion.

VI

Civil Rights

NOTE

The framers of the Constitution gave little thought to a bill of rights. Towards the close of the convention Mason of Virginia 'wished the plan had been prefaced with a Bill of Rights, & would second a Motion if made for the purpose.' He added that a bill of rights 'would give great quiet to the people. . .'[1] Gerry of Massachusetts moved for a committee to prepare a bill of rights, and Mason seconded the motion. Roger Sherman of Connecticut spoke against it. He was 'for securing the rights of the people where requisite' but he believed that a bill of rights was unnecessary. 'The State Declarations of Rights,' he said, 'are not repealed by this Constitution; and being in force are sufficient. . .' He believed that the 'Legislature may be safely trusted.'[2] Gerry's motion was defeated.

Why did the framers omit a bill of rights? Delegates to the Federal convention were asked this question when they returned to their home states. James Wilson, speaking before the Pennsylvania ratifying convention, said 'we are repeatedly called upon to give some reason why a bill of rights has not been annexed to the proposed plan. . .'[3]

Mr. Wilson could not speak for every member of the convention, but in his opinion 'such an idea never entered the mind of many of them.'[4] Apparently the subject was so unimportant he did not recollect 'to have heard the subject mentioned till within about three days of the time of our rising. . .' Wilson added that 'it appears from the example of other states, as well as from principle, that a bill of rights is neither an essential nor a necessary instrument in framing a system of government, since liberty may exist and be well secured without it.' Alexander Hamilton also considered a bill of rights unnecessary partly on the ground that the constitutions of several of the states were without a bill of rights. 'New York' he said, 'is of the number. And yet the opposers of the new system, in this State, who profess an unlimited admiration for its constitution, are among the most intemperate partisans of a bill of rights.'[5]

A bill of rights was also deemed to have been impracticable. Who, asked Wilson, 'will be bold enough to undertake to enumerate all the rights of the people?'[6] 'Enumerate all the rights of men! I am sure, Sir, that no gentleman in the late convention would have attempted such a thing. . .'[7]

[1] *The Records of the Federal Convention of* 1787, ed. by Max Farrand, New Haven, 1937, II, p. 587.
[2] Ibid. p. 588.
[3] Ibid. III, p. 143.
[4] Elliot's *Debates,* II, p. 435.
[5] The *Federalist,* ed. by Henry Cabot Lodge, New York, 1888, p. 533.
[6] *The Records of the Federal Convention of* 1787, op. cit. III, p. 144.
[7] Ibid. p. 162.

Both Wilson and Hamilton believed a bill of rights to be dangerous. If an enumeration of rights is made, Wilson asserted, and incorporated in a fundamental instrument of government, then 'it must be remembered that if the enumeration is not complete, everything not expressly mentioned will be presumed to be purposely omitted.'[8] Hamilton was not of the opinion that a provision concerning freedom of the press would confer a regulating power, but he considered it obvious that unscrupulous men might view such a restriction as a 'plausible pretence for claiming that power.'[9]

Furthermore, Hamilton considered certain provisions of the proposed Constitution to be of the nature of a bill of rights, providing greater security, or at least equal security, in comparison with the safeguards of the constitution of the state of New York.[10]

Again, Hamilton argued that bills of rights have no place in a constitutional government founded upon the consent of the people but only in the relations of king and subjects. Magna Carta, the Petition of Right, and the Bill of Rights were all 'stipulations between kings and their subjects, abridgements of prerogative in favor of privilege, reservations of rights not surrendered to the prince.'[11] The proposed Constitution, however, is not a princely concession. It is rather the positive act of 'We, The People,' the object of which is 'to secure the blessings of liberty to ourselves and our posterity. . .' Here, says Hamilton, 'is a better recognition of popular rights, than volumes of those aphorisms which make the principal figure in several of our State bills of rights, and which would sound much better in a treatise of ethics than in a constitution of government.'[12] Hamilton believed that no matter how high-sounding and fine such declarations of rights may be, respect for them 'must altogether depend on public opinion, and on the general spirit of the people and of the government.'[13]

Charles C. Pinckney of South Carolina noted that most bills of rights commence with a declaration that 'all men are by nature born free.' The Federal convention to his mind could only have made such a declaration with bad grace since 'a large part of our property consists in men who are actually born slaves.'[14]

The Federal convention completed its work 17 September 1787. The proposed Constitution was submitted to the Congress of the Confederation, and on the twenty-eighth of the month that body resolved unanimously, 'That the said report, with the resolutions and letter accompanying the same, be transmitted to the several legislatures, in order to be submitted to a Convention of delegates chosen in each state, by the people thereof, in conformity to the resolves of the Convention made and provided in that case.'[15]

Several of the states ratified the proposed Constitution without reservation or suggestion as to a bill of rights. A number ratified the Constitution, but recom-

[8] Ibid. p. 144.
[9] The *Federalist*, op. cit. p. 537.
[10] See Art. I, sec. 3, cl. 7; sec. 9, cl. 2, 3, 7; Art. III, sec. 2, cl. 3; sec. 3, cl. 1, 2.
[11] The *Federalist*, op. cit. p. 536.
[12] Ibid.
[13] Ibid.
[14] Elliot's *Debates*, IV, p. 316.
[15] Elliot's *Debates*, I, p. 319.

mended the early adoption of a bill of rights. And the first Congress under the new instrument of government submitted twelve proposed amendments to the state legislatures.[16] The first two proposed amendments were not ratified;[17] amendments 3 to 12 inclusive were adopted; and proposed amendment 3 became the First Amendment.

The subject of the Barnette case which follows is freedom of religion. In this case, which concerns Jehovah's Witnesses and the compulsory flag salute, the Supreme Court reversed its decision of 1940 upholding the flag salute.[18]

WEST VIRGINIA STATE BOARD OF EDUCATION ET AL. v. BARNETTE ET AL.
319 U.S. 624 (1943)

MR. JUSTICE JACKSON delivered the opinion of the Court.

Following the decision by this Court on June 3, 1940, in *Minersville School District* v. *Gobitis,* 310 U.S. 586, the West Virginia legislature amended its statutes to require all schools therein to conduct courses of instruction in history, civics, and in the Constitutions of the United States and of the State 'for the purpose of teaching, fostering and perpetuating the ideals, principles and spirit of Americanism, and increasing the knowledge of the organization and machinery of the government.' Appellant Board of Education was directed, with advice of the State Superintendent of Schools, to 'prescribe the courses of study covering these subjects' for public schools. The Act made it the duty of private, parochial, and denominational schools to prescribe courses of study 'similar to those required for the public schools.'

The Board of Education on January 9,

1942, adopted a resolution containing recitals taken largely from the Court's *Gobitis* opinion and ordering that the salute to the flag become 'a regular part of the program of activities in the public schools,' that all teachers and pupils 'shall be required to participate in the salute honoring the Nation represented by the Flag; provided, however, that refusal to salute the Flag be regarded as an act of insubordination, and shall be dealt with accordingly.'

The resolution originally required the 'commonly accepted salute to the Flag' which it defined. Objections to the salute as 'being too much like Hitler's' were raised by the Parent and Teachers Association, the Boy and Girl Scouts, the Red Cross, and the Federation of Women's Clubs. Some modification appears to have been made in deference to these objections, but no concession was made to Jehovah's Witnesses. What is now required is the 'stiff-arm' salute, the saluter to keep the

---

[16] *Documents Illustrative of the Formation of the Union of the American States,* Washington, 1927, pp. 1063-5.

[17] The rejected amendments are as follows: Article I: 'After the first enumeration required by the first Article of the Constitution, there shall be one Representative for every thirty thousand, until the number shall amount to one hundred, after which, the proportion shall be so regulated by Congress, that there shall be not less than one hundred Representatives, nor less than one Representative for every forty thousand persons, until the number of Representatives shall amount to two hundred, after which the proportion shall be so regulated by Congress, that there shall not be less than two hundred Representatives, nor more than one Representative for every fifty thousand persons.' Article II: 'No law, varying the compensation for the services of the Senators and Representatives, shall take effect, until an election of Representatives shall have intervened.' Ibid. pp. 1063-4.

[18] *Minersville School District* v. *Gobitis,* 310 U.S. 586.

right hand raised with palm turned up while the following is repeated: 'I pledge allegiance to the Flag of the United States of America and to the Republic for which it stands; one Nation, indivisible, with liberty and justice for all.'

Failure to conform is 'insubordination' dealt with by expulsion. Readmission is denied by statute until compliance. Meanwhile the expelled child is 'unlawfully absent' and may be proceeded against as a delinquent. His parents or guardians are liable to prosecution, and if convicted are subject to fine not exceeding $50 and jail term not exceeding thirty days.

Appellees, citizens of the United States and of West Virginia, brought suit in the United States District Court for themselves and others similarly situated asking its injunction to restrain enforcement of these laws and regulations against Jehovah's Witnesses. The Witnesses are an unincorporated body teaching that the obligation imposed by law of God is superior to that of laws enacted by temporal government. Their religious beliefs include a literal version of Exodus, Chapter 20, verses 4 and 5, which says: 'Thou shalt not make unto thee any graven image, or any likeness of anything that is in heaven above, or that is in the earth beneath, or that is in the water under the earth; thou shalt not bow down thyself to them nor serve them.' They consider that the flag is an 'image' within this command. For this reason they refuse to salute it.

Children of this faith have been expelled from school and are threatened with exclusion for no other cause. Officials threaten to send them to reformatories maintained for criminally inclined juveniles. Parents of such children have been prosecuted and are threatened with prosecutions for causing delinquency.

The Board of Education moved to dismiss the complaint setting forth these facts and alleging that the law and regulations are an unconstitutional denial of religious freedom, and of freedom of speech, and are invalid under the 'due process' and 'equal protection' clauses of the Fourteenth Amendment to the Federal Constitution. The cause was submitted on the pleadings to a District Court of three judges. It restrained enforcement as to the plaintiffs and those of that class. The Board of Education brought the case here by direct appeal.

This case calls upon us to reconsider a precedent decision, as the Court throughout its history often has been required to do. Before turning to the *Gobitis* case, however, it is desirable to notice certain characteristics by which this controversy is distinguished.

The freedom asserted by these appellees does not bring them into collision with rights asserted by any other individual. It is such conflicts which most frequently require intervention of the State to determine where the rights of one end and those of another begin. But the refusal of these persons to participate in the ceremony does not interfere with or deny rights of others to do so. Nor is there any question in this case that their behavior is peaceable and orderly. The sole conflict is between authority and rights of the individual. The State asserts power to condition access to public education on making a prescribed sign and profession and at the same time to coerce attendance by punishing both parent and child. The latter stand on a right of self-determination in matters that touch individual opinion and personal attitude.

As the present CHIEF JUSTICE said in dissent in the *Gobitis* case, the State may 'require teaching by instruction and study of all in our history and in the structure and organization of our government, including the guaranties of civil liberty, which tend to inspire patriotism and love of country.' 310 U.S. at 604. Here, however, we are dealing with a compulsion of students to declare a belief. They are not merely made acquainted with the flag salute so that they may be informed as to what it is or even what it means. The issue here is whether this slow and easily neglected route to aroused loyalties constitutionally may be short-cut by substituting a compulsory salute and slogan. This issue is not prejudiced by the Court's previous holding that where a State, without compelling attendance, extends college facilities to pupils who voluntarily enroll, it may prescribe military training as part of the course without offense to the Constitution. It was held that those who take advantage of its opportunities may not on ground of conscience refuse compliance with such conditions. *Hamilton* v. *Regents,* 293 U.S. 245. In the present case attendance is not optional. That case is also to be distinguished from the present one because, independently of college privileges or requirements, the State has power to raise militia and impose the duties of service therein upon its citizens.

There is no doubt that, in connection with the pledges, the flag salute is a form of utterance. Symbolism is a primitive but effective way of communicating ideas. The use of an emblem or flag to symbolize some system, idea, institution, or personality, is a short cut from mind to mind. Causes and nations, political parties, lodges and ecclesiastical groups seek to knit the loyalty of their followings to a flag or banner, a color or design. The State announces rank, function, and authority through crowns and maces, uniforms and black robes; the church speaks through the Cross, the Crucifix, the altar and shrine, and clerical raiment. Symbols of State often convey political ideas just as religious symbols come to convey theological ones. Associated with many of these symbols are appropriate gestures of acceptance or respect: a salute, a bowed or bared head, a bended knee. A person gets from a symbol the meaning he puts into it, and what is one man's comfort and inspiration is another's jest and scorn.

Over a decade ago Chief Justice Hughes led this Court in holding that the display of a red flag as a symbol of opposition by peaceful and legal means to organized government was protected by the free speech guaranties of the Constitution. *Stromberg* v. *California,* 283 U.S. 359. Here it is the State that employs a flag as a symbol of adherence to government as presently organized. It requires the individual to communicate by word and sign his acceptance of the political ideas it thus bespeaks. Objection to this form of communication when coerced is an old one, well known to the framers of the Bill of Rights.

It is also to be noted that the compulsory flag salute and pledge requires affirmation of a belief and an attitude of mind. It is not clear whether the regulation contemplates that pupils forego any contrary convictions of their own and become unwilling converts to the prescribed ceremony or whether it will be acceptable if they simulate assent by words without belief and by a gesture barren of meaning. It is now a commonplace that censorship or suppression of expression of opinion is tolerated by our Constitution only when the expression presents a clear and present danger of action of a kind the State is empowered to prevent and punish. It would seem that involuntary affirmation could be commanded only on even more immediate and urgent grounds than silence. But here the power of compulsion is invoked without any allegation that remaining passive during a flag salute ritual creates a clear and present danger that would justify an effort even to muffle expression. To sustain the compulsory flag salute we are required to say that a Bill of Rights which guards the individual's right to speak his own mind, left it open to public authorities to compel him to utter what is not in his mind.

Whether the First Amendment to the Constitution will permit officials to order observance of ritual of this nature does not depend upon whether as a voluntary exercise we would think it to be good, bad or merely innocuous. Any credo of nationalism is likely to include what some disapprove or to omit what others think essential, and to give off different overtones as it takes on different accents or interpretations. If official power exists to coerce acceptance of any patriotic creed, what it shall contain cannot be decided by courts, but must be largely discretionary with the ordaining authority, whose power to prescribe would no doubt include power to amend. Hence validity of the asserted power to force an American citizen publicly to profess any statement of belief or to engage in any ceremony of assent to one, presents questions of power that must be considered independently of any idea we may have as to the utility of the ceremony in question.

Nor does the issue as we see it turn on one's possession of particular religious views or the sincerity with which they are held. While religion supplies appellees' motive for enduring the discomforts of making the issue in this case, many citizens who do not share these religious views hold such a compulsory rite to infringe constitutional liberty of the individual. It is not necessary to inquire whether non-conformist beliefs will exempt from the duty to salute unless we first find power to make the salute a legal duty.

The *Gobitis* decision, however, *assumed*, as did the argument in that case and in this, that power exists in the State to impose the flag salute discipline upon school children in general. The Court only examined and rejected a claim based on religious beliefs of immunity from an unquestioned general rule. The question which underlies the flag salute controversy is whether such a ceremony so touching matters of opinion and political attitude may be imposed upon the individual by official authority under powers committed to any political organization under our Constitution. We examine rather than assume existence of this power and, against this broader definition of issues in this case, reëxamine specific grounds assigned for the *Gobitis* decision.

1. It was said that the flag-salute controversy confronted the Court with 'the problem which Lincoln cast in memorable dilemma: "Must a government of necessity be too *strong* for the liberties of its people, or too *weak* to maintain its own existence"?' and that the answer must be in favor of strength. *Minersville School District* v. *Gobitis, supra,* at 596.

We think these issues may be examined free of pressure or restraint growing out of such considerations.

It may be doubted whether Mr. Lincoln would have thought that the strength of government to maintain itself would be impressively vindicated by our confirming power of the State to expel a handful of children from school. Such oversimplification, so handy in political debate, often lacks the precision necessary to postulates of judicial reasoning. If validly applied to this problem, the utterance cited would resolve every issue of power in favor of those in authority and would require us to override every liberty thought to weaken or delay execution of their policies.

Government of limited power need not be anemic government. Assurance that rights are secure tends to diminish fear and jealousy of strong government, and by making us feel safe to live under it makes for its better support. Without promise of a limiting Bill of Rights it is doubtful if our Constitution could have mustered enough strength to enable its ratification. To enforce those rights today is not to choose weak government over strong government. It is only to adhere as a means of strength to individual freedom of mind in preference to officially disciplined uniformity for which history indicates a disappointing and disastrous end.

The subject now before us exemplifies this principle. Free public education, if faithful to the ideal of secular instruction and political neutrality, will not be partisan or enemy of any class, creed, party, or faction. If it is to impose any ideological discipline, however, each party or denomination must seek to control, or failing that, to weaken the influence of the educational system. Observance of the limitations of the Constitution will not weaken government in the field appropriate for its exercise.

2. It was also considered in the *Gobitis* case that functions of educational officers in States, counties and school districts were such that to interfere with their authority 'would in effect make us the school board for the country.' *Id.* at 598.

The Fourteenth Amendment, as now applied to the States, protects the citizen against the State itself and all of its creatures—Boards of Education not excepted. These have, of course, important, delicate, and highly discretionary functions, but none that they may not perform within the limits of the Bill of Rights. That they are educating the young for citizenship is reason for scrupulous protection of Constitutional freedoms of the individual, if we are not to strangle the free mind at its source and teach youth to discount important principles of our government as mere platitudes.

Such Boards are numerous and their territorial jurisdiction often small. But small and local authority may feel less sense of responsibility to the Constitution, and agencies of publicity may be less vigilant in calling it to account. The action of Congress in making flag observance voluntary and respecting the conscience of the objector in a matter so vital as raising the Army contrasts sharply with these local regulations in matters relatively trivial to the welfare of the nation. There are village tyrants as well as village Hampdens, but none who acts under color of law is beyond reach of the Constitution.

3. The *Gobitis* opinion reasoned that this is a field 'where courts possess no marked and certainly no controlling competence,' that it is committed to the legislatures as well as the courts to guard cherished liberties and that it is constitutionally appropriate to 'fight out the wise use of legislative authority in the forum of public opinion and before legislative assemblies rather than to transfer such a contest to the judicial arena,' since all the 'effective means of inducing political changes are left free.' *Id.* at 597-598, 600.

The very purpose of a Bill of Rights was to withdraw certain subjects from the vicissitudes of political controversy, to place them beyond the reach of majorities and officials and to establish them as legal principles to be applied by the courts. One's right to life, liberty, and property, to free speech, a free press, freedom of worship and assembly, and other fundamental rights may not be submitted to vote; they depend on the outcome of no elections.

In weighing arguments of the parties it is important to distinguish between the due process clause of the Fourteenth Amendment as an instrument for transmitting the principles of the First Amendment and those cases in which it is applied for its own sake. The test of legislation which collides with the Fourteenth Amendment because it also collides with the principles of the First, is much more definite than the test when only the Fourteenth is involved. Much of the vagueness of the due process clause disappears when the specific prohibitions of the First become its standard. The right of a State to regulate, for example, a public utility may well include, so far as the due process test is concerned, power to impose all of the restrictions which a legislature may have a 'rational basis' for adopting. But freedoms of speech and of press, of assembly, and of worship may not be infringed on such slender grounds. They are susceptible of restriction only to prevent grave and immediate danger to interests which the State may lawfully protect. It is important to note that while it is the Fourteenth Amendment which bears directly upon the State it is the more specific limiting principles of the First Amendment that finally govern this case.

Nor does our duty to apply the Bill of Rights to assertions of official authority depend upon our possession of marked competence in the field where the invasion of rights occurs. True, the task of translating the majestic generalities of the Bill of Rights, conceived as part of the pattern of liberal government in the eighteenth century, into concrete restraints on officials dealing with the problems of the twentieth century, is one to disturb self-confidence. These principles grew in soil which also produced a philosophy that the individual was the center of society, that his liberty was attainable through mere absence of governmental restraints, and that government should be entrusted with few controls and only the mildest supervision over men's affairs. We must transplant these rights to a soil in which the *laissez-faire* concept or principle of non-interference has withered at least as to economic affairs, and social advancements are increasingly sought through closer integration of society and through expanded and strengthened governmental controls. These changed conditions often deprive precedents of reliability and cast us more than we would choose upon our own judgment. But we act in these matters not by authority of our competence but by force of our commissions. We cannot, because of modest estimates of our competence in such specialties as public education, withhold the judgment that history authenticates as the function of this Court when liberty is infringed.

4. Lastly, and this is the very heart of the *Gobitis* opinion, it reasons that 'National unity is the basis of national security,' that the authorities have 'the right to select appropriate means for its attainment,' and hence reaches the conclusion that such compulsory measures toward 'national unity' are constitutional. *Id*. at 595. Upon the verity of this assumption depends our answer in this case.

National unity as an end which officials may foster by persuasion and example is not in question. The problem is whether under our Constitution compulsion as here employed is a permissible means for its achievement.

Struggles to coerce uniformity of sentiment in support of some end thought essential to their time and country have been waged by many good as well as by evil men. Nationalism is a relatively recent phenomenon but at other times and places the ends have been racial or territorial security, support of a dynasty or regime, and particular plans for saving souls. As first and moderate methods to attain unity have failed, those bent on its accomplishment must resort to an ever-increasing severity. As governmental pressure toward unity becomes greater, so strife becomes more bitter as to whose unity it shall be. Probably no deeper division of our people could proceed from any provocation than from finding it necessary to choose what doctrine and whose program public educational officials shall compel youth to unite in embracing. Ultimate futility of such attempts to compel coherence is the lesson of every such effort from the Roman drive to stamp out Christianity as a disturber of its pagan unity, the Inquisition, as a means to religious and dynastic unity, the Siberian exiles as a means to Russian unity, down to the fast failing efforts of our present totalitarian enemies. Those who begin coercive elimination of dissent soon find themselves exterminating dissenters. Compulsory unification of opinion achieves only the unanimity of the graveyard.

It seems trite but necessary to say that the First Amendment to our Constitution was designed to avoid these ends by avoiding these beginnings. There is no mysticism in the American concept of the State or of the nature or origin of its authority. We set up government by consent of the governed, and the Bill of Rights denies those in power any legal opportunity to coerce that consent. Authority here is to be controlled by public opinion, not public opinion by authority.

The case is made difficult not because the principles of its decision are obscure but because the flag involved is our own. Nevertheless, we apply the limitations of the Constitution with no fear that freedom to be intellectually and spiritually diverse or even contrary will disintegrate the social organization. To believe that patriotism will not flourish if patriotic ceremonies are voluntary and spontaneous instead of a compulsory routine is to make an unflattering estimate of the appeal of our institutions to free minds. We can have intellectual individualism and the rich cultural diversities that we owe to exceptional minds only at the price of occasional eccentricity and abnormal attitudes. When they are so harmless to others or to the State as those we deal with here, the price is not too great. But freedom to differ is not limited to things that do not matter much. That would be a mere shadow of freedom. The test of its substance is the right to differ as to things that touch the heart of the existing order.

If there is any fixed star in our constitutional constellation, it is that no official, high or petty, can prescribe what shall be orthodox in politics, nationalism, religion, or other matters of opinion or force citizens to confess by word or act their faith therein. If there are any circumstances which permit an exception, they do not now occur to us.

We think the action of the local authorities in compelling the flag salute and pledge transcends constitutional limitations on their power and invades the sphere of intellect and spirit which it is the purpose of the First Amendment to our Constitution to reserve from all official control.

The decision of this Court in *Minersville School District* v. *Gobitis* and the holdings of those few *per curiam* decisions which preceded and foreshadowed it are overruled, and the judgment enjoining enforcement of the West Virginia Regulation is

Affirmed.

Mr. Justice Roberts and Mr. Justice Reed adhere to the views expressed by the Court in *Minersville School District* v. *Gobitis,* 310 U.S. 586, and are of the opinion that the judgment below should be reversed.

Mr. Justice Black and Mr. Justice Douglas, concurring [with majority opinion]. . .

Mr. Justice Murphy, concurring [with majority opinion]. . .

Mr. Justice Frankfurter, dissenting. . .

NOTE

The guarantees of civil liberty in the Constitution serve to protect the individual from oppressive public authority. Freedom of speech and of the press and the right to worship as one pleases; the right to know the charges if one is accused of crime, to secure the assistance of counsel, to be protected in one's home and effects against unreasonable searches and seizures and from twice being put in danger of life and limb for the same offense; the right not to be deprived of life, liberty or property without due process of law, are among the individual rights guaranteed in the Constitution. They reflect the long struggle for individual liberty which extends back in English history at least to 1215 when King John put his mark to Magna Carta.

The Constitution as originally adopted contained few express safeguards against Federal encroachment upon individual liberty.[1] The first Congress proposed twelve amendments, ten of which were adopted by the states.[2] The first eight amendments are commonly called the Bill of Rights.

In *Barron* v. *Mayor and City Council of Baltimore*,[3] decided in 1833, the Supreme Court decided that the Bill of Rights operated to restrain the Federal government alone and not the states. Barron sought to recover damages because the corporation in diverting certain streams for public purposes had caused sand and earth to accumulate in the neighborhood of Barron's wharf, thus rendering it useless to larger vessels. Before the Supreme Court Barron argued, in part, that the authority exercised by the Mayor and City Council was repugnant to the Fifth Amendment of the Constitution which declares that 'private property shall not be taken for public use without just compensation.' He contended that the Fifth Amendment 'declares principles which regulate the legislation of the states, for the protection of the people in each and all the states. . .'[4]

The Supreme Court dismissed the case for want of jurisdiction. 'The constitution was ordained,' said Chief Justice Marshall, 'and established by the people of the United States for themselves, for their own government, and not for the government of the individual states. Each state established a constitution for itself and, in that constitution, provided such limitations and restrictions on the

---

[1] Art. I, § 9: 'The privilege of the writ of *habeas corpus* shall not be suspended, unless when in cases of rebellion or invasion the public safety may require it.' 'No bill of attainder or *ex post facto* law shall be passed.' 'No title of nobility shall be granted by the United States. . .' Art. III, § 2: 'The trial of all crimes, except in cases of impeachment, shall be by jury; and such trial shall be held in the State where the said crimes shall have been committed.' Art. III, § 3: 'Treason against the United States, shall consist only in levying war against them, or in adhering to their enemies, giving them aid and comfort. No person shall be convicted of treason unless on the testimony of two witnesses to the same overt act, or on confession in open court.'

[2] See *ante*, p. 73.   [3] 7 Pet. 243.   [4] Ibid. 246.

powers of its particular government as its judgment dictated. The people of the United States framed such a government for the United States as they supposed best adapted to their situation and best calculated to promote their interests. The powers they conferred on this government were to be exercised by itself; and the limitations on power, if expressed in general terms, are naturally, and, we think, necessarily applicable to the government created by the instrument. They are limitations of power granted in the instrument itself; not of distinct governments, framed by different persons and for different purposes.' [5]

'These amendments,' declared Marshall, 'contain no expression indicating an intention to apply them to the state governments. This court cannot so apply them.' [6]

Many years later, in *Gitlow* v. *New York,* [7] the Court for the first time held 'that freedom of speech and of the press—which are protected by the First Amendment from abridgment by Congress—are among the fundamental personal rights and "liberties" protected by the due process clause of the Fourteenth Amendment from impairment by the states.' [8] Freedom of religion, [9] of assembly, [10] and the right to secure the assistance of counsel [11] are likewise protected.

The opinion of the Court in *Palko* v. *Connecticut,* [12] which follows, presents an excellent discussion of the relationship of the due process clause of the Fourteenth Amendment to the first eight amendments. Palko argued that by virtue of the due process clause the entire Bill of Rights applied as a restraint upon the states.

PALKO v. CONNECTICUT
302 U.S. 319 (1937)

MR. JUSTICE CARDOZO delivered the opinion of the Court.

A statute of Connecticut permitting appeals in criminal cases to be taken by the state is challenged by appellant as an infringement of the Fourteenth Amendment of the Constitution of the United States. . .

Appellant was indicted in Fairfield County, Connecticut, for the crime of murder in the first degree. A jury found him guilty of murder in the second degree, and he was sentenced to confinement in the state prison for life. Thereafter the State of Connecticut, with the permission of the judge presiding at the trial, gave

notice of appeal to the Supreme Court of Errors. This it did pursuant to an act adopted in 1886. . . Upon such appeal, the Supreme Court of Errors reversed the judgment and ordered a new trial. *State* v. *Palko,* 121 Conn. 669; 186 Atl. 657. It found that there had been error of law to the prejudice of the state (1) in excluding testimony as to a confession by defendant; (2) in excluding testimony upon cross-examination of defendant to impeach his credibility, and (3) in the instructions to the jury as to the difference between first and second degree murder.

Pursuant to the mandate of the Supreme Court of Errors, defendant was

[5] Ibid. 247.   [6] Ibid. 250.   [7] 268 U.S. 652 (1925).
[8] Ibid. 666. See also *De Jonge* v. *Oregon,* 299 U.S. 353 (1937); *Grosjean* v. *American Press Co.,* 297 U.S. 233 (1936).
[9] See *Hamilton* v. *Regents,* 293 U.S. 245 (1934); *Cantwell* v. *Connecticut,* 310 U.S. 296 (1940).
[10] *De Jonge* v. *Oregon,* op. cit.
[11] *Powell* v. *Alabama,* 287 U.S. 45 (1932).   [12] 302 U.S. 319 (1937).

brought to trial again. Before a jury was impaneled and also at later stages of the case he made the objection that the effect of the new trial was to place him twice in jeopardy for the same offense, and in so doing to violate the Fourteenth Amendment of the Constitution of the United States. Upon the overruling of the objection the trial proceeded. The jury returned a verdict of murder in the first degree, and the court sentenced the defendant to the punishment of death. The Supreme Court of Errors affirmed the judgment of conviction. . . The case is here upon appeal. 28 U.S.C., § 344.

1. The execution of the sentence will not deprive appellant of his life without the process of law assured to him by the Fourteenth Amendment of the Federal Constitution.

The argument for appellant is that whatever is forbidden by the Fifth Amendment is forbidden by the Fourteenth also. The Fifth Amendment, which is not directed to the states, but solely to the federal government, creates immunity from double jeopardy. No person shall be 'subject for the same offense to be twice put in jeopardy of life or limb.' The Fourteenth Amendment ordains, 'nor shall any State deprive any person of life, liberty, or property, without due process of law.' To retry a defendant, though under one indictment and only one, subjects him, it is said, to double jeopardy in violation of the Fifth Amendment, if the prosecution is one on behalf of the United States. From this the consequence is said to follow that there is a denial of life or liberty without due process of law, if the prosecution is one on behalf of the People of a State. . .

We have said that in appellant's view the Fourteenth Amendment is to be taken as embodying the prohibitions of the Fifth. His thesis is even broader. Whatever would be a violation of the original bill of rights (Amendments I to VIII) if done by the federal government is now equally unlawful by force of the Fourteenth Amendment if done by a state. There is no such general rule.

The Fifth Amendment provides, among other things, that no person shall be held to answer for a capital or otherwise infamous crime unless on presentment or indictment of a grand jury. This court has held that, in prosecutions by a state, presentment or indictment by a grand jury may give way to informations at the instance of a public officer. *Hurtado* v. *California,* 110 U.S. 516; *Gaines* v. *Washington,* 277 U.S. 81, 86. The Fifth Amendment provides also that no person shall be compelled in any criminal case to be a witness against himself. This court has said that, in prosecutions by a state, the exemption will fail if the state elects to end it. *Twining* v. *New Jersey,* 211 U.S. 78. . . The Sixth Amendment calls for a jury trial in criminal cases and the Seventh for a jury trial in civil cases at common law where the value in controversy shall exceed twenty dollars. This court has ruled that consistently with those amendments trial by jury may be modified by a state or abolished altogether. *Walker* v. *Sauvinet,* 92 U.S. 90; *Maxwell* v. *Dow,* 176 U.S. 581; *New York Central R. Co.* v. *White,* 243 U.S. 188, 208; *Wagner Electric Mfg. Co.* v. *Lyndon,* 262 U.S. 226, 232. As to the Fourth Amendment, one should refer to *Weeks* v. *United States,* 232 U.S. 383, 398, and as to other provisions of the Sixth, to *West* v. *Louisiana,* 194 U.S. 258.

On the other hand, the due process clause of the Fourteenth Amendment may make it unlawful for a state to abridge by its statutes the freedom of speech which the First Amendment safeguards against encroachment by the Congress . . . or the like freedom of the press . . . or the free exercise of religion . . . or the right of peaceable assembly, without which speech would be unduly trammeled . . . or the right of one accused of crime to the benefit of counsel. . . In these and other situations immunities that are valid as against the federal government by force of the specific pledges of particular amendments have been found to be implicit in the concept of ordered liberty, and thus, through the Fourteenth Amendment, become valid as against the states.

The line of division may seem to be wavering and broken if there is a hasty catalogue of the cases on the one side and the other. Reflection and analysis will induce a different view. There emerges the perception of a rationalizing principle which gives to discrete instances a proper order and coherence. The right to trial by jury and the immunity from prosecution except as the result of an indictment may have value and importance. Even so, they are not of the very essence of a scheme of ordered liberty. To abolish them is not to violate a 'principle of justice so rooted in the traditions and conscience of our people as to be ranked as fundamental. . .' Few would be so narrow or provincial as to maintain that a fair and enlightened system of justice would be impossible without them. What is true of jury trials and indictments is true also, as the cases show, of the immunity from compulsory self-incrimination. . . This too might be lost, and justice still be done. Indeed, today as in the past there are students of our penal system who look upon the immunity as a mischief rather than a benefit, and who would limit its scope, or destroy it altogether. No doubt there would remain the need to give protection against torture, physical or mental. . . Justice, however, would not perish if the accused were subject to a duty to respond to orderly inquiry. The exclusion of these immunities and privileges from the privileges and immunities protected against the action of the states has not been arbitrary or casual. It has been dictated by a study and appreciation of the meaning, the essential implications, of liberty itself.

We reach a different plane of social and moral values when we pass to the privileges and immunities that have been taken over from the earlier articles of the federal bill of rights and brought within the Fourteenth Amendment by a process of absorption. These in their origin were effective against the federal government alone. If the Fourteenth Amendment has absorbed them, the process of absorption has had its source in the belief that neither liberty nor justice would exist if they were sacrificed. . . This is true, for illustration, of freedom of thought, and speech. Of that freedom one may say that it is the matrix, the indispensable condition, of nearly every other form of freedom. With rare aberrations a pervasive recognition of that truth can be traced in our history, political and legal. So it has come about that the domain of liberty, withdrawn by the Fourteenth Amendment from encroachment by the states, has been enlarged by latter-day judgments to include liberty of the mind as well as liberty of action. The extension became, indeed, a logical imperative when once it was recognized, as long ago it was, that liberty is something more than exemption from physical restraint, and that even in the field of substantive rights and duties the legislative judgment, if oppressive and arbitrary, may be overridden by the courts. . . Fundamental too in the concept of due process, and so in that of liberty, is the thought that condemnation shall be rendered only after trial. *Scott* v. *McNeal,* 154 U.S. 34; *Blackmer* v. *United States,* 284 U.S. 421. The hearing, moreover, must be a real one, not a sham or a pretense. *Moore* v. *Dempsey,* 261 U.S. 86; *Mooney* v. *Holohan,* 294 U.S. 103. For that reason, ignorant defendants in a capital case were held to have been condemned unlawfully when in truth, though not in form, they were refused the aid of counsel. *Powell* v. *Alabama* [287 U.S. 45]. . .

Our survey of the cases serves, we think, to justify the statement that the dividing line between them, if not unfaltering throughout its course, has been true for the most part to a unifying principle. On which side of the line the case made out by the appellant has appropriate location must be the next inquiry and the final one. Is that kind of double jeopardy to which the statute has subjected him a hardship so acute and shocking that our polity will not endure it? Does it violate those 'fundamental principles of liberty and justice which lie at the base of all our civil and political institutions'?. . . The answer surely must be 'no.' What the answer would have to be if the state were permitted after a trial free from error to try the accused over again or to bring another case against him, we have no occasion to consider. We deal with the statute before us and no other. The state is not attempting to wear the accused out by a multitude of cases with accumulated trials. It asks no more than this, that the case against him shall go on until there shall be a trial free from the corrosion of substantial legal error. . . This is not cruelty at all, nor even vexation in any immoderate degree. If the trial had been infected with error adverse to the accused, there might have been review at his instance, and as often as necessary to purge the vicious taint. A reciprocal privilege, subject at all times to the discretion of the presiding judge . . . has now been granted to the state. There is here no seismic innovation. The edifice of justice stands, its symmetry, to many, greater than before. . .

The judgment is

Affirmed.

NOTE

The Fourth Amendment to the Constitution of the United States was adopted in large part because of colonial experience with writs of assistance or general warrants by virtue of which British officers and agents searched the homes of the people for smuggled goods.

In the latter half of the eighteenth century the use of the general warrant was challenged in both England and in the colonies. John Wilkes, member of Parliament, in 1762, commenced the anonymous publication of a series of pamphlets entitled *The North Briton*. Number 45 of the series attacked bitterly a speech of the king. Believing that such criticism had gone too far, the Secretary of State, Lord Halifax, issued a warrant to four men commanding them 'to make strict and diligent search for the authors, printers, and publishers of a seditious and treasonable paper, entitled, *The North Briton, No.* 45 . . . and them, or any of them, having found, to apprehend and seize, together with their papers.'[1]

Under this general warrant the messengers of the Crown within three days arrested forty-nine persons on the ground of suspicion alone. The printers were finally detected and the name of John Wilkes revealed as the author of the objectionable pamphlet. Wilkes was arrested and taken before the Secretary of State. In the meantime, the four agents under direction of Wood, an undersecretary of state, opened all cabinets, chests, drawers, locked or not, in Wilkes' home and confiscated all papers found therein. Wilkes was committed to the Tower for a few days.

Wilkes brought suit for damages against Wood. 'The defendant,' declared Chief Justice Pratt, later Lord Camden, 'claimed a right, under precedents, to force persons' houses, break open escrutores (sic), seize their papers, et cetera upon a general warrant, where no inventory is made of the things thus taken away, and where no offenders' names are specified in the warrant, and therefore a discretionary power given to messengers to search wherever their suspicions may chance to fall. If such a power is truly invested in a secretary of state, and he can delegate this power, it certainly may affect the person and property of every man in this kingdom, and is totally subversive of the liberty of the subject.'[2]

Like Wilkes, John Entick was arrested on a warrant which was specific as to the person but general as to papers. Entick sued the messengers in trespass for the seizure of his papers.[3] Lord Camden delivered the judgment of the court

[1] Lasson, Nelson B., *The History and Development of the Fourth Amendment to the United States Constitution*, Baltimore, 1937, p. 43.

[2] *Wilkes* v. *Wood*, 19 State Trials 1153 (1763). See Adams, George Burton, and Stephens, H. Morse, *Select Documents of English Constitutional History*, New York, 1935, p. 492.

[3] *Entick* v. *Carrington*, 19 State Trials 1030 (1765). See Keir, D. L., and Lawson, F. H., *Cases in Constitutional Law*, London, 1933, p. 145.

for the plaintiff. Speaking of the power claimed by the government under the warrant, Lord Camden said that 'honestly exerted, it is a power to seize that man's papers, who is charged upon oath to be the author or publisher of a seditious libel; if oppressively, it acts against every man, who is so described in the warrant, though he be innocent. It is executed against the party, before he is heard or even summoned; and the information, as well as the informers, is unknown. It is executed by messengers . . . in the presence or the absence of the party, as the messengers shall think fit, and without a witness to testify what passes at the time of the transaction; so that when the papers are gone, as the only witnesses are the trespassers, the party injured is left without proof. If this injury falls upon an innocent person, he is as destitute of remedy as the guilty; and the whole transaction is so guarded against discovery, that if the officer should be disposed to carry off a bank-bill, he may do it with impunity, since there is no man capable of proving either the taker or the thing taken. It must not be here forgot that no subject whatsoever is privileged from this search. . .' [4] This decision settled the matter of the general warrant in England.

In the colonies there was a struggle against the use of the general warrant or writs of assistance. In 1760, George II died; according to the requirements of the law, all writs of assistance expired six months after the death of the sovereign. The merchants of Boston thereupon petitioned the court for a hearing on the question of granting new writs. James Otis, Jr., appeared for the merchants. He characterized the writ of assistance as 'the worst instrument of arbitrary power, the most destructive of English liberty and the fundamental principles of law, that ever was found in an English law-book.' [5] By virtue of this writ, Otis said, 'Custom-house officers may enter our houses, when they please; we are commanded to permit their entry. Their menial servants may enter, may break locks, bars, and everything in their way; and whether they break through malice or revenge, no man, no court, can inquire.' [6] Mr. Otis mentioned some facts. 'Mr. Pew,' he declared, 'had one of these writs, and when Mr. Ware succeeded him, he endorsed this writ over to Mr. Ware; so that these writs are negotiable from one officer to another; and so your Honors have no opportunity of judging the persons to whom this vast power is delegated.' [7] Otis related the story of Mr. Justice Walley who 'had called this same Mr. Ware before him, by a constable, to answer for a breach of Sabbath-day acts, or that of profane swearing. As soon as he was finished, Mr. Ware asked him if he had done. He replied, Yes. Well then, said Mr. Ware, I will show you a little of my power. I command you to permit me to search your house for uncustomed goods. And went on to search his house from the garret to the cellar; and then served the constable in the same manner.' [8]

The prohibition against unreasonable searches and seizures was first given constitutional stature in 1776 in the Virginia Bill of Rights.

The Fourth Amendment is an exception to the common law rule of evidence

---

[4] Keir and Lawson, Ibid. p. 146.
[5] Adams, John, *Works*, Boston, 1850, II, p. 523.
[6] Ibid. p. 524.
[7] Ibid. pp. 524-5.
[8] Ibid. p. 525.

which holds that evidence is not inadmissible simply because it has been illegally obtained.[9] When evidence is obtained by Federal agents in violation of the Fourth Amendment, the common law rule is inapplicable. Where government agents have not searched and seized evidence illegally, then the common law rule applies. For example, when a person, not a government agent, steals incriminating papers and turns them over to a Federal prosecuting attorney, the papers may be admitted in evidence; [10] had a Federal agent secured the same papers illegally, then the Fourth Amendment would protect him whose papers or other evidence had been taken.[11]

The courts have construed the Fourth Amendment as being intimately connected with that clause of the Fifth Amendment which provides that no person 'shall be compelled in any criminal case to be a witness against himself. . .' If a man's papers are seized in violation of the Fourth Amendment and used in evidence against him in a criminal case, he is subjected also to compulsory self-incrimination in violation of the Fifth Amendment.[12]

The admissibility of evidence procured by Federal agents through the tapping of telephone wires is the question in the case which follows.

OLMSTEAD v. UNITED STATES
277 U.S. 438 (1928)

Mr. Chief Justice Taft delivered the opinion of the Court.

These cases are here by certiorari from the Circuit Court of Appeals for the Ninth Circuit. 19 F. (2d) 842 and 850. The petition in No. 493 was filed August 30, 1927; in Nos. 532 and 533, September 9, 1927. They were granted with the distinct limitation that the hearing should be confined to the single question whether the use of evidence of private telephone conversations between the defendants and others, intercepted by means of wire tapping, amounted to a violation of the Fourth and Fifth Amendments.

The petitioners were convicted in the District Court for the Western District of Washington of a conspiracy to violate the National Prohibition Act by unlawfully possessing, transporting and importing intoxicating liquors and maintaining nui-

sances, and by selling intoxicating liquors. Seventy-two others in addition to the petitioners were indicted. Some were not apprehended, some were acquitted and others pleaded guilty.

The evidence in the records discloses a conspiracy of amazing magnitude to import, possess and sell liquor unlawfully. It involved the employment of not less than fifty persons, of two seagoing vessels for the transportation of liquor to British Columbia, of smaller vessels for coastwise transportation to the State of Washington, the purchase and use of a ranch beyond the suburban limits of Seattle, with a large underground cache for storage and a number of smaller caches in that city, the maintenance of a central office manned with operators, the employment of executives, salesmen, deliverymen, dispatchers, scouts, bookkeepers, collectors

---

[9] *Olmstead* v. *United States*, 277 U.S. 438 (1928).

[10] *Burdeau* v. *McDowell*, 256 U.S. 465 (1921).

[11] *Gouled* v. *United States*, 255 U.S. 298 (1921). *Davis* v. *United States*, 328 U.S. 582 (1946) and *Zap* v. *United States*, 328 U.S. 624 (1946), seem to limit the right relating to searches and seizures.

[12] Ibid.

and an attorney. In a bad month sales amounted to $176,000; the aggregate for a year must have exceeded two millions of dollars.

Olmstead was the leading conspirator and the general manager of the business. He made a contribution of $10,000 to the capital; eleven others contributed $1,000 each. The profits were divided one-half to Olmstead and the remainder to the other eleven. Of the several offices in Seattle the chief one was in a large office building. In this there were three telephones on three different lines. There were telephones in an office of the manager in his own home, at the homes of his associates, and at other places in the city. Communication was had frequently with Vancouver, British Columbia. Times were fixed for the deliveries of the 'stuff,' to places along Puget Sound near Seattle and from there the liquor was removed and deposited in the caches already referred to. One of the chief men was always on duty at the main office to receive orders by telephones and to direct their filling by a corps of men stationed in another room —the 'bull pen.' The call numbers of the telephones were given to those known to be likely customers. At times the sales amounted to 200 cases of liquor per day.

The information which led to the discovery of the conspiracy and its nature and extent was largely obtained by intercepting messages on the telephones of the conspirators by four federal prohibition officers. Small wires were inserted along the ordinary telephone wires from the residences of four of the petitioners and those leading from the chief office. The insertions were made without trespass upon any property of the defendants. They were made in the basement of the large office building. The taps from house lines were made in the streets near the houses.

The gathering of evidence continued for many months. Conversations of the conspirators of which refreshing stenographic notes were currently made, were testified to by the government witnesses. They revealed the large business transactions of the partners and their subordinates. Men at the wires heard the orders given for liquor by customers and the acceptances; they became auditors of the conversations between the partners. All this disclosed the conspiracy charged in the indictment. Many of the intercepted conversations were not merely reports but parts of the criminal acts. The evidence also disclosed the difficulties to which the conspirators were subjected, the reported news of the capture of vessels, the arrest of their men and the seizure of cases of liquor in garages and other places. It showed the dealing by Olmstead, the chief conspirator, with members of the Seattle police, the messages to them which secured the release of arrested members of the conspiracy, and also direct promises to officers of payments as soon as opportunity offered.

The Fourth Amendment provides— 'The right of the people to be secure in their persons, houses, papers, and effects against unreasonable searches and seizures shall not be violated; and no warrants shall issue but upon probable cause, supported by oath or affirmation and particularly describing the place to be searched and the persons or things to be seized.' And the Fifth: 'No person . . . shall be compelled, in any criminal case, to be a witness against himself.'

It will be helpful to consider the chief cases in this Court which bear upon the construction of these Amendments.

Boyd v. *United States,* 116 U.S. 616, was an information filed by the District Attorney in the federal court in a cause of seizure and forfeiture against thirty-five cases of plate glass, which charged that the owner and importer, with intent to defraud the revenue, made an entry of the imported merchandise by means of a fraudulent or false invoice. It became important to show the quantity and value of glass contained in twenty-nine cases previously imported. The fifth section of the

Act of June 22, 1874, provided that in cases not criminal under the revenue laws, the United States Attorney, whenever he thought an invoice, belonging to the defendant, would tend to prove any allegation made by the United States, might by a written motion describing the invoice and setting forth the allegation which he expected to prove, secure a notice from the court to the defendant to produce the invoice, and if the defendant refused to produce it, the allegations stated in the motion should be taken as confessed, but if produced, the United States Attorney should be permitted, under the direction of the court, to make an examination of the invoice, and might offer the same in evidence. This Act had succeeded the Act of 1867, which provided that in such cases the District Judge, on affidavit of any person interested, might issue a warrant to the marshal to enter the premises where the invoice was and take possession of it and hold it subject to the order of the judge. This had been preceded by the Act of 1863 of a similar tenor, except that it directed the warrant to the collector instead of the marshal. The United States Attorney followed the Act of 1874 and compelled the production of the invoice.

The court held the Act of 1874 repugnant to the Fourth and Fifth Amendments. As to the Fourth Amendment, Justice Bradley said (page 621):

'But, in regard to the Fourth Amendment, it is contended that, whatever might have been alleged against the constitutionality of the acts of 1863 and 1867, that of 1874, under which the order in the present case was made, is free from constitutional objection because it does not authorize the search and seizure of books and papers, but only requires the defendant or claimant to produce them. That is so; but it declares that if he does not produce them, the allegations which it is affirmed they will prove shall be taken as confessed. This is tantamount to compelling their production; for the prosecuting attorney will always be sure to state the evidence expected to be derived from them as strongly as the case will admit of. It is true that certain aggravating incidents of actual search and seizure, such as forcible entry into a man's house and searching amongst his papers, are wanting, and to this extent the proceeding under the Act of 1874 is a mitigation of that which was authorized by the former acts; but it accomplishes the substantial object of those acts in forcing from a party evidence against himself. It is our opinion, therefore, that a compulsory production of a man's private papers to establish a criminal charge against him, or to forfeit his property, is within the scope of the Fourth Amendment to the Constitution, in all cases in which a search and seizure would be; because it is a material ingredient, and effects the sole object and purpose of search and seizure.'

Concurring, Mr. Justice Miller and Chief Justice Waite said that they did not think the machinery used to get this evidence amounted to a search and seizure, but they agreed that the Fifth Amendment had been violated.

The statute provided an official demand for the production of a paper or document by the defendant for official search and use as evidence on penalty that by refusal he should be conclusively held to admit the incriminating character of the document as charged. It was certainly no straining of the language to construe the search and seizure under the Fourth Amendment to include such official procedure.

The next case, and perhaps the most important, is *Weeks* v. *United States,* 232 U.S. 383—a conviction for using the mails to transmit coupons or tickets in a lottery enterprise. The defendant was arrested by a police officer without a warrant. After his arrest other police officers and the United States marshal went to his house, got the key from a neighbor, entered the defendant's room and searched it, and took possession of various papers and articles. Neither the marshal nor the police officers had a search warrant. The defendant filed a petition in court asking the return of all his property. The court ordered the return of everything not pertinent to the charge, but denied return of relevant evidence. After the jury was sworn, the defendant again made objection, and on introduction of the papers contended that the search without warrant was a violation of the Fourth and Fifth Amendments and they were therefore inadmissible. This court held that such taking of papers by an official of the United States, acting under color of his office, was in violation of the constitutional rights of the defendant, and upon making seasonable application he was entitled to have them restored, and that by permitting their use upon the trial, the trial court erred.

The opinion cited with approval language of Mr. Justice Field in *Ex parte Jackson*, 96 U.S. 727, 733, saying that the Fourth Amendment as a principle of protection was applicable to sealed letters and packages in the mail and that, consistently with it, such matter could only be opened and examined upon warrants issued on oath or affirmation particularly describing the thing to be seized.

In *Silverthorne Lumber Company* v. *United States*, 251 U.S. 385, the defendants were arrested at their homes and detained in custody. While so detained, representatives of the Government without authority went to the office of their company and seized all the books, papers and documents found there. An application for return of the things was opposed by the District Attorney, who produced a subpoena for certain documents relating to the charge in the indictment then on file. The court said:

'Thus the case is not that of knowledge acquired through the wrongful act of a stranger, but it must be assumed that the Government planned or at all events ratified the whole performance.'

And it held that the illegal character of the original seizure characterized the entire proceeding and under the *Weeks* case the seized papers must be restored.

In *Amos* v. *United States*, 255 U.S. 313, the defendant was convicted of concealing whiskey on which the tax had not been paid. At the trial he presented a petition asking that private property seized in a search of his house and store 'within his curtilage,' without warrant should be returned. This was denied. A woman, who claimed to be his wife, was told by the revenue officers that they had come to search the premises for violation of the revenue law. She opened the door; they entered and found whiskey. Further searches in the house disclosed more. It was held that this action constituted a violation of the Fourth Amendment, and that the denial of the motion to restore the whiskey and to exclude the testimony was error.

In *Gouled* v. *The United States*, 255 U.S. 298, the facts were these: Gouled and two others were charged with conspiracy to defraud the United States. One pleaded guilty and another was acquitted. Gouled prosecuted error. The matter was presented here on questions propounded by the lower court. The first related to the admission in evidence of a paper surreptitiously taken from the office of the defendant by one acting under the direction of an officer of the Intelligence Department of the Army of the United States. Gouled was suspected of the crime. A private in the U. S. Army, pretending to make a friendly call on him, gained admission to his office and in his absence, without warrant of any character, seized and carried away several documents. One of these belonging to Gouled, was delivered to the United States Attorney and by him introduced in evidence. When produced, it was a surprise to the defendant. He had had no opportunity to make a previous motion to secure a return of it. The paper had no pecuniary value, but was relevant to the issue made on the trial. Admission of the paper was considered a violation of the Fourth Amendment.

Agnello v. *United States,* 269 U.S. 20, held that the Fourth and Fifth Amendments were violated by admission in evidence of contraband narcotics found in defendant's house, several blocks distant from the place of arrest, after his arrest, and seized there without a warrant. Under such circumstances the seizure could not be justified as incidental to the arrest.

There is no room in the present case for applying the Fifth Amendment unless the Fourth Amendment was first violated. There was no evidence of compulsion to induce the defendants to talk over their many telephones. They were continually and voluntarily transacting business without knowledge of the interception. Our consideration must be confined to the Fourth Amendment.

The striking outcome of the *Weeks* case and those which followed it was the sweeping declaration that the Fourth Amendment, although not referring to or limiting the use of evidence in courts, really forbade its introduction if obtained by government officers through a violation of the Amendment. Theretofore many had supposed that under the ordinary common law rules, if the tendered evidence was pertinent, the method of obtaining it was unimportant. This was held by the Supreme Judicial Court of Massachusetts in *Commonwealth* v. *Dana,* 2 Metcalf, 329, 337. There it was ruled that the only remedy open to a defendant whose rights under a state constitution equivalent of the Fourth Amendment had been invaded was by suit and judgment for damages, as Lord Camden held in *Entick* v. *Carrington,* 19 Howell State Trials, 1029. Mr. Justice Bradley made effective use of this case in *Boyd* v. *United States.* But in the *Weeks* case, and those which followed, this Court decided with great emphasis, and established as the law for the federal courts, that the protection of the Fourth Amendment would be much impaired un-

less it was held that not only was the official violator of the rights under the Amendment subject to action at the suit of the injured defendant, but also that the evidence thereby obtained could not be received.

The well known historical purpose of the Fourth Amendment, directed against general warrants and writs of assistance, was to prevent the use of governmental force to search a man's house, his person, his papers and his effects; and to prevent their seizure against his will. This phase of the misuse of governmental power of compulsion is the emphasis of the opinion of the Court in the *Boyd* case. This appears too in the *Weeks* case, in the *Silverthorne* case and in the *Amos* case.

Gouled v. *United States* carried the inhibition against unreasonable searches and seizures to the extreme limit. Its authority is not to be enlarged by implication and must be confined to the precise state of facts disclosed by the record. A representative of the Intelligence Department of the Army, having by stealth obtained admission to the defendant's office, seized and carried away certain private papers valuable for evidential purposes. This was held an unreasonable search and seizure within the Fourth Amendment. A stealthy entrance in such circumstances became the equivalent to an entry by force. There was actual entrance into the private quarters of defendant and the taking away of something tangible. Here we have testimony only of voluntary conversations secretly overheard.

The Amendment itself shows that the search is to be of material things—the person, the house, his papers or his effects. The description of the warrant necessary to make the proceeding lawful, is that it must specify the place to be searched and the person or *things* to be seized.

It is urged that the language of Mr. Justice Field in *Ex parte Jackson,* already quoted, offers an analogy to the interpretation of the Fourth Amendment in respect of wire tapping. But the analogy fails. The Fourth Amendment may have proper application to a sealed letter in the mail because of the constitutional provision for the Postoffice Department and the relations between the Government and those who pay to secure protection of their sealed letters. See Revised Statutes, §§ 3978 to 3988, whereby Congress monopolizes the carriage of letters and excludes from that business everyone else, and § 3929 which forbids any postmaster or other person to open any letter not addressed to himself. It is plainly within the words of the Amendment to say that the unlawful rifling by a government agent of a sealed letter is a search and seizure of the sender's papers or effects. The letter is a paper, an effect, and in the custody of a Government that forbids carriage except under its protection.

The United States takes no such care of telegraph or telephone messages as of mailed sealed letters. The Amendment does not forbid what was done here. There was no searching. There was no seizure. The evidence was secured by the use of the sense of hearing and that only. There was no entry of the houses or offices of the defendants.

By the invention of the telephone, fifty years ago, and its application for the purpose of extending communications, one can talk with another at a far distant place. The language of the Amendment can not be extended and expanded to include telephone wires reaching to the whole world from the defendant's house or office. The intervening wires are not part of his house or office any more than are the highways along which they are stretched.

This Court in *Carroll* v. *United States*, 267 U.S. 132, 149, declared:

'The Fourth Amendment is to be construed in the light of what was deemed an unreasonable search and seizure when it was adopted and in a manner which will conserve public interests as well as the interests and rights of individual citizens.'

Justice Bradley in the *Boyd* case, and Justice Clark in the *Gouled* case, said that the Fifth Amendment and the Fourth Amendment were to be liberally construed to effect the purpose of the framers of the Constitution in the interest of liberty. But that cannot justify enlargement of the language employed beyond the possible practical meaning of houses, persons, papers, and effects, or so to apply the words search and seizure as to forbid hearing or sight.

Hester v. *United States*, 265 U.S. 57, held that the testimony of two officers of the law who trespassed on the defendant's land, concealed themselves one hundred yards away from his house and saw him come out and hand a bottle of whiskey to another, was not inadmissible. While there was a trespass, there was no search of person, house, papers or effects. . .

Congress may of course protect the secrecy of telephone messages by making them, when intercepted, inadmissible in evidence in federal criminal trials, by direct legislation,[1] and thus depart from the common law of evidence. But the courts may not adopt such a policy by attributing an enlarged and unusual meaning to the Fourth Amendment. The reasonable view is that one who installs in his house a telephone instrument with connecting wires intends to project his voice to those quite outside, and that the wires beyond his house and messages while passing over them are not within the protection of the Fourth Amendment. Here those who intercepted the projected voices were not in the house of either party to the conversation.

Neither the cases we have cited nor any of the many federal decisions brought to our attention hold the Fourth Amendment

[1] Editors' Note: This was done in the Communications Act of 1934, § 605, 48 Stat. 1064, 1103. See *Nardone* v. *United States*, 302 U.S. 379 (1937); and *Nardone* v. *United States*, 308 U.S. 338 (1939).

to have been violated as against a defendant unless there has been an official search and seizure of his person, or such a seizure of his papers or his tangible material effects, or an actual physical invasion of his house 'or curtilage' for the purpose of making a seizure.

We think, therefore, that the wire tapping here disclosed did not amount to a search or seizure within the meaning of the Fourth Amendment.

What has been said disposes of the only question that comes within the terms of our order granting certiorari in these cases. But some of our number, departing from that order, have concluded that there is merit in the twofold objection overruled in both courts below that evidence obtained through intercepting of telephone messages by governing agents was inadmissible because the mode of obtaining it was unethical and a misdemeanor under the law of Washington. To avoid any misapprehension of our views of that objection we shall deal with it in both of its phases.

While a Territory, the English common law prevailed in Washington and thus continued after her admission in 1889. The rules of evidence in criminal cases in courts of the United States sitting there, consequently are those of the common law. . .

The common law rule is that the admissibility of evidence is not affected by the illegality of the means by which it was obtained. Professor Greenleaf in his work on evidence, vol. 1, 12th ed., by Redfield, § 254 (a) says:

'It may be mentioned in this place, that though papers and other subjects of evidence may have been *illegally taken* from the possession of the party against whom they are offered, or otherwise unlawfully obtained, this is no valid objection to their admissibility, if they are pertinent to the issue. The court will not take notice how they were obtained, whether lawfully or unlawfully, nor will it form an issue, to determine that question.'

Mr. Jones in his work on the same subject refers to Mr. Greenleaf's statement, and says:

'Where there is no violation of a constitutional guaranty, the verity of the above statement is absolute.' Vol. 5, § 2075, note 3.

The rule is supported by many English and American cases cited by Jones in vol. 5, § 2075, note 3, and § 2076, note 6; and by Wigmore, vol. 4, § 2183. It is recognized by this Court in *Adams* v. *New York,* 192 U.S. 585. The *Weeks* case, announced an exception to the common law rule by excluding all evidence in the procuring of which government officials took part by methods forbidden by the Fourth and Fifth Amendments. Many state courts do not follow the *Weeks* case. *People* v. *Defore,* 242 N.Y. 13. But those who do, treat it as an exception to the general common law rule and required by constitutional limitations. . . The common law rule must apply in the case at bar.

Nor can we, without the sanction of congressional enactment, subscribe to the suggestion that the courts have a discretion to exclude evidence, the admission of which is not unconstitutional, because unethically secured. This would be at variance with the common law doctrine generally supported by authority. There is no case that sustains, nor any recognized text book that gives color to such a view. Our general experience shows that much evidence has always been receivable although not obtained by conformity to the highest ethics. The history of criminal trials shows numerous cases of prosecutions of oath-bound conspiracies for murder, robbery, and other crimes, where officers of the law have disguised themselves and joined the organizations, taken the oaths and given themselves every appearance of active members engaged in the promotion of crime, for the purpose of securing evidence. Evidence secured by such means has always been received.

A standard which would forbid the reception of evidence if obtained by other than nice ethical conduct by government officials would make society suffer and give criminals greater immunity than has been known heretofore. In the absence of controlling legislation by Congress, those who realize the difficulties in bringing offenders to justice may well deem it wise that the exclusion of evidence should be confined to cases where rights under the Constitution would be violated by admitting it.

The statute of Washington, adopted in 1909, provides (Remington Compiled Statutes, 1922, § 2656 [18]) that:

'Every person . . . who shall intercept, read or in any manner interrupt or delay the sending of a message over any telegraph or telephone line . . . shall be guilty of a misdemeanor.'

This statute does not declare that evidence obtained by such interception shall be inadmissible, and by the common law, already referred to, it would not be. *People* v. *McDonald*, 177 App. Div. (N. Y.) 806. Whether the State of Washington may prosecute and punish federal officers violating this law and those whose messages were intercepted may sue them civilly is not before us. But clearly a statute, passed twenty years after the admission of the State into the Union can not affect the rules of evidence applicable in courts of the United States in criminal cases. Chief Justice Taney, in *United States* v. *Reid,* 12 How. 361, 363, construing the 34th section of the Judiciary Act, said:

'But it could not be supposed, without very plain words to show it, that Congress intended to give the states the power of prescribing the rules of evidence in trials for offenses against the United States. For this construction would place the criminal jurisprudence of one sovereignty under the control of another.' See also *Withaup* v. *United States,* 127 Fed. 530, 534.

The judgments of the Circuit Court of Appeals are affirmed. The mandates will go down forthwith under Rule 31.

Affirmed.

MR. JUSTICE HOLMES:

My brother BRANDEIS has given this case so exhaustive an examination that I desire to add but a few words. While I do not deny it, I am not prepared to say that the penumbra of the Fourth and Fifth Amendments covers the defendant, although I fully agree that Courts are apt to err by sticking too closely to the words of a law where those words import a policy that goes beyond them. *Gooch* v. *Oregon Short Line R. R. Co., 258 U.S. 22, 24. But I think, as MR. JUSTICE BRANDEIS says, that apart from the Constitution the Government ought not to use evidence obtained and only obtainable by a criminal act. There is no body of precedents by which we are bound, and which confines us to logical deduction from established rules. Therefore we must consider the two objects of desire, both of which we cannot have, and make up our minds which to choose. It is desirable that criminals should be detected, and to that end that all available evidence should be used. It also is desirable that the Government should not itself foster and pay for other crimes, when they are the means by which the evidence is to be obtained. If it pays its officers for having got evidence by crime I do not see why it may not as well pay them for getting it in the same way, and I can attach no importance to protestations of disapproval if it knowingly accepts and pays and announces that in future it will pay for the fruits. We have to choose, and for my part I think it a less evil that some criminals should escape than that the Government should play an ignoble part.

For those who agree with me, no distinction can be taken between the Government as prosecutor and the Government as judge. If the existing code does not permit district attorneys to have a hand in such dirty business it does not permit the judge to allow such iniquities to succeed. See *Silverthorne Lumber Co.* v. *United States,* 251 U.S. 385. And if all that I have said so far be accepted it makes no difference that in this case wire tapping is made a crime by the law of the State, not by the law of the United States. It is true that a State cannot make rules of evidence for Courts of the United States, but the State has authority over the conduct in question, and I hardly think that the United States would appear to greater advantage when paying for an odious crime against State law than when inciting to the disregard of its own. I am aware of the often repeated statement that in a criminal proceeding the Court will not take notice of the manner in which papers offered in evidence have been obtained. But that somewhat rudimentary mode of disposing of the question has been overthrown by *Weeks* v. *United States,* 232 U.S. 383 and the cases that have followed it. I have said that we are free to choose between two principles of policy. But if we are to confine ourselves to precedent and logic the reason for excluding evidence obtained by violating the Constitution seems to me logically to lead to excluding evidence obtained by a crime of the officers of the law.

MR. JUSTICE BRANDEIS, dissenting.

The defendants were convicted of conspiring to violate the National Prohibition Act. Before any of the persons now charged had been arrested or indicted, the telephones by means of which they habitually communicated with one another and with others had been tapped by federal officers. To this end, a lineman of long experience in wire-tapping was employed, on behalf of the Government and at its expense. He tapped eight telephones, some in the homes of the persons charged, some in their offices. Acting on behalf of the Government and in their official capacity, at least six other prohibition agents listened over the tapped wires and reported the messages taken. Their operations extended over a period of nearly five months. The typewritten record of the notes of conversations overheard occupies 775 typewritten pages. By objections seasonably made and persistently renewed, the defendants objected to the admission of the evidence obtained by wire-tapping, on the ground that the Government's wire-tapping constituted an unreasonable search and seizure, in violation of the Fourth Amendment; and that the use as evidence of the conversations overheard compelled the defendants to be witnesses against themselves, in violation of the Fifth Amendment.

The Government makes no attempt to defend the methods employed by its officers. Indeed, it concedes that if wire-tapping can be deemed a search and seizure within the Fourth Amendment, such wire-tapping as was practiced in the case at bar was an unreasonable search and seizure, and that the evidence thus obtained was inadmissible. But it relies on the language of the Amendment; and it claims that the protection given thereby cannot properly be held to include a telephone conversation.

'We must never forget,' said Mr. Chief Justice Marshall in *McCulloch* v. *Maryland,* 4 Wheat. 316, 407, 'that it is a constitution we are expounding.' Since then, this Court has repeatedly sustained the exercise of power by Congress, under various clauses of that instrument, over objects of which the Fathers could not have dreamed. . . We have likewise held that general limitations on the powers of Government, like those embodied in the due process clauses of the Fifth and Fourteenth Amendments, do not forbid the United States or the States from meeting modern conditions by regulations which 'a century ago, or even half a century ago, probably would have been rejected as arbitrary and oppressive.' *Village of Euclid* v. *Ambler Realty Co.,* 272 U.S. 365, 387; *Buck* v.

Bell, 274 U.S. 200. Clauses guaranteeing to the individual protection against specific abuses of power, must have a similar capacity of adaptation to a changing world. It was with reference to such a clause that this Court said in *Weems* v. *United States,* 217 U.S. 349, 373: 'Legislation, both statutory and constitutional, is enacted, it is true, from an experience of evils, but its general language should not, therefore, be necessarily confined to the form that evil had theretofore taken. Time works changes, brings into existence new conditions and purposes. Therefore a principle to be vital must be capable of wider application than the mischief which gave it birth. This is peculiarly true of constitutions. They are not ephemeral enactments, designed to meet passing occasions. They are, to use the words of Chief Justice Marshall "designed to approach immortality as nearly as human institutions can approach it." The future is their care and provision for events of good and bad tendencies of which no prophecy can be made. In the application of a constitution, therefore, our contemplation cannot be only of what has been but of what may be. Under any other rule a constitution would indeed be as easy of application as it would be deficient in efficacy and power. Its general principles would have little value and be converted by precedent into impotent and lifeless formulas. Rights declared in words might be lost in reality.'

When the Fourth and Fifth Amendments were adopted, 'the form that evil had theretofore taken,' had been necessarily simple. Force and violence were then the only means known to man by which a Government could directly effect self-incrimination. It could compel the individual to testify—a compulsion effected, if need be, by torture. It could secure possession of his papers and other articles incident to his private life—a seizure effected, if need be, by breaking and entry. Protection against such invasion of 'the sanctities of a man's home and the privacies of life' was provided in the Fourth and Fifth Amendments by specific language. *Boyd* v. *United States,* 116 U.S. 616, 630. But 'time works changes, brings into existence new conditions and purposes.' Subtler and more far-reaching means of invading privacy have become available to the Government. Discovery and invention have made it possible for the Government, by means far more effective than stretching upon the rack, to obtain disclosure in court of what is whispered in the closet.

Moreover, 'in the application of a constitution, our contemplation cannot be only of what has been but of what may be.' The progress of science in furnishing the Government with means of espionage is not likely to stop with wire-tapping. Ways may some day be developed by which the Government, without removing papers from secret drawers, can reproduce them in court, and by which it will be enabled to expose to a jury the most intimate occurrences of the home. Advances in the psychic and related sciences may bring means of exploring unexpressed beliefs, thoughts and emotions. 'That places the liberty of every man in the hands of every petty officer' was said by James Otis of much lesser intrusions than these. To Lord Camden, a far slighter intrusion seemed 'subversive of all the comforts of society.' Can it be that the Constitution affords no protection against such invasions of individual security?

A sufficient answer is found in *Boyd* v. *United States,* 116 U.S. 616, 627-630, a case that will be remembered as long as civil liberty lives in the United States. This Court there reviewed the history that lay behind the Fourth and Fifth Amendments. We said with reference to Lord Camden's judgment in *Entick* v. *Carrington,* 19 Howell's State Trials, 1030: 'The principles laid down in this opinion affect the very essence of constitutional liberty and security. They reach farther than the concrete form of the case there before the court, with its adventitious circumstances; they apply to all invasions on the part of the Government and its employees of the sanctities of a man's home and the privacies of life. It is not the breaking of his doors, and the rummaging of his drawers, that constitutes the essence of the offence; but it is the invasion of his indefeasible right of personal security, personal liberty and private property, where that right has never been forfeited by his conviction of some public offence,—it is the invasion of this sacred right which underlies and constitutes the essence of Lord Camden's judgment. Breaking into a house and opening boxes and drawers are circumstances of aggravation; but any forcible and compulsory extortion of a man's own testimony or of his private papers to be used as evidence of a crime or to forfeit his goods, is within the condemnation of that judgment. In this regard the Fourth and Fifth Amendments run almost into each other.'

In *Ex parte Jackson*, 96 U.S. 727, it was held that a sealed letter entrusted to the mail is protected by the Amendments. The mail is a public service furnished by the Government. The telephone is a public service furnished by its authority. There is, in essence, no difference between the sealed letter and the private telephone message. As Judge Rudkin said below: 'True the one is visible, the other invisible; the one is tangible, the other intangible; the one is sealed and the other unsealed, but these are distinctions without a difference.' The evil incident to invasion of the privacy of the telephone is far greater than that involved in tampering with the mails. Whenever a telephone line is tapped, the privacy of the persons at both ends of the line is invaded and all conversations between them upon any subject, and although proper, confidential and privileged, may be overheard. Moreover, the tapping of one man's telephone line involves the tapping of the telephone of every other person whom he may call or

who may call him. As a means of espionage, writs of assistance and general warrants are but puny instruments of tyranny and oppression when compared with wiretapping.

Time and again, this Court in giving effect to the principle underlying the Fourth Amendment, has refused to place an unduly literal construction upon it. This was notably illustrated in the *Boyd* case itself. Taking language in its ordinary meaning, there is no 'search' or 'seizure' when a defendant is required to produce a document in the orderly process of a court's procedure. 'The right of the people to be secure in their persons, houses, papers, and effects, against unreasonable searches and seizures,' would not be violated, under any ordinary construction of language, by compelling obedience to a subpoena. But this Court holds the evidence inadmissible simply because the information leading to the issue of the subpoena has been unlawfully secured. *Silverthorne Lumber Co.* v. *United States*, 251 U.S. 385. Literally, there is no 'search' or 'seizure' when a friendly visitor abstracts papers from an office; yet we held in *Gouled* v. *United States*, 255 U.S. 298, that evidence so obtained could not be used. No court which looked at the words of the Amendment rather than at its underlying purpose would hold, as this Court did in *Ex parte Jackson*, 96 U.S. 727, 733, that its protection extended to letters in the mails. The provision against self-incrimination in the Fifth Amendment has been given an equally broad construction. The language is: 'No person . . . shall be compelled in any criminal case to be a witness against himself.' Yet we have held, not only that the protection of the Amendment extends to a witness before a grand jury, although he has not been charged with crime, *Counselman* v. *Hitchcock*, 142 U.S. 547, 562, 586, but that: 'It applies alike to civil and criminal proceedings, wherever the answer might tend to subject to criminal responsibility him who gives it. The privilege protects a mere witness as fully as it does one who is also a party defendant.' *McCarthy* v. *Arndstein,* 266 U.S. 34, 40. The narrow language of the Amendment has been consistently construed in the light of its object, 'to insure that a person should not be compelled, when acting as a witness in any investigation, to give testimony which might tend to show that he himself had committed a crime. The privilege is limited to criminal matters, but it is as broad as the mischief against which it seeks to guard.' *Counselman* v. *Hitchcock, supra,* p. 562.

Decisions of this Court applying the principle of the *Boyd* case have settled these things. Unjustified search and seizure violates the Fourth Amendment, whatever the character of the paper; whether the paper when taken by the federal officers was in the home, in an office or elsewhere; whether the taking was effected by force, by fraud, or in the orderly process of a court's procedure. From these decisions, it follows necessarily that the Amendment is violated by the officer's reading the paper without a physical seizure, without his even touching it; and that use, in any criminal proceeding, of the contents of the paper so examined—as where they are testified to by a federal officer who thus saw the document or where, through knowledge so obtained, a copy has been procured elsewhere—any such use constitutes a violation of the Fifth Amendment.

The protection guaranteed by the Amendments is much broader in scope. The makers of our Constitution undertook to secure conditions favorable to the pursuit of happiness. They recognized the significance of man's spiritual nature, of his feelings and of his intellect. They knew that only a part of the pain, pleasure and satisfactions of life are to be found in material things. They sought to protect Americans in their beliefs, their thoughts, their emotions and their sensations. They

conferred, as against the Government, the right to be let alone—the most comprehensive of rights and the right most valued by civilized men. To protect that right, every unjustifiable intrusion by the Government upon the privacy of the individual, whatever the means employed, must be deemed a violation of the Fourth Amendment. And the use, as evidence in a criminal proceeding, of facts ascertained by such intrusion must be deemed a violation of the Fifth.

Applying to the Fourth and Fifth Amendments the established rule of construction, the defendants' objections to the evidence obtained by wire-tapping must, in my opinion, be sustained. It is, of course, immaterial where the physical connection with the telephone wires leading into the defendants' premises was made. And it is also immaterial that the intrusion was in aid of law enforcement. Experience should teach us to be most on our guard to protect liberty when the Government's purposes are beneficent. Men born to freedom are naturally alert to repel invasion of their liberty by evil-minded rulers. The greatest dangers to liberty lurk in insidious encroachment by men of zeal, well-meaning but without understanding.

Independently of the constitutional question, I am of opinion that the judgment should be reversed. By the laws of Washington, wire-tapping is a crime. Pierce's Code, 1921, § 8976 (18). To prove its case, the Government was obliged to lay bare the crimes committed by its officers on its behalf. A federal court should not permit such a prosecution to continue. . .

The situation in the case at bar differs widely from that presented in *Burdeau* v. *McDowell,* 256 U.S. 465. There, only a single lot of papers was involved. They had been obtained by a private detective while acting on behalf of a private party; without the knowledge of any federal official; long before anyone had thought of instituting a federal prosecution. Here, the evidence obtained by crime was obtained at the Government's expense, by its officers, while acting on its behalf; the officers who committed these crimes are the same officers who were charged with the enforcement of the Prohibition Act; the crimes of these officers were committed for the purpose of securing evidence with which to obtain an indictment and to secure a conviction. The evidence so obtained constitutes the warp and woof of the Government's case. The aggregate of the Government evidence occupies 306 pages of the printed record. More than 210 of them are filled by recitals of the details of the wire-tapping and of facts ascertained thereby. There is literally no other evidence of guilt on the part of some of the defendants except that illegally obtained by these officers. As to nearly all the defendants (except those who admitted guilt), the evidence relied upon to secure a conviction consisted mainly of that which these officers had so obtained by violating the state law.

As Judge Rudkin said below: 'Here we are concerned with neither eavesdroppers nor thieves. Nor are we concerned with the acts of private individuals. . . We are concerned only with the acts of federal agents whose powers are limited and controlled by the Constitution of the United States.' The Eighteenth Amendment has not in terms empowered Congress to authorize anyone to violate the criminal laws of a State. And Congress has never purported to do so. . . The terms of appointment of federal prohibition agents do not purport to confer upon them authority to violate any criminal law. Their superior officer, the Secretary of the Treasury, has not instructed them to commit crime on behalf of the United States. It may be assumed that the Attorney General of the United States did not give any such instruction.

When these unlawful acts were committed, they were crimes only of the officers individually. The Government was

innocent, in legal contemplation; for no federal official is authorized to commit a crime on its behalf. When the Government, having full knowledge, sought, through the Department of Justice, to avail itself of the fruits of these acts in order to accomplish its own ends, it assumed moral responsibility for the officers' crimes. . . And if this Court should permit the Government, by means of its officers' crimes, to effect its purpose of punishing the defendants, there would seem to be present all the elements of a ratification. If so, the Government itself would become a lawbreaker.

Will this Court by sustaining the judgment below sanction such conduct on the part of the Executive? The governing principle has long been settled. It is that a court will not redress a wrong when he who invokes its aid has unclean hands. The maxim of unclean hands comes from courts of equity. But the principle prevails also in courts of law. Its common application is in civil actions between private parties. Where the Government is the actor, the reasons for applying it are even more persuasive. Where the remedies invoked are those of the criminal law, the reasons are compelling.

The door of a court is not barred because the plaintiff has committed a crime. The confirmed criminal is as much entitled to redress as his most virtuous fellow citizen; no record of crime, however long, makes one an outlaw. The court's aid is denied only when he who seeks it has violated the law in connection with the very transaction as to which he seeks legal redress. Then aid is denied despite the defendant's wrong. It is denied in order to maintain respect for law; in order to promote confidence in the administration of justice; in order to preserve the judicial process from contamination. The rule is one, not of action, but of inaction. It is sometimes spoken of as a rule of substantive law. But it extends to matters of procedure as well. A defense may be waived. It is waived when not pleaded. But the objection that the plaintiff comes with unclean hands will be taken by the court itself. It will be taken despite the wish to the contrary of all the parties to the litigation. The court protects itself.

Decency, security and liberty alike demand that government officials shall be subjected to the same rules of conduct that are commands to the citizen. In a government of laws, existence of the government will be imperiled if it fails to observe the law scrupulously. Our Government is the potent, the omnipresent teacher. For good or for ill, it teaches the whole people by its example. Crime is contagious. If the Government becomes a lawbreaker, it breeds contempt for law; it invites every man to become a law unto himself; it invites anarchy. To declare that in the administration of the criminal law the end justifies the means—to declare that the Government may commit crimes in order to secure the conviction of a private criminal—would bring terrible retribution. Against that pernicious doctrine this Court should resolutely set its face.

Mr. Justice Butler, dissenting. . .

Mr. Justice Stone, dissenting. . .

VII

The Suffrage

NOTE

In *Smith* v. *Allwright,* decided in 1944, the Court declared invalid the 'white primary,' which was one of several means introduced at various times, especially in Southern states to keep Negroes from voting. Literacy tests and poll taxes have proved an effective suffrage restriction on both white and Negro.[1] The Constitution of Mississippi provides that the applicant for registration shall 'be able to read any section of the Constitution of this State; or he shall be able to understand the same when read to him, or give a reasonable interpretation thereof.'[2] This law is administered by election officials and the decision of 'pass or fail' is open to wide discretion. This provision was held valid in *Williams* v. *Mississippi.*[3] To restrict voting to those who are literate is within the power of the state and subject to the state's definition of literacy. It could not be shown to the satisfaction of the Court that color played any part in the administration of the Mississippi tests. Similar literacy tests are required in other states.

The 'grandfather clauses' were declared unconstitutional in *Guinn* v. *United States.*[4] The enactments varied, but the one which reached the Supreme Court was the provision in the Oklahoma Constitution which exempted applicants for registration from the literacy test if they were descendants of any person who was entitled to vote under any form of government or who resided in a foreign land prior to 1 January 1866.[5] Under this law most white persons could be registered without the literacy test and by the use of the literacy test most Negroes could be eliminated. The Court held that this law was in intent directed toward 'a previous condition of servitude' and thus, a violation of the Fifteenth Amendment regardless of the fact that there was no specific mention of 'race, color or previous condition of servitude.' A 1916 literacy law in Oklahoma omitted the ancestral exemptions but provided that all persons registered in 1914 should remain permanently on the rolls without taking the literacy test. This law was held invalid in *Lane* v. *Wilson*[6] since these persons were registered under an unconstitutional law as determined by the Guinn case. Although these laws were finally held invalid they were in effect for voting purposes for some time. The 'grandfather' provision was used in Oklahoma from 1910 to 1914 and in some other states for a longer period. The unconstitutional permanent registration feature was in effect in Oklahoma from 1916 to 1938.

[1] On several occasions bills have been introduced into Congress to forbid the poll tax as a restriction on voting. These measures have been debated widely in regard to the power of Congress so to restrict state laws.

[2] Art. XII, sec. 244.

[3] 170 U.S. 213 (1898).

[4] 238 U.S. 347 (1915).

[5] Art. III, sec. 4a.

[6] 307 U.S. 268 (1939).

The power of Congress to control the conduct of federal elections stems from Article 1, sec. 4: 'The times, places, and manner of holding elections for Senators and Representatives shall be prescribed in each State by the legislature thereof; but the Congress may at any time by law make or alter such regulations, except as to the places of choosing Senators.' The Court in *Ex parte Yarbrough* [7] upheld the conviction under federal statute of certain members of the Ku Klux Klan for intimidation of Negroes in a Georgia election for Congressmen. The Court, however, in *Newberry* v. *United States* [8] held that Senator Truman H. Newberry could not be convicted for spending more money in the primary campaign than was authorized by the Federal Corrupt Practices Act. Mr. Newberry was charged with spending some $195,000 in his 1918 campaign to defeat Henry Ford for the Republican nomination for the United States Senate in Michigan. Four justices including Justice McReynolds who wrote the official opinion claimed that the constitutional provisions and hence this statute applied only to *general* elections and not to *primaries*. Four justices dissented from this opinion and the fifth justice who decided in favor of Newberry based his opinion on a different consideration. [9]

Inspired by this decision the State of Texas instituted the principle of the 'white primary.' If the primary is not an election as was implied by the Newberry case then the restrictions of the Fifteenth Amendment may not apply to the primary elections. The first of these Texas statutes providing that no Negro should participate in a Democratic party primary was held invalid in *Nixon* v. *Herndon* [10] as a violation of the 'equal protection of the laws' clause of the Fourteenth Amendment. To exclude Negro citizens from participation in a Democratic primary on the basis of race is considered to be an unreasonable classification in state law. The Fifteenth Amendment was not considered.

After this decision Texas passed a statute delegating to the State Executive Committee of the Democratic party power to set voting qualifications in the party's primary. Acting under this authority the Committee adopted a resolution restricting participation to 'white Democrats.' In *Nixon* v. *Condon* [11] the Court held this statute invalid on the ground that the Committee had by virtue of the delegation become the representative of the state and hence subject to the same constitutional limitations as the legislature. [12]

After this decision the Texas Legislature repealed the statute in question but at the same time retained many other regulations of the primary. The State Democratic Convention thereupon passed a resolution permitting only white citizens to participate in party activities including the nomination of candidates. The Supreme Court in *Grovey* v. *Townsend* [13] upheld this regulation as the valid right of any voluntary private association to determine its own member-

[7] 110 U.S. 651 (1884).　　　　　　　　[8] 256 U.S. 232 (1921).

[9] The United States Senate after lengthy debate seated Mr. Newberry. Later he resigned his position because of the criticism his constituency reflected against the party in the election of 1922. *Congressional Record,* 67th Cong., 3d sess. (Nov. 21, 1922), p. 15.

[10] 273 U.S. 536 (1927).　　　　　　　[12] See Note on delegation, *post,* p. 132.
[11] 286 U.S. 73 (1932).　　　　　　　　[13] 295 U.S. 45 (1935).

ship. This restriction was held to be not state action but private action and hence not subject to the Fourteenth Amendment. Since it was a primary and not a general election, the Fifteenth Amendment was held not to apply.

In *United States* v. *Classic* [14] the Court faced directly the question of congressional control over primary elections. Political observers have long recognized that, especially in one-party states, a candidate's election is guaranteed by his success in the primary. If the provisions of the Federal Criminal Code on the manner of holding elections are not to apply to the primary, then the voter in many areas has been denied effective participation in the choice of federal officers. The primary election has become such an essential part of the whole process of electing federal officers that it must be within the authority of Congress to pass laws for the regulation of the primary as well as the general election in order to uphold the constitutional rights of qualified voters to select representatives in Congress.

The Supreme Court recognized this observation when Classic and others, Commissioners of Elections in New Orleans were convicted under the United States Criminal Code for wilfully altering and falsely counting ballots cast in a Democratic Congressional primary election in Louisiana in 1940.

In the following case, Dr. Smith, a Negro citizen of Texas, urged that this decision provided a basis for a reconsideration of the principles laid down in *Grovey* v. *Townsend*.

SMITH v. ALLWRIGHT
321 U.S. 649 (1944)

Mr. Justice Reed delivered the opinion of the Court.

This writ of certiorari brings here for review a claim for damages in the sum of $5,000 on the part of petitioner, a Negro citizen of the 48th precinct of Harris County, Texas, for the refusal of respondents, election and associate election judges respectively of that precinct, to give petitioner a ballot or to permit him to cast a ballot in the primary election of July 27, 1940, for the nomination of Democratic candidates for the United States Senate and House of Representatives, and Governor and other state officers. The refusal is alleged to have been solely because of the race and color of the proposed voter.

The actions of respondents are said to violate §§ 31 and 43 of Title 8 [1] of the United States Code in that petitioner was deprived of rights secured by §§ 2 and 4

[14] 313 U.S. 299 (1941).
[1] 8 U.S.C. § 31:
'All citizens of the United States who are otherwise qualified by law to vote at any election by the people in any State, Territory, district, county, city, parish, township, school district, municipality, or other territorial subdivision, shall be entitled and allowed to vote at all such elections, without distinction of race, color, or previous condition of servitude; any constitution, law, custom, usage, or regulation of any State or Territory, or by or under its authority, to the contrary notwithstanding.'

§ 43: 'Every person who, under color of any statute, ordinance, regulation, custom, or usage, of any State or Territory, subjects, or causes to be subjected, any citizen of the United States or other person within the jurisdiction thereof to the deprivation of any rights, privileges, or immunities secured by the Constitution and laws, shall be liable to the party injured in an action at law, suit in equity, or other proper proceeding for redress.'

of Article I [2] and the Fourteenth, Fifteenth and Seventeenth Amendments to the United States Constitution.[3] The suit was filed in the District Court of the United States for the Southern District of Texas, which had jurisdiction under Judicial Code § 24, subsection 14.

The District Court denied the relief sought and the Circuit Court of Appeals quite properly affirmed its action on the authority of *Grovey* v. *Townsend*, 295 U.S. 45.[4] We granted the petition for certiorari to resolve a claimed inconsistency between the decision in the *Grovey* case and that of *United States* v. *Classic*, 313 U.S. 299. 319 U.S. 738.

The State of Texas by its Constitution and statutes provides that every person, if certain other requirements are met which are not here in issue, qualified by residence in the district or county 'shall be deemed a qualified elector.' Constitution of Texas, Article vi, § 2; Vernon's Civil Statutes (1939 ed.), Article 2955. Primary elections for United States Senators, Congressmen and state officers are provided for by Chapters Twelve and Thirteen of the statutes. Under these chapters, the Democratic party was required to hold the primary which was the occasion of the alleged wrong to petitioner. A summary of the state statutes regulating primaries appears in the footnote.[5] These nominations are to be made by the qualified voters of the party. Art. 3101.

The Democratic party of Texas is held by the Supreme Court of that State to be a 'voluntary association,' *Bell* v. *Hill,* 123 Tex. 531, 534, protected by § 27 of the Bill of Rights, Art. 1, Constitution of Texas, from interference by the State except that:

'In the interest of fair methods and a fair expression by their members of their preferences in the selection of their nominees, the State may regulate such elections by proper laws.' p. 545.

That court stated further:

'Since the right to organize and maintain a political party is one guaranteed by the Bill of Rights of this State, it necessarily follows that every privilege essential or reasonably appropriate to the exercise of that right is likewise guaranteed,—including, of course, the privilege of deter-

---

[2] Constitution, Art. 1:

'Section 2. The House of Representatives shall be composed of Members chosen every second Year by the People of the several States, and the Electors in each State shall have the Qualifications requisite for Electors of the most numerous Branch of the State Legislature.'

'Section 4. The Times, Places and Manner of holding Elections for Senators and Representatives, shall be prescribed in each State by the Legislature thereof; but the Congress may at any time by Law make or alter such Regulations, except as to the Places of chusing Senators.'

[3] Constitution:

Article xiv. 'Section 1. All persons born or naturalized in the United States, and subject to the jurisdiction thereof, are citizens of the United States and of the State wherein they reside. No State shall make or enforce any law which shall abridge the privileges or immunities of citizens of the United States; nor shall any State deprive any person of life, liberty, or property, without due process of law; nor deny to any person within its jurisdiction the equal protection of the laws.'

Article xv. 'Section 1. The right of citizens of the United States to vote shall not be denied or abridged by the United States or by any State on account of race, color, or previous condition of servitude.

'Section 2. The Congress shall have power to enforce this article by appropriate legislation.'

Article xvii. 'The Senate of the United States shall be composed of two Senators from each State, elected by the people thereof, for six years; and each Senator shall have one vote. The electors in each State shall have the qualifications requisite for electors of the most numerous branch of the State legislatures.'

[4] *Smith* v. *Allwright*, 131 F. 2d 593.

[5] Editors' Note: In the Court's footnote more than fifty sections of the Texas Statutes are quoted giving detailed regulations for the conduct of the primary.

mining the policies of the party and its membership. Without the privilege of determining the policy of a political association and its membership, the right to organize such an association would be a mere mockery. We think these rights,—that is, the right to determine the membership of a political party and to determine its policies, of necessity are to be exercised by the state convention of such party, and cannot, under any circumstances, be conferred upon a state or governmental agency.' p. 546. . .

The Democratic party on May 24, 1932, in a state convention adopted the following resolution, which has not since been 'amended, abrogated, annulled or avoided':

'Be it resolved that all white citizens of the State of Texas who are qualified to vote under the Constitution and laws of the State shall be eligible to membership in the Democratic party and, as such, entitled to participate in its deliberations.'

It was by virtue of this resolution that the respondents refused to permit the petitioner to vote.

Texas is free to conduct her elections and limit her electorate as she may deem wise, save only as her action may be affected by the prohibitions of the United States Constitution or in conflict with powers delegated to and exercised by the National Government.[6] The Fourteenth Amendment forbids a State from making or enforcing any law which abridges the privileges or immunities of citizens of the United States and the Fifteenth Amendment specifically interdicts any denial or abridgement by the State of the right of citizens to vote on account of color. Respondents appeared in the District Court and the Circuit Court of Appeals and defended on the ground that the Democratic party of Texas is a voluntary organization with members banded together

for the purpose of selecting individuals of the group representing the common political beliefs as candidates in the general election. As such a voluntary organization, it was claimed, the Democratic party is free to select its own membership and limit to whites participation in the party primary. Such action, the answer asserted, does not violate the Fourteenth, Fifteenth or Seventeenth Amendment as officers of government cannot be chosen at primaries and the Amendments are applicable only to general elections where governmental officers are actually elected. Primaries, it is said, are political party affairs, handled by party, not governmental, officers. No appearance for respondents is made in this Court. Arguments presented here by the Attorney General of Texas and the Chairman of the State Democratic Executive Committee of Texas, as amici curiae, urged substantially the same grounds as those advanced by the respondents.

The right of a Negro to vote in the Texas primary has been considered heretofore by this Court. The first case was *Nixon* v. *Herndon*, 273 U.S. 536. At that time, 1924, the Texas statute, Art. 3093a, afterwards numbered Art. 3107 (Rev. Stat. 1925) declared 'in no event shall a Negro be eligible to participate in a Democratic Party primary election in the State of Texas.' Nixon was refused the right to vote in a Democratic primary and brought a suit for damages against the election officers under R. S. §§ 1979 and 2004, the present §§ 43 and 31 of Title 8, U.S.C., respectively. It was urged to this Court that the denial of the franchise to Nixon violated his Constitutional rights under the Fourteenth and Fifteenth Amendments. Without consideration of the Fifteenth, this Court held that the action of Texas in denying the ballot to Negroes by statute was in violation of the equal protection clause of the Fourteenth

[6] Cf. *Parker* v. *Brown*, 317 U.S. 341, 359-60.

Amendment and reversed the dismissal of the suit.

The legislature of Texas reenacted the article but gave the State Executive Committee of a party the power to prescribe the qualifications of its members for voting or other participation. This article remains in the statutes. The State Executive Committee of the Democratic party adopted a resolution that white Democrats and none other might participate in the primaries of that party. Nixon was refused again the privilege of voting in a primary and again brought suit for damages by virtue of § 31. Title 8, U.S.C. This Court again reversed the dismissal of the suit for the reason that the Committee action was deemed to be state action and invalid as discriminatory under the Fourteenth Amendment. The test was said to be whether the Committee operated as representative of the State in the discharge of the State's authority. *Nixon* v. *Condon,* 286 U.S. 73. The question of the inherent power of a political party in Texas 'without restraint by any law to determine its own membership' was left open. *Id.,* 84-5.

In *Grovey* v. *Townsend,* 295 U.S. 45, this Court had before it another suit for damages for the refusal in a primary of a county clerk, a Texas officer with only public functions to perform, to furnish petitioner, a Negro, an absentee ballot. The refusal was solely on the ground of race. This case differed from *Nixon* v. *Condon, supra,* in that a state convention of the Democratic party had passed the resolution of May 24, 1932, hereinbefore quoted. It was decided that the determination by the state convention of the membership of the Democratic party made a significant change from a determination by the Executive Committee. The former was party action, voluntary in character. The latter, as had been held in the *Condon* case, was action by authority of the State. The managers of the primary election were therefore declared not to be state

officials in such sense that their action was state action. A state convention of a party was said not to be an organ of the State. This Court went on to announce that to deny a vote in a primary was a mere refusal of party membership with which 'the State need have no concern,' *loc. cit.* at 55, while for a State to deny a vote in a general election on the ground of race or color violated the Constitution. Consequently, there was found no ground for holding that the county clerk's refusal of a ballot because of racial ineligibility for party membership denied the petitioner any right under the Fourteenth or Fifteenth Amendment.

Since *Grovey* v. *Townsend* and prior to the present suit, no case from Texas involving primary elections has been before this Court. We did decide, however, *United States* v. *Classic,* 313 U.S. 299. We there held that § 4 of Article 1 of the Constitution authorized Congress to regulate primary as well as general elections, 313 U.S. at 316, 317, 'where the primary is by law made an integral part of the election machinery.' 313 U.S. at 318. Consequently, in the *Classic* case, we upheld the applicability to frauds in a Louisiana primary of §§ 19 and 20 of the Criminal Code. Thereby corrupt acts of election officers were subjected to Congressional sanctions because that body had power to protect rights of federal suffrage secured by the Constitution in primary as in general elections. 313 U.S. at 323. This decision depended, too, on the determination that under the Louisiana statutes the primary was a part of the procedure for choice of federal officials. By this decision the doubt as to whether or not such primaries were a part of 'elections' subject to federal control, which had remained unanswered since *Newberry* v. *United States,* 256 U.S. 232, was erased. The *Nixon Cases* were decided under the equal protection clause of the Fourteenth Amendment without a determination of the status of the primary as a part of the electoral process. The exclusion of Negroes from the primaries by action of the State was held invalid under that Amendment. The fusing by the *Classic* case of the primary and general elections into a single instrumentality for choice of officers has a definite bearing on the permissibility under the Constitution of excluding Negroes from primaries. This is not to say that the *Classic* case cuts directly into the rationale of *Grovey* v. *Townsend*. This latter case was not mentioned in the opinion. *Classic* bears upon *Grovey* v. *Townsend* not because exclusion of Negroes from primaries is any more or less state action by reason of the unitary character of the electoral process but because the recognition of the place of the primary in the electoral scheme makes clear that state delegation to a party of the power to fix the qualifications of primary elections is delegation of a state function that may make the party's action the action of the State. When *Grovey* v. *Townsend* was written, the Court looked upon the denial of a vote in a primary as a mere refusal by a party of party membership. 295 U.S. at 55. As the Louisiana statutes for holding primaries are similar to those of Texas, our ruling in *Classic* as to the unitary character of the electoral process calls for a reexamination as to whether or not the exclusion of Negroes from a Texas party primary was state action.

The statutes of Texas relating to primaries and the resolution of the Democratic party of Texas extending the privileges of membership to white citizens only are the same in substance and effect today as they were when *Grovey* v. *Townsend* was decided by a unanimous Court. The question as to whether the exclusionary action of the party was the action of the State persists as the determinative factor. In again entering upon consideration of the inference to be drawn as to state action from a substantially similar factual situation, it should be noted that *Grovey* v. *Townsend* upheld exclusion of

Negroes from primaries through the denial of party membership by a party convention. A few years before, this Court refused approval of exclusion by the State Executive Committee of the party. A different result was reached on the theory that the Committee action was state authorized and the Convention action was unfettered by statutory control. Such a variation in the result from so slight a change in form influences us to consider anew the legal validity of the distinction which has resulted in barring Negroes from participating in the nominations of candidates of the Democratic party in Texas. Other precedents of this Court forbid the abridgement of the right to vote. *United States* v. *Reese*, 92 U.S. 214, 217; *Neal* v. *Delaware*, 103 U.S. 370, 388; *Guinn* v. *United States*, 238 U.S. 347, 361; *Myers* v. *Anderson*, 238 U.S. 368, 379; *Lane* v. *Wilson*, 307 U.S. 268.

It may now be taken as a postulate that the right to vote in such a primary for the nomination of candidates without discrimination by the State, like the right to vote in a general election, is a right secured by the Constitution. *United States* v. *Classic*, 313 U.S. at 314; *Myers* v. *Anderson*, 238 U.S. 368; *Ex parte Yarbrough*, 110 U.S. 651, 663 *et seq.* By the terms of the Fifteenth Amendment that right may not be abridged by any State on account of race. Under our Constitution the great privilege of the ballot may not be denied a man by the State because of his color.

We are thus brought to an examination of the qualifications for Democratic primary electors in Texas, to determine whether state action or private action has excluded Negroes from participation. Despite Texas' decision that the exclusion is produced by private or party action, *Bell* v. *Hill, supra,* federal courts must for themselves appraise the facts leading to that conclusion. It is only by the performance of this obligation that a final and uniform interpretation can be given to the Constitution, the 'supreme Law of the Land.' . . . Texas requires electors in a primary to pay a poll tax. Every person who does so pay and who has the qualifications of age and residence is an acceptable voter for the primary. Art. 2955. As appears above in the summary of the statutory provisions . . . Texas requires by the law the election of the county officers of a party. These compose the county executive committee. The county chairmen so selected are members of the district executive committee and choose the chairman for the district. Precinct primary election officers are named by the county executive committee. Statutes provide for the election by the voters of precinct delegates to the county convention of a party and the selection of delegates to the district and state conventions by the county convention. The state convention selects the state executive committee. No convention may place in platform or resolution any demand for specific legislation without endorsement of such legislation by the voters in a primary. Texas thus directs the selection of all party officers.

Primary elections are conducted by the party under state statutory authority. The county executive committee selects precinct election officials and the county, district or state executive committees, respectively, canvass the returns. These party committees or the state convention certify the party's candidates to the appropriate officers for inclusion on the official ballot for the general election. No name which has not been so certified may appear upon the ballot for the general election as a candidate of a political party. No other name may be printed on the ballot which has not been placed in nomination by qualified voters who must take oath that they did not participate in a primary for the selection of a candidate for the office for which the nomination is made.

The state courts are given exclusive original jurisdiction of contested elections and of mandamus proceedings to compel party officers to perform their statutory duties.

We think that this statutory system for the selection of party nominees for inclusion on the general election ballot makes the party which is required to follow these legislative directions an agency of the State in so far as it determines the participants in a primary election. The party takes its character as a state agency from the duties imposed upon it by state statutes; the duties do not become matters of private law because they are performed by a political party. The plan of the Texas primary follows substantially that of Louisiana, with the exception that in Louisiana the State pays the cost of the primary while Texas assesses the cost against candidates. In numerous instances, the Texas statutes fix or limit the fees to be charged. Whether paid directly by the State or through state requirements, it is state action which compels. When primaries become a part of the machinery for choosing officials, state and national, as they have here, the same tests to determine the character of discrimination or abridgement should be applied to the primary as are applied to the general election. If the State requires a certain electoral procedure, prescribes a general election ballot made up of party nominees so chosen and limits the choice of the electorate in general elections for state offices, practically speaking, to those whose names appear on such a ballot, it endorses, adopts and enforces the discrimination against Negroes, practiced by a party entrusted by Texas law with the determination of the qualifications of participants in the primary. This is state action within the meaning of the Fifteenth Amendment. *Guinn v. United States,* 238 U.S. 347, 362.

The United States is a constitutional democracy. Its organic law grants to all citizens a right to participate in the choice of elected officials without restriction by any State because of race. This grant to the people of the opportunity for choice is not to be nullified by a State through casting its electoral process in a form which permits a private organization to practice racial discrimination in the election. Constitutional rights would be of little value if they could be thus indirectly denied. *Lane* v. *Wilson,* 307 U.S. 268, 275.

The privilege of membership in a party may be, as this Court said in *Grovey* v. *Townsend,* 295 U.S. 45, 55, no concern of a State. But when, as here, that privilege is also the essential qualification for voting in a primary to select nominees for a general election, the State makes the action of the party the action of the State. In reaching this conclusion we are not unmindful of the desirability of continuity of decision in constitutional questions. However, when convinced of former error, this Court has never felt constrained to follow precedent. In constitutional questions, where correction depends upon amendment and not upon legislative action this Court throughout its history has freely exercised its power to reexamine the basis of its constitutional decisions. This has long been accepted practice, and this practice has continued to this day. This is particularly true when the decision believed erroneous is the application of a constitutional principle rather than an interpretation of the Constitution to extract the principle itself.[7] Here we are applying, contrary to the recent decision in *Grovey* v. *Townsend,* the well-established principle of the Fifteenth Amendment, forbidding the abridgement by State of a citizen's right to vote. *Grovey* v. *Townsend* is overruled.

Judgment reversed.

MR. JUSTICE FRANKFURTER concurs in the result.

MR. JUSTICE ROBERTS:

In *Mahnich* v. *Southern Steamship Co.,* 321 U.S. 96, 105, I have expressed my views with respect to the present policy of the court freely to disregard and to overrule considered decisions and the rules of law announced in them. This tendency, it seems to me, indicates an intolerance for what those who have composed this court in the past have conscientiously and deliberately concluded, and involves an assumption that knowledge and wisdom reside in us which was denied to our predecessors. I shall not repeat what I there said for I consider it fully applicable to the instant decision, which but points the moral anew.

A word should be said with respect to the judicial history forming the background of *Grovey* v. *Townsend,* 295 U.S. 45, which is now overruled.

In 1923 Texas adopted a statute which declared that no negro should be eligible to participate in a Democratic primary election in that State. A negro, a citizen of the United States and of Texas, qualified to vote, except for the provisions of the statute, was denied the opportunity to vote in a primary election at which candidates were to be chosen for the offices of senator and representative in the Congress of the United States. He brought action against the judges of election in a United States court for damages for their refusal to accept his ballot. This court unanimously reversed a judgment dismissing the complaint and held that the judges acted pursuant to state law and that the State of Texas, by its statute, had denied the voter the equal protection secured by the Fourteenth Amendment. *Nixon* v. *Herndon,* 273 U.S. 536 (1927).

In 1927 the legislature of Texas repealed the provision condemned by this court and enacted that every political party in the State might, through its Executive Committee, prescribe the qualifications of its own members and determine in its own way who should be qualified to vote or participate in the party, except that no denial of participation could be decreed

---

[7] Cf. Dissent in *Burnet* v. *Coronado Oil & Gas Co.,* 285 U.S. 393 at 410.

by reason of former political or other affiliation. Thereupon the State Executive Committee of the Democratic party in Texas adopted a resolution that white Democrats, and no other, should be allowed to participate in the party's primaries.

A negro, whose primary ballot was rejected pursuant to the resolution, sought to recover damages from the judges who had rejected it. The United States District Court dismissed his action, and the Circuit Court of Appeals affirmed; but this court reversed the judgment and sustained the right of action by a vote of 5 to 4. *Nixon* v. *Condon,* 286 U.S. 73 (1932).

The opinion was written with care. The court refused to decide whether a political party in Texas had inherent power to determine its membership. The court said, however: 'Whatever inherent power a state political party has to determine the content of its membership resides in the state convention,' and referred to the statutes of Texas to demonstrate that the State had left the Convention free to formulate the party faith. Attention was directed to the fact that the statute under attack did not leave to the party convention the definition of party membership but placed it in the party's State Executive Committee which could not, by any stretch of reasoning, be held to constitute the party. The court held, therefore, that the State Executive Committee acted solely by virtue of the statutory mandate and as delegate of state power, and again struck down the discrimination against negro voters as deriving force and virtue from state action,—that is, from statute.

In 1932 the Democratic Convention of Texas adopted a resolution that 'all white citizens of the State of Texas who are qualified to vote under the Constitution and laws of the State shall be eligible to membership in the Democratic party and

as such entitled to participate in its deliberations.'

A negro voter qualified to vote in a primary election, except for the exclusion worked by the resolution, demanded an absentee ballot which he was entitled to mail to the judges at a primary election except for the resolution. The county clerk refused to furnish him a ballot. He brought an action for damages against the clerk in a state court. That court, which was the tribunal having final jurisdiction under the laws of Texas, dismissed his complaint and he brought the case to this court for review. After the fullest consideration by the whole court[8] an opinion was written representing its unanimous views and affirming the judgment. *Grovey* v. *Townsend,* 295 U.S. 45 (1935).

I believe it will not be gainsaid the case received the attention and consideration which the questions involved demanded and the opinion represented the views of all the justices. It appears that those views do not now commend themselves to the court. I shall not restate them. They are exposed in the opinion and must stand or fall on their merits. Their soundness, however, is not a matter which presently concerns me.

The reason for my concern is that the instant decision, overruling that announced about nine years ago, tends to bring adjudications of this tribunal into the same class as a restricted railroad ticket, good for this day and train only. I have no assurance, in view of current decisions, that the opinion announced today may not shortly be repudiated and overruled by justices who deem they have new light on the subject. In the present term the court has overruled three cases.

In the present case, as in *Mahnich* v. *Southern S. S. Co., supra,* the court below relied, as it was bound to, upon our pre-

[8] The Court was composed of Hughes, C. J., Van Devanter, McReynolds, Brandeis, Sutherland, Butler, Stone, Roberts and Cardozo, J. J.

vious decision. As that court points out, the statutes of Texas have not been altered since *Grovey* v. *Townsend* was decided. The same resolution is involved as was drawn in question in *Grovey* v. *Townsend*. Not a fact differentiates that case from this except the names of the parties.

It is suggested that *Grovey* v. *Townsend* was overruled *sub silentio* in *United States* v. *Classic,* 313 U.S. 299. If so, the situation is even worse than that exhibited by the outright repudiation of an earlier decision, for it is the fact that, in the *Classic* case, *Grovey* v. *Townsend* was distinguished in brief and argument by the Government without suggestion that it was wrongly decided, and was relied on by the appellees, not as a controlling decision, but by way of analogy. The case is not mentioned in either of the opinions in the *Classic* case. Again and again it is said in the opinion of the court in that case that the voter who was denied the right to vote was a fully qualified voter. In other words, there was no question of his being a person entitled under state law to vote in the primary. The offense charged was the fraudulent denial of his conceded right by an election officer because of his race. Here the question is altogether different. It is whether, in a Democratic primary, he who tendered his vote was a member of the Democratic party.

I do not stop to call attention to the material differences between the primary election laws of Louisiana under consideration in the *Classic* case and those of Texas which are here drawn in question. These differences were spelled out in detail in the Government's brief in the *Classic* case and emphasized in its oral argument. It is enough to say that the Louisiana statutes required the primary to be conducted by state officials and made it a state election, whereas, under the Texas statute, the primary is a party election conducted at the expense of members of the party and by officials chosen by the party. If this court's opinion in the *Classic* case discloses its method of overruling earlier decisions, I can only protest that, in fairness, it should rather have adopted the open and frank way of saying what it was doing than, after the event, characterize its past action as overruling *Grovey* v. *Townsend* though those less sapient never realized the fact.

It is regrettable that in an era marked by doubt and confusion, an era whose greatest need is steadfastness of thought and purpose, this court, which has been looked to as exhibiting consistency in adjudication, and a steadiness which would hold the balance even in the face of temporary ebbs and flows of opinion, should now itself become the breeder of fresh doubt and confusion in the public mind as to the stability of our institutions.

VIII

The Power of Congress to Investigate

NOTE

The power of Congress to investigate, as a derivative of its power to make law, is the concern of the Supreme Court in *McGrain* v. *Daugherty,* decided in 1927.

This power to investigate is not a broad, general power. Its use extends only so far as to enable Congress properly to exercise its legislative function. 'A legislative body,' said Mr. Justice Van Devanter in the McGrain case, 'cannot legislate wisely or effectively in the absence of information respecting the conditions which the legislation is intended to affect or change; and where the legislative body does not itself possess the requisite information . . . recourse must be had to others who do possess it.' To get necessary information, Congress may subpoena, and finally compel, witnesses to appear and to give information. However, this does not mean that Congress may embark upon 'fishing expeditions' amongst the private papers, records, or affairs of either an individual or a corporation with the hope of finding incriminating evidence.

Professor Dimock declares that there are 'three principal functions of Congressional investigating committees, namely, the membership function, the law-making function, and the power of investigating the administration in order to determine whether or not the legislature's will has been carried out lawfully, economically, and efficiently.' [1]

The constitutional bases of the first function are to be found in the first article of the Constitution: 'Each House shall be the judge of the elections, returns and qualifications of its own members'; 'Each House may determine the rules of its proceedings, punish its members for disorderly behaviour, and, with the concurrence of two-thirds, expel a member'; 'They shall in all cases, except treason, felony and breach of the peace, be privileged from arrest during their attendance at the session of their respective Houses, and in going to and returning from the same; and for any speech or debate in either House they shall not be questioned in any other place.' The first two clauses are the bases of the power to investigate the qualifications or conduct of Senators and Representatives. A recent instance of the exercise of its power under the first clause was the investigation into the ways and means of Senator Bilbo's election in Mississippi. The third clause, especially the latter part, relates to privileges and immunities of members and to contempts against either House.

The constitutional bases of the second function, namely, the law-making

[1] Dimock, Marshall Edward, *Congressional Investigating Committees,* Baltimore, 1929, p. 44. We have omitted here the question of congressional investigations in connection with impeachment proceedings.

function of congressional investigating committees, are likewise to be found in the first article of the Constitution: 'All legislative powers herein granted shall be vested in a Congress of the United States . . .'; in addition, it is provided that Congress shall have power 'To make all laws which shall be necessary and proper for carrying into execution the foregoing powers, and all other powers vested by this Constitution in the Government of the United States, or in any department or officer thereof.'

With an eye to immediate or future legislation, congressional investigating committees have delved into problems of national significance such as corporate combinations in restraint of trade, the concentration of economic power, and the relations of labor and management.

As to the third function, that is, investigations of the executive departments and government agencies, Congress 'must learn the needs of the departments in legislating . . . ,' and assure itself 'that the departments are conducted in accordance with law and policy.'[2] When 'Congress suspects,' says Dimock, 'for good and sufficient reason, that irregularities are taking place in a department, it is its duty and privilege under the Constitution to investigate as a means to "other action."'[3]

The Senate investigation which commenced in 1922 of the lease of naval oil reserves to private operators is a case in point. The Committee on Public Lands under the direction of Senator Thomas J. Walsh, after months of study and interrogation, brought to light an unsavory tale of corruption which involved a former Secretary of the Interior, Albert B. Fall, and two oil operators, Harry F. Sinclair and Edward L. Doheny. Fall was sentenced to a year in jail and fined $100,000.

What are the end results of congressional investigations? McGeary in his study of the investigatory power finds that a law may be enacted or an executive official disciplined. He emphasizes, however, the fact that the results may be less tangible. 'An inquiry may,' he says, '. . . gather information which, although it is not used at once, may serve as a partial basis for legislation in later years.'[4] Also, one purpose of public inquiries 'is to mould public opinion . . . yet the actual effect of an investigation in shaping opinion can only be surmised.'[5] Finally, declares McGeary, 'one fruit of investigations is that they help to restrain wrongdoing, both public and private.'[6]

McGRAIN v. DAUGHERTY
273 U.S. 135 (1927)

Appeal from the United States District Court for the Southern District of Ohio. . .

Mr. Justice Van Devanter delivered the opinion of the court.

This is an appeal from the final order

[2] Ibid. p. 28.   [3] Ibid.
[4] McGeary, M. Nelson, *The Development of Congressional Investigative Power,* New York, 1940, p. 85.
[5] Ibid.   [6] Ibid.

in a proceeding in *habeas corpus* discharging a recusant witness held in custody under process of attachment issued from the United States Senate in the course of an investigation which it was making of the administration of the Department of Justice. A full statement of the case is necessary.

The Department of Justice is one of the great executive departments established by congressional enactment and has charge, among other things, of the initiation and prosecution of all suits, civil and criminal, which may be brought in the right and name of the United States to compel obedience or punish disobedience to its laws, to recover property obtained from it by unlawful or fraudulent means, or to safeguard its rights in other respects; and also of the assertion and protection of its interests when it or its officers are sued by others. The Attorney General is the head of the department, and its functions are all to be exercised under his supervision and direction.

Harry M. Daugherty became the Attorney General March 5, 1921, and held that office until March 28, 1924, when he resigned. Late in that period various charges of misfeasance and nonfeasance in the Department of Justice after he became its supervising head were brought to the attention of the Senate by individual senators and made the basis of an insistent demand that the department be investigated to the end that the practices and deficiencies which, according to the charges, were operating to prevent or impair its right administration might be definitely ascertained and that appropriate and effective measures might be taken to remedy or eliminate the evil. The Senate regarded the charges as grave and requiring legislative attention and action. Accordingly it formulated, passed, and invited the House of Representatives to pass (and that body did pass) two measures taking important litigation then in immediate contemplation out of the control of the Department

of Justice and placing the same in charge of special counsel to be appointed by the President; and also adopted a resolution authorizing and directing a select committee of five senators—

'to investigate circumstances and facts, and report the same to the Senate, concerning the alleged failure of Harry M. Daugherty, Attorney General of the United States, to prosecute properly violators of the Sherman Anti-trust Act and the Clayton Act against monopolies and unlawful restraint of trade; the alleged neglect and failure of the said Harry M. Daugherty, Attorney General of the United States, to arrest and prosecute Albert B. Fall, Harry F. Sinclair, E. L. Doheny, C. R. Forbes, and their co-conspirators in defrauding the Government, as well as the alleged neglect and failure of the said Attorney General to arrest and prosecute many others for violations of Federal statutes, and his alleged failure to prosecute properly, efficiently, and promptly, and to defend, all manner of civil and criminal actions wherein the Government of the United States is interested as a party plaintiff or defendant. And said committee is further directed to inquire into, investigate, and report to the Senate the activities of the said Harry M. Daugherty, Attorney General, and any of his assistants in the Department of Justice which would in any manner tend to impair their efficiency or influence as representatives of the Government of the United States.'

The resolution also authorized the committee to send for books and papers, to subpoena witnesses, to administer oaths, and to sit at such times and places as it might deem advisable.

In the course of the investigation the committee issued and caused to be duly served on Mally S. Daugherty—who was a brother of Harry M. Daugherty and president of the Midland National Bank of Washington Court House, Ohio—a subpoena commanding him to appear before the committee for the purpose of giving testimony bearing on the subject under investigation, and to bring with him the 'deposit ledgers of the Midland National Bank since November 1, 1920; also note files and transcript of owners of every safety vault; also records of income drafts; also records of any individual account or accounts showing withdrawals of amounts of $25,000 or over during above period.' The witness failed to appear.

A little later in the course of the investigation the committee issued and caused to be duly served on the same witness another subpoena commanding him to appear before it for the purpose of giving testimony relating to the subject under consideration—nothing being said in this subpoena about bringing records, books, or papers. The witness again failed to appear; and no excuse was offered by him for either failure.

The committee then made a report to the Senate stating that the subpoenas had been issued, that according to the officer's returns—copies of which accompanied the report—the witness was personally served; and that he had failed and refused to appear. After a reading of the report, the Senate adopted a resolution reciting these facts and proceeding as follows:

'Whereas the appearance and testimony of the said M. S. Daugherty is material and necessary in order that the committee may properly execute the functions imposed upon it and may obtain information necessary as a basis for such legislative and other action as the Senate may deem necessary and proper: Therefore be it

'Resolved, That the President of the Senate pro tempore issue his warrant commanding the Sergeant at Arms or his deputy to take into custody the body of the said M. S. Daugherty wherever found, and to bring the said M. S. Daugherty before the bar of the Senate, then and there to answer such questions pertinent to the matter under inquiry as the Senate may order the President of the Senate pro tem-

pore to propound; and to keep the said M. S. Daugherty in custody to await the further order of the Senate.'

It will be observed from the terms of the resolution that the warrant was to be issued in furtherance of the effort to obtain the personal testimony of the witness and, like the second subpoena, was not intended to exact from him the production of the various records, books, and papers named in the first subpoena.

The warrant was issued agreeably to the resolution and was addressed simply to the Sergeant at Arms. That officer on receiving the warrant indorsed thereon a direction that it be executed by John J. McGrain, already his deputy, and delivered it to him for execution.

The deputy, proceeding under the warrant, took the witness into custody at Cincinnati, Ohio, with the purpose of bringing him before the bar of the Senate as commanded; whereupon the witness petitioned the federal district court in Cincinnati for a writ of *habeas corpus*. The writ was granted and the deputy made due return setting forth the warrant and the cause of the detention. After a hearing the court held the attachment and detention unlawful and discharged the witness, the decision being put on the ground that the Senate in directing the investigation and in ordering the attachment exceeded its powers under the Constitution, 299 F. 620. The deputy prayed and was allowed a direct appeal to this Court under section 238 of the Judicial Code as then existing.

We have given the case earnest and prolonged consideration because the principal questions involved are of unusual importance and delicacy. They are (a) whether the Senate—or the House of Representatives, both being on the same plane in this regard—has power, through its own process, to compel a private individual to appear before it or one of its committees and give testimony needed to enable it efficiently to exercise a legislative function belonging to it under the Constitution, and (b) whether it sufficiently appears that the process was being employed in this instance to obtain testimony for that purpose. . .

In approaching the principal questions, which remain to be considered, two observations are in order. One is that we are not now concerned with the direction in the first subpoena that the witness produce various records, books, and papers of the Midland National Bank. That direction was not repeated in the second subpoena; and is not sought to be enforced by the attachment. This was recognized by the court below, 299 Fed. 623, and is conceded by counsel for the appellant. The other is that we are not now concerned with the right of the Senate to propound or the duty of the witness to answer specific questions, for as yet no questions have been propounded to him. He is asserting—and is standing on his assertion— that the Senate is without power to interrogate him, even if the questions propounded be pertinent and otherwise legitimate—which for present purposes must be assumed.

The first of the principal questions— the one which the witness particularly presses on our attention—is, as before shown, whether the Senate—or the House of Representatives, both being on the same plane in this regard—has power, through its own process, to compel a private individual to appear before it or one of its committees and give testimony needed to enable it efficiently to exercise a legislative function belonging to it under the Constitution.

The Constitution provides for a Congress consisting of a Senate and House of Representatives and invests it with 'all legislative powers' granted to the United States, and with power 'to make all laws which shall be necessary and proper' for carrying into execution these powers and 'all other powers' vested by the Constitution in the United States or in any department or officer thereof. Art. 1, secs. 1, 8.

Other provisions show that, while bills can become laws only after being considered and passed by both houses of Congress, each house is to be distinct from the other, to have its own officers and rules, and to exercise its legislative function independently. Art. 1, secs. 2, 3, 5, 7. But there is no provision expressly investing either house with power to make investigations and exact testimony to the end that it may exercise its legislative function advisedly and effectively. So the question arises whether this power is so far incidental to the legislative function as to be implied.

In actual legislative practice power to secure needed information by such means has long been treated as an attribute of the power to legislate. It was so regarded in the British Parliament and in the Colonial legislatures before the American Revolution; and a like view has prevailed and been carried into effect in both houses of Congress and in most of the state legislatures.

This power was both asserted and exerted by the House of Representatives in 1792, when it appointed a select committee to inquire into the St. Clair expedition and authorized the committee to send for necessary persons, papers and records. Mr. Madison, who had taken an important part in framing the Constitution only five years before, and four of his associates in that work, were members of the House of Representatives at the time, and all voted for the inquiry. 3 Cong. Ann. 494. Other exertions of the power by the House of Representatives, as also by the Senate, are shown in the citations already made. Among those by the Senate, the inquiry ordered in 1859 respecting the raid by John Brown and his adherents on the armory and arsenal of the United States at Harper's Ferry is of special significance. The resolution directing the inquiry authorized the committee to send for persons and papers, to inquire into the facts pertaining to the raid and the means by which it was organized and supported, and to report what legislation, if any, was necessary to preserve the peace of the country and protect the public property. The resolution was briefly discussed and adopted without opposition. Cong. Globe, 36th Cong., 1st Sess., pp. 141, 152. Later on the committee reported that Thaddeus Hyatt, although subpoenaed to appear as a witness, had refused to do so; whereupon the Senate ordered that he be attached and brought before it to answer for his refusal. When he was brought in he answered by challenging the power of the Senate to direct the inquiry and exact testimony to aid it in exercising its legislative function. The question of power thus presented was thoroughly discussed by several senators—Mr. Sumner of Massachusetts taking the lead in denying the power and Mr. Fessenden of Maine in supporting it. Sectional and party lines were put aside and the question was debated and determined with special regard to principle and precedent. The vote was taken on a resolution pronouncing the witness's answer insufficient and directing that he be committed until he should signify that he was ready and willing to testify. The resolution was adopted—44 senators voting for it and 10 against. Cong. Globe, 36 Cong., 1st Sess., pp. 1100-1109, 3006-7. . . .

The deliberate solution of the question on that occasion has been accepted and followed on other occasions by both houses of Congress, and never has been rejected or questioned by either.

The state courts quite generally have held that the power to legislate carries with it by necessary implication ample authority to obtain information needed in the rightful exercise of that power and to employ compulsory process for the purpose. . .

We have referred to the practice of the two houses of Congress; and we now shall notice some significant congressional enactments. . . January 24, 1857, c. 19, 11 Stat. 155, it passed 'An Act more effectually to enforce the attendance of witnesses on the summons of either house of Congress, and to compel them to discover testimony.' This act provided, first, that any person summoned as a witness to give testimony or produce papers in any matter under inquiry before either house of Congress, or any committee of either house, who should wilfully make default, or, if appearing, should refuse to answer any question pertinent to the inquiry, should, in addition to the pains and penalties then existing, be deemed guilty of a misdemeanor and be subject to indictment and punishment as there prescribed; and, secondly, that no person should be excused from giving evidence in such an inquiry on the ground that it might tend to incriminate or disgrace him, nor be held to answer criminally, or be subjected to any penalty or forfeiture, for any fact or act as to which he was required to testify, excepting that he might be subjected to prosecution for perjury committed while so testifying. January 24, 1862, c. 11, 12 Stat. 333, Congress modified the immunity provision in particulars not material here. These enactments are now embodied in §§ 101-4 and 859 of Revised Statutes. They show very plainly that Congress intended thereby (a) to recognize the power of either house to institute inquiries and exact evidence touching subjects within its jurisdiction and on which it was disposed to act; (b) to recognize that such inquiries may be conducted through committees; (c) to subject defaulting and contumacious witnesses to indictment and punishment in the courts, and thereby to enable either house to exert the power of inquiry 'more effectually'; and (d) to open the way for obtaining evidence in such an inquiry, which otherwise could not be obtained, by exempting witnesses required to give evidence therein from criminal and penal prosecutions in respect of matters disclosed by their evidence.

Four decisions of this Court are cited

and more or less relied on, and we now turn to them.

The first decision was in *Anderson* v. *Dunn,* 6 Wheat. 204. The question there was whether, under the Constitution, the House of Representatives has power to attach and punish a person other than a member for contempt of its authority—in fact, an attempt to bribe one of its members. The Court regarded the power as essential to the effective exertion of other powers expressly granted, and therefore as implied. The argument advanced to the contrary was that as the Constitution expressly grants to each house power to punish or expel its own members and says nothing about punishing others, the implication or inference, if any, is that power to punish one who is not a member is neither given nor intended. The Court answered this by saying:

(page 225) 'There is not in the whole of that admirable instrument, a grant of powers which does not draw after it others, not expressed, but vital to their exercise; not substantive and independent, indeed, but auxiliary and subordinate.'

(page 233) 'This argument proves too much; for its direct application would lead to the annihilation of almost every power of Congress. To enforce its laws upon any subject without the sanction of punishment, is obviously impossible. Yet there is an express grant of power to punish in one class of cases and one only, and all the punishing power exercised by Congress, in any cases, except those which relate to piracy and offenses against the laws of nations, is derived from implication. Nor did the idea ever occur to any one, that the express grant in one class of cases repelled the assumption of the punishing power in any other. The truth is, that the exercise of the powers given over their own members, was of such a delicate nature, that a constitutional provision became necessary to assert or communicate it. Constituted, as that body is, of the delegates of confederated States, some such provision was necessary to guard against their mutual jealousy, since every proceeding against a representative would indirectly affect the honor or interests of the state which sent him.'

The next decision was in *Kilbourn* v. *Thompson,* 103 U.S. 168. The question there was whether the House of Representatives had exceeded its power in directing one of its committees to make a particular investigation. The decision was that it had. The principles announced and applied in the case are—that neither house of Congress possesses a 'general power of making inquiry into the private affairs of the citizen'; that the power actually possessed is limited to inquiries relating to matters of which the particular house 'has jurisdiction' and in respect of which it rightfully may take other action; that if the inquiry relates to 'a matter wherein relief or redress could be had only by a judicial proceeding' it is not within the range of this power, but must be left to the courts, conformably to the constitutional separation of governmental powers; and that for the purpose of determining the essential character of the inquiry recourse may be had to the resolution or order under which it is made. The court examined the resolution which was the basis of the particular inquiry, and ascertained therefrom that the inquiry related to a private real-estate pool or partnership in the District of Columbia. Jay Cooke & Co. had had an interest in the pool, but had become bankrupts, and their estate was in course of administration in a federal bankruptcy court in Pennsylvania. The United States was one of their creditors. The trustee in the bankruptcy proceeding had effected a settlement of the bankrupts' interest in the pool, and of course his action was subject to examination and approval or disapproval by the bankruptcy court. Some of the creditors, including the United States, were dissatisfied with the settlement. In these circumstances, disclosed in the preamble, the resolution directed the committee 'to inquire into the matter and history of said real-estate pool and the character of said settlement, with the amount of property involved in which Jay Cooke & Co. were interested, and the amount paid or to be paid in said settlement, with power to send for persons and papers and report to the House.' The Court pointed out that the resolution contained no suggestion of contemplated legislation; that the matter was one in respect to which no valid legislation could be had; that the bankrupt's estate and the trustee's settlement were still pending in the bankruptcy court; and that the United States and other creditors were free to press their claims in that proceeding. And on these grounds the Court held that in undertaking the investigation 'the House of Representatives not only exceeded the limit of its own authority but assumed a power which could only be properly exercised by another branch of the government, because it was in its nature clearly judicial.'

The case has been cited at times, and is cited to us now, as strongly intimating, if not holding, that neither house of Congress has power to make inquiries and exact evidence in aid of contemplated legislation. There are expressions in the opinion which, separately considered, might bear such an interpretation; but that this was not intended is shown by the immediately succeeding statement (p. 189) that 'This latter proposition is one which we do not propose to decide in the present case because we are able to decide the case without passing upon the existence or non-existence of such a power in aid of the legislative function.'

Next in order is *In re Chapman*, 166 U.S. 661. The inquiry there in question was conducted under a resolution of the Senate and related to charges, published in the press, that senators were yielding to corrupt influences in considering a tariff bill then before the Senate and were speculating in stocks the value of which would be affected by pending amendments to the bill. Chapman appeared before the committee in response to a subpoena, but refused to answer questions pertinent to the inquiry, and was indicted and convicted under the act of 1857 for his refusal. The Court sustained the constitutional validity of the act of 1857, and, after referring to the constitutional provision empowering either house to punish its members for disorderly behavior and by a vote of two-thirds to expel a member, held that the inquiry related to the integrity and fidelity of senators in the discharge of their duties, and therefore to a matter 'within the range of the constitutional powers of the Senate' and in respect of which it could compel witnesses to appear and testify. . .

The case is relied on here as fully sustaining the power of either house to conduct investigations and exact testimony from witnesses for legislative purposes. In the course of the opinion (p. 671) it is said that disclosures by witnesses may be compelled constitutionally 'to enable the respective bodies to discharge their legitimate functions, and that it was to effect this that the act of 1857 was passed'; and also 'We grant that Congress could not divest itself or either of its houses of the essential and inherent power to punish for contempt, in cases to which the power of either house properly extended; but, because Congress, by the act of 1857, sought to aid each of the houses in the discharge of its constitutional functions, it does not follow that any delegation of the power in each to punish for contempt was involved.' The terms 'legitimate functions' and 'constitutional functions' are broad and might well be regarded as including the legislative function, but as the case in hand did not call for any expression respecting that function, it hardly can be said that these terms were purposely used as including it.

The latest case is *Marshall* v. *Gordon*, 243 U.S. 521. The question there was whether the House of Representatives exceeded its power in punishing, as for a contempt of its authority, a person—not a member—who had written, published, and sent to the chairman of one of its committees an ill-tempered and irritating letter respecting the action and purposes of the committee. Power to make inquiries and obtain evidence by compulsory process was not involved. The Court recognized distinctly that the House of Representatives has implied power to punish a person not a member for contempt, as was ruled in *Anderson* v. *Dunn, supra,* but held that its action in this instance was without constitutional justification. The decision was put on the ground that the letter, while offensive and vexatious, was not calculated or likely to affect the House in any of its proceedings or in the exercise of any of its functions—in short, that the act which was punished as a contempt was not of such a character as to bring it within the rule that an express power draws after it others which are necessary and appropriate to give effect to it.

While these cases are not decisive of the question we are considering, they definitely settle two propositions which we recognize as entirely sound and having a bearing on its solution: One, that the two houses of Congress, in their separate relations, possess not only such powers as are expressly granted to them by the Constitution, but such auxiliary powers as are necessary and appropriate to make the express powers effective; and, the other, that neither house is invested with 'general' power to inquire into private affairs and compel disclosures but only with such limited power of inquiry as is shown to exist when the rule of constitutional interpretation just stated is rightly applied. . .

With this review of the legislative practice, congressional enactments, and court decisions, we proceed to a statement of our conclusions on the question.

We are of opinion that the power of inquiry—with process to enforce it—is an essential and appropriate auxiliary to the legislative function. . .

We are further of opinion that the provisions of the Constitution are not of doubtful meaning, but, as was held by this Court in the cases we have reviewed, are intended to be effectively exercised, and therefore to carry with them such auxiliary powers as are necessary and appropriate to that end. While the power to exact information in aid of the legislative function was not involved in those cases, the rule of interpretation applied there is applicable here. A legislative body cannot legislate wisely or effectively in the absence of information respecting the conditions which the legislation is intended to affect or change; and where the legislative body does not itself possess the requisite information—which not infrequently is true—recourse must be had to others who do possess it. Experience has taught that mere requests for such information often are unavailing, and also that information which is volunteered is not always accurate or complete; so some means of compulsion are essential to obtain what is needed. All this was true before and when the Constitution was framed and adopted. In that period the power of inquiry—with enforcing process—was regarded and employed as a necessary and appropriate attribute of the power to legislate—indeed, was treated as inhering in it. Thus there is ample warrant for thinking, as we do, that the constitutional provisions which commit the legislative function to the two houses are intended to include this attribute to the end that the function may be effectively exercised.

The contention is earnestly made on behalf of the witness that this power of inquiry, if sustained, may be abusively and oppressively exerted. If this be so, it affords no ground for denying the power. The same contention might be directed against the power to legislate and, of course, would be unavailing. We must assume, for present purposes, that neither house will be disposed to exert the power beyond its proper bounds, or without due regard to the rights of witnesses. But if, contrary to this assumption, controlling limitations or restrictions are disregarded, the decisions in *Kilbourn* v. *Thompson* and *Marshall* v. *Gordon* point to admissible measures of relief. And it is a necessary deduction from the decisions in *Kilbourn* v. *Thompson* and *In re Chapman* that a witness rightfully may refuse to answer where the bounds of the power are exceeded or the questions are not pertinent to the matter under inquiry.

We come now to the question whether it sufficiently appears that the purpose for which the witness' testimony was sought was to obtain information in aid of the legislative function. The court below answered the question in the negative and put its decision largely on this ground, as is shown by the following excerpts from its opinion (299 Fed. 638, 639, 640):

'It will be noted that in the second resolution the Senate has expressly avowed that the investigation is in aid of other action than legislation. Its purpose is to "obtain information necessary as a basis for such legislative and other action as the Senate may deem necessary and proper." This indicates that the Senate is contemplating the taking of action other than legislative, as the outcome of the investigation, at least the possibility of so doing. The extreme personal cast of the original resolutions; the spirit of hostility towards the then Attorney General which they breathe; that it was not avowed that legislative action was had in view until after the action of the Senate had been challenged; and that the avowal then was coupled with an avowal that other action was had in view—are calculated to create the impression that the idea of legislative action being in contemplation was an afterthought.

'That the Senate has in contemplation the possibility of taking action other than legislation as an outcome of the investigation, as thus expressly avowed, would seem of itself to invalidate the entire proceeding. But, whether so or not, the Senate's action is invalid and absolutely void, in that, in ordering and conducting the investigation, it is exercising the judicial function, and power to exercise that function, in such a case as we have here, has not been conferred upon it expressly or by fair implication. What it is proposing to do is to determine the guilt of the Attorney General of the shortcomings and wrongdoings set forth in the resolutions. It is "to hear, adjudge, and condemn." In so doing it is exercising the judicial function.

'What the Senate is engaged in doing is not investigating the Attorney General's office; it is investigating the former Attorney General. What it has done is to put him on trial before it. In so doing it is exercising the judicial function. This it has no power to do.'

We are of opinion that the court's ruling on this question was wrong, and that it sufficiently appears, when the proceedings are rightly interpreted, that the object of the investigation and of the effort to secure the witness's testimony was to obtain information for legislative purposes.

It is quite true that the resolution directing the investigation does not in terms avow that it is intended to be in aid of legislation; but it does show that the subject to be investigated was the administration of the Department of Justice— whether its functions were being properly discharged or were being neglected or misdirected, and particularly whether the Attorney General and his assistants were performing or neglecting their duties in respect of the institution and prosecution of proceedings to punish crimes and enforce appropriate remedies against the wrongdoers—specific instances of alleged neglect being recited. Plainly the subject was one on which legislation could be had and would be materially aided by the information which the investigation was calculated to elicit. This becomes manifest when it is reflected that the functions of the Department of Justice, the powers and duties of the Attorney General and the duties of his assistants are all subject to regulation by congressional legislation, and that the department is maintained and its activities are carried on under such appropriations as in the judgment of Congress are needed from year to year.

The only legitimate object the Senate could have in ordering the investigation was to aid it in legislating; and we think the subject-matter was such that the presumption should be indulged that this was the real object. An express avowal of the object would have been better; but in view of the particular subject-matter was not indispensable. . .

The second resolution—the one directing that the witness be attached—declares that his testimony is sought with the purpose of obtaining 'information necessary as a basis for such legislative and other action as the Senate may deem necessary and proper.' This avowal of contemplated legislation is in accord with what we think is the right interpretation of the earlier resolution directing the investigation. The

suggested possibility of 'other action' if deemed 'necessary or proper' is of course open to criticism in that there is no other action in the matter which would be within the power of the Senate. But we do not assent to the view that this indefinite and untenable suggestion invalidates the entire proceeding. The right view in our opinion is that it takes nothing from the lawful object avowed in the same resolution and rightly inferable from the earlier one. It is not as if an inadmissible or unlawful object were affirmatively and definitely avowed.

We conclude that the investigation was ordered for a legitimate object; that the witness wrongfully refused to appear and testify before the committee and was lawfully attached; that the Senate is entitled to have him give testimony pertinent to the inquiry, either at its bar or before the committee; and that the district court erred in discharging him from custody under the attachment. . .

Final order reversed.

Mr. Justice Stone did not participate in the consideration or decision of the case.

IX

The President's Removal Power

NOTE

In *Humphrey's Executor* v. *United States,* decided in 1935, the Court considered the President's power to remove members of an independent regulatory commission. Controversy over the legitimate power to remove administrative officials has centered upon four broad theories.[1]

1. Since the Constitution specifically mentions only impeachment as a method of removal, a few historians believe that, unless removed by impeachment or by the common law judicial process, officers are entitled to complete their terms of appointment. Others argue, however, that additional removal power does exist under the Constitution.

2. One theory is that the removal power is inherent in the office of the 'executive' and in the power of the President to 'take care that the laws be faithfully executed.'[2] This philosophy was expounded by Madison and others in the debates in the first Congress. This opinion was also held by President Jackson and was set forth in his Message of Protest in 1834. The doctrine appeared again in the debates on the Tenure of Office Act in 1867.

3. Another theory places the removal power with the appointing authority. If an officer is appointed by the President with the advice and consent of the Senate, his removal can be effected only by action of both. Hamilton stated this doctrine in the Federalist papers although he may have changed his opinion later.[3]

The Supreme Court on one occasion held that 'in the absence of all constitutional or statutory provision as to the removal of such [inferior] officers, it would seem to be a sound and necessary rule to consider the power of removal as incident to the power of appointment.'[4]

4. Still another group believes that the removal power belongs solely with Congress under the latter's authority 'to make all laws which shall be necessary and proper for carrying into execution the foregoing powers.'[5] Congress may place the removal power in any hands it deems expedient and may restrict the President's removal power in any manner. It was this doctrine which Henry Clay expounded in his controversies with Jackson in 1834 and the same philoso-

---

[1] A thorough analysis of the removal power is given in Corwin, Edward S., *The President: Office and Powers,* New York, 1940, pp. 84-96. For a discussion of the views of the early period and for explanation of the common law process, see *Ex parte Hennen,* 13 Pet. 225 (1839).

[2] For an historical analysis of this view see the opinion in *Myers* v. *United States,* 272 U.S. 52 (1926).

[3] *The Federalist, A Commentary on the Constitution of the United States,* Philadelphia, 1865, II, p. 568.

[4] Syllabus of *Ex parte Hennen,* 13 Pet. 225, 230.

[5] *Constitution of the United States,* Art. 1, sec. 8.

phy won the debates on the Tenure of Office Act insofar as the constitutionality question was a matter under consideration.

The Supreme Court avoided facing squarely the question of the President's removal power until 1926. Since that date, in two important cases, *Myers* v. *United States* [6] and the present case, the Court has discussed the power at length.

The Myers case questioned the constitutionality of a Tenure of Office Act passed by Congress in 1876 which provided that first, second, and third class postmasters be removed by the President by and with the advice and consent of the Senate. President Wilson removed Mr. Myers, a first class postmaster in Portland, Oregon, at the end of two and one half years without senatorial consent. Myers sued for his salary which amounted to $8,838.72 in the United States Court of Claims. The case was appealed to the Supreme Court. The Department of Justice for the first time appeared in Court to argue against the constitutionality of a statute.[7] A majority of the Court held that the President's authority to remove the postmaster was incidental to his executive power and was necessary in order that the laws be faithfully executed.

The Myers decision was written by Chief Justice Taft who as President of the United States had doubtless experienced difficulties in 'executing' the office with unsatisfactory subordinates. Brandeis and McReynolds each wrote a dissent, investigated the same historical documents, and reached conclusions contrary to those of the majority. Justice Holmes filed a separate dissent.

In 1941 the Supreme Court denied certiorari in *Morgan* v. *United States* [8] after a lower court had approved President Roosevelt's authority to remove Arthur E. Morgan, Chairman of the Tennessee Valley Authority.[9] The statute creating the TVA provides for the removal of board members by concurrent resolution of Congress. The President is required to remove board members if they use political tests for the selection or promotion of employees.[10] The Court held, however, that these provisions were not exclusive. The fact that certain reasons for removal are specified does not prevent the President from removing for other reasons unless it is so stated.

The statute creating the Federal Trade Commission restricts the President's power to remove except for 'inefficiency, neglect of duty, or malfeasance in office.' [11] There is no provision either in the statute or tradition for reviewing the President's reasons; he may remove an official by simply stating that he is 'inefficient.' The President's moral integrity and political pressures are the only checks. Since the Court in the following case seems to imply exact distinction between administrative agencies which are quasi-legislative and quasi-judicial in nature as opposed to those that are purely executive, the application of the principle is difficult. It would seem that the Court preferred to avoid using this

[6] 272 U.S. 52 (1926).
[7] Cushman, Robert E., *Leading Constitutional Decisions,* 7th ed., New York, 1941, p. 161.
[8] 312 U.S. 701 (1941).   [10] 48 Stat. 58, secs. 4 (f) and 6 (1933).
[9] 115 Fed. (2d) 427 (1939).   [11] 38 Stat. 717, sec. 1 (1914).

criterion in the TVA case and chose to find other grounds on which to uphold the President's power.

HUMPHREY'S EXECUTOR v. UNITED STATES
295 U.S. 602 (1935)

MR. JUSTICE SUTHERLAND delivered the opinion of the Court.

Plaintiff brought suit in the Court of Claims against the United States to recover a sum of money alleged to be due the deceased for salary as a Federal Trade Commissioner from October 8, 1933, when the President undertook to remove him from office, to the time of his death on February 14, 1934. The court below has certified to this court two questions (Act of February 13, 1925, § 3 (a), c. 229, 43 Stat. 936, 939; 28 U.S.C. § 288), in respect of the power of the President to make the removal. The material facts which give rise to the questions are as follows:

William E. Humphrey, the decedent, on December 10, 1931, was nominated by President Hoover to succeed himself as a member of the Federal Trade Commission, and was confirmed by the United States Senate. He was duly commissioned for a term of seven years expiring September 25, 1938; and, after taking the required oath of office, entered upon his duties. On July 25, 1933, President Roosevelt addressed a letter to the commissioner asking for his resignation, on the ground 'that the aims and purposes of the Administration with respect to the work of the Commission can be carried out most effectively with personnel of my own selection,' but disclaiming any reflection upon the commissioner personally or upon his services. The commissioner replied, asking time to consult his friends. After some further correspondence upon the subject, the President on August 31, 1933, wrote the commissioner expressing the hope that the resignation would be forthcoming and saying:

'You will, I know, realize that I do not feel that your mind and my mind go along together on either the policies or the administering of the Federal Trade Commission, and, frankly, I think it is best for the people of this country that I should have a full confidence.'

The commissioner declined to resign; and on October 7, 1933, the President wrote him:

'Effective as of this date you are hereby removed from the office of Commissioner of the Federal Trade Commission.'

Humphrey never acquiesced in this action, but continued thereafter to insist that he was still a member of the commission, entitled to perform its duties and receive the compensation provided by law at the rate of $10,000 per annum. Upon these and other facts set forth in the certificate, which we deem it unnecessary to recite, the following questions are certified:

'1. Do the provisions of section 1 of the Federal Trade Commission Act, stating that "any commissioner may be removed by the President for inefficiency, neglect of duty, or malfeasance in office," restrict or limit the power of the President to remove a commissioner except upon one or more of the causes named?

'If the foregoing question is answered in the affirmative, then—

'2. If the power of the President to remove a commissioner is restricted or limited as shown by the foregoing interrogatory and the answer made thereto, is such a restriction or limitation valid under the Constitution of the United States?'

The Federal Trade Commission Act, c. 311, 38 Stat. 717, 15 U.S.C. §§ 41, 42, creates a commission of five members to be appointed by the President by and with the advice and consent of the Senate, and section 1 provides:

'Not more than three of the commissioners shall be members of the same political party. The first commissioners appointed shall continue in office for terms of three, four, five, six, and seven years, respectively, from the date of the taking effect of this Act [September 26, 1914], the term of each to be designated by the President, but their successors shall be appointed for terms of seven years, except that any person chosen to fill a vacancy shall be appointed only for the unexpired term of the commissioner whom he shall succeed. The commission shall choose a chairman from its own membership. No commissioner shall engage in any other business, vocation, or employment. Any commissioner may be removed by the President for inefficiency, neglect of duty, or malfeasance in office. . .'

Section 5 of the act in part provides:

'That unfair methods of competition in commerce are hereby declared unlawful.

'The commission is empowered and directed to prevent persons, partnerships, or corporations, except banks, and common carriers subject to the Acts to regulate commerce, from using unfair methods of competition in commerce.'

In exercising this power, the commission must issue a complaint stating its charges and giving notice of hearing upon a day to be fixed. A person, partnership, or corporation proceeded against is given the right to appear at the time and place fixed and show cause why an order to cease and desist should not be issued. There is provision for intervention by others interested. If the commission finds the method of competition is one prohibited by the act, it is directed to make a report in writing stating its findings as to the facts, and to issue and cause to be served a cease and desist order. If the order is disobeyed, the commission may apply to the appropriate circuit court of appeals for its enforcement. The party subject to the order may seek and obtain a review in the circuit court of appeals in a manner provided by the act.

Section 6, among other things, gives the commission wide powers of investigation in respect of certain corporations subject to the act, and in respect of other matters, upon which it must report to Congress with recommendations. Many such investigations have been made, and some have served as the basis of congressional legislation.

Section 7 provides:

'That in any suit in equity brought by or under the direction of the Attorney General as provided in the anti-trust Acts, the court may, upon the conclusion of the testimony therein, if it shall be then of opinion that the complainant is entitled to relief, refer said suit to the commission, as a master in chancery, to ascertain and report an appropriate form of decree therein. The commission shall proceed upon such notice to the parties and under such rules of procedure as the court may prescribe, and upon the coming in of such report such exceptions may be filed and such proceedings had in relation thereto as upon the report of a master in other equity causes, but the court may adopt or reject such report, in whole or in part, and enter such decree as the nature of the case may in its judgment require.'

First. The question first to be considered is whether, by the provisions of section 1 of the Federal Trade Commission Act already quoted, the President's power is limited to removal for the specific causes enumerated therein. The negative contention of the government is based principally upon the decision of this court in *Shurtleff* v. *United States,* 189 U.S. 311. That case involved the power of the President to remove a general appraiser of merchandise appointed under the Act of June 10, 1890, 26 Stat. 131. Section 12 of the act provided for the appointment by the President, by and with the advice and consent of the Senate, of nine general appraisers of merchandise, who 'may be removed from office at any time by the President for inefficiency, neglect of duty, or malfeasance in office.' The President removed Shurtleff without assigning any cause therefor. The Court of Claims dismissed plaintiff's petition to recover salary, upholding the President's power to remove for causes other than those stated. In this court Shurtleff relied upon the maxim *expressio unius est exclusio alterius;* but this court held that, while the rule expressed in the maxim was a very proper one and founded upon justifiable reasoning in many instances, it 'should not be accorded controlling weight when to do so would involve the alteration of the universal practice of the government for over a century, and the consequent curtailment of the powers of the executive in such an unusual manner.' What the court meant by this expression appears from a reading of the opinion. That opinion—after saying that no term of office was fixed by the act and that, with the exception of judicial officers provided for by the Constitution, no civil officer had ever held office by life tenure since the foundation of the government—points out that to construe the statute as contended for by Shurtleff would give the appraiser the right to hold office during his life or until found guilty of some act specified in the statute, the result of which would be a complete revolution in respect of the general tenure of office, effected by implication with regard to that particular office only.

'We think it quite inadmissible,' the court said (pp. 316, 318), 'to attribute an intention on the part of Congress to make such an extraordinary change in the usual rule governing the tenure of office, and one which is to be applied to this particular office only, without stating such intention in plain and explicit language, instead of leaving it to be implied from doubtful inferences. . . We cannot bring ourselves to the belief that Congress ever intended this result while omitting to use language which would put that intention beyond doubt.'

These circumstances, which led the court to reject the maxim as inapplicable, are exceptional. In the face of the unbroken precedent against life tenure, except in the case of the judiciary, the conclusion that Congress intended that, from among all other civil officers, appraisers alone should be selected to hold office for life was so extreme as to forbid, in the opinion of the court, any ruling which would produce that result if it reasonably could be avoided. The situation here presented is plainly and wholly different. The statute fixes a term of office, in accordance with many precedents. The first commissioners appointed are to continue in office for terms of three, four, five, six, and seven years, respectively; and their successors are to be appointed for terms of seven years—any commissioner being subject to removal by the President for inefficiency, neglect of duty, or malfeasance in office. The words of the act are definite and unambiguous.

The government says the phrase 'continue in office' is of no legal significance and, moreover, applies only to the first Commissioners. We think it has significance. It may be that, literally, its application is restricted as suggested; but it, nevertheless, lends support to a view contrary to that of the government as to the meaning of the entire requirement in respect of tenure; for it is not easy to suppose that Congress intended to secure the first commissioners against removal except for the causes specified and deny like security to their successors. Putting this phrase aside, however, the fixing of a definite term subject to removal for cause, unless there be some countervailing provision or circumstance indicating the contrary, which here we are unable to find, is enough to establish the legislative intent that the term is not to be curtailed in the absence of such cause. But if the intention of Congress that no removal should be made during the specified term except for one or more of the enumerated causes were not clear upon the face of the statute, as we think it is, it would be made clear by a consideration of the character of the commission and the legislative history which accompanied and preceded the passage of the act.

The commission is to be non-partisan; and it must, from the very nature of its duties, act with entire impartiality. It is charged with the enforcement of no policy except the policy of the law. Its duties are neither political nor executive, but predominantly quasi-judicial and quasi-legislative. Like the Interstate Commerce Commission, its members are called upon to exercise the trained judgment of a body of experts 'appointed by law and informed by experience.' *Illinois Central R. Co.* v. *Interstate Commerce Comm'n,* 206 U.S. 441, 454; *Standard Oil Co.* v. *United States,* 283 U.S. 235, 238-239.

The legislative reports in both houses of Congress clearly reflect the view that a fixed term was necessary to the effective and fair administration of the law. In the report to the Senate (No. 597, 63d Cong., 2d Sess., pp. 10-11) the Senate Committee on Interstate Commerce, in support of the bill which afterwards became the act in question, after referring to the provision fixing the term of office at seven years, so arranged that the membership would not be subject to complete change at any one time, said:

'The work of this commission will be of a most exacting and difficult character, demanding persons who have experience in the problems to be met—that is, a proper knowledge of both the public requirements and the practical affairs of industry. It is manifestly desirable that the terms of the commissioners shall be long enough to give them an opportunity to acquire the expertness in dealing with these special questions concerning industry that comes from experience.'

The report declares that one advantage which the commission possessed over the Bureau of Corporations (an executive subdivision in the Department of Commerce which was abolished by the act) lay in the fact of its independence, and that it was essential that the commission should not be open to the suspicion of partisan direction. The report quotes (p. 22) a statement to the committee by Senator Newlands, who reported the bill, that the tribunal should be of high character and 'independent of any department of the government . . . a board or commission of dignity, permanence, and ability, independent of executive authority, except in its selection, and independent in character.'

The debates in both houses demonstrate that the prevailing view was that the commission was not to be 'subject to anybody in the government but . . . only to the people of the United States'; free from 'political domination or control' or the 'probability or possibility of such a thing'; to be 'separate and apart from any existing department of the government—not subject to the orders of the President.'

More to the same effect appears in the debates, which were long and thorough and contain nothing to the contrary. While the general rule precludes the use of these debates to explain the meaning of the words of the statute, they may be considered as reflecting light upon its general purposes and the evils which it sought to remedy. *Federal Trade Comm'n* v. *Raladam Co.,* 283 U.S. 643, 650.

Thus, the language of the act, the legislative reports, and the general purposes of the legislation as reflected by the debates, all combine to demonstrate the Congressional intent to create a body of experts who shall gain experience by length of service—a body which shall be independent of executive authority, *except in its selection,* and free to exercise its judgment without the leave or hindrance of any other official or any department of the government. To the accomplishment of these purposes, it is clear that Congress was of opinion that length and certainty of tenure would vitally contribute. And to hold that, nevertheless, the members of the commission continue in office at the mere will of the President, might be to thwart, in large measure, the very ends which Congress sought to realize by definitely fixing the term of office.

We conclude that the intent of the act is to limit the executive power of removal to the causes enumerated, the existence of none of which is claimed here; and we pass to the second question.

Second. To support its contention that the removal provision of section 1, as we have just construed it, is an unconstitutional interference with the executive power of the President, the government's chief reliance is *Myers* v. *United States,* 272 U.S. 52. . . The narrow point actually decided was only that the President had power to remove a postmaster of the first class, without the advice and consent of the Senate as required by act of Congress. In the course of the opinion of the court, expressions occur which tend to sustain the government's contention, but these are beyond the point involved and, therefore, do not come within the rule of *stare decisis*. In so far as they are out of harmony with the views here set forth, these expressions are disapproved. . .

The office of a postmaster is so essentially unlike the office now involved that the decision in the *Myers* case cannot be accepted as controlling our decision here. A postmaster is an executive officer restricted to the performance of executive functions. He is charged with no duty at all related to either the legislative or judicial power. The actual decision in the *Myers* case finds support in the theory that such an officer is merely one of the units in the executive department and, hence, inherently subject to the exclusive and illimitable power of removal by the Chief Executive, whose subordinate and aid he is. Putting aside *dicta,* which may

be followed if sufficiently persuasive but which are not controlling, the necessary reach of the decision goes far enough to include all purely executive officers. It goes no farther;—much less does it include an officer who occupies no place in the executive department and who exercises no part of the executive power vested by the Constitution in the President.

The Federal Trade Commission is an administrative body created by Congress to carry into effect legislative policies embodied in the statute in accordance with the legislative standard therein prescribed, and to perform other specified duties as a legislative or as a judicial aid. Such a body cannot in any proper sense be characterized as an arm or an eye of the executive. Its duties are performed without executive leave and, in the contemplation of the statute, must be free from executive control. In administering the provisions of the statute in respect of 'unfair methods of competition'—that is to say in filling in and administering the details embodied by that general standard—the commission acts in part quasi-legislatively and in part quasi-judicially. In making investigations and reports thereon for the information of Congress under section 6, in aid of the legislative power, it acts as a legislative agency. Under section 7, which authorizes the commission to act as a master in chancery under rules prescribed by the court, it acts as an agency of the judiciary. To the extent that it exercises any executive function—as distinguished from executive power in the constitutional sense—it does so in the discharge and effectuation of its quasi-legislative or quasi-judicial powers, or as an agency of the legislative or judicial departments of the government.

If Congress is without authority to prescribe causes for removal of members of the trade commission and limit executive power of removal accordingly, that power at once becomes practically all-inclusive in respect of civil officers with the exception of the judiciary provided for by the Constitution. The Solicitor General, at the bar, apparently recognizing this to be true, with commendable candor, agreed that his view in respect of the removability of members of the Federal Trade Commission necessitated a like view in respect of the Interstate Commerce Commission and the Court of Claims. We are thus confronted with the serious question whether not only the members of these quasi-legislative and quasi-judicial bodies, but the judges of the legislative Court of Claims, exercising judicial power (*Williams* v. *United States,* 289 U.S. 553, 565-567), continue in office only at the pleasure of the President.

We think it plain under the Constitution that illimitable power of removal is not possessed by the President in respect of officers of the character of those just named. The authority of Congress, in creating quasi-legislative or quasi-judicial agencies, to require them to act in discharge of their duties independently of executive control cannot well be doubted; and that authority includes, as an appropriate incident, power to fix the period during which they shall continue in office and to forbid their removal except for cause in the meantime. For it is quite evident that one who holds his office only during the pleasure of another, cannot be depended upon to maintain an attitude of independence against the latter's will.

The fundamental necessity of maintaining each of the three general departments of government entirely free from the control or coercive influence, direct or indirect, of either of the others, has often been stressed and is hardly open to serious question. So much is implied in the very fact of the separation of the powers of these departments by the Constitution; and in the rule which recognizes their essential co-equality. The sound application of a principle that makes one master in his own house precludes him from imposing his control in the house of another who is

master there. James Wilson, one of the framers of the Constitution and a former justice of this court, said that the independence of each department required that its proceedings 'should be free from the remotest influence, direct or indirect, of either of the other two powers.' Andrews, The Works of James Wilson (1896), vol. I, p. 367. And Mr. Justice Story in the first volume of his work on the Constitution, 4th ed., § 530, citing No. 48 of the Federalist, said that neither of the departments in reference to each other 'ought to possess, directly or indirectly, an overruling influence in the administration of their respective powers.' And see *O'Donoghue* v. *United States* [289 U.S. 516], at pp. 530-31.

The power of removal here claimed for the President falls within this principle, since its coercive influence threatens the independence of a commission, which is not only wholly disconnected from the executive department, but which, as already fully appears, was created by Congress as a means of carrying into operation legislative and judicial powers, and as an agency of the legislative and judicial departments.

In the light of the question now under consideration, we have reexamined the precedents referred to in the *Myers* case, and find nothing in them to justify a conclusion contrary to that which we have reached. The so-called 'decision of 1789' had relation to a bill proposed by Mr. Madison to establish an executive Department of Foreign Affairs. The bill provided that the principal officer was 'to be removable from office by the President of the United States.' This clause was changed to read 'whenever the principal officer shall be removed from office by the President of the United States,' certain things should follow, thereby, in connection with the debates, recognizing and confirming, as the court thought in the *Myers* case, the sole power of the President in the matter. We shall not discuss the subject further, since it is so fully covered by the opinions in the *Myers* case, except to say that the office under consideration by Congress was not only purely executive, but the officer one who was responsible to the President, and to him alone, in a very definite sense. A reading of the debates shows that the President's illimitable power of removal was not considered in respect of other than executive officers. And it is pertinent to observe that when, at a later time, the tenure of office for the Comptroller of the Treasury was under consideration, Mr. Madison quite evidently thought that, since the duties of that office were not purely of an executive nature but partook of the judiciary quality as well, a different rule in respect of executive removal might well apply. 1 Annals of Congress, cols. 611-12.

In *Marbury* v. *Madison* [1 Cranch 137], pp. 162, 165-6, it is made clear that Chief Justice Marshall was of opinion that a justice of the peace for the District of Columbia was not removable at the will of the President; and that there was a distinction between such an officer and officers appointed to aid the President in the performance of his constitutional duties. In the latter case, the distinction he saw was that 'their acts are his acts' and his will, therefore, controls; and, by way of illustration, he adverted to the act establishing the Department of Foreign Affairs, which was the subject of the 'decision of 1789.'

The result of what we now have said is this: Whether the power of the President to remove an officer shall prevail over the authority of Congress to condition the power by fixing a definite term and precluding a removal except for cause, will depend upon the character of the office; the *Myers* decision, affirming the power of the President alone to make the removal, is confined to purely executive officers; and as to officers of the kind here under consideration, we hold that no removal can be made during the prescribed term for which the officer is appointed, except for one or more of the causes named in the applicable statute.

To the extent that, between the decision in the *Myers* case, which sustains the unrestrictable power of the President to remove purely executive officers, and our present decision that such power does not extend to an office such as that here involved, there shall remain a field of doubt, we leave such cases as may fall within it for future consideration and determination as they may arise.

In accordance with the foregoing, the questions submitted are answered.

Question No. 1, Yes.
Question No. 2, Yes.

Mr. Justice McReynolds agrees that both questions should be answered in the affirmative. A separate opinion in *Myers* v. *United States*, 272 U.S. 52, 178, states his views concerning the power of the President to remove appointees.

X

The Delegation of Legislative Power

NOTE

It is a maxim of constitutional law in the United States that power conferred upon the legislature to make laws shall not be delegated to any other authority.[1] This principle stems from two sources—the constitutional doctrine of separation of powers and the principle of popular sovereignty applied to the law of agency. The doctrine of separation of powers is derived, in part, from Article 1, § 1 of the Constitution that 'All legislative powers herein granted shall be vested in a Congress. . .' The law of agency contains the maxim, *delegatus non potest delegare,* or delegated power shall not be delegated.[2] Since Congress derives its original power from a grant of the sovereign people, it is serving merely as a legal agent and in that capacity is not entitled to delegate away its function. In spite of these two maxims, Congress has delegated policy formation to administrators. The Court, while continuing to hold that the delegation of legislative power is illegal, has by a process of judicial sophistry upheld most such delegations as being not 'legislative' power but merely 'quasi-legislative' power. The line of demarcation is important but is most flexible and seems to be dictated more at times by expediency and the judge's philosophy than by any consistent logic.

With the extension of governmental authority it has become impossible for Congress to have either the time or the expert knowledge for making minute regulations. The complexity of industrial and social problems necessitates the use of technical experts in the constant detailed adjustment of governmental regulations to changing conditions. In the early history of the United States there was substantial delegation of power to the President. It later was extended to subordinate officials. There was a marked increase of the practice during the Civil War and Reconstruction periods. The development of the independent regulatory commissions commencing with the Interstate Commerce Commission in 1887 marked the extension of quasi-legislative and quasi-judicial authority in an agency which was more nearly the tool of the legislature.[3] In the twentieth century, highlighted by two major wars and the period of New Deal legislation, the practice of delegating discretion to the President, to subordinate officials, to commissions and even to private groups has greatly increased.[4] Yet, paralleling

---

[1] See Cooley, Thomas M., *A Treatise on the Constitutional Limitations,* 7th ed., Boston, 1903, p. 163.

[2] See Duff, P. W., and Whiteside, Horace E., 'Delegata Potestas Non Potest Delegari,' in *Selected Essays on Constitutional Law,* Chicago, 1938, IV, pp. 291-316.

[3] Note the distinctions made in *Humphrey's Executor* v. *United States,* 295 U.S. 602 (1935). See also Cushman, Robert E., *The Independent Regulatory Commissions,* New York, 1941.

[4] Woody, Carroll H., *The Growth of the Federal Government 1915-1932,* New York, 1934. Carr, Cecil T., *Delegated Legislation,* Cambridge, 1921. Weeks, O. Douglas, 'Legislative Power Versus Dele-

this trend, there has been a tendency in some areas for statutes to contain regulations of such detailed nature as to permit administrators no discretion in the execution of the law.

In weighing the desirability of administrative discretion some critics hold that Congress has abdicated to 'bureaucrats' its power to make laws. Administrators, to these critics, have become a 'new despotism' composed of dictatorial men who carry on 'star chamber' proceedings and act without reference to the 'rule of law.'[5] Others, who welcome the extension of administrative discretion, argue that 'government by experts' should replace 'government by windbags.' They talk about 'politicians' and 'verbose legislatures' in terms which might seem to imply the need for re-enactment of the so-called Henry viii clauses.[6] Between these two extremes the law and practice in the United States has drawn a flexible line in which the standard or overall policy is established by Congress while the administrative details are determined by technical experts.[7]

In *Hampton* v. *United States,* decided in 1928, the Court presents the legal arguments for delegation and traces a few of the earlier cases. In 1935 the Supreme Court for the first time declared invalid an act of Congress on the basis of illegal delegation of legislative authority to the President.[8] In sec. 9 (c) of the National Industrial Recovery Act of 1933 Congress authorized the President to forbid the shipment in interstate commerce of oil which had been produced or transported in violation of state law. No standards were set as to the conditions under which the President was to exercise this authority. The Court by an eight to one decision held such delegation as unlimited in scope and a violation of the doctrine of separation of powers. The law applied to only one clearly defined subject and permitted only two choices on the part of the President, namely, to prohibit or not to prohibit the shipment of 'hot oil' in interstate commerce. Justice Cardozo in a dissenting opinion maintained that there was adequate definition and limitation. He said: 'Discretion is not unconfined and vagrant. It is canalized within banks that keep it from overflowing.'[9]

In *Schechter* v. *United States*[10] the Court unanimously held other parts of the National Industrial Recovery Act unconstitutional. Provision had been made for systems of Codes of Fair Competition which were to be formulated by representatives of industry and approved by the President. Justice Cardozo in distinguishing this practice from that on 'hot oil' said: 'Here, in the case before us, is an attempted delegation not confined to any single act nor to any class or group of acts identified or described by reference to a standard. Here in effect

gated Legislative Power,' in *Selected Essays on Constitutional Law*, op. cit., pp. 228-50. Comer, J. P., *Legislative Functions of National Administrative Authorities*, New York, 1927.

[5] Hewart, Lord, *The New Despotism*, London, 1929. Beck, James M., *Our Wonderland of Bureaucracy*, New York, 1932. Sullivan, Lawrence, *The Dead Hand of Bureaucracy*, Indianapolis, 1940.

[6] A fifteenth century piece of English legislation which made it possible for administrators to modify Acts of Parliament in any manner they found necessary for putting the law into operation.

[7] See Committee on Ministers' Powers, *Report*, London, 1932, and Attorney General's Committee on Administrative Procedure, *Final Report*, Washington, 1941.

[8] *Panama Refining Company* v. *Ryan*, 293 U.S. 388 (1935).

[9] Ibid. p. 440.

[10] 295 U.S. 495 (1935).

is a roving commission to inquire into evils and upon discovery correct them.'[11]

Several times since the Schechter case the question of delegation has been before the Court and in general approved although not always by unanimous agreement of the justices.[12] In *Yakus* v. *United States*[13] the Court held that the Emergency Price Control Act of 1942 did not delegate illegal authority to the Price Administrator when it authorized him to set prices which would be 'fair and equitable.' In *Opp Cotton Mills* v. *Administrator of Wage and Hour Division*[14] the Fair Labor Standards Act of 1938 was upheld on the matter of delegation. In this act the administrator was authorized to set the wage after consultation with representatives of the industry, investigation of the industry, and public hearings.

A summary of the delegation cases indicates some general practices.[15] The Court will uphold delegation to a clearly defined governmental agency in preference to private groups but private groups may be used in an advisory capacity. The legislature may not give away unlimited discretion to determine policy, but it may delegate the power to make a technical finding upon which the policy must depend. Some writers call this *contingent* legislation.[16] The Court points out that: 'The legislature cannot delegate its power to make a law; but it can make a law to delegate a power to determine some fact or state of things upon which the law makes, or intends to make, its own action depend.'[17]

The Hampton case goes a step further in permitting *supplementary* legislation but still requires that the statute define the subject and provide a primary standard or criterion to guide the administrators in the formulation of the rule. The Court will always question whether Congress has the authority under the Constitution because it is obvious that no agency can give away authority which it does not possess.

J. W. HAMPTON, JR., & COMPANY v. UNITED STATES
276 U.S. 394 (1928)

MR. CHIEF JUSTICE TAFT delivered the opinion of the Court.

J. W. Hampton, Jr., & Company made an importation into New York of barium dioxide, which the collector of customs assessed at the dutiable rate of six cents per pound. This was two cents per pound more than that fixed by statute, par. 12, ch. 356, 42 Stat. 858, 860. The rate was raised by the collector by virtue of the proclamation of the President, 45 Treas. Dec. 669, T.D. 40216, issued under, and by authority of, § 315 of Title III of the Tariff Act of September 21, 1922, ch. 356, 42 Stat. 858, 941, which is the so-called flexible tariff provision. Protest was made

---

[11] Ibid. p. 551.

[12] See *Mulford* v. *Smith*, 307 U.S. 38 (1939), Note, *post*, p. 204, for a discussion of delegation in the field of agriculture.

[13] 321 U.S. 414 (1944).   [14] 312 U.S. 126 (1941).

[15] See Hart, James, *An Introduction to Administrative Law*, New York, 1940, p. 169.

[16] Ibid. p. 154.

[17] *Field* v. *Clark*, 143 U.S. 649, 694 (1892), citing *Locke's Appeal*, 72 Pa. 491, 498 (1873).

and an appeal was taken under § 514, Part 3, Title IV, ch. 356, 42 Stat. 969-70. The case came on for hearing before the United States Customs Court, 49 Treas. Dec. 593. A majority held the Act constitutional. Thereafter the case was appealed to the United States Court of Customs Appeals. On the 16th day of October, 1926, the Attorney General certified that in his opinion the case was of such importance as to render expedient its review by this Court. Thereafter the judgment of the United States Customs Court was affirmed. 14 Ct. Cust. App. 350. On a petition to this Court for certiorari, filed May 10, 1927, the writ was granted, 274 U.S. 735. The pertinent parts of § 315 of Title III of the Tariff Act, ch. 356, 42 Stat. 858, 941 U.S.C., Tit. 19, §§ 154, 156, are as follows:

'Section 315(a). That in order to regulate the foreign commerce of the United States and to put into force and effect the policy of the Congress by this Act intended, whenever the President, upon investigation of the differences in costs of production of articles wholly or in part the growth or product of the United States and of like or similar articles wholly or in part the growth or product of competing foreign countries, shall find it thereby shown that the duties fixed in this Act do not equalize the said differences in costs of production in the United States and the principal competing country he shall, by such investigation, ascertain said differences and determine and proclaim the changes in classifications or increases or decreases in any rate of duty provided in this Act shown by said ascertained differences in such costs of production necessary to equalize the same. Thirty days after the date of such proclamation or proclamations, such changes in classification shall take effect, and such increased or decreased duties shall be levied, collected, and paid on such articles when imported from any foreign country into the United States or into any of its possessions (except the Philippine Islands, the Virgin Islands, and the islands of Guam and Tutuila): *Provided,* That the total increase or decrease of such rates of duty shall not exceed 50 per centum of the rates specified in Title 1 of this Act, or in any amendatory Act. . .

'(c). That in ascertaining the differences in costs of production, under the provisions of subdivisions (a) and (b) of this section, the President, in so far as he finds it practicable, shall take into consideration (1) the differences in conditions in production, including wages, costs of material, and other items in costs of production of such or similar articles in the United States and in competing foreign countries; (2) the differences in the wholesale selling prices of domestic and foreign articles in the principal markets of the United States; (3) advantages granted to a foreign producer by a foreign government, or by a person, partnership, corporation, or association in foreign country; and (4) any other advantages or disadvantages in competition.

'Investigations to assist the President in ascertaining differences in costs of production under this section shall be made by the United States Tariff Commission, and no proclamation shall be issued under this section until such investigation shall have been made. The commission shall give reasonable public notice of its hearings and shall give reasonable opportunity to parties interested to be present, to produce evidence, and to be heard. The commission is authorized to adopt such reasonable procedure, rules, and regulations as it may deem necessary.

'The President, proceeding as hereinbefore provided for in proclaiming rates of duty, shall, when he determines that it is shown that the differences in costs of production have changed or no longer exist which led to such proclamation, accordingly as so shown, modify or terminate the same. Nothing in this section shall be construed to authorize a transfer of an article from the dutiable list to the free list or from the free list to the dutiable list, nor a change in form of duty. Whenever it is provided in any paragraph of Title I of this Act, that the duty or duties shall not exceed a specified ad valorem rate upon the articles provided for in such paragraph, no rate determined under the provision of this section upon such articles shall exceed the maximum ad valorem rate so specified.'

The President issued his proclamation May 19, 1924. After reciting part of the foregoing from § 315, the proclamation continued as follows:

'Whereas, under and by virtue of said section of said act, the United States Tariff Commission has made an investigation to assist the President in ascertaining the differences in costs of production of and of all other facts and conditions enumerated in said section with respect to . . . barium dioxide. . .

'Whereas in the course of said investigation a hearing was held, of which reasonable public notice was given and at which parties interested were given a reasonable opportunity to be present, to produce evidence, and to be heard;

'And whereas the President upon said investigation . . . has thereby found that the principal competing country is Germany, and that the duty fixed in said title and act does not equalize the differences in costs of production in the United States and in . . . Germany, and has ascertained and determined the increased rate of duty necessary to equalize the same.

'Now, therefore, I, Calvin Coolidge, President of the United States of America, do hereby determine and proclaim that the increase in the rate of duty provided in the said act shown by said ascertained differences in said costs of production necessary to equalize the same is as follows:

' "An increase in said duty on barium dioxide (within the limit of total increase provided for in said act) from 4 cents per pound to 6 cents per pound.

' "In witness whereof, I have hereunto set my hand and caused the seal of the United States to be affixed.

' "Done at the City of Washington this nineteenth day of May in the year of our Lord one thousand nine hundred and twenty-four, and of the Independence of the United States of America the one hundred and forty-eighth.

' "Calvin Coolidge.

' "By the President: Charles E. Hughes, Secretary of State." '

The issue here is as to the constitutionality of § 315, upon which depends the authority for the proclamation of the President and for two of the six cents per pound duty collected from the petitioner. The contention of the taxpayers is twofold—first, they argue that the section is invalid in that it is a delegation to the President of the legislative power, which by Article 1, § 1 of the Constitution, is vested in Congress, the power being that declared in § 8 of Article 1, that the Congress shall have power to lay and collect taxes, duties, imposts and excises. The second objection is that, as § 315 was enacted with the avowed intent and for the purpose of protecting the industries of the United States, it is invalid because the Constitution gives power to lay such taxes only for revenue.

First. It seems clear what Congress intended by § 315. Its plan was to secure by law the imposition of customs duties on articles of imported merchandise which should equal the difference between the cost of producing in a foreign country the articles in question and laying them down for sale in the United States, and the cost of producing and selling like or similar articles in the United States, so that the duties not only secure revenue but at the same time enable producers to compete on terms of equality with foreign producers in the markets of the United States. It may be that it is difficult to fix with exactness this difference, but the difference which is sought in the statute is perfectly clear and perfectly intelligible. Because of the difficulty in practically determining what that difference is, Congress seems to have doubted that the information in its possession was such as to enable it to make the adjustment accurately, and also to have apprehended that with changing conditions the difference might vary in such a way that some readjustments would be necessary to give effect to the principle on which the statute proceeds. To avoid such difficulties, Congress adopted in § 315 the method of describing with clearness what its policy and plan was and then authorizing a member of the executive branch to carry out this policy and plan, and to find the changing difference from time to time, and to make the adjustments necessary to conform the duties to the standard underlying that policy and plan. As it was a matter of great importance, it concluded to give by statute to the President, the chief of the executive branch, the function of determining the difference as it might vary. He was provided with a body of investigators who were to assist him in obtaining needed data and ascertaining the facts justifying readjustments. There was no specific provision by which action by the President might be invoked under this Act, but it was presumed that the President would through this body of advisers keep himself advised of the necessity for investigation or change, and then would proceed to pursue his duties under the Act and reach such conclusion as he might find justified by the investigation, and proclaim the same if necessary.

The Tariff Commission does not itself fix duties, but before the President reaches a conclusion on the subject of investigation, the Tariff Commission must make an investigation and in doing so must give notice to all parties interested and an opportunity to adduce evidence and to be heard.

The well-known maxim *Delegata potestas non potest delegari,* applicable to the law of agency in the general and common law, is well understood and has had wider application in the construction of our Federal and State Constitutions than it has in private law. The Federal Constitution and State Constitutions of this country divide the governmental power into three branches. The first is the legislative, the second is the executive, and the third is the judicial, and the rule is that in the actual administration of the government Congress or the Legislature should exercise the legislative power, the President or the State executive, the Governor, the executive power, and the Courts or the judiciary the judicial power, and in carrying out that constitutional division into three branches it is a breach of the National fundamental law if Congress gives up its legislative power and transfers it to the President, or to the Judicial branch, or if by law it attempts to invest itself or its members with either executive power or judicial power. This is not to say that the three branches are not co-ordinate parts of one government and that each in the field of its duties may not invoke the action of the two other branches in so far as the action invoked shall not be an assumption of the constitutional field of action of another branch. In determining what it may do in seeking assistance from another branch, the extent and character of that assistance must be fixed according to common sense and the inherent necessities of the governmental co-ordination.

The field of Congress involves all and many varieties of legislative action, and Congress has found it frequently necessary to use officers of the Executive Branch, within defined limits, to secure the exact effect intended by its acts of legislation, by vesting discretion in such officers to make public regulations interpreting a statute and directing the details of its execution, even to the extent of providing for penalizing a breach of such regulations. . .

Congress may feel itself unable conveniently to determine exactly when its exercise of the legislative power should become effective, because dependent on future conditions, and it may leave the determination of such time to the decision of an Executive, or, as often happens in matters of state legislation, it may be left to a popular vote of the residents of a district to be effected by the legislation. While in a sense one may say that such residents are exercising legislative power, it is not an exact statement, because the power has already been exercised legislatively by the body vested with that power under the Constitution, the condition of its legislation going into effect being made dependent by the legislature on the expression of the voters of a certain district. As Judge Ranney of the Ohio Supreme Court in *Cincinnati, Wilmington and Zanesville Railroad Co.* v. *Commissioners,* 1 Ohio St. 77, 88, said in such a case: 'The true distinction, therefore, is, between the delegation of power to make the law, which necessarily involves a discretion as to what it shall be, and conferring an authority or discretion as to its execution, to be exercised under and in pursuance of the law. The first cannot be done; to the latter no valid objection can be made.' See also *Moers* v. *Reading,* 21 Penn. St. 188, 202; *Locke's Appeal,* 72 Penn. St. 491, 498.

Again, one of the great functions conferred on Congress by the Federal Constitution is the regulation of interstate commerce and rates to be exacted by interstate carriers for the passenger and merchandise traffic. The rates to be fixed are myriad. If Congress were to be required to fix every rate, it would be impossible to exercise the power at all. Therefore, common sense requires that in the fixing of such rates, Congress may provide a Commission, as it does, called the Interstate Commerce Commission, to fix those rates, after hearing evidence and argument concerning them from interested parties, all in accord with a general rule that Congress first lays down, that rates shall be just and reasonable considering the service given, and not discriminatory. As said by this Court in *Interstate Commerce Commission* v. *Goodrich Transit Co.,* 224 U.S. 194, 214, 'The Congress may not delegate its purely legislative power to a commission, but, having laid down the general rules of action under which a commission shall proceed, it may require of that commission the application of such rules to particular situations and the investigation of facts, with a view to making orders in a particular matter within the rules laid down by the Congress.'

The principle upon which such a power is upheld in state legislation as to fixing railway rates is admirably stated by Judge Mitchell, in the case of *State* v. *Chicago, Milwaukee & St. Paul Railway Company,* 38 Minn. 281, 298 to 302. The learned Judge says on page 301:

'If such a power is to be exercised at all, it can only be satisfactorily done by a board or commission, constantly in session, whose time is exclusively given to the subject, and who, after investigation of the facts, can fix rates with reference to the peculiar circumstances of each road, and each particular kind of business, and who can change or modify these rates to suit the ever-varying conditions of traffic. . . Our legislature has gone a step further than most others, and vested our commission with full power to determine what rates are equal and reasonable in each particular case. Whether this was wise or not is not for us to say; but in doing so we can not see that they have transcended their constitutional authority. They have not delegated to the commission any authority or discretion as to what the law shall be,—which would not be allowable, —but have merely conferred upon it an authority and discretion, to be exercised in the execution of the law, and under and in pursuance of it, which is entirely permissible. The legislature itself has passed upon the expediency of the law, and what it shall be. The commission is intrusted with no authority or discretion upon these questions.' See also the language of Justices Miller and Bradley in the same case in this Court. 134 U.S. 418, 459, 461, 464.

It is conceded by counsel that Congress may use executive officers in the application and enforcement of a policy declared in law by Congress, and authorize such officers in the application of the Congressional declaration to enforce it by regulation equivalent to law. But it is said that this never has been permitted to be done where Congress has exercised the power to levy taxes and fix customs duties. The authorities make no such distinction. The same principle that permits Congress to exercise its rate making power in interstate commerce, by declaring the rule which shall prevail in the legislative fixing of rates, and enables it to remit to a rate-making body created in accordance with its provisions the fixing of such rates, justifies a similar provision for the fixing of customs duties on imported merchandise. If Congress shall lay down by legislative act an intelligible principle to which the person or body authorized to fix such rates is directed to conform, such legislative action is not a forbidden delegation of legislative power. If it is thought wise to vary the customs duties according to changing conditions of production at home and abroad, it may authorize the Chief Executive to carry out this purpose, with the advisory assistance of a Tariff Commission appointed under Congressional authority. This conclusion is amply sustained by a case in which there was no advisory commission furnished the President—a case to which this Court gave the fullest consideration nearly forty years ago. In *Field* v. *Clark*, 143 U.S. 649, 680, the third section of the Act of October 1, 1890, contained this provision:

'That with a view to secure reciprocal trade with countries producing the following articles, and for this purpose, on and after the first day of January, eighteen hundred and ninety-two, whenever, and so often as the President shall be satisfied that the government of any country producing and exporting sugars, molasses, coffee, tea and hides, raw and uncured, or any of such articles, imposes duties or other exactions upon the agricultural or other products of the United States, which in view of the free introduction of such sugar, molasses, coffee, tea and hides into the United States he may deem to be reciprocally unequal and unreasonable, he shall have the power and it shall be his duty to suspend, by proclamation to that effect, the provisions of this act relating to the free introduction of such sugar, molasses, coffee, tea and hides, the production of such country, for such time as he shall deem just, and in such case and during such suspension duties shall be levied, collected, and paid upon sugar, molasses, coffee, tea and hides, the product of or exported from such designated country as follows, namely:'

Then followed certain rates of duty to be imposed. It was contended that this section delegated to the President both legislative and treaty-making powers and was unconstitutional. After an examination of all the authorities, the Court said that while Congress could not delegate legislative power to the President, this Act did not in any real sense invest the President with the power of legislation, because nothing involving the expediency or just operation of such legislation was left to the determination of the President; that the legislative power was exercised when Congress declared that the suspension should take effect upon a named contingency. What the President was required to do was merely in execution of the act of Congress. It was not the making of law. He was the mere agent of the law-making department to ascertain and declare the event upon which its expressed will was to take effect.

Second. The second objection to § 315 is that the declared plan of Congress, either expressly or by clear implication, formulates its rule to guide the President and his advisory Tariff Commission as one directed to a tariff system of protection that will avoid damaging competition to the country's industries by the importation of goods from other countries at too low a rate to equalize foreign and domestic competition in the markets of the United States. It is contended that the only power of Congress in the levying of customs duties is to create revenue, and that it is unconstitutional to frame the customs duties with any other view than that of revenue raising. It undoubtedly is true that during the political life of this country there has been much discussion between parties as to the wisdom of the policy of protection, and we may go further and say as to its constitutionality, but no historian, whatever his view of the wisdom of the policy of protection, would contend that Congress, since the first revenue Act, in 1789, has not assumed that it was within its power in making provision for the collection of revenue, to put taxes upon importations and to vary the subjects of such taxes or rates in an effort to encourage the growth of the industries of the Nation by protecting home production against foreign competition. It is enough to point out that the second act adopted by the Congress of the United States, July 4, 1789, ch. 2, 1 Stat. 24, contained the following recital.

'SEC. 1. Whereas it is necessary for the support of government, for the discharge of the debts of the United States, and the encouragement and protection of manufactures, that duties be laid on goods, wares and merchandises imported: Be it enacted, et cetera.'

In this first Congress sat many members of the Constitutional Convention of 1787. This Court has repeatedly laid down the principle that a contemporaneous legislative exposition of the Constitution when the founders of our Government and framers of our Constitution were actively participating in public affairs, long acquiesced in, fixes the construction to be given its provisions. *Myers* v. *United States,* 272 U.S. 52, 175, and cases cited. The enactment and enforcement of a number of customs revenue laws drawn with a motive of maintaining a system of protection, since the revenue law of 1789, are matters of history.

More than a hundred years later, the titles of the Tariff Acts of 1897 and 1909 declared the purpose of those acts, among other things, to be that of encouraging the industries of the United States. The title of the Tariff Act of 1922, of which § 315 is a part, is 'An Act to provide revenue, to regulate commerce with foreign countries, to encourage the industries of the United States and for other purposes.' Whatever we may think of the wisdom of a protection policy, we cannot hold it unconstitutional.

So long as the motive of Congress and the effect of its legislative action are to secure revenue for the benefit of the general government, the existence of other motives in the selection of the subjects of taxes cannot invalidate Congressional action. As we said in the *Child Labor Tax Case,* 259 U.S. 20, 38: 'Taxes are occasionally imposed in the discretion of the legislature on proper subjects with the primary motive of obtaining revenue from them, and with the incidental motive of discouraging them by making their continuance onerous. They do not lose their character as taxes because of the incidental motive.' And so here, the fact that Congress declares that one of its motives in fixing the rates of duty is so to fix them that they shall encourage the industries of this country in the competition with producers in other countries in the sale of goods in this country, can not invalidate a revenue act so framed. Section 315 and its provisions are within the power of Congress. The judgment of the Court of Customs Appeals is affirmed.

Affirmed.

XI

The Taxing Power

NOTE

The Constitution provides that 'The Congress shall have power to lay and collect taxes, duties, imposts and excises, to pay the debts and provide for the common defense and general welfare of the United States.' It is therefore apparent that Congress is authorized to 'provide' in some way or other 'for the general welfare.'

From the very beginning of our constitutional system there has been some controversy over the interpretation of this clause. Opinions on the subject reflect the many approaches to the problem of the proper functions of government in general and, more particularly, the proper functions of the Federal government. It has been a basic source from which a large amount of socio-economic legislation has derived. Accordingly, some of the history of this doctrinal struggle will serve to place *United States* v. *Butler,* decided in 1936, in its proper setting.

Three more or less distinct views of the meaning of the general welfare clause have at one time or another been advanced and supported by reputable authorities. The first of these is an extreme view. It declares that the general welfare clause is an entirely separate clause granting Congress a separate, substantive power to act as it may see fit for the common defense and general welfare. It would endow Congress with power to regulate many matters not specifically referred to in the Constitution. Logic does not support this interpretation. To accept it would be to ignore normal grammatical construction, since the words in question are part of a sentence dealing with the collection of taxes. Furthermore, it is unlikely that the framers of the Constitution would have enumerated the powers of the central government in such detail if a general, undefined power to legislate for the general welfare had been intended in addition to the powers enumerated.

The second view has come to be identified with James Madison; it approaches the opposite extreme. In a letter to Andrew Stevenson, 27 November 1830,[1] he described the general welfare clause as simply a qualification upon the taxing power and denied that it granted any separate, substantive power. Moreover, it should be construed as ancillary to the other specifically granted powers, i.e., Federal taxation may be imposed only for the collection of money to be expended for the execution of the other explicit powers of Congress.

In the *Federalist* Madison elaborated upon this position and elsewhere insisted that 'Money cannot be applied to the general welfare, otherwise than by application of it to some particular measure conducive to general welfare.

[1] *The Records of the Federal Convention of 1787*, ed. by Max Farrand, New Haven, 1937, III, p. 483.

Whenever, therefore, money has been raised by the General Authority, and is to be applied to a particular measure, a question arises whether the particular measure be within the enumerated authorities vested in Congress. If it be, the money requisite for it may be applied to it; if it be not, no such application can be made.'[2] Such an interpretation makes the scope of the Federal government's power to tax and spend coextensive with the scope of its other powers and renders the general welfare clause somewhat superfluous.

Intermediate between these two extreme views of the general welfare clause is the interpretation placed upon it by Alexander Hamilton and later adopted by Joseph Story. Favoring a strong central government, the Federalists considered Congress as having authority to tax and spend for anything that fell in the category of the general welfare and insisted that the only limitation upon this authority was that it must serve a public purpose.

In his famous *Report on Manufactures,* 1791, Hamilton wrote: 'It is therefore of necessity left to the discretion of the national legislature to pronounce upon the objects which concern the national welfare, and for which, under that description, an appropriation of money is requisite and proper. . . The only qualification of the generality of the phrase in question which seems to be admissible is this: That the object to which an appropriation of money is to be made must be general, and not local; its operation extending in fact or by possibility, throughout the Union, and not being confined to a particular spot.'[3]

Thus, while it confers no separate, substantive power of regulation upon Congress, the general welfare clause does amplify the taxing power and extends the purposes of spending beyond the narrow fields of the enumerated powers. As thus expressed, this Hamiltonian view, elaborated by Judge Story, was for the first time explicitly adopted by the United States Supreme Court in *United States* v. *Butler.* However, despite its acceptance of the Hamilton-Story doctrine, the Court found the Agricultural Adjustment Act of 1933 to be unconstitutional.[4] The processing taxes imposed by the Act were held not to be taxes in the proper sense; instead, they were levies placed upon one class for the benefit of another. No decision was announced as to whether appropriations for the aid of agriculture would withstand the requirement that expenditures be for the general and not for the particular welfare. Furthermore, the Act was unconstitutional because it sought to regulate a matter (agricultural production) which fell within the reserved powers of the states.

UNITED STATES v. BUTLER
297 U.S. 1 (1936)

Mr. Justice Roberts delivered the opinion of the Court.

In this case we must determine whether certain provisions of the Agricultural Ad-

---

[2] *Works,* ed. by Gaillard Hunt, New York, 1906, vi, p. 357. See also the *Federalist,* No. 41.

[3] *Works,* ed. by Henry Cabot Lodge, New York, 1904, iv, p. 70.

[4] A new Agricultural Adjustment Act was passed in 1938 with objectives similar to those in the Act of 1933. Based upon the commerce power rather than the taxing power, it was upheld in *Mulford* v. *Smith, post,* p. 206.

justment Act, 1933, conflict with the Federal Constitution.

Title 1 of the statute is captioned 'Agricultural Adjustment.' Section 1 recites that an economic emergency has arisen, owing to disparity between the prices of agricultural and other commodities, with consequent destruction of farmers' purchasing power and breakdown in orderly exchange, which, in turn, have affected transactions in agricultural commodities with a national public interest and burdened and obstructed the normal currents of commerce, calling for the enactment of legislation.

Section 2 declares it to be the policy of Congress:

'To establish and maintain such balance between the production and consumption of agricultural commodities, and such marketing conditions therefor, as will re-establish prices to farmers at a level that will give agricultural commodities a purchasing power with respect to articles that farmers buy, equivalent to the purchasing power of agricultural commodities in the base period.'

The base period, in the case of cotton, and all other commodities except tobacco, is designated as that between August, 1909, and July, 1914.

The further policies announced are an approach to the desired equality by gradual correction of present inequalities 'at as rapid a rate as is deemed feasible in view of the current consumptive demand in domestic and foreign markets,' and the protection of consumers' interest by readjusting farm production at such level as will not increase the percentage of the consumers' retail expenditures for agricultural commodities or products derived therefrom, which is returned to the farmer, above the percentage returned to him in the base period.

Section 8 provides, amongst other things, that 'In order to effectuate the declared policy,' the Secretary of Agriculture shall have power

'(1). To provide for reduction in the acreage or reduction in the production for market, or both, of any basic agricultural commodity, through agreements with producers or by other voluntary methods, and to provide for rental or benefit payments in connection therewith or upon that part of the production of any basic agricultural commodity required for domestic consumption, in such amounts as the Secretary deems fair and reasonable, to be paid out of any moneys available for such payments. . .'

'(2). To enter into marketing agreements with processors, associations of producers, and others engaged in the handling, in the current of interstate or foreign commerce of any agricultural commodity or product thereof, after due notice and opportunity for hearing to interested parties. . .'

'(3). To issue licenses permitting processors, associations of producers, and others to engage in the handling, in the current of interstate or foreign commerce, of any agricultural commodity or product thereof, or any competing commodity or product thereof.'

It will be observed that the Secretary is not required, but is permitted, if, in his uncontrolled judgment, the policy of the act will so be promoted, to make agreements with individual farmers for a reduction of acreage or production upon such terms as he may think fair and reasonable.

Section 9 (a) enacts:

'To obtain revenue for extraordinary expenses incurred by reason of the national economic emergency, there shall be levied processing taxes as hereinafter provided. When the Secretary of Agriculture determines that rental or benefit payments are to be made with respect to any basic agricultural commodity, he shall proclaim such determination, and a processing tax shall be in effect with respect to such commodity from the beginning of the marketing year therefor next following the date of such proclamation. The processing tax shall be levied, assessed, and collected upon the first domestic processing of the commodity, whether of domestic production or imported, and shall be paid by the processor. . .'

Section 9 (b) fixes the tax 'at such rate as equals the difference between the current average farm price for the commodity and the fair exchange value,' with power in the Secretary, after investigation, notice, and hearing, to readjust the tax so as to prevent the accumulation of surplus stocks and depression of farm prices.

Section 9 (c) directs that the fair exchange value of a commodity shall be such a price as will give that commodity the same purchasing power with respect to articles farmers buy as it had during the base period and that the fair exchange value and the current average farm price of a commodity shall be ascertained by the Secretary from available statistics in his department.

Section 12 (a) appropriates $100,000,000 'to be available to the Secretary of Agriculture for administrative expenses under this title and for rental and benefit payments . . .'; and § 12 (b) appropriates the proceeds derived from all taxes imposed under the act 'to be available to the Secretary of Agriculture for expansion of markets and removal of surplus agricultural products . . . administrative expenses, rental and benefit payments, and refunds on taxes.'

Section 15 (d) permits the Secretary, upon certain conditions, to impose compensating taxes on commodities in competition with those subject to the processing tax.

By § 16 a floor tax is imposed upon the sale or other disposition of any article processed wholly or in chief value from any commodity with respect to which a processing tax is to be levied in amount equivalent to that of the processing tax which would be payable with respect to the commodity from which the article is processed if the processing had occurred on the date when the processing tax becomes effective.

On July 14, 1933, the Secretary of Agriculture, with the approval of the President, proclaimed that he had determined rental and benefit payments should be made with respect to cotton; that the marketing year for that commodity was to begin August 1, 1933; and calculated and fixed the rates of processing and floor taxes on cotton in accordance with the terms of the act.

The United States presented a claim to the respondents as receivers of the Hoosac Mills Corporation for processing and floor taxes on cotton levied under §§ 9 and 16 of the act. The receivers recommended that the claim be disallowed. The District Court found the taxes valid and ordered them paid. Upon appeal the Circuit Court of Appeals reversed the order. . .

First. At the outset the United States contends that the respondents have no standing to question the validity of the tax. The position is that the act is merely a revenue measure levying an excise upon the activity of processing cotton,—a proper subject for the imposition of such a tax,—the proceeds of which go into the federal treasury and thus become available for appropriation for any purpose. It is said that what the respondents are endeavoring to do is to challenge the intended use of the money pursuant to Congressional appropriation when, by confession, that money will have become the property of the Government and the taxpayer will no longer have any interest in it. *Massachusetts* v. *Mellon,* 262 U.S. 447, is claimed to foreclose litigation by the respondents or other taxpayers, as such, looking to restraint of the expenditure of government funds. That case might be an authority in the petitioners' favor if we were here concerned merely with a suit by a taxpayer to restrain the expenditure of the public moneys. It was there held that a taxpayer of the United States may not question expenditures from its treasury on the ground that the alleged unlawful diversion will deplete the public funds and thus increase the burden of future taxation. Obviously the asserted interest of a taxpayer in the federal government's funds and the supposed increase of the future burden of taxation is minute and indeterminable. But here the respondents who are called upon to pay moneys as taxes, resist the exaction as a step in an unauthorized plan. This circumstance clearly distinguishes the case. The Government in substance and effect asks us to separate the Agricultural Adjustment Act into two statutes, the one levying an excise on processors of certain commodities, the other appropriating the public moneys independently of the first. Passing the novel suggestion that two statutes enacted as parts of a single scheme should be tested as if they were distinct and unrelated, we think the legislation now before us is not susceptible of such separation and treatment.

The tax can only be sustained by ignoring the avowed purpose and operation of the act, and holding it a measure merely laying an excise upon processors to raise revenue for the support of government. Beyond cavil the sole object of the legislation is to restore the purchasing power of agricultural products to a parity with that prevailing in an earlier day; to take money from the processor and bestow it upon farmers who will reduce their acreage for the accomplishment of the proposed end, and, meanwhile to aid these farmers during the period required to bring the prices of their crops to the desired level.

The tax plays an indispensable part in the plan of regulation. As stated by the Agricultural Adjustment Administrator, it is 'the heart of the law'; a means of 'accomplishing one or both of two things intended to help farmers attain parity prices and purchasing power.' A tax auto-

matically goes into effect for a commodity when the Secretary of Agriculture determines that rental or benefit payments are to be made for reduction of production of that commodity. The tax is to cease when rental or benefit payments cease. The rate is fixed with the purpose of bringing about crop-reduction and price-raising. It is to equal the difference between the 'current average farm price' and 'fair exchange value.' It may be altered to such amount as will prevent accumulation of surplus stocks. If the Secretary finds the policy of the act will not be promoted by the levy of the tax for a given commodity, he may exempt it. (§ 11.) The whole revenue from the levy is appropriated in aid of crop control; none of it is made available for general governmental use. The entire agricultural adjustment program embodied in Title I of the act is to become inoperative when, in the judgment of the President, the national economic emergency ends; and as to any commodity he may terminate the provisions of the law, if he finds them no longer requisite to carrying out the declared policy with respect to such commodity. (§ 13.)

The statute not only avows an aim foreign to the procurement of revenue for the support of government, but by its operation shows the exaction laid upon processors to be the necessary means for the intended control of agricultural production. . .

It is inaccurate and misleading to speak of the exaction from processors prescribed by the challenged act as a tax, or to say that as a tax it is subject to no infirmity. A tax, in the general understanding of the term, and as used in the Constitution, signifies an exaction for the support of the Government. The word has never been thought to connote the expropriation of money from one group for the benefit of another. We may concede that the latter sort of imposition is constitutional when imposed to effectuate regulation of a matter in which both groups are interested and in respect of which there is a power of legislative regulation. But manifestly no justification for it can be found unless as an integral part of such regulation. The exaction cannot be wrested out of its setting, denominated an excise for raising revenue and legalized by ignoring its purpose as a mere instrumentality for bringing about a desired end. To do this would be to shut our eyes to what all others than we can see and understand. *Child Labor Tax Case,* 259 U.S. 20, 37.

We conclude that the act is one regulating agricultural production; that the tax is a mere incident of such regulation and that the respondents have standing to challenge the legality of the exaction. . .

Second. The Government asserts that even if the respondents may question the propriety of the appropriation embodied in the statute their attack must fail because Article 1, § 8 of the Constitution authorizes the contemplated expenditure of the funds raised by the tax. This contention presents the great and the controlling question in the case. We approach its decision with a sense of our grave responsibility to render judgment in accordance with the principles established for the governance of all three branches of the Government.

There should be no misunderstanding as to the function of this court in such a case. It is sometimes said that the court assumes a power to overrule or control the action of the people's representatives. This is a misconception. The Constitution is the supreme law of the land ordained and established by the people. All legislation must conform to the principles it lays down. When an act of Congress is appropriately challenged in the courts as not conforming to the constitutional mandate the judicial branch of the Government has only one duty,—to lay the article of the Constitution which is invoked beside the statute which is challenged and to decide whether the latter squares with the former. All the court does, or can do, is to an-

nounce its considered judgment upon the question. The only power it has, if such it may be called, is the power of judgment. This court neither approves nor condemns any legislative policy. Its delicate and difficult office is to ascertain and declare whether the legislation is in accordance with, or in contravention of, the provisions of the Constitution; and, having done that, its duty ends.

The question is not what power the Federal Government ought to have but what powers in fact have been given by the people. It hardly seems necessary to reiterate that ours is a dual form of government; that in every state there are two governments,—the state and the United States. Each State has all governmental powers save such as the people, by their Constitution, have conferred upon the United States, denied to the States, or reserved to themselves. The federal union is a government of delegated powers. It has only such as are expressly conferred upon it and such as are reasonably to be implied from those granted. In this respect we differ radically from nations where all legislative power, without restriction or limitation, is vested in a parliament or other legislative body subject to no restrictions except the discretion of its members.

Article 1, § 8, of the Constitution vests sundry powers in the Congress. But two of its clauses have any bearing upon the validity of the statute under review.

The third clause endows the Congress with power 'to regulate Commerce . . . among the several States.' Despite a reference in its first section to a burden upon, and an obstruction of the normal currents of commerce, the act under review does not purport to regulate transactions in interstate or foreign commerce. Its stated purpose is the control of agricultural production, a purely local activity, in an effort to raise the prices paid the farmer. Indeed, the Government does not attempt to uphold the validity of the act on the basis of the commerce clause, which, for the purpose of the present case, may be put aside as irrelevant.

The clause thought to authorize the legislation,—the first,—confers upon the Congress power 'to lay and collect Taxes, Duties, Imposts and Excises, to pay the Debts and provide for the common Defense and general Welfare of the United States. . .' It is not contended that this provision grants power to regulate agricultural production upon the theory that such legislation would promote the general welfare. The Government concedes that the phrase 'to provide for the general welfare' qualifies the power 'to lay and collect taxes.' The view that the clause grants power to provide for the general welfare, independently of the taxing power, has never been authoritatively accepted. Mr. Justice Story points out that if it were adopted 'it is obvious that under color of the generality of the words, to "provide for the common defence and general welfare," the government of the United States is, in reality, a government of general and unlimited powers, notwithstanding the subsequent enumeration of specific powers.' The true construction undoubtedly is that the only thing granted is the power to tax for the purpose of providing funds for payment of the nation's debts and making provision for the general welfare.

Nevertheless the Government asserts that warrant is found in this clause for the adoption of the Agricultural Adjustment Act. The argument is that Congress may appropriate and authorize the spending of moneys for the 'general welfare'; that the phrase should be liberally construed to cover anything conducive to national welfare; that decision as to what will promote such welfare rests with Congress alone, and the courts may not review its determination; and finally that the appropriation under attack was in fact for the general welfare of the United States.

The Congress is expressly empowered to lay taxes to provide for the general wel-

fare. Funds in the Treasury as a result of taxation may be expended only through appropriation. (Art. 1, § 9, cl. 7.) They can never accomplish the objects for which they were collected unless the power to appropriate is as broad as the power to tax. The necessary implication from the terms of the grant is that the public funds may be appropriated 'to provide for the general welfare of the United States.' These words cannot be meaningless, else they would not have been used. The conclusion must be that they were intended to limit and define the granted power to raise and to expend money. How shall they be construed to effectuate the intent of the instrument?

Since the foundation of the Nation sharp differences of opinion have persisted as to the true interpretation of the phrase. Madison asserted it amounted to no more than a reference to the other powers enumerated in the subsequent clause of the same section; that, as the United States is a government of limited and enumerated powers, the grant of power to tax and spend for the general national welfare must be confined to the enumerated legislative fields committed to the Congress. In this view the phrase is mere tautology, for taxation and appropriations are or may be necessary incidents of the exercise of any of the enumerated legislative powers. Hamilton, on the other hand, maintained the clause confers a power separate and distinct from those later enumerated, is not restricted in meaning by the grant of them, and Congress consequently has a substantive power to tax and to appropriate, limited only by the requirement that it shall be exercised to provide for the general welfare of the United States. Each contention has had the support of those whose views are entitled to weight. This court has noticed the question, but has never found it necessary to decide which is the true construction. Mr. Justice Story, in his Commentaries, espouses the Hamiltonian position. We shall not review the writings of public men and commentators or discuss the legislative practice. Study of all these leads us to conclude that the reading advocated by Mr. Justice Story is the correct one. While, therefore, the power to tax is not unlimited, its confines are set in the clause which confers it, and not in those of § 8 which bestow and define the legislative powers of the Congress. It results that the power of Congress to authorize expenditure of public moneys for public purposes is not limited by the direct grants of legislative power found in the Constitution.

But the adoption of the broader construction leaves the power to spend subject to limitations.

As Story says:

'The Constitution was, from its very origin, contemplated to be the frame of a national government, of special and enumerated powers, and not of general and unlimited powers.'

Again he says:

'A power to lay taxes for the common defence and general welfare of the United States is not in common sense a general power. It is limited to those objects. It cannot constitutionally transcend them.'

That the qualifying phrase must be given effect all advocates of broad construction admit. Hamilton, in his well known Report on Manufactures, states that the purpose must be 'general, and not local.' Monroe, an advocate of Hamilton's doctrine, wrote: 'Have Congress a right to raise and appropriate the money to any and to every purpose according to their will and pleasure? They certainly have not.' Story says that if the tax be not proposed for the common defence or general welfare, but for other objects wholly extraneous, it would be wholly indefensible upon constitutional principles. And he makes it clear that the powers of taxation and appropriation extend only to matters of national, as distinguished from local welfare.

As elsewhere throughout the Constitution the section in question lays down principles which control the use of the power, and does not attempt meticulous or detailed directions. Every presumption is to be indulged in favor of faithful compliance by Congress with the mandates of the fundamental law. Courts are reluctant to adjudge any statute in contravention of them. But under our frame of government, no other place is provided where the citizen may be heard to urge that the law fails to conform to the limits set upon the use of a granted power. When such a contention comes here we naturally require a showing that by no reasonable possibility can the challenged legislation fall within the wide range of discretion permitted to the Congress. How great is the extent of that range, when the subject is the promotion of the general welfare of the United States, we hardly need remark. But, despite the breadth of the legislative discretion, our duty to hear and to render judgment remains. If the statute plainly violates the stated principle of the Constitution we must so declare.

We are not now required to ascertain the scope of the phrase 'general welfare of the United States' or to determine whether an appropriation in aid of agriculture falls within it. Wholly apart from that question, another principle embedded in our Constitution prohibits the enforcement of the Agricultural Adjustment Act. The act invades the reserved rights of the states. It is a statutory plan to regulate and control agricultural production, a matter beyond the powers delegated to the federal government. The tax, the appropriation of the funds raised, and the direction for their disbursement, are but parts of the plan. They are but means to an unconstitutional end.

From the accepted doctrine that the United States is a government of delegated powers, it follows that those not expressly granted, or reasonably to be implied from such as are conferred, are reserved to the states or to the people. To forestall any suggestion to the contrary, the Tenth Amendment was adopted. The same proposition, otherwise stated, is that powers not granted are prohibited. None to regulate agricultural production is given, and therefore legislation by Congress for that purpose is forbidden.

It is an established principle that the attainment of a prohibited end may not be accomplished under the pretext of the exertion of powers which are granted.

'Should Congress, in the execution of its powers, adopt measures which are prohibited by the Constitution; or should Congress, under the pretext of executing its powers, pass laws for the accomplishment of objects not intrusted to the government; it would become the painful duty of this tribunal, should a case requiring such a decision come before it, to say that such an act was not the law of the land.' *McCulloch* v. *Maryland,* 4 Wheat. 316, 423.

'Congress cannot, under the pretext of executing delegated power, pass laws for the accomplishment of objects not entrusted to the Federal Government. And we accept as established doctrine that any provision of an act of Congress ostensibly enacted under power granted by the Constitution, not naturally and reasonably adapted to the effective exercise of such power but solely to the achievement of something plainly within power reserved to the States, is invalid and cannot be enforced.' *Linder* v. *United States,* 268 U.S. 5, 17.

These principles are as applicable to the power to lay taxes as to any other federal power. Said the court, in *McCulloch* v. *Maryland, supra,* 421:

'Let the end be legitimate, let it be within the scope of the Constitution, and all means which are appropriate, which are plainly adapted to that end, which are not prohibited, but consist with the letter and spirit of the constitution, are constitutional.'

The power of taxation, which is expressly granted, may, of course, be adopted as a means to carry into operation another power also expressly granted. But resort to the taxing power to effectuate an end which is not legitimate, not within the scope of the Constitution, is obviously inadmissible. . . .

In the *Child Labor Tax Case,* 259 U.S. 20 and in *Hill* v. *Wallace,* 259 U.S. 44, this court had before it statutes which purported to be taxing measures. But their purpose was found to be to regulate the conduct of manufacturing and trading, not in interstate commerce, but in the states,—matters not within any power conferred upon Congress by the Constitution —and the levy of the tax a means to force compliance. The court held this was not a constitutional use, but an unconstitutional abuse of the power to tax. In *Linder* v. *United States, supra,* we held that the power to tax could not justify the regulation of the practice of a profession, under the pretext of raising revenue. In *United States* v. *Constantine,* 296 U.S. 287, we declared that Congress could not, in the guise of a tax, impose sanctions for violation of state law respecting the local sale of liquor. These decisions demonstrate that Congress could not, under the pretext of raising revenue, lay a tax on processors who refuse to pay a certain price for cotton, and exempt those who agree so to do, with the purpose of benefiting producers.

Third. If the taxing power may not be used as the instrument to enforce a regulation of matters of state concern with respect to which the Congress has no authority to interfere, may it, as in the present case, be employed to raise the money necessary to purchase a compliance which the Congress is powerless to command? The Government asserts that whatever might be said against the validity of the plan if compulsory, it is constitutionally sound because the end is accomplished by voluntary co-operation. There are two sufficient answers to the contention. The regulation is not in fact voluntary. The farmer, of course, may refuse to comply, but the price of such refusal is the loss of benefits. The amount offered is intended to be sufficient to exert pressure on him to agree to the proposed regulation. The power to confer or withhold unlimited benefits is the power to coerce or destroy. If the cotton grower elects not to accept the benefits, he will receive less for his crops; those who receive payments will be able to undersell him. The result may well be financial ruin. The coercive purpose and intent of the statute is not obscured by the fact that it has not been perfectly successful. It is pointed out that, because there still remained a minority whom the rental and benefit payments were insufficient to induce to surrender their independence of action, the Congress has gone further and, in the Bankhead Cotton Act, used the taxing power in a more directly minatory fashion to compel submission. This progression only serves more fully to expose the coercive purpose of the so-called tax imposed by the present act. It is clear that the Department of Agriculture has properly described the plan as one to keep a non-co-operating minority in line. This is coercion by economic pressure. The asserted power of choice is illusory. . .

But if the plan were one for purely voluntary co-operation it would stand no better so far as federal power is concerned. At best it is a scheme for purchasing with federal funds submission to federal regulation of a subject reserved to the states.

It is said that Congress has the undoubted right to appropriate money to executive officers for expenditure under contracts between the government and individuals; that much of the total expenditures is so made. But appropriations and expenditures under contracts for proper governmental purposes cannot justify contracts which are not within federal power. And contracts for the reduction of acreage and the control of production are outside the range of that power. An appropria-

tion to be expended by the United States under contracts calling for violation of a state law clearly would offend the Constitution. Is a statute less objectionable which authorizes expenditure of federal moneys to induce action in a field in which the United States has no power to intermeddle? The Congress cannot invade state jurisdiction to compel individual action; no more can it purchase such action.

We are referred to numerous types of federal appropriation which have been made in the past, and it is asserted no question has been raised as to their validity. We need not stop to examine or consider them. As was said in *Massachusetts v. Mellon, supra* (p. 487):

'. . . as an examination of the acts of Congress will disclose, a large number of statutes appropriating or involving the expenditure of moneys for non-federal purposes have been enacted and carried into effect.'

As the opinion points out, such expenditures have not been challenged because no remedy was open for testing their constitutionality in the courts.

We are not here concerned with a conditional appropriation of money, nor with a provision that if certain conditions are not complied with the appropriation shall no longer be available. By the Agricultural Adjustment Act the amount of the tax is appropriated to be expended only in payment under contracts whereby the parties bind themselves to regulation by the Federal Government. There is an obvious difference between a statute stating the conditions upon which moneys shall be expended and one effective only upon assumption of a contractual obligation to submit to a regulation which otherwise could not be enforced. Many examples pointing the distinction might be cited. We are referred to appropriations in aid of education, and it is said that no one has doubted the power of Congress to stipulate the sort of education for which money shall be expended. But an appropriation to an educational institution which by its terms is to become available only if the beneficiary enters into a contract to teach doctrines subversive of the Constitution is clearly bad. An affirmance of the authority of Congress so to condition the expenditure of an appropriation would tend to nullify all constitutional limitations upon legislative power.

But it is said that there is a wide difference in another respect, between compulsory regulation of the local affairs of a state's citizens and the mere making of a contract relating to their conduct; that, if any state objects, it may declare the contract void and thus prevent those under the state's jurisdiction from complying with its terms. The argument is plainly fallacious. The United States can make the contract only if the federal power to tax and to appropriate reaches the subject matter of the contract. If this does reach the subject matter, its exertion cannot be displaced by state action. To say otherwise is to deny the supremacy of the laws of the United States; to make them subordinate to those of a State. This would reverse the cardinal principle embodied in the Constitution and substitute one which declares that Congress may only effectively legislate as to matters within federal competence when the States do not dissent.

Congress has no power to enforce its commands on the farmer to the ends sought by the Agricultural Adjustment Act. It must follow that it may not indirectly accomplish those ends by taxing and spending to purchase compliance. The Constitution and the entire plan of our government negative any such use of the power to tax and to spend as the act undertakes to authorize. It does not help to declare that local conditions throughout the nation have created a situation of national concern; for this is but to say that whenever there is a widespread similarity of local conditions, Congress may ignore constitutional limitations upon its own powers and usurp those reserved to the states. If, in lieu of compulsory regulation of subjects within the states' reserved jurisdiction, which is prohibited, the Congress could invoke the taxing and spending power as a means to accomplish the same end, clause 1 of § 8 of Article 1 would become the instrument for total subversion of the governmental powers reserved to the individual states.

If the act before us is a proper exercise of the federal taxing power, evidently the regulation of all industry throughout the United States may be accomplished by similar exercises of the same power. It would be possible to exact money from one branch of an industry and pay it to another branch in every field of activity which lies within the province of the states. The mere threat of such a procedure might well induce the surrender of rights and the compliance with federal regulation as the price of continuance in business. A few instances will illustrate the thought.

Let us suppose Congress should determine that the farmer, the miner or some other producer of raw materials is receiving too much for his products, with consequent depression of the processing industry and idleness of its employes. Though, by confession, there is no power vested in Congress to compel by statute a lowering of the prices of the raw material, the same result might be accomplished, if the questioned act be valid, by taxing the producer upon his output and appropriating the proceeds to the processors, either with or without conditions imposed as the consideration for payment of the subsidy.

We have held in *Schechter Poultry Corp.* v. *United States,* 295 U.S. 495, that Congress has no power to regulate wages and hours of labor in a local business. If the petitioner is right, this very end may be accomplished by appropriating money to be paid to employers from the federal treasury under contracts whereby they agree to comply with certain standards fixed by federal law or by contract.

Should Congress ascertain that sugar refiners are not receiving a fair profit, and that this is detrimental to the entire industry, and in turn has its repercussions in trade and commerce generally, it might, in analogy to the present law, impose an excise of two cents a pound on every sale of the commodity and pass the funds collected to such refiners, and such only, as will agree to maintain a certain price.

Assume that too many shoes are being manufactured throughout the nation; that the market is saturated, the price depressed, the factories running halftime, the employes suffering. Upon the principle of the statute in question Congress might authorize the Secretary of Commerce to enter into contracts with shoe manufacturers providing that each shall reduce his output and that the United States will pay him a fixed sum proportioned to such reduction, the money to make the payments to be raised by a tax on all retail shoe dealers or their customers.

Suppose that there are too many garment workers in the large cities; that this results in dislocation of the economic balance. Upon the principle contended for an excise might be laid on the manufacture of all garments manufactured and the proceeds paid to those manufacturers who agree to remove their plants to cities having not more than a hundred thousand population. Thus, through the asserted power of taxation, the federal government, against the will of individual states, might completely redistribute the industrial population.

A possible result of sustaining the claimed federal power would be that every business group which thought itself under-privileged might demand that a tax be laid on its vendors or vendees, the proceeds to be appropriated to the redress of its deficiency of income.

These illustrations are given, not to suggest that any of the purposes mentioned are unworthy, but to demonstrate the scope of the principle for which the Government contends; to test the principle by its applications; to point out that, by the exercise of the asserted power, Congress would, in effect, under the pretext of exercising the taxing power, in reality accomplish prohibited ends. It cannot be said that they envisage improbable legislation. The supposed cases are no more improbable than would the present act have been deemed a few years ago.

Until recently no suggestion of the existence of any such power in the Federal Government has been advanced. The expressions of the framers of the Constitution, the decisions of this court interpreting that instrument, and the writings of great commentators will be searched in vain for any suggestion that there exists in the clause under discussion or elsewhere in the Constitution, the authority whereby every provision and every fair implication from that instrument may be subverted, the independence of the individual states obliterated, and the United States converted into a central government exercising uncontrolled police power in every state of the Union, superseding all local control or regulation of the affairs or concerns of the states.

Hamilton himself, the leading advocate of broad interpretation of the power to tax and to appropriate for the general welfare, never suggested that any power granted by the Constitution could be used for the destruction of local self-government in the states. Story countenances no such doctrine. It seems never to have occurred to them, or to those who have agreed with them, that the general welfare of the United States, (which has aptly been termed 'an indestructible Union, composed of indestructible States,') might be served by obliterating the constituent members of the Union. But to this fatal conclusion the doctrine contended for would inevitably lead. And its sole premise is that, though the makers of the Constitution, in erecting the federal government, intended sedulously to limit and define its powers, so as to reserve to the states and the people sovereign power, to be wielded by the states and their citizens and not to be invaded by the United States, they nevertheless by a single clause gave power to the Congress to tear down the barriers, to invade the states' jurisdiction, and to become a parliament of the whole people, subject to no restrictions save such as are self-imposed. The argument when seen in its true character and in the light of its inevitable results must be rejected.

Since, as we have pointed out, there was no power in the Congress to impose the contested exaction, it could not lawfully ratify or confirm what an executive officer had done in that regard. Consequently the Act of 1935 does not affect the rights of the parties.

The judgment is

Affirmed.

Mr. JUSTICE STONE, dissenting.

I think the judgment should be reversed. . .

[The] pivot on which the decision of the Court is made to turn . . . is that a levy unquestionably within the taxing power of Congress may be treated as invalid because it is a step in a plan to regulate agricultural production and is thus a forbidden infringement of state power. The levy is not any the less an exercise of taxing power because it is intended to defray an expenditure for the general welfare rather than for some other support of government. Nor is the levy and collection of the tax pointed to as effecting the regulation. While all federal taxes inevitably have some influence on the internal economy of the states, it is not contended that the levy of a processing tax upon manufacturers using agricultural products as raw material has any perceptible regulatory effect upon either their production or manufacture. The tax is

unlike the penalties which were held invalid in the *Child Labor Tax Case,* 259 U.S. 20, in *Hill* v. *Wallace,* 259 U.S. 44, in *Linder* v. *United States,* 268 U.S. 5, 17, and in *United States* v. *Constantine,* 296 U.S. 287, because they were themselves the instruments of regulation by virtue of their coercive effect on matters left to the control of the states. Here regulation, if any there be, is accomplished not by the tax but by the method by which its proceeds are expended, and would equally be accomplished by any like use of public funds, regardless of their source.

The method may be simply stated. Out of the available fund payments are made to such farmers as are willing to curtail their productive acreage, who in fact do so and who in advance have filed their written undertaking to do so with the Secretary of Agriculture. In saying that this method of spending public moneys is an invasion of the reserved powers of the states, the Court does not assert that the expenditure of public funds to promote the general welfare is not a substantive power specifically delegated to the national government, as Hamilton and Story pronounced it to be. It does not deny that the expenditure of funds for the benefit of farmers and in aid of a program of curtailment of production of agricultural products, and thus of a supposedly better ordered national economy, is within the specifically granted power. But it is declared that state power is nevertheless infringed by the expenditure of the proceeds of the tax to compensate farmers for the curtailment of their cotton acreage. Although the farmer is placed under no legal compulsion to reduce acreage, it is said that the mere offer of compensation for so doing is a species of economic coercion which operates with the same legal force and effect as though the curtailment were made mandatory by Act of Congress. In any event it is insisted that even though not coercive the expenditure of public funds to induce the recipients to curtail production is itself an infringement of state power, since the federal government cannot invade the domain of the states by the 'purchase' of performance of acts which it has no power to compel.

Of the assertion that the payments to farmers are coercive, it is enough to say that no such contention is pressed by the taxpayer, and no such consequences were to be anticipated or appear to have resulted from the administration of the Act. The suggestion of coercion finds no support in the record or in any data showing the actual operation of the Act. Threat of loss, not hope of gain, is the essence of economic coercion. . .

It is upon the contention that state power is infringed by purchased regulation of agricultural production that chief reliance is placed. It is insisted that, while the Constitution gives to Congress, in specific and unambiguous terms, the power to tax and spend, the power is subject to limitations which do not find their origin in any express provision of the Constitution and to which other expressly delegated powers are not subject.

The Constitution requires that public funds shall be spent for a defined purpose, the promotion of the general welfare. Their expenditure usually involves payment on terms which will insure use by the selected recipients within the limits of the constitutional purpose. Expenditures would fail of their purpose and thus lose their constitutional sanction if the terms of payment were not such that by their influence on the action of the recipients the permitted end would be attained. The power of Congress to spend is inseparable from persuasion to action over which Congress has no legislative control. Congress may not command that the science of agriculture be taught in state universities. But if it would aid the teaching of that science by grants to state institutions, it is appropriate, if not necessary, that the grant be on the condition, incorporated in the Morrill Act, 12 Stat. 503, 26 Stat. 417, that

it be used for the intended purpose. Similarly it would seem to be compliance with the Constitution, not violation of it, for the government to take and the university to give a contract that the grant would be so used. It makes no difference that there is a promise to do an act which the condition is calculated to induce. Condition and promise are alike valid since both are in furtherance of the national purpose for which the money is appropriated. . .

The limitation now sanctioned must lead to absurd consequences. The government may give seeds to farmers, but may not condition the gift upon their being planted in places where they are most needed or even planted at all. The government may give money to the unemployed, but may not ask that those who get it shall give labor in return, or even use it to support their families. It may give money to sufferers from earthquake, fire, tornado, pestilence or flood, but may not impose conditions—health precautions designed to prevent the spread of disease, or induce the movement of population to safer or more sanitary areas. All that, because it is purchased regulation infringing state powers, must be left for the states, who are unable or unwilling to supply the necessary relief. The government may spend its money for vocational rehabilitation, 48 Stat. 389, but it may not, with the consent of all concerned, supervise the process which it undertakes to aid. It may spend its money for the suppression of the boll weevil, but may not compensate the farmers for suspending the growth of cotton in the infected areas. It may aid state reforestation and forest fire preventing agencies, 43 Stat. 653, but may not be permitted to supervise their conduct. It may support rural schools, 39 Stat. 929, 45 Stat. 1151, 48 Stat. 792, but may not condition its grant by the requirement that certain standards be maintained. It may appropriate moneys to be expended by the Reconstruction Finance Corporation 'to aid in financing agriculture, commerce and industry,' and to facilitate 'the exportation of agricultural and other products.' Do all its activities collapse because, in order to effect the permissible purpose, in myriad ways the money is paid out upon terms and conditions which influence action of the recipients within the states, which Congress cannot command? The answer would seem plain. If the expenditure is for a national public purpose, that purpose will not be thwarted because payment is on condition which will advance that purpose. The action which Congress induces by payments of money to promote the general welfare, but which it does not command or coerce, is but an incident to a specifically granted power, but a permissible means to a legitimate end. If appropriation in aid of a program of curtailment of agricultural production is constitutional, and it is not denied that it is, payment to farmers on condition that they reduce their crop acreage is constitutional. It is not any the less so because the farmer at his own option promises to fulfill the condition.

That the governmental power of the purse is a great one is not now for the first time announced. Every student of the history of government and economics is aware of its magnitude and of its existence in every civilized government. Both were well understood by the framers of the Constitution when they sanctioned the grant of the spending power to the federal government, and both were recognized by Hamilton and Story, whose views of the spending power as standing on a parity with the other powers specifically granted, have hitherto been generally accepted.

The suggestion that it must now be curtailed by judicial fiat because it may be abused by unwise use hardly rises to the dignity of argument. So may judicial power be abused. 'The power to tax is the power to destroy,' but we do not, for that reason, doubt its existence, or hold that its efficacy is to be restricted by its incidental or collateral effects upon the

states. . . . The power to tax and spend is not without constitutional restraints. One restriction is that the purpose must be truly national. Another is that it may not be used to coerce action left to state control. Another is the conscience and patriotism of Congress and the Executive. 'It must be remembered that legislators are the ultimate guardians of the liberties and welfare of the people in quite as great a degree as the courts.' Justice Holmes, in *Missouri, Kansas & Texas Ry. Co.* v. *May,* 194 U.S. 267, 270.

A tortured construction of the Constitution is not to be justified by recourse to extreme examples of reckless congressional spending which might occur if courts could not prevent—expenditures which, even if they could be thought to effect any national purpose, would be possible only by action of a legislature lost to all sense of public responsibility. Such suppositions are addressed to the mind accustomed to believe that it is the business of courts to sit in judgment on the wisdom of legislative action. Courts are not the only agency of government that must be assumed to have capacity to govern. Congress and the courts both unhappily may falter or be mistaken in the performance of their constitutional duty. But interpretation of our great charter of government which proceeds on any assumption that the responsibility for the preservation of our institutions is the exclusive concern of any one of the three branches of government, or that it alone can save them from destruction is far more likely, in the long run, 'to obliterate the constituent members' of 'an indestructible union of indestructible states' than the frank recognition that language, even of a constitution, may mean what it says: that the power to tax and spend includes the power to relieve a nationwide economic maladjustment by conditional gifts of money.

Mr. Justice Brandeis and Mr. Justice Cardozo join in this opinion.

NOTE

Sonzinsky v. *United States* (1937) presents an instance of the use of the federal power to tax for purposes other than revenue. In general, the purpose of taxation is revenue; oftentimes, however, the tax power is used for purposes of prohibition and regulation.

In *Veazie Bank* v. *Fenno* [1] the Supreme Court upheld an act of Congress imposing a ten per cent tax upon the note issues of banks chartered by the states. The tax was a tax only in form; its intent was not to raise revenue but to drive out of circulation the paper money of the state banks and thus protect the note issues of the recently established national banks.[2] It was argued by counsel for the bank that the law was unconstitutional since so excessive a tax indicated a purpose on the part of Congress to destroy the franchise of the bank. 'The first answer to this,' said Chief Justice Chase, 'is that the judicial cannot prescribe to the legislative departments of the government limitations upon the exercise of its acknowledged powers. The power to tax may be exercised oppressively upon persons, but the responsibility of the legislature is not to the courts, but to the people by whom its members are elected.'[3] The second answer was that under the Constitution Congress is given power to regulate the currency.

By taxing white phosphorus matches two cents per hundred matches, Congress eliminated their manufacture entirely.[4] The use of white phosphorus in the making of matches was extremely dangerous to workers in the industry.

The White Phosphorus Match Act was never reviewed by the Supreme Court, but a roughly similar act was sustained by the Court. In the Oleomargarine Acts of 1886 and 1902, Congress sought to regulate the sale of oleomargarine colored to resemble butter. A tax of ten cents per pound upon colored oleomargarine was alleged to be so high as to make it impossible to sell such a product in competition with butter, and that the effect of the tax would be the destruction of the oleomargarine industry. In *McCray* v. *United States,*[5] the Supreme Court speaking through Mr. Justice White sustained the tax. 'The act before us,' he said, 'is on its face an act for levying taxes, and although it may operate in so doing to prevent deception in the sale of oleomargarine as and for butter, its primary object must be assumed to be the raising of revenue.'[6] As for the allegation that the tax was imposed not to raise revenue but for

[1] 8 Wall. 533 (1869).
[2] 12 Stat. 665 (1863); 14 Stat. 98, 146 (1866).
[3] 8 Wall. 548.
[4] 37 Stat. 81 (1912).
[5] 195 U.S. 27 (1904).
[6] Ibid. 51. Here Mr. Justice White is quoting Chief Justice Fuller in *In re Kollock*, 165 U.S. 526 (1897).

other purposes, Mr. Justice White said: 'The decisions of this court from the beginning lend no support whatever to the assumption that the judiciary may restrain the exercise of lawful power on the assumption that a wrongful purpose or motive has caused the power to be exerted.'[7]

The Harrison Narcotics Act[8] of 1914 placed a special tax upon the manufacture, importation, and sale of opium or coca leaves or their compounds or derivatives. The act required every person subject to the tax to register with the Collector of Internal Revenue and forbade him to sell the drug or its derivatives except upon a written order of the person to whom the sale was made. Similar requirements were made as to sales upon prescriptions of a physician and as to the dispensing of such drugs directly to a patient by a physician. The purpose of the act was, obviously, the regulation and control of a known evil. One Doremus, a physician who had registered and paid the tax as required by the act, was indicted for supplying a known drug addict with heroin, not for the purpose of treating disease, and without requiring the written order prescribed by the act. Upon demurrer to the indictment, the District Court held the pertinent section of the act to be unconstitutional on the ground that it was not a revenue measure. The lower court also held it to be an invasion of the reserved powers of the states.

The District Court's decision was reversed, and the act sustained, by the Supreme Court in *United States* v. *Doremus*.[9] 'If the legislation enacted,' said Mr. Justice Day, 'has some reasonable relation to the exercise of the taxing authority conferred by the Constitution, it cannot be invalidated because of the supposed motives which induced it. . . Nor is it sufficient to invalidate the taxing authority given to the Congress by the Constitution that the same business may be regulated by the police power of the State.'[10] The act 'may not be declared unconstitutional,' he continued, 'because its effect may be to accomplish another purpose as well as the raising of revenue. If the legislation is within the taxing authority of Congress—that is sufficient to sustain it.'[11]

In the case which follows the Supreme Court had before it the question of the validity of the National Firearms Act[12] of 1934. This act, patterned closely upon the Harrison Narcotics Act, was a federal response to widespread interstate criminal activity. That the primary purpose of the act was not revenue is clear. Its object was to regulate and to control the traffic in firearms, in part through licensing the dealer.

SONZINSKY v. UNITED STATES
300 U.S. 506 (1937)

Mr. Justice Stone delivered the opinion of the Court.

The question for decision is whether § 2 of the National Firearms Act of June 26, 1934, c. 757, 48 Stat. 1236, 26 U.S.C., §§ 1132-1132q, which imposes a $200 an-

---

[7] Ibid. 56.
[8] 38 Stat. 785.

[9] 249 U.S. 86 (1919).
[10] Ibid. 93-4.

[11] Ibid. 94.
[12] 48 Stat. 1236.

nual license tax on dealers in firearms, is a constitutional exercise of the legislative power of Congress.

Petitioner was convicted by the District Court for Eastern Illinois on two counts of an indictment, the first charging him with violation of § 2, by dealing in firearms without payment of the tax. On appeal the Court of Appeals set aside the conviction on the second count and affirmed on the first. 86 F. (2d) 486. On petition of the accused we granted certiorari, limited to the question of the constitutional validity of the statute in its application under the first count in the indictment.

Section 2 of the National Firearms Act requires every dealer in firearms to register with the Collector of Internal Revenue in the district where he carries on business, and to pay a special excise tax of $200 a year. Importers or manufacturers are taxed $500 a year. Section 3 imposes a tax of $200 on each transfer of a firearm, payable by the transferor, and § 4 prescribes regulations for the identification of purchasers. The term 'firearm' is defined by § 1 as meaning a shotgun or a rifle having a barrel less than eighteen inches in length, or any other weapon, except a pistol or revolver, from which a shot is discharged by an explosive, if capable of being concealed on the person, or a machine gun, and includes a muffler or silencer for any firearm. As the conviction for non-payment of the tax exacted by § 2 has alone been sustained, it is unnecessary to inquire whether the different tax levied by § 3 and the regulations pertaining to it are valid. Section 16 declares that the provisions of the Act are separable. Each tax is on a different activity and is collectible independently of the other. Full effect may be given to the license tax standing alone, even though all other provisions are invalid. . .

In the exercise of its constitutional power to lay taxes, Congress may select the subjects of taxation, choosing some and

omitting others. See *Flint* v. *Stone Tracy Co.,* 220 U.S. 107, 158; *Nicol* v. *Ames,* 173 U.S. 509, 516; *Bromley* v. *McCaughn,* 280 U.S. 124. Its power extends to the imposition of excise taxes upon the doing of business. See *License Tax Cases,* 5 Wall. 462; *Spreckles Sugar Refining Co.* v. *McClain,* 192 U.S. 397, 412; *United States* v. *Doremus,* 249 U.S. 86, 94. Petitioner does not deny that Congress may tax his business as a dealer in firearms. He insists that the present levy is not a true tax, but a penalty imposed for the purpose of suppressing traffic in a certain noxious type of firearms, the local regulation of which is reserved to the states because not granted to the national government. To establish its penal and prohibitive character, he relies on the amounts of the tax imposed by § 2 on dealers, manufacturers and importers, and of the tax imposed by § 3 on each transfer of a 'firearm,' payable by the transferor. The cumulative effect on the distribution of a limited class of firearms, of relatively small value, by the successive imposition of different taxes, one on the business of the importer or manufacturer, another on that of the dealer, and a third on the transfer to a buyer, is said to be prohibitive in effect and to disclose unmistakably the legislative purpose to regulate rather than to tax.

The case is not one where the statute contains regulatory provisions related to a purported tax in such a way as has enabled this Court to say in other cases that the latter is a penalty resorted to as a means of enforcing the regulations. See *Child Labor Tax Case,* 259 U.S. 20, 35; *Hill* v. *Wallace,* 259 U.S. 44; *Carter* v. *Carter Coal Co.,* 298 U.S. 238. Nor is the subject of the tax described or treated as criminal by the taxing statute. Compare *United States* v. *Constantine,* 296 U.S. 287. Here § 2 contains no regulation other than the mere registration provisions, which are obviously supportable as in aid of a revenue purpose. On its face it is only a taxing measure, and we are asked to say that the tax, by virtue of its deterrent effect on the activities taxed, operates as a regulation which is beyond the congressional power.

Every tax is in some measure regulatory. To some extent it interposes an economic impediment to the activity taxed as compared with others not taxed. But a tax is not any the less a tax because it has a regulatory effect, *United States* v. *Doremus, supra,* 93, 94; *Nigro* v. *United States,* 276 U.S. 332, 353, 354; *License Tax Cases, supra;* see *Child Labor Tax Case, supra,* 38; and it has long been established that an Act of Congress which on its face purports to be an exercise of the taxing power is not any the less so because the tax is burdensome or tends to restrict or suppress the thing taxed. *Veazie Bank* v. *Fenno,* 8 Wall. 533, 548; *McCray* v. *United States,* 195 U.S. 27, 60-61; cf. *Alaska Fish Co.* v. *Smith,* 255 U.S. 44, 48.

Inquiry into the hidden motives which may move Congress to exercise a power constitutionally conferred upon it is beyond the competency of courts. *Veazie Bank* v. *Fenno, supra; McCray* v. *United States, supra,* 56-59; *United States* v. *Doremus, supra,* 93-94. . . They will not undertake, by collateral inquiry as to the measure of the regulatory effect of a tax, to ascribe to Congress an attempt, under the guise of taxation, to exercise another power denied by the Federal Constitution. *McCray* v. *United States, supra.* . .

Here the annual tax of $200 is productive of some revenue.[1] We are not free to speculate as to the motives which moved Congress to impose it, or as to the extent to which it may operate to restrict the activities taxed. As it is not attended by an offensive regulation, and since it operates as a tax, it is within the national taxing power. . .

We do not discuss petitioner's contentions which he failed to assign as error below.

Affirmed.

---

[1] The $200 tax was paid by 27 dealers in 1934, and by 22 dealers in 1935. Annual Report of the Commissioner of Internal Revenue, Fiscal Year Ended 30 June 1935, pp. 129-31; *id.,* Fiscal Year ended 30 June 1936, pp. 139-41.

NOTE

In *State of New York* v. *United States,* decided in 1946, the Supreme Court upheld a non-discriminatory Federal excise tax on the sale, by the State of New York, of bottled mineral waters taken from State-owned springs.

The power to tax is a power exercised concurrently by both Federal and state governments. This power exercised by one government may not be used to destroy or to curtail the functions of the other. Thus, in *McCulloch* v. *Maryland*[1] the Supreme Court held invalid a state tax upon the note issues of the Second National Bank, on the ground that the tax was a tax upon a legitimate function of the Federal government. In *Dobbins* v. *Commissioners of Erie County*[2] the Court decided that the salary of a Federal officer, in this case the captain of a United States revenue cutter, was immune from state taxation.

Conversely, in *Collector* v. *Day,*[3] the Supreme Court held the salary of a state judge to be immune from Federal taxation. The Constitution contains no express provision which prohibits the Federal government from taxing the instrumentalities of the states; nor does the Constitution forbid expressly state taxation of Federal instrumentalities. 'In both cases,' said Mr. Justice Nelson, 'the exemption rests upon necessary implication, and is upheld by the great law of self-preservation. . .'[4] The Court cited *McCulloch* v. *Maryland* and *Dobbins* v. *Commissioners of Erie County,* and referred to *Veazie Bank* v. *Fenno*[5] as a pertinent illustration of the position taken by John Marshall in the McCulloch case, namely, 'That the power to tax involves the power to destroy.'

Mr. Justice Bradley in his dissent in *Collector* v. *Day* anticipated future difficulties. 'In my judgment,' he declared, 'the limitation of the power of taxation in the general government, which the present decision establishes, will be found very difficult of control. Where are we to stop in enumerating the functions of the State governments which will be interfered with by Federal taxation? If a State incorporates a railroad to carry out its purposes of internal improvement, or a bank to aid its financial arrangements, reserving, perhaps, a percentage on the stock or profits, for the supply of its own treasury, will the bonds or stock of such an institution be free from Federal taxation? How can we now tell what the effect of this decision will be? I cannot but regard it as founded on a fallacy, and that it will lead to mischievous consequences.'[6]

Immunity from Federal taxation was extended in *Pollock* v. *Farmers' Loan & Trust Co.,*[7] to interest derived from state and local bonds.

[1] 4 Wheat. 316 (1819).
[2] 16 Pet. 435 (1842).
[3] 11 Wall. 113 (1871).
[4] Ibid. 127.

[5] 8 Wall. 533 (1869). See *ante,* p. 156.
[6] 11 Wall. 113, 129.
[7] 157 U.S. 429 (1895); 158 U.S. 601 (1895).

As a consequence of these parent decisions a large possible source of revenue was ruled to be exempt from Federal and state taxing powers. However, with increasing expansion of Federal and state governments, and with, during the depression, a decreasing area of taxation, the Federal government and the states sought new revenue sources and found them, in part, in the hitherto tax-exempt salaries of government employees.

The Supreme Court in *Helvering* v. *Gerhardt,* decided in 1938, approved the imposition of the Federal income tax upon the salaries of a construction engineer and two assistant general managers employed by the Port of New York Authority. Mr. Justice Stone, speaking for the Court, declared that 'we decide only that the present tax neither precludes nor threatens unreasonably to obstruct any function essential to the continued existence of the state government.' [8]

The implied constitutional immunity from income taxation of the salaries of officers or employees of the national or a state government or their instrumentalities set forth in *Collector* v. *Day* was expressly overruled in *Graves* v. *New York ex rel. O'Keefe,* [9] decided in 1939. Here the Court was presented with the question whether a non-discriminatory state income tax on the salary of an employee of the Home Owners' Loan Corporation, a Federal instrumentality, unconstitutionally burdened the Federal government. 'Assuming, as we do,' said Mr. Justice Stone for the majority, 'that the Home Owners' Loan Corporation is clothed with the same immunity from state taxation as the government itself, we cannot say that the present tax on the income of its employees lays any unconstitutional burden upon it. All the reasons for refusing to imply a constitutional prohibition of federal income taxation of salaries of state employees, stated at length in the *Gerhardt* case, are of equal force when immunity is claimed from state income tax on salaries paid by the national government or its agencies.' [10]

An exception to the rule of *Collector* v. *Day* came in 1905 in *South Carolina* v. *United States.* [11] Here South Carolina had established by law dispensaries for the wholesale and retail sale of liquor. The dispensers made no profits for the profits were appropriated by the State; in other words, the State had entered the liquor business. In this case, South Carolina sued to recover the amounts paid for license taxes as required by Federal law. The State argued that the Federal government had no power to tax a function of the state. This argument was rejected by the Supreme Court. Suppose, queried the Court, with the thought of mingling profit and regulation the state should take possession of tobacco, oleomargarine, and all other objects of internal revenue; if one state finds such ordinary business profitable, other states may follow, and 'the whole body of internal revenue tax be thus stricken down.' 'If,' said Mr. Justice Brewer, 'the power of the state is carried to the extent suggested, and with it is relief from

[8] 304 U.S. 405, 424.
[9] 306 U.S. 466. *New York ex rel. Rogers* v. *Graves,* 299 U.S. 401 (1937), was also overruled. In this case, the salary of the general counsel of the Panama Railroad Co. had been held exempt from payment of a state income tax.
[10] 306 U.S. 486.   [11] 199 U.S. 437 (1905).

all federal taxation, the national government would be largely crippled in its revenues.' In sustaining the tax, the Court declared that 'whenever a State engages in a business which is of a private nature that business is not withdrawn from the taxing power of the Nation.'[12] This is not always a simple rule to apply in practice, but the courts have held that the operation for profit by the state of a bank, a street-railway system, or a public wharf was not strictly and normally a governmental function. In connection with athletic contests in which the teams of the educational institutions of the state participated, Georgia claimed that the exaction of the Federal admissions tax unconstitutionally burdened a governmental function of the State. 'Where a State,' said Mr. Justice Roberts, 'embarks in a business which would normally be taxable, the fact that in doing so it is exercising a governmental power does not render the activity immune from federal taxation.'[13]

The following case provides a recent pronouncement on the subject of Federal taxation of state enterprise. As Mr. Justice Frankfurter says, 'on the basis of authority the case is quickly disposed of . . . but there comes a time when even the process of empiric adjudication calls for a more rational disposition than that the immediate case is not different from preceding cases.'[14]

NEW YORK ET AL. v. UNITED STATES
326 U.S. 572 (1946)

Mr. Justice Frankfurter announced the judgment of the Court and delivered an opinion in which Mr. Justice Rutledge joined.

Section 615 (a) (5) of the 1932 Revenue Act, 47 Stat. 169, 264, imposed a tax on mineral waters. The United States brought this suit to recover taxes assessed against the State of New York on the sale of mineral waters taken from Saratoga Springs, New York. The State claims immunity from this tax on the ground that 'in the bottling and sale of the said waters the defendant State of New York was engaged in the exercise of a usual, traditional and essential governmental function.' The claim was rejected by the District Court and judgment went for the United States. 48 F. Supp. 15. The judgment was affirmed by the Circuit Court of Appeals for the Second Circuit. 140 F. 2d 608.

The strong urging of New York for further clarification of the amenability of States to the taxing power of the United States led us to grant certiorari. 322 U.S. 724. After the case was argued at the 1944 Term, reargument was ordered.

On the basis of authority the case is quickly disposed of. When States sought to control the liquor traffic by going into the liquor business, they were denied immunity from federal taxes upon the liquor business. *South Carolina* v. *United States,* 199 U.S. 437; *Ohio* v. *Helvering,* 292 U.S. 360. And in rejecting a claim of immunity from federal taxation when Massachusetts took over the street railways of Boston, this Court a decade ago said: 'We see no reason for putting the operation of a street railway [by a State] in a different category from the sale of liquors.' *Helvering* v. *Powers,* 293 U.S. 214, 227. We certainly see no reason for putting soft drinks

---

[12] Ibid. 463. See also *Ohio* v. *Helvering,* 292 U.S. 360 (1934).
[13] *Allen* v. *Regents,* 304 U.S. 439, 451 (1938).
[14] 326 U.S. 572, 574-5 (1946).

in a different constitutional category from hard drinks. See also *Allen* v. *Regents*, 304 U.S. 439.

One of the greatest sources of strength of our law is that it adjudicates concrete cases and does not pronounce principles in the abstract. But there comes a time when even the process of empiric adjudication calls for a more rational disposition than that the immediate case is not different from preceding cases. The argument pressed by New York and the forty-five other States who, as *amici curiae*, have joined her deserves an answer.

Enactments levying taxes made in pursuance of the Constitution are, as other laws are, 'the supreme Law of the Land.' Art. vi, Constitution of the United States; *Flint* v. *Stone Tracy Co.*, 220 U.S. 107, 153. The first of the powers conferred upon Congress is the power 'To lay and collect Taxes, Duties, Imposts and Excises. . .' Art. i, § 8. By its terms the Constitution has placed only one limitation upon this power, other than limitations upon methods of laying taxes not here relevant: Congress can lay no tax 'on Articles exported from any State.' Art. i, § 9. Barring only exports, the power of Congress to tax 'reaches every subject.' *License Tax Cases*, 5 Wall. 462, 471. But the fact that ours is a federal constitutional system, as expressly recognized in the Tenth Amendment, carries with it implications regarding the taxing power as in other aspects of government. See, *e.g.*, *Hopkins Savings Assn.* v. *Cleary*, 296 U.S. 315. Thus, for Congress to tax State activities while leaving untaxed the same activities pursued by private persons would do violence to the presuppositions derived from the fact that we are a Nation composed of States.

But the fear that one government may cripple or obstruct the operations of the other early led to the assumption that there was a reciprocal immunity of the instrumentalities of each from taxation by the other. It was assumed that there was an equivalence in the implications of taxation by a State of the governmental activities of the National Government and the taxation by the National Government of State instrumentalities. This assumed equivalence was nourished by the phrase of Chief Justice Marshall that 'the power to tax involves the power to destroy.' *McCulloch* v. *Maryland*, 4 Wheat. 316, 431. To be sure, it was uttered in connection with a tax of Maryland which plainly discriminated against the use by the United States of the Bank of the United States as one of its instruments. What he said may not have been irrelevant in its setting. But Chief Justice Marshall spoke at a time when social complexities did not so clearly reveal as now the practical limitations of a rhetorical absolute. See Holmes, J., in *Long* v. *Rockwood*, 277 U.S. 142, 148, and *Panhandle Oil Co.* v. *Mississippi*, 277 U.S. 218, 223. The phrase was seized upon as the basis of a broad doctrine of intergovernmental immunity, while at the same time an expansive scope was given to what were deemed to be 'instrumentalities of government' for purposes of tax immunity. As a result, immunity was until recently accorded to all officers of one government from taxation by the other, and it was further assumed that the economic burden of a tax on any interest derived from a government imposes a burden on that government so as to involve an interference by the taxing government with the functioning of the other government. . .

To press a juristic principle designed for the practical affairs of government to abstract extremes is neither sound logic nor good sense. And this Court is under no duty to make law less than sound logic and good sense. When this Court for the first time relieved State officers from a non-discriminatory Congressional tax, not because of anything said in the Constitution but because of the supposed implications of our federal system, Mr. Justice Bradley pointed out the invalidity of the notion of reciprocal intergovernmental immunity. The considerations bearing upon taxation by the States of activities or agencies of the federal government are not correlative with the considerations bearing upon federal taxation of State agencies or activities. The federal government is the government of all the States, and all the States share in the legislative process by which a tax of general applicability is laid. 'The taxation by the State governments of the instruments employed by the general government in the exercise of its powers,' said Mr. Justice Bradley, 'is a very different thing. Such taxation involves an interference with the powers of a government in which other States and their citizens are equally interested with the State which imposes the taxation.' Since then we have moved away from the theoretical assumption that the National Government is burdened if its functionaries, like other citizens, pay for the upkeep of their State governments, and we have denied the implied constitutional immunity of federal officials from State taxes. . .

In the meantime, cases came here, as we have already noted, in which States claimed immunity from a federal tax imposed generally on enterprises in which the State itself was also engaged. This problem did not arise before the present century, partly because State trading did not actively emerge until relatively recently, and partly because of the narrow scope of federal taxation. In *South Carolina* v. *United States,* 199 U.S. 437, immunity from a federal tax on a dispensary system, whereby South Carolina monopolized the sale of intoxicating liquors, was denied by drawing a line between taxation of the historically recognized governmental functions of a State, and business engaged in by a State of a kind which theretofore had been pursued by private enterprise. The power of the federal government thus to tax a liquor business conducted by the State was derived from an appeal to the Constitution 'in the light of condi-

tions surrounding at the time of its adoption.' *South Carolina* v. *United States, supra,* at 457. That there is a constitutional line between the State as government and the State as trader, was still more recently made the basis of a decision sustaining a liquor tax against Ohio. 'If a state chooses to go into the business of buying and selling commodities, its right to do so may be conceded so far as the Federal Constitution is concerned; but the exercise of the right is not the performance of a governmental function. . . When a state enters the market place seeking customers it divests itself of its *quasi* sovereignty *pro tanto,* and takes on the character of a trader, so far, at least, as the taxing power of the federal government is concerned.' *Ohio* v. *Helvering, supra,* at 369. When the *Ohio* case was decided it was too late in the day not to recognize the vast extension of the sphere of government, both State and National, compared with that with which the Fathers were familiar. It could hardly remain a satisfactory constitutional doctrine that only such State activities are immune from federal taxation as were engaged in by the States in 1787. Such a static concept of government denies its essential nature. 'The science of government is the most abstruse of all sciences; if, indeed, that can be called a science which has but few fixed principles, and practically consists in little more than the exercise of a sound discretion, applied to the exigencies of the state as they arise. It is the science of experiment.' *Anderson* v. *Dunn,* 6 Wheat. 204, 226.

When this Court came to sustain the federal taxing power upon a transportation system operated by a State, it did so in ways familiar in developing the law from precedent to precedent. It edged away from reliance on a sharp distinction between the 'governmental' and the 'trading' activities of a State, by denying immunity from federal taxation to a State when it 'is undertaking a business enterprise of a sort that is normally within the reach of the federal taxing power and is distinct from the usual governmental functions that are immune from federal taxation in order to safeguard the necessary independence of the State.' *Helvering* v. *Powers, supra,* at 227. But this likewise does not furnish a satisfactory guide for dealing with such a practical problem as the constitutional power of the United States over State activities. To rest the federal taxing power on what is 'normally' conducted by private enterprise in contradiction to the 'usual' governmental functions is too shifting a basis for determining constitutional power and too entangled in expediency to serve as a dependable legal criterion. The essential nature of the problem cannot be hidden by an attempt to separate manifestations of indivisible governmental powers. . .

The present case illustrates the sterility of such an attempt. New York urges that in the use it is making of Saratoga Springs it is engaged in the disposition of its natural resources. And so it is. But in doing so it is engaged in an enterprise in which the State sells mineral waters in competition with private waters, the sale of which Congress has found necessary to tap as a source of revenue for carrying on the National Government. To say that the States cannot be taxed for enterprises generally pursued, like the sale of mineral water, because it is somewhat connected with a State's conservation policy, is to invoke an irrelevance to the federal taxing power. Liquor control by a State certainly concerns the most important of a State's natural resources—the health and well-being of its people. . . If in its wisdom a State engages in the liquor business and may be taxed by Congress as others engaged in the liquor business are taxed, so also Congress may tax the States when they go into the business of bottling water as others in the mineral water business are taxed even though a State's sale of its mineral waters has relation to its conservation policy.

In the older cases, the emphasis was on immunity from taxation. The whole tendency of recent cases reveals a shift in emphasis to that of limitation upon immunity. They also indicate an awareness of the limited role of courts in assessing the relative weight of the factors upon which immunity is based. Any implied limitation upon the supremacy of the federal power to levy a tax like that now before us, in the absence of discrimination against State activities, brings fiscal and political factors into play. The problem cannot escape issues that do not lend themselves to judgment by criteria and methods of reasoning that are within the professional training and special competence of judges. Indeed the claim of implied immunity by States from federal taxation raises questions not wholly unlike provisions of the Constitution, such as that of Art. IV, § 4, guaranteeing States a republican form of government, see *Pacific States Tel. & Tel. Co.* v. *Oregon,* 223 U.S. 118, which this Court has deemed not within its duty to adjudicate.

We have already held that by engaging in the railroad business a State cannot withdraw the railroad from the power of the federal government to regulate commerce. *United States* v. *California,* 297 U.S. 175. See also *University of Illinois* v. *United States,* 289 U.S. 48. Surely the power of Congress to lay taxes has impliedly no less a reach than the power of Congress to regulate commerce. There are, of course, State activities and State-owned property that partake of uniqueness from the point of view of intergovernmental relations. These inherently constitute a class by themselves. Only a State can own a Statehouse; only a State can get income by taxing. These could not be included for purposes of federal taxation in any abstract category of taxpayers without taxing the State as a State. But so long as Congress generally taps a source of revenue by whomsoever earned and not uniquely capable of being earned only by a State, the Constitution of the United States does not forbid it merely because its incidence falls also on a State. If Congress desires, it may of course leave untaxed enterprises pursued by States for the public good while it taxes like enterprises organized for private ends. . . If Congress makes no such differentiation and, as in this case, taxes all vendors of mineral water alike, whether State vendors or private vendors, it simply says, in effect, to a State: 'You may carry out your own notions of social policy in engaging in what is called business, but you must pay your share in having a nation which enables you to pursue your policy.' After all, the representatives of all the States, having, as the appearance of the Attorneys General of forty-six States at the bar of this Court shows, common interests, alone can pass such a taxing measure and they alone in their wisdom can grant or withhold immunity from federal taxation of such State activities.

The process of Constitutional adjudication does not thrive on conjuring up horrible possibilities that never happen in the real world and devising doctrines sufficiently comprehensive in detail to cover the remotest contingency. Nor need we go beyond what is required for a reasoned disposition of the kind of controversy now before the Court. The restriction upon States not to make laws that discriminate against interstate commerce is a vital constitutional principle, even though 'discrimination' is not a code of specifics but a continuous process of application. So we decide enough when we reject limitations upon the taxing power of Congress derived from such untenable criteria as 'proprietary' against 'governmental' activities of the States, or historically sanctioned activities of government, or activities conducted merely for profit, and find no restriction upon Congress to include the States in levying a tax exacted equally from private persons upon the same subject matter.

Judgment affirmed.

Mr. Justice Jackson took no part in the consideration or decision of this case.

[Mr. Justice Rutledge concurred in the opinion of Mr. Justice Frankfurter and in the result and read a brief opinion. Chief Justice Stone, Mr. Justice Reed, Mr. Justice Murphy and Mr. Justice Burton concurred in the result, the Chief Justice reading an opinion.]

Mr. Justice Douglas, with whom Mr. Justice Black concurs, dissenting.

I

If *South Carolina* v. *United States,* 199 U.S. 437, is to stand, the present judgment would have to be affirmed. For I agree that there is no essential difference between a federal tax on South Carolina's liquor business and a federal tax on New York's mineral water business. Whether *South Carolina* v. *United States* reaches the right result is another matter. . .

I do not believe *South Carolina* v. *United States* states the correct rule. A State's project is as much a legitimate governmental activity whether it is traditional, or akin to private enterprise, or conducted for profit. Cf. *Helvering* v. *Gerhardt,* 304 U.S. 405, 426-427. A State may deem it as essential to its economy that it own and operate a railroad, a mill, or an irrigation system as it does to own and operate bridges, street lights, or a sewage disposal plant. What might have been viewed in an earlier day as an improvident or even dangerous extension of state activities may today be deemed indispensable. But as Mr. Justice White said in his dissent in *South Carolina* v. *United States,* any activity in which a State engages within the limits of its police power is a legitimate governmental activity. Here a State is disposing of some of its natural resources. Tomorrow it may issue securities, sell power from its public power project, or manufacture fertilizer. Each is an exercise of its power of sovereignty. Must it pay the federal government for the privilege of exercising that inherent power? If the Constitution grants it immunity from a tax on the issuance of securities, on what grounds can it be forced to pay a tax when it sells power or disposes of other natural resources?

II

One view, just announced, purports to reject the distinction which *South Carolina* v. *United States* drew between those activities of a State which are and those which are not strictly governmental, usual, or traditional. But it is said that a federal tax on a State will be sustained so long as Congress 'does not attempt to tax a State because it is a State.' Yet if that means that a federal real estate tax of general application (apportioned) would be valid if applied to a power dam owned by a State but invalid if applied to a Statehouse, the old doctrine has merely been poured into a new container. If, on the other hand, any federal tax on any state activity were sustained unless it discriminated against the State, then a constitutional rule would be fashioned which would undermine the sovereignty of the States as it has been understood throughout our history. Any such change should be accomplished only by constitutional amendment. The doctrine of state immunity is too intricately involved in projects which have been launched to be whittled down by judicial fiat.

III

Woodrow Wilson stated the starting point for me when he said that 'the States of course possess every power that government has ever anywhere exercised, except only those powers which their own constitutions or the Constitution of the United States explicitly or by plain inference withhold. They are the ordinary governments of the country; the federal government is its instrument only for particular purposes.' The Supremacy Clause, Article VI, clause 2, applies to federal laws within the powers delegated to Congress by the States. But it is antagonistic to the very implications of our federal system to say that the power of Congress to lay and collect taxes, Article 1, § 8, includes the power to tax any state activity or function so long as the tax does not discriminate against the States. As stated in *United States* v. *Railroad Co.,* 17 Wall. 322, 327-328, 'The right of the States to administer their own affairs through their legislative, executive, and judicial departments, in their own manner through their own agencies, is conceded by the uniform decisions of this court and by the practice of the Federal government from its organization. This carries with it an exemption of those agencies and instruments, from the taxing power of the Federal government. If they may be taxed lightly, they may be taxed heavily; if justly, oppressively. Their operation may be impeded and may be destroyed, if any interference is permitted. . .'

A tax is a powerful, regulatory instrument. Local government in this free land does not exist for itself. The fact that local government may enter the domain of private enterprise and operate a project for profit does not put it in the class of private business enterprise for tax purposes. Local government exists to provide for the welfare of its people, not for a limited group of stockholders. If the federal government can place the local governments on its tax collector's list, their capacity to serve the needs of their citizens is at once hampered or curtailed. The field of federal excise taxation alone is practically without limits. Many state activities are in marginal enterprises where private capital refuses to venture. Add to the cost of these projects a federal tax and the social program may be destroyed before it can be launched. In any case, the repercussions of such a fundamental change on the credit of the States and on their programs to take care of the needy and to build for the future would be considerable. To say the present tax will be sustained because it does not impair the

State's functions of government is to conclude either that the sale by the State of
its mineral water is not a function of government or that the present tax is so slight
as to be no burden. The former obviously
is not true. The latter overlooks the fact
that the power to tax lightly is the power
to tax severely. The power to tax is indeed
one of the most effective forms of regulation. And no more powerful instrument
for centralization of government could be
devised. For with the federal government
immune and the States subject to tax,
the economic ability of the federal government to expand its activities at the expense
of the States is at once apparent. That is
the result whether the rule of *South Carolina* v. *United States* be perpetuated or a
new rule of discrimination be adopted. . .

The immunity of the States from federal
taxation is no less clear because it is implied. The States on entering the Union
surrendered some of their sovereignty. It
was further curtailed as various Amendments were adopted. But the Tenth
Amendment provides that 'The powers
not delegated to the United States by the
Constitution, nor prohibited by it to the
States, are reserved to the States respectively, or to the people.' The Constitution
is a compact between sovereigns. The
power of one sovereign to tax another is
an innovation so startling as to require
explicit authority if it is to be allowed.
If the power of the federal government to
tax the States is conceded, the reserved
power of the States guaranteed by the
Tenth Amendment does not give them
the independence which they have always
been assumed to have. They are relegated
to a more servile status. They become subject to interference and control both in the
functions which they exercise and the
methods which they employ. They must
pay the federal government for the privilege of exercising the powers of sovereignty guaranteed them by the Constitution, whether, as here, they are disposing
of their natural resources, or tomorrow

they issue securities or perform any other
acts within the scope of their police power.

Of course, the levying of the present tax
does not curtail the business of the state
government more than it does the like
business of the citizen. But the same might
be true in the case of many state activities
which have long been assumed to be immune from federal taxation. When a
municipality acquires a water system or
an electric power plant and transmission
facilities, it withdraws projects from the
field of private enterprise. Is the tax immunity to be denied because a tax on the
municipality would not curtail the municipality more than it would the prior private
owner? Is the municipality to be taxed
whenever it engages in an activity which
once was in the field of private enterprise
and therefore was once taxable? Every
expansion of state activity since the adoption of the Constitution limits the reach
of federal taxation if state immunity is
recognized. Yet none would concede that
the sovereign powers of the States were
limited to those which they exercised in
1787. Nor can it be said that if the present
tax is not sustained there will be withdrawn from the taxing power of the federal government a subject of taxation
which has been traditionally within that
power from the beginning. Not until
South Carolina v. *United States* was it
held that so-called business activities of a
State were subject to federal taxation.
That was after the turn of the present
century. Thus the major objection to the
suggested test is that it disregards the
Tenth Amendment, places the sovereign
States on the same plane as private citizens, and makes the sovereign States pay
the federal government for the privilege
of exercising the powers of sovereignty
guaranteed them by the Constitution.

That this idea is hostile to the view of
the Framers of the Constitution is evident
from Hamilton's discussion of the taxing
power of the federal government in the
Federalist, Nos. 30-36 (Sesquicentennial

Ed. 1937) pp. 183-224. He repeatedly stated that the taxing powers of the States and of the federal government were to be 'concurrent'—'the only admissible substitute for an entire subordination, in respect to this branch of power, of the State authority to that of the Union' (pp. 202-3). He also stated, 'The convention thought the concurrent jurisdiction preferable to that subordination; and it is evident that it has at least the merit of reconciling an indefinite constitutional power of taxation in the Federal government with an adequate and independent power in the States to provide for their own necessities' (p. 209). On such assurances could it possibly be thought that the States were so subordinate that their activities could be taxed by the federal government?

In *M'Culloch* v. *Maryland*, 4 Wheat. 316, the Court held unconstitutional a state tax on notes of the Bank of the United States. The statement of Chief Justice Marshall (pp. 429-30) is adequate to sustain the case for the reciprocal immunity of the state and federal governments:

'If we measure the power of taxation residing in a State, by the extent of sovereignty which the people of a single State possess, and can confer on its government, we have an intelligible standard, applicable to every case to which the power may be applied. We have a principle which leaves the power of taxing the people and property of a State unimpaired; which leaves to a State the command of all its resources, and which places beyond its reach, all those powers which are conferred by the people of the United States on the government of the Union, and all those means which are given for the purpose of carrying those powers into execution. We have a principle which is safe for the States, and safe for the Union. We

are relieved, as we ought to be, from clashing sovereignty; from interfering powers; from a repugnancy between a right in one government to pull down what there is an acknowledged right in another to build up; from the incompatibility of a right in one government to destroy what there is a right in another to preserve. We are not driven to the perplexing inquiry, so unfit for the judicial department, what degree of taxation is the legitimate use, and what degree may amount to the abuse of the power.'

IV

Those who agreed with *South Carolina* v. *United States* had the fear that an expanding program of state activity would dry up sources of federal revenues and thus cripple the national government. 199 U.S. pp. 454-5. That was in 1905. That fear is expressed again today when we have the federal income tax, from which employees of the States may not claim exemption on constitutional grounds. *Helvering* v. *Gerhardt, supra*. The fear of depriving the national government of revenue if the tax immunity of the States is sustained has no more place in the present decision than the spectre of socialism, the fear of which, said Holmes, 'was translated into doctrines that had no proper place in the Constitution or the common law.'

There is no showing whatsoever that an expanding field of state activity even faintly promises to cripple the federal government in its search for needed revenues. If the truth were known, I suspect it would show that the activity of the States in the fields of housing, public power and the like have increased the level of income of the people and have raised the standards of marginal or sub-marginal groups. Such conditions affect favorably, not adversely, the tax potential of the federal government.

XII

The Currency

NOTE

The constitutional interpretation of Congress's power over money and banking has led to some of the most dramatic episodes in United States history. In *McCulloch* v. *Maryland*,[1] upholding the national bank, Chief Justice Marshall gave one of his most significant opinions and introduced the doctrine of resulting and implied powers. In 1862 under the stress of War, Congress, with the reluctant advice of Salmon P. Chase, Secretary of the Treasury, passed the Legal Tender Act authorizing the issuance of treasury notes to be used in payment of public and private debts. The legality of this measure was brought to the Court in 1869 and in *Hepburn* v. *Griswold*[2] was held unconstitutional by a vote of four to three with Chase, now Chief Justice, handing down a decision against the Act which as Secretary of the Treasury he had recommended. Within fifteen months the Hepburn decision was reversed by a five to four vote in the *Legal Tender Cases*.[3]

The background of these cases aroused much popular concern and many heated and hair-splitting debates among lawyers. Discussion centered, in part, upon the accusation that President Grant had 'packed the Court.' In order to restrict the appointing power of President Johnson, Congress in 1866 exercised its control over Supreme Court membership by requiring that no vacancies in the Court be filled until the number had dropped to six. After Grant was elected this law was rescinded and the size of the Court restored to nine. When the latter law took effect in December, 1869, there were eight justices on the Court but Justice Grier, who was failing physically and mentally, was urged by his colleagues to resign. Justice Grier tendered his resignation to take effect on 1 February 1870, thus giving Grant the opportunity to make two appointments. In December the President presented to the Senate the names of Edwin M. Stanton, Secretary of War, and Ebenezer Rockwood Hoar, Attorney General. The Senate confirmed Stanton immediately but he died four days later. The Senate later rejected Mr. Hoar. Consequently when the Hepburn decision was handed down on 7 February 1870, there were still two vacancies on the Court. On the same day of this momentous decision Grant sent to the Senate the names of William Strong, lower court judge from Pennsylvania, who had already handed down a decision favoring the paper money, and Joseph P. Bradley, a 'radical' Republican highly favored by Mr. Hoar, the Attorney General. Shortly after their confirmation by the Senate, Hoar requested and was granted a reconsideration of the Legal

[1] 4 Wheat. 316 (1819). See Note, *ante*, p. 15.
[2] 8 Wall. 603 (1870).
[3] *Knox* v. *Lee* and *Parker* v. *Davis*, 12 Wall. 457 (1871).

Tender Act. In the *Legal Tender Cases* the two new appointees joined the three minority justices of the Hepburn case and by a five to four decision upheld the Legal Tender Act.

Justice Strong in the majority decision of the *Legal Tender Cases* supported the Congressional action on the theory of resulting powers and sovereign rights: 'to levy and collect taxes, to coin money and regulate its value, to raise and support armies, or to provide for and maintain a navy, are instruments for the paramount object, which was to establish a government, sovereign within its sphere, with capability of self-preservation. . .'[4] In addition to establishing the right to issue the greenbacks from this group of powers, Justice Bradley in a concurring opinion went into a more dangerous discussion that Congress holds this power as 'one of those vital and essential powers inhering in every national sovereignty and necessary to its self-preservation.'[5] This power to exercise authority not specifically delegated but merely coming from inherent rights of a sovereign has been used on a few occasions in the field of foreign relations[6] but is rarely if ever used in connection with a domestic issue.

The Court in the *Legal Tender Cases* was, as is often true, in the awkward position of trying to right what may be a legal wrong after it has been in *de facto* existence for a number of years. Chase, in explaining why he favored this measure when he was Secretary of the Treasury, argued that he had done so out of a sense of expediency at a time when constitutional limits of legislative and executive power had given way to war necessity.[7] It is possible that expediency was in the minds of the majority justices also when they considered the political and financial chaos that might result from the repudiation of legal tender that had been the basis of economic transactions for almost a decade. Justice Miller's opinion in this case is a classic presentation of the limits of the Court's authority to declare invalid measures which the legislature has found necessary to the conduct of war.

There is no provision in the Constitution which prohibits Congress from impairing the obligation of contracts, although there is such limitation on the power of the state governments.[8] In *Bronson* v. *Rodes,*[9] however, it was decided that the Legal Tender Act did not apply to private contracts which specified payment in gold. Private contracts after this decision more frequently included the gold clause

[4] *Legal Tender Cases,* 12 Wall. 457, 532-3.

[5] Ibid. 564. Justice Strong also said: 'They tend plainly to show that, in the judgment of those who adopted the Constitution, there were powers created by it, neither expressly specified nor deducible from any one specific power, or ancillary to it alone, but which grew out of the aggregate of powers conferred upon the government, or out of the sovereignty instituted.' Ibid. 535.

[6] In *Fong Yue Ting* v. *United States,* 149 U.S. 698 (1893), the Court upheld the power of Congress to exclude foreigners as essential to the rights of any sovereign nation.

[7] Warren, Charles, *The Supreme Court in United States History,* Boston, 1922, III, p. 234. It should be noted that 'it is constitutional heresy to claim that an Act unconstitutional in normal times becomes constitutional because Congress deems that an emergency exists. The reverse of this doctrine has been firmly established ever since the Civil War.' *Perry* v. *United States,* 294 U.S. 330, 335 (1935), citing among others *Ex parte Milligan,* 4 Wall. 2 (1866).

[8] *Constitution of the United States,* Art. I, § 10.

[9] 7 Wall. 229 (1869).

provision. In *Juilliard* v. *Greenman* [10] the Court held that this power to issue paper money could be used in peace time as well as war time.

Norman v. *Baltimore and Ohio Railroad Company* is one of three Gold Clause decisions handed down on 18 February 1935 concerning the legality of the money and banking legislation passed during the early days of the New Deal. A series of dramatic events after President Roosevelt's inauguration on 4 March 1933 culminated in a Congressional Joint Resolution forbidding the holding or dealing in gold by private individuals, thus giving the government a monopoly of the gold supply. The Resolution then repudiated all contracts, public or private, that called for payment in gold. Through its power to regulate currency the government depreciated the gold content of the legal tender. The contestants in the three cases sought, therefore, to get full gold value payment for their contracts which specified gold. Two of the cases involved public obligations—one a gold certificate issued by the Treasury [11] and the other a Fourth Liberty Loan bond. [12]

NORMAN v. BALTIMORE & OHIO RAILROAD CO.
294 U.S. 240 (1934)

Mr. Chief Justice Hughes delivered the opinion of the Court.

These cases present the question of the validity of the Joint Resolution of the Congress, of June 5, 1933, with respect to the 'gold clauses' of private contracts for the payment of money. 48 Stat. 112.

This Resolution . . . declares that 'every provision contained in or made with respect to any obligation which purports to give the obligee a right to require payment in gold or a particular kind of coin or currency, or in an amount in money of the United States measured thereby' is 'against public policy.' Such provisions in obligations thereafter incurred are prohibited. The Resolution provides that 'Every obligation, heretofore or hereafter incurred, whether or not any such provision is contained therein or made with respect thereto, shall be discharged upon payment, dollar for dollar, in any coin or currency which at the time of payment is legal tender for public and private debts.'

In No. 270, the suit was brought upon a coupon of a bond made by the Baltimore and Ohio Railroad Company under date of February 1, 1930, for the payment of $1,000 on February 1, 1960, and interest from date at the rate of 4½ per cent per annum, payable semi-annually. The bond provided that the payment of principal and interest 'will be made . . . in gold coin of the United States of America of or equal to the standard of weight and fineness existing on February 1, 1930.' The coupon in suit, for $22.50 was payable on February 1, 1934. The complaint alleged that on February 1, 1930, the standard weight and fineness of a gold dollar of the United States as a unit of value 'was fixed to consist of twenty-five and eight-tenths grains of gold, nine-tenths fine,' pursuant to the Act of Congress of March 14, 1900 (31 Stat. 45); and that by the Act of Congress known as the 'Gold Reserve Act of 1934' (January 30, 1934, 48 Stat. 337), and by the order of the President under that Act, the standard unit of value of a gold dollar of the United States 'was fixed to consist of fifteen and five-twenty-firsts grains of gold, nine-

---

[10] 110 U.S. 421 (1884).
[11] *Nortz* v. *United States*, 294 U.S. 317 (1935).

[12] *Perry* v. *United States*, 294 U.S. 330 (1935).

tenths fine,' from and after January 31, 1934. On presentation of the coupon, defendant refused to pay the amount in gold, or the equivalent of gold in legal tender of the United States which was alleged to be, on February 1, 1934, according to the standard of weight and fineness existing on February 1, 1930, the sum of $38.10, and plaintiff demanded judgment for that amount.

Defendant answered that by Acts of Congress, and, in particular, by the Joint Resolution of June 5, 1933, defendant had been prevented from making payment in gold coin 'or otherwise than dollar for dollar, in coin or currency of the United States (other than gold coin and gold certificates)' which at the time of payment constituted legal tender. Plaintiff, challenging the validity of the Joint Resolution under the Fifth and Tenth Amendments, and Article 1, § 1, of the Constitution of the United States, moved to strike the defense. The motion was denied. Judgment was entered for plaintiff for $22.50, the face of the coupon, and was affirmed upon appeal. The Court of Appeals of the State considered the federal question and decided that the Joint Resolution was valid. 265 N.Y. 37; 191 N.E. 726. This Court granted a writ of certiorari, October 8, 1934. . .

The Joint Resolution of June 5, 1933, was one of a series of measures relating to the currency. These measures disclose not only the purposes of the Congress but also the situations which existed at the time the Joint Resolution was adopted and when payments under the 'gold clauses' were sought. On March 6, 1933, the President, stating that there had been 'heavy and unwarranted withdrawals of gold and currency from our banking institutions for the purpose of hoarding' and 'extensive speculative activity abroad in foreign exchange' which had resulted 'in severe drains on the Nation's stocks of gold,' and reciting the authority conferred by § 5 (b) of the Act of October 6, 1917 (40 Stat.

411), declared 'a bank holiday' until March 9, 1933. On the same date, the Secretary of the Treasury, with the President's approval, issued instructions to the Treasurer of the United States to make payments in gold in any form only under license issued by the Secretary.

On March 9, 1933, the Congress passed the Emergency Banking Act. 48 Stat. 1. All orders issued by the President or the Secretary of the Treasury since March 4, 1933, under the authority conferred by § 5(b) of the Act of October 6, 1917, were confirmed. That section was amended so as to provide that during any period of national emergency declared by the President, he might 'investigate, regulate or prohibit,' by means of licenses or otherwise, 'any transactions in foreign exchange, transfers of credit between or payments by banking institutions as defined by the President, and export, hoarding, melting, or earmarking of gold or silver coin or bullion or currency, by any person within the United States or any place subject to the jurisdiction thereof.' The Act also amended § 11 of the Federal Reserve Act (39 Stat. 752) so as to authorize the Secretary of the Treasury to require all persons to deliver to the Treasurer of the United States 'any or all gold coin, gold bullion, and gold certificates' owned by them, and that the Secretary should pay therefor 'an equivalent amount of any other form of coin or currency coined or issued under the laws of the United States.' By Executive Order of March 10, 1933, the President authorized banks to be reopened, as stated, but prohibited the removal from the United States, or any place subject to its jurisdiction, of 'any gold coin, gold bullion, or gold certificates, except in accordance with regulations prescribed by or under license issued by the Secretary of the Treasury.' By further Executive Order of April 5, 1933, forbidding hoarding, all persons were required to deliver, on or before May 1, 1933, to stated banks 'all gold coin, gold bullion and gold certificates,' with certain exceptions, the holder to receive 'an equivalent amount of any other form of coin or currency coined or issued under the laws of the United States.' Another Order of April 20, 1933, contained further requirements with respect to the acquisition and export of gold and to transactions in foreign exchange.

By § 43 of the Agricultural Adjustment Act of May 12, 1933 (48 Stat. 51), it was provided that the President should have authority, upon the making of prescribed findings and in the circumstances stated, 'to fix the weight of the gold dollar in grains nine tenths fine and also to fix the weight of the silver dollar in grains nine tenths fine at a definite fixed ratio in relation to the gold dollar at such amounts as he finds necessary from his investigation to stabilize domestic prices or to protect the foreign commerce against the adverse effect of depreciated foreign currencies,' and it was further provided that the 'gold dollar, the weight of which is so fixed, shall be the standard unit of value,' and that 'all forms of money shall be maintained at a parity with this standard,' but that 'in no event shall the weight of the gold dollar be fixed so as to reduce its present weight by more than 50 per centum.'

Then followed the Joint Resolution of June 5, 1933. There were further Executive Orders of August 28 and 29, 1933, October 25, 1933, and January 12 and 15, 1934, relating to the hoarding and export of gold coin, gold bullion and gold certificates, to the sale and export of gold recovered from natural deposits, and to transactions in foreign exchange, and orders of the Secretary of the Treasury, approved by the President, on December 28, 1933, and January 15, 1934, for the delivery of gold coin, gold bullion and gold certificates to the United States Treasury.

On January 30, 1934, the Congress passed the 'Gold Reserve Act of 1934' (48 Stat. 337) which, by § 13, ratified and confirmed all the actions, regulations and orders taken or made by the President and the Secretary of the Treasury under the Act of March 9, 1933, or under § 43 of the Act of May 12, 1933, and, by § 12, with respect to the authority of the President to fix the weight of the gold dollar, provided that it should not be fixed 'in any event at more than 60 per centum of its present weight.' On January 31, 1934, the President issued his proclamation declaring that he fixed 'the weight of the gold dollar to be 15 5/21 grains nine tenths fine,' from and after that date.

We have not attempted to summarize all the provisions of these measures. We are not concerned with their wisdom. The question before the Court is one of power, not of policy. And that question touches the validity of these measures at but a single point, that is, in relation to the Joint Resolution denying effect to 'gold clauses' in existing contracts. The Resolution must, however, be considered in its legislative setting and in the light of other measures *in pari materia*.

First. The interpretation of the gold clauses in suit. In the case of the *Baltimore and Ohio Railroad Company,* the obligor considers the obligation to be one 'for the payment of money and not for the delivery of a specified number of grains or ounces of gold'; that it is an obligation payable in money of the United States and not less so because payment is to be made 'in a particular kind of money'; that it is not a 'commodity contract' which could be discharged by 'tender of bullion.' At the same time, the obligor contends that, while the Joint Resolution is constitutional in either event, the clause is a 'gold coin' and not a 'gold value' clause; that is, it does not imply 'a payment in the "equivalent" of gold in case performance by payment in gold coin is impossible.' The parties, runs the argument, intended that the instrument should be negotiable and hence it should not be regarded as one 'for the payment of an indeterminate sum ascertainable only at date of payment.' And in the reference to the standard of weight and fineness, the words 'equal to' are said to be synonymous with 'of'. . .

We are of the opinion that the gold clauses now before us were not contracts for payment in gold coin as a commodity, or in bullion, but were contracts for the payment of money. The bonds were severally for the payment of one thousand dollars. We also think that, fairly construed, these clauses were intended to afford a definite standard or measure of value, and thus to protect against a depreciation of the currency and against the discharge of the obligation by a payment of lesser value than that prescribed. When these contracts were made they were not repugnant to any action of the Congress. In order to determine whether effect may now be given to the intention of the parties in the face of the action taken by the Congress, or the contracts may be satisfied by the payment dollar for dollar, in legal tender, as the Congress has now prescribed, it is necessary to consider (1) the power of the Congress to establish a monetary system and the necessary implications of that power; (2) the power of the Congress to invalidate the provisions of existing contracts which interfere with the exercise of its constitutional authority; and (3) whether the clauses in question do constitute such an interference as to bring them within the range of that power.

Second. The power of the Congress to establish a monetary system. It is unnecessary to review the historic controversy as to the extent of this power, or again to go over the ground traversed by the Court in reaching the conclusion that the Congress may make treasury notes legal tender in payment of debts previously contracted, as well as of those subsequently contracted, whether that authority be exercised in course of war or in time of peace. *Knox* v. *Lee*, 12 Wall. 457; *Juilliard* v. *Greenman*, 110 U.S. 421. We need only consider

certain postulates upon which that conclusion rested.

The Constitution grants to the Congress power 'To coin money, regulate the value thereof, and of foreign coin.' Art. 1, § 8, par. 5. But the Court in the legal tender cases did not derive from that express grant alone the full authority of the Congress in relation to the currency. The Court found the source of that authority in all the related powers conferred upon the Congress and appropriate to achieve 'the great objects for which the government was framed,'—'a national government, with sovereign powers.' . . . The broad and comprehensive national authority over the subjects of revenue, finance and currency is derived from the aggregate of the powers granted to the Congress, embracing the powers to lay and collect taxes, to borrow money, to regulate commerce with foreign nations, and among the several States, to coin money, regulate the value thereof, and of foreign coin, and fix the standards of weights and measures, and the added express power 'to make all laws which shall be necessary and proper for carrying into execution' the other enumerated powers. *Juilliard* v. *Greenman, supra,* pp. 439, 440.

The Constitution 'was designed to provide the same currency, having a uniform legal value in all the States.' It was for that reason that the power to regulate the value of money was conferred upon the Federal government, while the same power, as well as the power to emit bills of credit, was withdrawn from the States. The States cannot declare what shall be money, or regulate its value. Whatever power there is over the currency is vested in the Congress. *Knox* v. *Lee, supra,* p. 545. . .

Moreover, by virtue of this national power, there attach to the ownership of gold and silver those limitations which public policy may require by reason of their quality as legal tender and as a medium of exchange. *Ling Su Fan* v.

United States, 218 U.S. 302, 310. Those limitations arise from the fact that the law 'gives to such coinage a value which does not attach as a mere consequence of intrinsic value.' Their quality as legal tender is attributed by the law, aside from their bullion value. Hence the power to coin money includes the power to forbid mutilation, melting and exportation of gold and silver coin,—'to prevent its outflow from the country of its origin.' *Id.,* p. 311.

Dealing with the specific question as to the effect of the legal tender acts upon contracts made before their passage, that is, those for the payment of money generally, the Court, in the legal tender cases, recognized the possible consequences of such enactments in frustrating the expected performance of contracts,—in rendering them 'fruitless or partially fruitless.' The Court pointed out that the exercise of the powers of Congress may affect 'apparent obligations' of contracts in many ways. The Congress may pass bankruptcy acts. The Congress may declare war, or, even in peace, pass non-intercourse acts, or direct an embargo, which may operate seriously upon existing contracts. And the Court reasoned that if the legal tender acts 'were justly chargeable with impairing contract obligations, they would not, for that reason, be forbidden, unless a different rule is to be applied to them from that which has hitherto prevailed in the construction of other powers granted by the fundamental law.' The conclusion was that contracts must be understood as having been made in reference to the possible exercise of the rightful authority of the Government, and that no obligation of a contract 'can extend to the defeat' of that authority. *Knox* v. *Lee, supra,* pp. 549-51.

On similar ground, the Court dismissed the contention under the Fifth Amendment forbidding the taking of private property for public use without just compensation or the deprivation of it without due process of law. . .

The question of the validity of the Joint Resolution of June 5, 1933, must be determined in the light of these settled principles.

Third. The power of the Congress to invalidate the provisions of existing contracts which interfere with the exercise of its constitutional authority. The instant cases involve contracts between private parties, but the question necessarily relates as well to the contracts or obligations of States and municipalities, or of their political subdivisions, that is, to such engagements as are within the reach of the applicable national power. The Government's own contracts—the obligations of the United States—are in a distinct category and demand separate consideration. See *Perry* v. *United States,* decided this day, *post,* p. 330.

The contention is that the power of Congress, broadly sustained by the decisions we have cited in relation to private contracts for the payment of money generally, does not extend to the striking down of express contracts for gold payments. The acts before the Court in the legal tender cases, as we have seen, were not deemed to go so far. Those acts left in circulation two kinds of money, both lawful and available, and contracts for payments in gold, one of these kinds, were not disturbed. The Court did not decide that the Congress did not have the constitutional power to invalidate existing contracts of that sort, if they stood in the way of the execution of the policy of Congress in relation to the currency. . .

Here, the Congress has enacted an express interdiction. The argument against it does not rest upon the mere fact that the legislation may cause hardship or loss. Creditors who have not stipulated for gold payments may suffer equal hardship or loss with creditors who have so stipulated. The former, admittedly, have no constitutional grievance. And, while the latter may not suffer more, the point is pressed that their express stipulations for gold payments constitute property, and that creditors who have not such stipulations are without that property right. And the contestants urge that the Congress is seeking not to regulate the currency, but to regulate contracts, and thus has stepped beyond the power conferred.

This argument is in the teeth of another established principle. Contracts, however express, cannot fetter the constitutional authority of the Congress. Contracts may create rights of property, but when contracts deal with a subject matter which lies within the control of the Congress, they have a congenital infirmity. Parties cannot remove their transactions from the reach of dominant constitutional power by making contracts about them. See *Hudson Water Co.* v. *McCarter,* 209 U.S. 349, 357.

This principle has familiar illustration in the exercise of the power to regulate commerce. If shippers and carriers stipulate for specified rates, although the rates may be lawful when the contracts are made, if Congress through the Interstate Commerce Commission exercises its authority and prescribes different rates, the latter control and override inconsistent stipulations in contracts previously made. . .

The same reasoning applies to the constitutional authority of the Congress to regulate the currency and to establish the monetary system of the country. If the gold clauses now before us interfere with the policy of the Congress in the exercise of that authority they cannot stand.

Fourth. The effect of the gold clauses in suit in relation to the monetary policy adopted by the Congress. Despite the wide range of the discussion at the bar and the earnestness with which the arguments against the validity of the Joint Resolution have been pressed, these contentions necessarily are brought, under the dominant principles to which we have referred, to a single and narrow point. That point is whether the gold clauses do constitute an actual interference with the monetary policy of the Congress in the light of its broad power to determine that policy. Whether they may be deemed to be such

an interference depends upon an appraisement of economic conditions and upon determinations of questions of fact. With respect to those conditions and determinations, the Congress is entitled to its own judgment. We may inquire whether its action is arbitrary or capricious, that is, whether it has reasonable relation to a legitimate end. If it is an appropriate means to such an end, the decisions of the Congress as to the degree of the necessity for the adoption of that means, is final. *McCulloch* v. *Maryland, supra,* pp. 421, 423; *Juilliard* v. *Greenman, supra,* p. 450; *Stafford* v. *Wallace,* 258 U.S. 495, 521; *Everard's Breweries* v. *Day,* 265 U.S. 545, 559, 562.

The Committee on Banking and Currency of the House of Representatives stated in its report recommending favorable action upon the Joint Resolution (H.R. Rep. No. 169, 73d Cong., 1st Sess.):

'The occasion for the declaration in the resolution that the gold clauses are contrary to public policy arises out of the experiences of the present emergency. These gold clauses render ineffective the power of the Government to create a currency and determine the value thereof. If the gold clause applied to a very limited number of contracts and security issues, it would be a matter of no particular consequence, but in this country virtually all obligations, almost as a matter of routine, contain the gold clause. In the light of this situation two phenomena which have developed during the present emergency make the enforcement of the gold clauses incompatible with the public interest. The first is the tendency which has developed internally to hoard gold; the second is the tendency for capital to leave the country. Under these circumstances no currency system, whether based upon gold or upon any other foundation, can meet the requirements of a situation in which many billions of dollars of securities are expressed in a particular form of the circulating medium, particularly when it is the medium upon which the entire credit and currency structure rests.'

And the Joint Resolution itself recites the determination of the Congress in these words:

'Whereas the existing emergency has disclosed that provisions of obligations which purport to give the obligee a right to require payment in gold or a particular kind of coin or currency of the United States, or in an amount in money of the United States measured thereby, obstruct the power of the Congress to regulate the value of the money of the United States, and are inconsistent with the declared policy of the Congress to maintain at all times the equal power of every dollar, coined or issued by the United States, in the markets and in the payment of debts.'

Can we say that this determination is so destitute of basis that the interdiction of the gold clauses must be deemed to be without any reasonable relation to the monetary policy adopted by the Congress? . . .

The devaluation of the dollar placed the domestic economy upon a new basis. In the currency as thus provided, States and municipalities must receive their taxes; railroads, their rates and fares; public utilities, their charges for services. The income out of which they must meet their obligations is determined by the new standard. Yet, according to the contentions before us, while that income is thus controlled by law, their indebtedness on their 'gold bonds' must be met by an amount of currency determined by the former gold standard. Their receipts, in this view, would be fixed on one basis; their interest charges, and the principal of their obligations, on another. It is common knowledge that the bonds issued by these obligors have generally contained gold clauses, and presumably they account for a large part of the outstanding obligations of that sort. It is also common knowledge that a similar situation exists with respect to numerous industrial corporations that have is-

sued their 'gold bonds' and must now receive payments for their products in the existing currency. It requires no acute analysis or profound economic inquiry to disclose the dislocation of the domestic economy which would be caused by such a disparity of conditions in which, it is insisted, those debtors under gold clauses should be required to pay one dollar and sixty-nine cents in currency while respectively receiving their taxes, rates, charges and prices on the basis of one dollar of that currency.

We are not concerned with consequences, in the sense that consequences, however serious, may excuse an invasion of constitutional right. We are concerned with the constitutional power of the Congress over the monetary system of the country and its attempted frustration. Exercising that power, the Congress has undertaken to establish a uniform currency, and parity between kinds of currency, and to make that currency, dollar for dollar, legal tender for the payment of debts. In the light of abundant experience, the Congress was entitled to choose such a uniform monetary system, and to reject a dual system, with respect to all obligations within the range of the exercise of its constitutional authority. The contention that these gold clauses are valid contracts and cannot be struck down proceeds upon the assumption that private parties, and States and municipalities, may make and enforce contracts which may limit that authority. Dismissing that untenable assumption, the facts must be faced. We think that it is clearly shown that these clauses interfere with the exertion of the power granted to the Congress and certainly it is not established that the Congress arbitrarily or capriciously decided that such an interference existed.

The judgment and decree, severally under review, are affirmed. . .

Mr. Justice McReynolds, Mr. Justice Van Devanter, Mr. Justice Sutherland, and Mr. Justice Butler dissent. . .

XIII

Interstate Commerce

NOTE

The commerce clause was first interpreted by the Supreme Court in 1824 in *Gibbons* v. *Ogden*. This is the parent decision of a great mass of subsequent decisions justifying federal control on the basis of the commerce power.

Under the Articles of Confederation, each state tended to further its own prosperity at the expense of other states. 'Any state,' says Farrand, 'which enjoyed superior conditions to a neighboring state was only too apt to take advantage of that fact. Some of the states, as James Madison described it, "having no convenient ports for foreign commerce, were subject to be taxed by their neighbors, through whose ports their commerce was carried on. New Jersey, placed between Philadelphia and New York, was likened to a cask tapped at both ends; and North Carolina, between Virginia and South Carolina, to a patient bleeding at both arms." The Americans were an agricultural and a trading people. Interference with the arteries of commerce was cutting off the very life-blood of the nation, and something had to be done. The articles of confederation provided no remedy. . .'[1] The gentlemen who met in Philadelphia in the summer of 1787, however, were resourceful. In an effort to improve interstate trade relations, to ensure the development of improved arteries of commerce, to provide a larger market for the products of farm and what little industry there was, the Congress was empowered in the Constitution 'to regulate commerce . . . among the several states. . .'

Towards the end of the 18th century, Robert R. Livingston of New York became interested in the development of a vessel propelled by steam. In 1798, he prevailed upon the New York Legislature to grant to him the exclusive right for twenty years to operate steam vessels on the waters of the State, provided that within a year he could produce a steam vessel whose progress should not be less than four miles an hour against the current of the Hudson.[2] Not meeting the requirement of the proviso, Livingston secured a renewal of the grant. Though the vessel was not built, the legislature continued to renew the grant. In the meantime, Livingston had met Robert Fulton. Impressed with the latter's achievements in developing a steam-propelled vessel, Livingston and Fulton formed a partnership.

In 1803, the legislature granted monopoly privileges to Livingston and Fulton.[3] Again the grant lapsed and again it was renewed. Finally, on 17 April 1807, their vessel successfully made the run from New York to Albany.

[1] Farrand, Max, *The Framing of the Constitution of the United States,* New Haven, 1926, p. 7.
[2] Act of 27 March, Laws of New York, 21st sess., chap. 55.
[3] Act of 5 April, Laws of New York, 26th sess., chap. 94.

The New York legislature on 11 April 1808 passed an act which provided that 'whenever Robert R. Livingston and Robert Fulton, and such persons as they may associate with them, shall establish one, or more steam-boats or vessels, other than that already established, they shall, for each and every additional boat, be entitled to five years prolongation of their grant or contract with this state: *Provided nevertheless,* That the whole term of their exclusive privileges shall not exceed thirty years, after the passage of this act.'[4] The act provided further 'That no person or persons, without the license of . . . ,' Livingston and Fulton, 'shall set in motion, or navigate upon the waters of this state . . . any boat or vessel moved by steam or fire. . .'[5]

Aaron Ogden purchased from the monopoly the right to operate steam ferry boats from New York to various points on the New Jersey shore. Ogden combined with Thomas Gibbons who operated a steam vessel between New Jersey landings. The combination provided only for the exchange of passengers at Elizabethtown Point in New Jersey; but, in a sense, Gibbons was carrying passengers from New York to points in New Jersey not served by Ogden directly. This practice was considered a violation of the right purchased by Ogden from the monopoly, and the latter sought an injunction against Ogden and Gibbons. In the Court of Chancery Ogden declared that his license applied only to the waters of New York and had no application to the waters of New Jersey. Gibbons argued that he operated under a coasting license procured from the Federal government in accord with an act of Congress.[6] He denied that the monopoly had the exclusive privilege of running steam vessels between New York and New Jersey. The Court of Chancery declared that by act of 6 April 1808 New York had asserted jurisdiction over the whole Hudson River. 'I shall therefore deny the motion,' said Chancellor James Kent, 'as against the defendant Ogden, who navigates his boat under authority from the plaintiff, and who does not appear, in any instance, to have exceeded that authority; and I shall grant the motion, as against the defendant Gibbons, so far only as to enjoin him from navigating the waters in the Bay of New York or Hudson River between Staten Island and Powles Hook.'[7]

Gibbons, thereupon, began to run steam vessels regularly between New York and New Jersey, in competition with Ogden. The latter sued for an injunction to restrain his former partner. Gibbons in defense asserted his right to run his

[4] Laws of New York, 31st sess., chap. 225.

[5] Ibid. Not content with monopoly privileges in New York, Livingston and Fulton placed steam vessels on the Mississippi, and in 1811, procured a monopoly from the territorial legislature of Orleans; thus, the most important artery of trade in middle America came under the control of Livingston and Fulton. And the monopoly virus spread. Samuel Howard of Savannah was granted exclusive rights to transport merchandise upon Georgia waters in all vessels propelled by steam. Massachusetts by act of February 1815 granted similar privileges to Langdon Sullivan. New Hampshire provided the same accommodation to the same Sullivan. Vermont, also, granted navigation privileges in that part of Lake Champlain which came under her jurisdiction to a monopoly. Such conditions were hardly conducive to a free flow of interstate commerce. See Beveridge, Albert J., *The Life of John Marshall*, Boston, 1929, IV, pp. 414-15.

[6] 1 Stat. 305-18 (1793).

[7] *Livingston* v. *Ogden and Gibbons*, 4 Johnson's Chancery Reports, 48, 52-53 (1819).

vessels between the two states on the ground that he was licensed to do so by the Federal Government. 'The Act of Congress (passed 18 Feb. 1793, chap. 8),' declared Kent, 'referred to in the answer, provides for the enrolling and licensing ships and vessels to be employed in the coasting trade and fisheries. Without being enrolled and licensed, they are not entitled to the privileges of American vessels, but must pay the same fees and tonnage as foreign vessels; and if they have on board articles of foreign growth and manufacture, or distilled spirits, they are liable to forfeiture. I do not perceive that this Act confers any right incompatible with an exclusive right in Livingston and Fulton to navigate steamboats upon the waters of this State. . .'[8]

Gibbons then appealed to the highest court in the state, the Court for the Trial of Impeachments and the Correction of Errors. This court rejected the arguments of Gibbons and affirmed the decree of the Court of Chancery.[9] Gibbons then appealed to the Supreme Court of the United States.

'[A]re these laws [granting monopoly privileges to Livingston and Fulton],' queried Daniel Webster as counsel for Gibbons, 'such as the legislature of New York had a right to pass? If so, do they, secondly, in their operation, interfere with any right enjoyed under the constitution and laws of the United States, and are they, therefore, void, as far as such interference extends?'

GIBBONS v. OGDEN
9 Wheaton 1 (1824)

MARSHALL, C. J., delivered the opinion of the Court.

The appellant contends that this decree is erroneous, because the laws which purport to give the exclusive privilege it sustains, are repugnant to the constitution and laws of the United States.

They are said to be repugnant:

1st. To that clause in the constitution which authorizes Congress to regulate commerce. . .

As preliminary to the very able discussions of the constitution, which we have heard from the bar, and as having some influence on its construction, reference has been made to the political situation of these states, anterior to its formation. It has been said, that they were sovereign, were completely independent, and were connected with each other only by a league. This is true. But when these allied sovereigns converted their league into a government, when they converted their congress of ambassadors, deputed to deliberate on their common concerns, and to recommend measures of general utility, into a legislature, empowered to enact laws on the most interesting subjects, the whole character in which the states appear, underwent a change, the extent of which must be determined by a fair consideration of the instrument by which that change was effected.

This instrument contains an enumeration of powers expressly granted by the people to their government. It has been said, that these powers ought to be construed strictly. But why ought they to be so construed? Is there one sentence in the constitution which gives countenance to this rule? In the last of the enumerated powers, that which grants, expressly, the

[8] *Ogden* v. *Gibbons*, 4 Johnson's Chancery Reports, 150, 156 (1819).
[9] *Gibbons* v. *Ogden*, 17 Johnson's Chancery Reports (Court of Errors), 488 (1820).

means for carrying all others into execution, congress is authorized 'to make all laws which shall be necessary and proper' for the purpose. But this limitation on the means which may be used, is not extended to the powers which are conferred; nor is there one sentence in the constitution which has been pointed out by the gentlemen of the bar, or which we have been able to discern, that prescribes this rule. We do not, therefore, think ourselves justified in adopting it. . . If, from the imperfection of human language, there should be serious doubts respecting the extent of any given power, it is a well-settled rule that the objects for which it was given, especially, when those objects are expressed in the instrument itself, should have great influence in the construction. We know of no reason for excluding this rule from the present case. . .

The words are, 'congress shall have power to regulate commerce with foreign nations, and among the several states, and with the Indian tribes.' The subject to be regulated is commerce; and our constitution being, as was aptly said at the bar, one of enumeration, and not of definition, to ascertain the extent of the power, it becomes necessary to settle the meaning of the word. The counsel for the appellee would limit it to traffic, to buying and selling, or the interchange of commodities, and do not admit that it comprehends navigation. This would restrict a general term, applicable to many objects, to one of its significations. Commerce, undoubtedly, is traffic, but it is something more—it is intercourse. It describes the commercial intercourse between nations, and parts of nations, in all its branches, and is regulated by prescribing rules for carrying on that intercourse. The mind can scarcely conceive a system for regulating commerce between nations, which shall exclude all laws concerning navigation, which shall be silent on the admission of the vessels of the one nation into the ports of the other, and be confined to prescribing rules for the conduct of individuals, in the actual employment of buying and selling, or of barter. If commerce does not include navigation, the government of the Union has no direct power over that subject, and can make no law prescribing what shall constitute American vessels, or requiring that they shall be navigated by American seamen. Yet this power has been exercised from the commencement of the government, has been exercised with the consent of all, and has been understood by all to be a commercial regulation. All America understands, and has uniformly understood, the word 'commerce' to comprehend navigation. It was so understood, and must have been so understood, when the constitution was framed. The power over commerce, including navigation, was one of the primary objects for which the people of America adopted their government, and must have been contemplated in forming it. The convention must have used the word in that sense, because all have understood it in that sense; and the attempt to restrict it comes too late.

If the opinion that 'commerce' as the word is used in the constitution, comprehends navigation also, requires any additional confirmation, that additional confirmation is, we think, furnished by the words of the instrument itself. It is a rule of construction, acknowledged by all, that the exceptions from a power mark its extent; for it would be absurd, as well as useless, to except from a granted power, that which was not granted—that which the words of the grant could not comprehend, if, then, there are in the constitution plain exceptions from the power over navigation, plain inhibitions to the exercise of that power in a particular way, it is a proof that those who made these exceptions, and prescribed these inhibitions, understood the power to which they applied as being granted. The 9th section of the last [1] article declares that 'no preference

[1] Editors' note: This is an error; the *first* Article was intended.

shall be given, by any regulation of commerce or revenue, to the ports of one state over those of another.' This clause cannot be understood as applicable to those laws only which are passed for the purposes of revenue, because it is expressly applied to commercial regulations; and the most obvious preference which can be given to one port over another, in regulating commerce, relates to navigation. But the subsequent part of the sentence is still more explicit. It is, 'nor shall vessels bound to or from one state, be obliged to enter, clear, or pay duties in another.' These words have a direct reference to navigation.

The universally acknowledged power of the government to impose embargoes, must also be considered as showing, that all America is united in that construction which comprehends navigation in the word commerce. Gentlemen have said, in argument, that this is a branch of the war-making power, and that an embargo is an instrument of war, not a regulation of trade. That it may be, and often is, used as an instrument of war, cannot be denied. An embargo may be imposed, for the purpose of facilitating the equipment or manning of a fleet, or for the purpose of concealing the progress of an expedition preparing to sail from a particular port. In these, and in similar cases, it is a military instrument, and partakes of the nature of war. But all embargoes are not of this description. They are sometimes resorted to, without a view to war, and with a single view to commerce. In such case, an embargo is no more a war measure, than a merchantman is a ship of war, because both are vessels which navigate the ocean with sails and seamen. . .

The word used in the constitution, then, comprehends, and has been always understood to comprehend, navigation within its meaning; and a power to regulate navigation, is as expressly granted, as if that term had been added to the word 'commerce.' To what commerce does this power extend? The constitution informs us, to commerce 'with foreign nations, and among the several states, and with the Indian tribes.' It has, we believe, been universally admitted, that these words comprehend every species of commercial intercourse between the United States and foreign nations. No sort of trade can be carried on between this country and any other, to which this power does not extend. It has been truly said, that commerce, as the word is used in the constitution, is a unit, every part of which is indicated by the term.

If this be the admitted meaning of the word, in its application to foreign nations, it must carry the same meaning throughout the sentence, and remain a unit, unless there be some plain intelligible cause which alters it. The subject to which the power is next applied, is to commerce, 'among the several states.' The word 'among' means intermingled with. A thing which is among others, is intermingled with them. Commerce among the states, cannot stop at the external boundary line of each state, but may be introduced into the interior. It is not intended to say, that these words comprehend that commerce, which is completely internal, which is carried on between man and man in a state, or between different parts of the same state, and which does not extend to or affect other states. Such a power would be inconvenient, and is certainly unnecessary. Comprehensive as the word 'among' is, it may very properly be restricted to that commerce which concerns more states than one. The phrase is not one which would probably have been selected to indicate the completely interior traffic of a state, because it is not an apt phrase for that purpose; and the enumeration of the particular classes of commerce to which the power was to be extended, would not have been made, had the intention been to extend the power to every description. The enumeration presupposes something not enumerated; and that something, if we regard the language or the subject of the sentence, must be the exclusively internal commerce of a state. The genius and character of the whole government seem to be, that its action is to be applied to all the external concerns of the nation, and to those internal concerns which affect the states generally; but not to those which are completely within a particular state, which do not affect other states, and with which it is not necessary to interfere, for the purpose of executing some of the general powers of the government. The completely internal commerce of a state, then, may be considered as reserved for the state itself.

But in regulating commerce with foreign nations, the power of congress does not stop at the jurisdictional lines of the several states. It would be a very useless power, if it could not pass those lines. The commerce of the United States with foreign nations, is that of the whole United States; every district has a right to participate in it. The deep streams which penetrate our country in every direction, pass through the interior of almost every state in the Union, and furnish the means of exercising this right. If congress has the power to regulate it, that power must be exercised whenever the subject exists. If it exists within the states, if a foreign voyage may commence or terminate at a port within a state, then the power of congress may be exercised within a state. . .

We are now arrived at the inquiry— what is this power? It is the power to regulate; that is, to prescribe the rule by which commerce is to be governed. This power, like all others vested in congress, is complete in itself, may be exercised to its utmost extent, and acknowledges no limitations, other than are prescribed in the constitution. These are expressed in plain terms, and do not affect the questions which arise in this case, or which have

been discussed at the bar. If, as has always been understood, the sovereignty of congress, though limited to specified objects, is plenary as to those objects, the power over commerce with foreign nations, and among the several states, is vested in congress as absolutely as it would be in a single government, having in its constitution the same restrictions on the exercise of the power as are found in the constitution of the United States. . .

But it has been urged, with great earnestness, that although the power of congress to regulate commerce with foreign nations, and among the several states, be co-extensive with the subject itself, and have no other limits than are prescribed in the constitution, yet the states may severally exercise the same power, within their respective jurisdictions. In support of this argument, it is said, that they possessed it as an inseparable attribute of sovereignty, before the formation of the constitution, and still retain it, except so far as they have surrendered it by that instrument; that this principle results from the nature of the government, and is secured by the tenth amendment; that an affirmative grant of power is not exclusive, unless in its own nature it be such that the continued exercise of it by the former possessor is inconsistent with the grant, and that this is not of that description. The appellant, conceding these postulates, except the last, contends, that full power to regulate a particular subject, implies the whole power, and leaves no residuum; that a grant of the whole is incompatible with the existence of a right in another to any part of it. Both parties have appealed to the constitution, to legislative acts, and judicial decisions; and have drawn arguments from all these sources, to support and illustrate the propositions they respectively maintain.

The grant of the power to lay and collect taxes is, like the power to regulate commerce, made in general terms, and has never been understood to interfere with the exercise of the same power by the states; and hence has been drawn an argument which has been applied to the question under consideration. But the two grants are not, it is conceived, similar in their terms or their nature. Although many of the powers formerly exercised by the states, are transferred to the government of the Union, yet the state governments remain, and constitute a most important part of our system. The power of taxation is indispensable to their existence, and is a power which, in its own nature, is capable of residing in, and being exercised by, different authorities, at the same time. . . When, then, each government exercises the power of taxation, neither is exercising the power of the other. But when a state proceeds to regulate commerce with foreign nations, or among the several states, it is exercising the very power that is granted to congress, and is doing the very thing which congress is authorized to do. There is no analogy, then, between the power of taxation and the power of regulating commerce.

In discussing the question, whether this power is still in the states, in the case under consideration, we may dismiss from it the inquiry, whether it is surrendered by the mere grant to congress, or is retained until congress shall exercise the power. We may dismiss that inquiry, because it has been exercised, and the regulations which congress deemed it proper to make, are now in full operation. The sole question is, can a state regulate commerce with foreign nations and among the states, while congress is regulating it?

The counsel for the respondent answer this question in the affirmative, and rely very much on the restrictions in the 10th section, as supporting their opinion. They say, very truly, that limitations of a power furnish a strong argument in favor of the existence of that power, and that the section which prohibits the states from laying duties on imports or exports, proves that this power might have been exercised, had it not been expressly forbidden; and, consequently, that any other commercial regulation, not expressly forbidden, to which the original power of the state was competent, may still be made. That this restriction shows the opinion of the convention, that a state might impose duties on exports and imports, if not expressly forbidden, will be conceded; but that it follows, as a consequence, from this concession, that a state may regulate commerce with foreign nations and among the states, cannot be admitted.

We must first determine, whether the act of laying 'duties or imposts on imports or exports' is considered, in the constitution as a branch of the taxing power, or of the power to regulate commerce. We think it very clear, that it is considered as a branch of the taxing power. It is so treated in the first clause of the 8th section: 'Congress shall have power to lay and collect taxes, duties, imposts and excises'; and before commerce is mentioned, the rule by which the exercise of this power must be governed, is declared. It is, that all duties, imposts and excises shall be uniform. In a separate clause of the enumeration, the power to regulate commerce is given, as being entirely distinct from the right to levy taxes and imposts, and as being a new power, not before conferred. The constitution, then, considers these powers as substantive, and distinct from each other; and so places them in the enumeration it contains. The power of imposing duties on imports is classed with the power to levy taxes, and that seems to be its natural place. But the power to levy taxes could never be considered as abridging the right of the states on that subject; and they might, consequently, have exercised it, by levying duties on imports or exports, had the constitution contained no prohibition on this subject. This prohibition, then, is an exception from the acknowledged power of the states to levy taxes, not from the questionable power to regulate commerce. . .

These restrictions, then, are on the taxing power, not on that to regulate commerce; and presuppose the existence of that which they restrain, not of that which they do not purport to restrain.

But the inspection laws are said to be regulations of commerce, and are certainly recognized in the constitution, as being passed in the exercise of a power remaining with the states. That inspection laws may have a remote and considerable influence on commerce, will not be denied; but that a power to regulate commerce is the source from which the right to pass them is derived, cannot be admitted. The object of inspection laws, is to improve the quality of articles produced by the labor of a country; to fit them for exportation; or, it may be, for domestic use. They act upon the subject, before it becomes an article of foreign commerce, or of commerce among the states, and prepare it for that purpose. They form a portion of that immense mass of legislation which embraces everything within the territory of a state, not surrendered to the general government; all which can be most advantageously exercised by the states themselves. Inspection laws, quarantine laws, health laws of every description, as well as laws for regulating the internal commerce of a state, and those which respect turnpike-roads, ferries, etc. are component parts of this mass.

No direct general power over these objects is granted to congress; and, consequently, they remain subject to state legislation. If the legislative power of the Union can reach them, it must be for national purposes; it must be, where the power is expressly given for a special purpose, or is clearly incidental to some power which is expressly given. It is obvious, that the government of the Union, in the exercise of its express powers, that, for example, of regulating commerce with foreign nations and among the states, may use means that may also be employed by a state, in the exercise of its acknowledged powers; that, for example, of regulating commerce within the state. If congress license vessels to sail from one port to another, in the same state, the act is supposed to be, necessarily, incidental to the power expressly granted to congress, and implies no claim of a direct power to regulate the purely internal commerce of a state, or to act directly on its system of police. So, if a state, in passing laws on subjects acknowledged to be within its control, and with a view to those subjects, shall adopt a measure of the same character with one which congress may adopt, it does not derive its authority from the particular power which has been granted, but from some other, which remains with the state, and may be executed by the same means. All experience shows, that the same measures, or measures scarcely distinguishable from each other, may flow from distinct powers; but this does not prove that the powers themselves are identical. Although the means used in their execution may sometimes approach each other so nearly as to be confounded, there are other situations in which they are sufficiently distinct, to establish their individuality.

In our complex system, presenting the rare and difficult scheme of one general government, whose action extends over the whole, but which possesses only certain enumerated powers; and of numerous state governments, which retain and exercise all powers not delegated to the Union, contests respecting power must arise. Were it even otherwise, the measures taken by the respective governments to execute their acknowledged powers, would often be of the same description, and might, sometimes, interfere. This, however, does not prove that the one is exercising, or has a right to exercise, the powers of the other.

The acts of congress, passed in 1796 and 1799 (1 U.S. Stat. 474, 619), empowering and directing the officers of the general government to conform to, and assist in the execution of the quarantine and health laws of a state, proceed, it is said, upon the idea that these laws are constitutional. It is undoubtedly true, that they do proceed upon that idea; and the constitutionality of such laws has never, so far we are informed, been denied. But they do not imply an acknowledgment that a state may rightfully regulate commerce with foreign nations, or among the states; for they do not imply that such laws are an exercise of that power, or enacted with a view to it. On the contrary, they are treated as quarantine and health laws, are so denominated in the acts of congress, and are considered as flowing from the acknowledged power of a state, to provide for the health of its citizens. But as it was apparent, that some of the provisions made for this purpose, and in virtue of this power, might interfere with, and be affected by the laws of the United States, made for the regulation of commerce, congress, in that spirit of harmony and conciliation which ought always to characterize the conduct of governments standing in the relation which that of the Union and those of the states bear to each other, has directed its officers to aid in the execution of these laws; and has, in some measure, adapted its own legislation to this object, by making provisions in aid of those of the states. But in making these provisions, the opinion is unequivocably manifested, that congress may control the state laws, so far as it may be necessary to control them, for the regulation of commerce. . .

It has been said, that the act of August 7th, 1789, acknowledges a concurrent power in the states to regulate the conduct of pilots, and hence is inferred an admission of their concurrent right with congress to regulate commerce with foreign nations, and amongst the states. But this inference is not, we think, justified by the fact. Although congress cannot enable a state to legislate, congress may adopt the provisions of a state on any subject. When the government of the Union was brought into existence, it found a system for the

regulation of its pilots in full force in every state. The act which has been mentioned, adopts this system, and gives it the same validity as if its provisions had been specially made by congress. But the act, it may be said, is prospective also, and the adoption of laws to be made in future, presupposes the right in the maker to legislate on the subject. The act unquestionably manifests an intention to leave this subject entirely to the states, until congress should think proper to interpose; but the very enactment of such a law indicates an opinion that it was necessary; that the existing system would not be applicable to the new state of things, unless expressly applied to it by congress. But this section is confined to pilots within the 'bays, inlets, rivers, harbors and ports of the United States,' which are, of course, in whole or in part, also within the limits of some particular state. The acknowledged power of a state to regulate its police, its domestic trade, and to govern its own citizens, may enable it to legislate on this subject, to a considerable extent; and the adoption of its system by congress, and the application of it to the whole subject of commerce, does not seem to the court to imply a right in the states so to apply it of their own authority. But the adoption of the state system being temporary, being only 'until further legislative provision shall be made by congress,' shows, conclusively, an opinion that congress could control the whole subject, and might adopt the system of the states, or provide one of its own. . .

It has been contended by the counsel for the appellant, that, as the word 'to regulate' implies in its nature, full power over the thing to be regulated, it excludes, necessarily, the action of all others that would perform the same operation on the same thing. That regulation is designed for the entire result, applying to those parts which remain as they were, as well as to those which are altered. It produces a uniform whole, which is as much disturbed and deranged by changing what the regulating power designs to leave untouched, as that on which it has operated. There is great force in this argument, and the court is not satisfied that it has been refuted.

Since, however, in exercising the power of regulating their own purely internal affairs, whether of trading or police, the states may sometimes enact laws, the validity of which depends on their interfering with, and being contrary to, an act of congress passed in pursuance of the constitution, the court will enter upon the inquiry, whether the laws of New York, as expounded by the highest tribunal of that state, have, in their application to this case, come into collision with an act of congress, and deprived a citizen of a right to which that act entitles him. Should this collision exist, it will be immaterial, whether those laws were passed in virtue of a concurrent power 'to regulate commerce with foreign nations and among the several states,' or, in virtue of a power to regulate their domestic trade and police. In one case and the other, the acts of New York must yield to the law of congress; and the decision sustaining the privilege they confer, against a right given by a law of the Union, must be erroneous. . .

In pursuing this inquiry at the bar, it has been said, that the constitution does not confer the right of intercourse between state and state. That right derives its source from those laws whose authority is acknowledged by civilized man through-out the world. This is true. The constitution found it an existing right, and gave to congress the power to regulate it. In the exercise of this power, congress has passed 'an act for enrolling or licensing ships or vessels to be employed in the coasting trade and fisheries, and for regulating the same.' The counsel for the respondent contend, that this act does not give the right to sail from port to port, but confines itself to regulating a preexisting right, so far only as to confer certain privileges on enrolled and licensed vessels in its exercise. . . This act demonstrates the opinion of congress, that steamboats may be enrolled and licensed, in common with vessels using sails. They are, of course, entitled to the same privileges, and can no more be restrained from navigating waters, and entering ports which are free to such vessels, than if they were wafted on their voyage by the winds, instead of being propelled by the agency of fire. The one element may be as legitimately used as the other, for every commercial purpose authorized by the laws of the Union; and the act of a state inhibiting the use of either, to any vessel having a license under the act of congress, comes, we think, in direct collision with that act. . .

Reversed.

[MR. JUSTICE JOHNSON wrote a concurring opinion.]

NOTE

The case which follows provides an example of the use of the commerce clause to restrict the powers of the state. It is in the field of commerce, particularly, that the Supreme Court, in a quasi-arbitral role, endeavors to balance national and state interests. This is clear if *Baldwin* v. *Seelig* and *Parker* v. *Brown* [1] are compared.

The Seelig Company of New York purchased milk in Vermont; the milk was shipped to New York in cans, a small quantity of which was sold in bottles, and the remainder sold to hotels, restaurants, and stores in the original containers. Seelig refused to pay the Vermont producers the minimum price established for New York producers by the New York Milk Control Board acting in accordance with law. As a consequence, the Milk Board refused to license Seelig's business. Seelig sought an injunction in a Federal District Court to restrain the enforcement of the statute, alleging its unconstitutionality under the commerce clause. The District Court granted a decree in Seelig's favor concerning the milk sold in the original container, but denied relief in regard to milk sold in bottles. Both parties then appealed to the Supreme Court: Baldwin, Commissioner of Agriculture and Markets, sought a reversal of the District Court's decision regarding milk sold in the original cans; Seelig sought a reversal of the lower court's refusal to issue an injunction restraining enforcement of the act in regard to milk sold in bottles. This controversy raised the question of the original package doctrine.

The Constitution provides that Congress shall have power to regulate commerce among the several states and foreign commerce. The Supreme Court interpreted the words 'commerce,' 'commerce among the several states,' and 'to regulate,' in the early case of *Gibbons* v. *Ogden*.[2] The question was bound to arise, however, concerning the point at which interstate commerce passed over into intrastate commerce; in other words, when did interstate commerce end and thus permit state regulation or taxation?

Chief Justice Marshall answered the question partially in *Brown* v. *Maryland*,[3] with his statement of what came to be called the original package doctrine. This case did not involve interstate commerce but foreign commerce. A Maryland statute forbade, without a license from the State, the wholesale disposal of goods imported from foreign countries. The Court held the State statute to be unconstitutional, first, because it conflicted with the power of Congress to regulate foreign commerce; and second, because it violated that clause of the Constitu-

---

[1] 317 U.S. 341 (1943). See *post*, p. 198. [3] 12 Wheat. 419 (1827).
[2] See *ante*, p. 181.

tion which prohibits the states from taxing imports without the consent of Congress. In the course of his opinion, Chief Justice Marshall said: 'When the importer has so acted upon the thing imported, that it has become incorporated and mixed up with the mass of property in the country, it has, perhaps, lost its distinctive character as an import, and has become subject to the taxing power of the state; but while remaining the property of the importer, in his warehouse, in the original form or package in which it was imported, a tax upon it is too plainly a duty on imports, to escape the prohibition in the constitution.'[4] In an *obiter dictum,* Marshall declared that 'we suppose the principles laid down in this case, to apply equally to importations from a sister state.'[5]

The original package doctrine was not applied to interstate commerce until 1890 in the case of *Leisy* v. *Hardin.*[6] Iowa by law prohibited the sale of intoxicating liquors, including the sale of liquor or beer by the importer to the dispensers, but the Supreme Court held this prohibition to be unconstitutional. The plaintiffs were citizens of Illinois; they imported into Iowa beer which they sold in the original packages; they had a right to do so; finally, 'they had the right to sell it, by which act alone it (the beer) would become mingled in the common mass of property within the State,'[7] and thus subject to state regulation or taxation.[8]

The original package doctrine is a rough rule of thumb and it was presented as such in *Brown* v. *Maryland.* However, it is not always simple to apply; in some cases, there is no original package to be broken.

It was contended in one case that the original packages were not the larger boxes or cases in which goods were imported, but the smaller packages contained therein, and that until these were broken, the state could not impose a tax upon them. The Supreme Court, however, held that the larger case was the original package.[9]

In *Austin* v. *Tennessee,*[10] the defendant was convicted of attempting to evade a Tennessee law prohibiting the sale of cigarettes. He had sold cigarettes in unbroken packages of ten, the packages having been shipped from North Carolina in baskets. 'The whole theory,' said the Court, 'of the exemption of the original package from the operation of state laws is based upon the idea that the property is imported in the ordinary form in which, from time to time immemorial, foreign goods have been brought into the country.'[11] The Court declared that 'If there be any original package at all in this case we think it is the basket and not the paper box.'[12]

---

[4] Ibid. 441-2.   [5] Ibid. 449.   [6] 135 U.S. 100.

[7] Ibid. 124. 'Sale,' said Marshall in *Brown* v. *Maryland,* 'is the object of importation, and is an essential ingredient of that intercourse, of which importation constitutes a part.' 12 Wheat. 419, 447.

[8] If Congress wishes it may forbid the importation of intoxicating liquors into 'dry' states. Webb-Kenyon Act of 1913, 37 Stat. 699, upheld in *Clark Distilling Co.* v. *Western Maryland Railroad,* 242 U.S. 311 (1917). In *Whitfield* v. *Ohio,* 297 U.S. 431 (1936), the Court upheld the Hawes-Cooper Convict-made Goods Act, 45 Stat. 1084, which provided that convict-made goods when shipped into a state shall be subject to the laws of that state, and 'shall not be exempt therefrom by reason of being introduced in the original package or otherwise.'

[9] *May & Co.* v. *New Orleans,* 178 U.S. 496 (1900).   [11] Ibid. 359.

[10] 179 U.S. 343 (1900).   [12] Ibid.

When a new automobile is transported from the factory in one state to the dealer in another state, obviously the original package doctrine is not applicable.

In addition, by virtue of the police power, and if a menace to health and safety, a state may forbid the importation of diseased meat and explosives even while in the original package.

The original package doctrine is not a hard and fast rule for the transactions of interstate commerce; in fact, it is flexible and has been spoken of as a rule of judicial convenience. In *Baldwin* v. *Seelig,* Mr. Justice Cardozo asserts that 'the test of the original package is not an ultimate principle. It is an illustration of a principle. . . It marks a convenient boundary and one sufficiently precise save in exceptional conditions. What is ultimate is the principle that one state in its dealings with another may not place itself in a position of economic isolation.'

BALDWIN v. G. A. F. SEELIG, INC.

294 U.S. 511 (1935)

MR. JUSTICE CARDOZO delivered the opinion of the Court.

Whether and to what extent the New York Milk Control Act (N.Y. Laws of 1933, c. 158; Laws of 1934, c. 126) may be applied against a dealer who has acquired title to the milk as the result of a transaction in interstate commerce is the question here to be determined.

G. A. F. Seelig, Inc. (appellee in No. 604 and appellant in No. 605) is engaged in business as a milk dealer in the city of New York. It buys its milk, including cream, in Fair Haven, Vermont, from the Seelig Creamery Corporation, which in turn buys from the producers on the neighboring farms. The milk is transported to New York by rail in forty-quart cans, the daily shipment amounting to about 200 cans of milk and 20 cans of cream. Upon arrival in New York about 90% is sold to customers in the original cans, the buyers being chiefly hotels, restaurants and stores. About 10% is bottled in New York, and sold to customers in bottles. By concession, title passes from the Seelig Creamery to G. A. F. Seelig, Inc. at Fair Haven, Vermont. For convenience the one company will be referred to as the Creamery and the other as Seelig. The New York Milk Control Act with

the aid of regulations made thereunder has set up a system of minimum prices to be paid by dealers to producers. The validity of that system in its application to producers doing business in New York State has support in our decisions. *Nebbia* v. *New York,* 291 U.S. 502; *Hegeman Farms Corp.* v. *Baldwin,* 293 U.S. 163. . . From the farms of New York the inhabitants of the so-called Metropolitan Milk District, comprising the City of New York and certain neighboring communities, derive about 70% of the milk requisite for their use. To keep the system unimpaired by competition from afar, the Act has a provision whereby the protective prices are extended to that part of the supply (about 30%) which comes from other states. The substance of the provision is that, so far as such a prohibition is permitted by the Constitution, there shall be no sale within the state of milk bought outside unless the price paid to the producers was one that would be lawful upon a like transaction within the state. . .

Seelig buys its milk from the Creamery in Vermont at prices lower than the minimum payable to producers in New York. The Commissioner of Farms and Markets refuses to license the transaction of its business unless it signs an agreement to conform to the New York statute and regulations in the sale of the imported product. This the applicant declines to do. Because of that refusal other public officers, parties to these appeals, announce a purpose to prosecute for trading without a license and to recover heavy penalties. This suit has been brought to restrain the enforcement of the Act in its application to the complainant, repugnancy being charged between its provisions when so applied and limitations imposed by the Constitution of the United States. United States Constitution, Art. 1, § 8, clause 3; Fourteenth Amendment, § 1. A District Court of three judges, organized in accordance with § 266 of the Judicial Code (28 U.S.C. § 380), has granted a final decree restraining the enforcement of the Act in so far as sales are made by the complainant while the milk is in the cans or other original packages in which it was brought into New York, but refusing an injunction as to milk taken out of the cans for bottling, and thereafter sold in bottles. See opinion on application for interlocutory injunction:—7 F. Supp. 776; and cf. 293 U.S. 522. The case is here on cross-appeals. 28 U.S.C. § 380.

First. An injunction was properly granted restraining the enforcement of the Act in its application to sales in the original packages.

New York has no power to project its legislation into Vermont by regulating the price to be paid in that state for milk acquired there. So much is not disputed. New York is equally without power to prohibit the introduction within her territory of milk of wholesome quality acquired in Vermont, whether at high prices or at low ones. This again is not disputed. Accepting those postulates, New York asserts her power to outlaw milk so introduced by prohibiting its sale thereafter if the price that has been paid for it to the farmers of Vermont is less than would be owing in like circumstances to farmers in New York. The importer in that view

may keep his milk or drink it, but sell it he may not.

Such a power, if exerted, will set a barrier to traffic between one state and another as effective as if customs duties, equal to the price differential, had been laid upon the thing transported. Imposts or duties upon commerce with other countries are placed by an express prohibition of the Constitution, beyond the power of a state, 'except what may be absolutely necessary for executing its inspection laws.' Constitution, Art. 1, § 10, clause 2; *Woodruff* v. *Parham,* 8 Wall. 123. Imposts and duties upon interstate commerce are placed beyond the power of a state, without mention of an exception, by the provision committing commerce of that order to the power of Congress. Constitution, Art. 1, § 8, clause 3. 'It is the established doctrine of this court that a state may not, in any form or under any guise, directly burden the prosecution of interstate business.' *International Textbook Co.* v. *Pigg,* 217 U.S. 91, 112. . . Nice distinctions have been made at times between direct and indirect burdens. They are irrelevant when the avowed purpose of the obstruction, as well as its necessary tendency, is to suppress or mitigate the consequences of competition between the states. Such an obstruction is direct by the very terms of the hypothesis. We are reminded in the opinion below that a chief occasion of the commerce clauses was 'the mutual jealousies and aggressions of the States, taking form in customs barriers and other economic retaliation.' Farrand, *Records of the Federal Convention,* vol. II, p. 308; vol. III, pp. 478, 547, 548; *The Federalist,* No. XLII; Curtis, *History of the Constitution,* vol. I, p. 502; *Story on the Constitution,* § 259. If New York, in order to promote the economic welfare of her farmers, may guard them against competition with the cheaper prices of Vermont, the door has been opened to rivalries and reprisals that were meant to be averted by subjecting commerce between the states to the power of the nation.

The argument is pressed upon us, however, that the end to be served by the Milk Control Act is something more than the economic welfare of the farmers or of any other class or classes. The end to be served is the maintenance of a regular and adequate supply of pure and wholesome milk, the supply being put in jeopardy when the farmers of the state are unable to earn a living income. *Nebbia* v. *New York, supra.* Price security, we are told, is only a special form of sanitary security; the economic motive is secondary and subordinate; the state intervenes to make its inhabitants healthy, and not to make them rich. On that assumption we are asked to say that intervention will be upheld as a valid exercise by the state of its internal police power, though there is an incidental obstruction to commerce between one state and another. This would be to eat up the rule under the guise of an exception. Economic welfare is always related to health, for there can be no health if men are starving. Let such an exception be admitted, and all that a state will have to do in times of stress and strain is to say that its farmers and merchants and workmen must be protected against competition from without, lest they go upon the poor relief lists or perish altogether. To give entrance to that excuse would be to invite a speedy end of our national solidarity. The Constitution was framed under the dominion of a political philosophy less parochial in range. It was framed upon the theory that the peoples of the several states must sink or swim together, and that in the long run prosperity and salvation are in union and not division.

We have dwelt up to this point upon the argument of the state that economic security for farmers in the milk-shed may be a means of assuring to consumers a steady supply of a food of prime necessity. There is, however, another argument which seeks to establish a relation between the well-being of the producer and the quality of the product. We are told that farmers who are underpaid will be tempted to save the expense of sanitary precautions. This temptation will affect the farmers outside New York as well as those within it. For that reason the exclusion of milk paid for in Vermont below the New York minimum will tend, it is said, to impose a higher standard of quality and thereby promote health. We think the argument will not avail to justify impediments to commerce between the states. There is neither evidence nor presumption that the same minimum prices established by order of the Board for producers in New York are necessary also for producers in Vermont. But apart from such defects of proof, the evils springing from uncared for cattle must be remedied by measures of repression more direct and certain than the creation of a parity of prices between New York and other states. Appropriate certificates may be exacted from farmers in Vermont and elsewhere (*Mintz* v. *Baldwin,* 289 U.S. 346; *Reid* v. *Colorado,* 187 U.S. 137); milk may be excluded if necessary safeguards have been omitted; but commerce between the states is burdened unduly when one state regulates by indirection the prices to be paid to producers in another, in the faith that augmentation of prices will lift up the level of economic welfare, and that this will stimulate the observance of sanitary requirements in the preparation of the product. The next step would be to condition importation upon proof of a satisfactory wage scale in factory or shop, or even upon proof of the profits of the business. Whatever relation there may be between earnings and sanitation is too remote and indirect to justify obstructions to the normal flow of commerce in its movement between states. . . One state may not put pressure of that sort upon others to reform their economic standards. If farmers or manufacturers in Vermont are abandoning farms or factories, or are failing to maintain them properly, the legislature of Vermont and not that of New York must supply the fitting remedy.

Many cases from our reports are cited by counsel for the state. They do not touch the case at hand. The line of division between direct and indirect restraints of commerce involves in its marking a reference to considerations of degree. Even so, the borderland is wide between the restraints upheld as incidental and those attempted here. Subject to the paramount power of the Congress, a state may regulate the importation of unhealthy swine or cattle . . . or decayed or noxious foods. *Crossman* v. *Lurman,* 192 U.S. 189; *Savage* v. *Jones,* 225 U.S. 501; *Price* v. *Illinois,* 238 U.S. 446. Things such as these are not proper subjects of commerce, and there is no unreasonable interference when they are inspected and excluded. So a state may protect its inhabitants against the fraudulent substitution, by deceptive coloring or otherwise, of one article for another. *Plumley* v. *Massachusetts,* 155 U.S. 461; *Hebe Co.* v. *Shaw,* 248 U.S. 297; *Hygrade Provision Co.* v. *Sherman,* 266 U.S. 497. It may give protection to travelers against the dangers of overcrowded highways (*Bradley* v. *Public Utilities Comm'n,* 289 U.S. 92) and protection to its residents against unnecessary noises. *Hennington* v. *Georgia,* 163 U.S. 229. . . At times there are border cases, such as *Silz* v. *Hesterberg,* 211 U.S. 31, where the decision in all likelihood was influenced, even if it is not wholly explained, by a recognition of the special and restricted nature of rights of property in game. Interference was there permitted with sale and importation, but interference for a close season and no longer, and in aid of a policy of conservation common to many states. . . None of these statutes—inspection laws, game laws, laws intended to curb fraud or exterminate disease—approaches in drastic quality the statute here in controversy which would neutralize the economic consequences of free trade among the states.

Second. There was error in refusing an injunction to restrain the enforcement of the Act in its application to milk in bottles to be sold by the importer.

The test of the 'original package,' which came into our law with *Brown* v. *Maryland,* 12 Wheat. 419, is not inflexible and final for the transactions of interstate commerce, whatever may be its validity for commerce with other countries. . . There are purposes for which merchandise, transported from another state, will be treated as a part of the general mass of property at the state of destination though still in the original containers. This is so, for illustration, where merchandise so contained is subjected to a non-discriminatory property tax which it bears equally with other merchandise produced within the state. *Sonneborn Bros.* v. *Cureton,* 262 U.S. 506; *Texas Co.* v. *Brown,* 258 U.S. 466, 475; *American Steel & Wire Co.* v. *Speed,* 192 U.S. 500. There are other purposes for which the same merchandise will have the benefit of the protection appropriate to interstate commerce, though the original packages have been broken and the contents subdivided. 'A state tax upon merchandise brought in from another State, or upon its sales, whether in original packages or not, after it has reached its destination and is in a state of rest, is lawful only when the tax is not discriminating in its incidence against the merchandise because of its origin in another State.' *Sonneborn Bros.* v. *Cureton, supra,* at p. 516. . . In brief, the test of the original package is not an ultimate principle. It is an illustration of a principle. *Pennsylvania Gas Co.* v. *Public Service Comm'n,* 225 N.Y. 397, 403; 122 N.E. 260. It marks a convenient boundary and one sufficiently precise save in exceptional conditions. What is ultimate is the principle that one state in its dealings with another may not place itself in a position of economic isolation. Formulas and catchwords are subordinate to this overmastering requirement. Neither the power to tax nor the police power may be used by the state of destination with the aim and effect of establishing an economic barrier against competition with the products of another state or the labor of its residents. Restrictions so contrived are an unreasonable clog upon the mobility of commerce. They set up what is equivalent to a rampart of customs duties designed to neutralize advantages belonging to the place of origin. They are thus hostile in conception as well as burdensome in result. The form of the packages in such circumstances is immaterial, whether they are original or broken. The importer must be free from imposts framed for the very purpose of suppressing competition from without and leading inescapably to the suppression so intended.

The statute here in controversy will not survive that test. A dealer in milk buys it in Vermont at prices there prevailing. He brings it to New York, and is told he may not sell it if he removes it from the can and pours it into bottles. He may not do this for the reason that milk in Vermont is cheaper than milk in New York at the regimented prices, and New York is moved by the desire to protect her inhabitants from the cut prices and other consequences of Vermont competition. To overcome that competition a common incident of ownership—the privilege of sale in convenient receptacles—is denied to one who has bought in interstate commerce. He may not sell on any terms to any one, whether the orders were given in advance or came to him thereafter. The decisions of this court as to the significance of the original package in interstate transactions were not meant to be a cover for retortion or suppression.

The distinction is clear between a statute so designed and statutes of the type considered in *Leisy* v. *Hardin,* 135 U.S. 100, to take one example out of many available. By the teaching of that decision intoxicating liquors are not subject to license or prohibition by the state of destination without congressional consent.[1] They become subject, however, to such laws when the packages are broken. There is little, if any, analogy between restrictions of that type and those in controversy here. In licensing or prohibiting the sale of intoxicating liquors a state does not attempt to neutralize economic advantages belonging to the place of origin. What it does is no more than to apply its domestic policy, rooted in its conceptions of morality and order, to property which for such a purpose may fairly be deemed to have passed out of commerce and to be commingled in an absorbing mass. So also the analogy is remote between restrictions like the present ones upon the sale of imported milk and restrictions affecting sales in unsanitary sweat-shops. It is one thing for a state to exact adherence by an importer to fitting standards of sanitation before the products of the farm or factory may be sold in its markets. It is a very different thing to establish a wage scale or a scale of prices for use in other states, and to bar the sale of the products, whether in the original packages or in others, unless the scale has been observed.

The decree in No. 604 is affirmed, and that in No. 605 reversed, and the cause remanded for proceedings in accordance with this opinion.

No. 604. Affirmed.
No. 605. Reversed.

[1] The rule is different today under the Twenty-first Amendment. Art. xxi, § 2.

NOTE

In *Parker* v. *Brown,* decided in 1943, the Supreme Court upheld a California agricultural proration program [1] designed to restrict competition and to maintain producers' prices. Under the act a proration program was instituted which required, in this case, raisin growers to turn over two-thirds of their individual crops to a central committee which controlled the marketing of the crop to the packers. About 95% of the raisin crop was destined for interstate and foreign commerce. The act was alleged to be invalid under the Sherman Act,[2] the Agricultural Marketing Agreement Act of 1937,[3] and the commerce clause of the Constitution. Invocation of the commerce clause failed to persuade the Court of the program's unconstitutionality.

Gibbons v. *Ogden* opened, but did not decide, the question of the validity of state regulation of interstate commerce in the absence of congressional legislation. This question came before the Supreme Court in 1851 in *Cooley* v. *Board of Port Wardens.*[4] Here the Court sustained a Pennsylvania statute regulating pilots of vessels entering and leaving the port of Philadelphia. The act, obviously, was a regulation of interstate and foreign commerce. Speaking for a majority of the Court, Mr. Justice Curtis set forth an interpretation of the commerce clause which has never been directly repudiated. He said: 'Either absolutely to affirm, or deny that the nature of this power requires exclusive legislation by Congress, is to lose sight of the nature of the subjects of this power, and to assert concerning all of them, what is really applicable but to a part. Whatever subjects of this power are in their nature national, or admit only of one uniform system, or plan of regulation, may justly be said to be of such a nature as to require exclusive legislation by Congress. That this cannot be affirmed of laws for the regulation of pilots and pilotage, is plain.'[5] This principle implies that the state possesses a concurrent power to regulate interstate commerce in areas where Congress has not acted.

The rule set forth in the Cooley case is at present little relied upon as a source of state power to regulate any part of interstate commerce;[6] such power is generally derived from either the state taxing power or the police power.

The state may not tax the commerce among the states nor foreign commerce. But short of the regulation of interstate commerce which the Constitution gives to Congress, a state may, for example, impose a non-discriminatory tax upon the instrumentalities of that commerce. A state tax on net income derived wholly

[1] Agricultural Prorate Act, Statutes of California of 1933, as amended, 1935, 1938, 1939, 1941.
[2] 15 U.S.C. § 1.
[3] 50 Stat. 246 (1937).
[4] 12 How. 299 (1851).
[5] Ibid. 319.
[6] However, see *California* v. *Thompson*, 313 U.S. 109 (1941).

from interstate commerce is legitimate. A state tax, first upon the storage of gasoline brought into the state by an interstate railroad, and second, upon its withdrawal for use in both intrastate and interstate commerce, was deemed valid. A non-discriminatory municipal sales tax upon coal shipped from Pennsylvania and delivered in New York City was held not to be a burden upon interstate commerce. 'If, as guides to decision,' said Mr. Justice Stone, 'we look to the purpose of the commerce clause to protect interstate commerce from discriminatory or destructive state action, and at the same time to the purpose of the state taxing power under which interstate commerce admittedly must bear its fair share of state tax burdens, and to the necessity of judicial reconciliation of these competing demands, we can find no adequate ground for saying that the present tax is a regulation which, in the absence of Congressional action the commerce clause forbids.'[7]

The police power may be defined as the power of a state to promote the public health and safety, the morals, the convenience, and general welfare of its people. In the exercise of this power the state restricts personal freedom and property rights, and sometimes imposes burdens upon, or affects, interstate commerce. In the latter connection, where the burden is only incidental, and the restriction warranted by local needs, the Supreme Court will hold such legislation valid. The Court's function, says Professor Corwin, 'in the handling of this type of case is that of an arbitral, rather than of a strictly judicial, body.'[8]

On the basis of the police power the state may license trainmen engaged in interstate commerce in order to insure their skill and fitness. The state may prescribe regulations for the payment of wages to interstate train crews. It may require interstate passenger cars to be heated. It may regulate the speed of interstate trains within city limits. It may require interstate railroads to eliminate dangerous grade crossings. It may enact local quarantine laws applicable to goods moving in interstate commerce as a means of protecting public health. The state may regulate pilots and pilotage in its harbors.

Despite the absence of controlling Federal law, the state may not regulate interstate commerce so as to restrict materially its flow or to deprive it of necessary regulatory uniformity by 'simply invoking the convenient apologetics of the police power.'[9] Thus, a state may not as a safety measure require interstate trains to reduce speed almost to a stop at grade crossings when compliance with the act increased the running time more than six hours over a distance of one hundred and twenty-three miles. As applied to interstate trains, a state statute making it unlawful to operate a passenger train of more than fourteen cars, or a freight train of more than seventy, would contravene the commerce clause.

It was in the exercise of the police power that California enacted the Agricultural Prorate Act. The object of the act was the conservation of the agricultural wealth of the State, and the prevention of economic waste in the marketing of its agricultural products.

[7] *McGoldrick* v. *Berwind-White Co.*, 309 U.S. 33, 49-50 (1940).
[8] Corwin, Edward S., *The Constitution and What It Means Today*, Princeton, 1946, p. 45.
[9] Mr. Justice Holmes in *Kansas City Southern R. Co.* v. *Kaw Valley District*, 233 U.S. 75, 79 (1914).

PARKER v. BROWN
317 U.S. 341 (1943)

Appeal from a decree of a district court of three judges enjoining the enforcement, against the appellee, of a marketing program adopted pursuant to the California Agricultural Prorate Act. . .

Mr. Chief Justice Stone delivered the opinion of the Court.

The questions for our consideration are whether the marketing program adopted for the 1940 raisin crop under the California Agricultural Prorate Act is rendered invalid (1) by the Sherman Act, or (2) by the Agricultural Marketing Agreement Act of 1937, as amended, 7 U.S.C. §§ 601, *et seq.*, or (3) by the Commerce Clause of the Constitution. . .

Validity of the Prorate Program under the Sherman Act.

Section 1 of the Sherman Act, 15 U.S.C. § 1, makes unlawful 'every contract, combination . . . or conspiracy, in restraint of trade or commerce among the several States.' And § 2, 15 U.S.C. § 2, makes it unlawful to 'monopolize, or attempt to monopolize, or combine or conspire with any other person or persons, to monopolize any part of the trade or commerce among the several States.' We may assume for present purposes that the California prorate program would violate the Sherman Act if it were organized and made effective solely by virtue of a contract, combination or conspiracy of private persons, individual or corporate. . .

But it is plain that the prorate program here was never intended to operate by force of individual agreement or combination. It derived its authority and its efficacy from the legislative command of the state and was not intended to operate or become effective without that command. We find nothing in the language of the Sherman Act or in its history which sug-

gests that its purpose was to restrain a state or its officers or agents from activities directed by its legislature. . . The sponsor of the bill which was ultimately enacted as the Sherman Act declared that it prevented only 'business combinations.' 21 Cong. Rec. 2562, 2457; see also at 2459, 2461. . .

The state in adopting and enforcing the prorate program made no contract or agreement and entered into no conspiracy in restraint of trade or to establish monopoly but, as sovereign, imposed the restraint as an act of government which the Sherman Act did not undertake to prohibit. . .

Validity of the Program under the Agricultural Marketing Agreement Act

The Agricultural Marketing Agreement Act of 1937, 50 Stat. 246, 7 U.S.C. §§ 601 *et seq.*, authorizes the Secretary of Agriculture to issue orders limiting the quantity of specified agricultural products, including fruits, which may be marketed 'in the current of . . . or so as directly to burden, obstruct, or affect interstate or foreign commerce.' Such orders may allot the amounts which handlers may purchase from any producer by means which equalize the amount marketed among producers; may provide for the control and elimination of surpluses and for the establishment of reserve pools of the regulated produce. § 8c (6). The federal statute differs from the California Prorate Act in that its sanction falls upon handlers alone while the state act (§ 22.5 (3)) applies to growers and extends also to handlers so far as they may unlawfully receive or have in their possession within the state any commodity subject to a prorate program. . .

The declared objective of the California Act is to prevent excessive supplies of agricultural commodities from 'adversely affecting' the market, and although the statute speaks in terms of 'economic stability' and 'agricultural waste' rather than of price, the evident purpose and effect of the regulation is to 'conserve agricultural wealth of the state' by raising and maintaining prices, but 'without permitting unreasonable profits to producers.' § 10. The only possibility of conflict would seem to be if a state program were to raise prices beyond the parity price prescribed by the federal act, a condition which has not occurred.

That the Secretary has reason to believe that the state act will tend to effectuate the policies of the federal act so as not to require the issuance of an order under the latter is evidenced by the approval given by the Department of Agriculture to the state program by the loan agreement between the state and the Commodity Credit Corporation. By § 302 of the Agricultural Adjustment Act of 1938, 52 Stat. 43, 7 U.S.C. § 1302 (a), the Commodity Credit Corporation is authorized 'upon the recommendation of the Secretary and with the approval of the President, to make available loans on agricultural commodities. . .' The 'amount, terms, and conditions' of such loans are to be 'fixed by the Secretary, subject to the approval of the Corporation and the President.' Under this authority the Commodity Credit Corporation made loans of $5,146,000 to Zone No. 1, secured by a pledge of 109,000 tons of 1940 crop raisins in the surplus and stabilization pools. These loans were ultimately liquidated by sales of 76,000 tons to packers and 33,000 tons to the Federal Surplus Marketing Administration, an agency of the Department of Agriculture, for relief distribution and for export under the Lend-Lease program. The loans were conditional upon the adoption by the state of the present seasonal marketing program. We are informed by the Government, which at our request filed a brief amicus curiae, that under the loan agreement prices and sales policies as to the pledged raisins were to be controlled by a committee appointed by the Secretary, and that officials of the Department of Agriculture collaborated in drafting the 1940 state raisin program.

Section 302 of the Agricultural Adjustment Act of 1938 requires the Commodity Credit Corporation to make non-recourse loans to producers of certain agricultural products at specified percentages of the parity price, and authorizes loans on any agricultural commodity. The Government informs us that in making loans under the latter authority, § 302 has been construed by the Department of Agriculture as requiring the loans to be made only in order to effectuate the policy of federal agricultural legislation. Section 2 of the Agricultural Adjustment Act of 1938 declares it to be the policy of Congress to achieve the statutory objectives through loans. The Agricultural Adjustment Act of 1938 and the Agricultural Marketing Agreement Act of 1937 were both derived from the Agricultural Adjustment Act of 1933, 48 Stat. 31, and are coördinate parts of a single plan for raising farm prices to parity levels. The conditions imposed by the Secretary of Agriculture in the loan agreement with the State of California, and the collaboration of federal officials in the drafting of the program, must be taken as an expression of opinion by the Department of Agriculture that the state program thus aided by the loan is consistent with the policies of the Agricultural Adjustment and Agricultural Marketing Agreement Acts. We find no conflict between the two acts and no such occupation of the legislative field by the mere adoption of the Agricultural Marketing Agreement Act, without the issuance of any order by the Secretary putting it into effect, as would preclude the effective operation of the state act.

We have no occasion to decide whether

the same conclusion would follow if the state program had not been adopted with the collaboration of officials of the Department of Agriculture and aided by loans from the Commodity Credit Corporation recommended by the Secretary of Agriculture.

Validity of the Program under the Commerce Clause

The court below found that approximately 95 per cent of the California raisin crop finds its way into interstate or foreign commerce. It is not denied that the proration program is so devised as to compel the delivery by each producer, including appellee, of over two-thirds of his 1940 raisin crop to the program committee, and to subject it to the marketing control of the committee. The program, adopted through the exercise of the legislative power delegated to state officials, has the force of law. It clothes the committee with power and imposes on it the duty to control marketing of the crop so as to enhance the price or at least to maintain prices by restraints on competition of producers in the sale of their crop. The program operates to eliminate competition of the producers in the terms of sale of the crop, including price. And since 95 per cent of the crop is marketed in interstate commerce, the program may be taken to have a substantial effect on the commerce, in placing restrictions on the sale and marketing of a product to buyers who eventually sell and ship it in interstate commerce.

The question is thus presented whether in the absence of Congressional legislation prohibiting or regulating the transactions affected by the state program, the restrictions which it imposes upon the sale within the state of a commodity by its producer to a processor who contemplates doing, and in fact does, work upon the commodity before packing and shipping it in interstate commerce, violate the Commerce Clause.

The governments of the states are sovereign within their territory save only as they are subject to the prohibitions of the Constitution or as their action in some measure conflicts with powers delegated to the National Government, or with Congressional legislation enacted in the exercise of those powers. This Court has repeatedly held that the grant of power to Congress by the Commerce Clause did not wholly withdraw from the states the authority to regulate the commerce with respect to matters of local concern, on which Congress has not spoken. *Minnesota Rate Cases,* 230 U.S. 352, 399-400; *South Carolina Highway Dept.* v. *Barnwell Bros.,* 303 U.S. 177, 187, *et seq.; California* v. *Thompson,* 313 U.S. 109, 113-14 and cases cited; *Duckworth* v. *Arkansas,* 314 U.S. 390. *A fortiori* there are many subjects and transactions of local concern not themselves interstate commerce or a part of its operations which are within the regulatory and taxing power of the states, so long as state action serves local ends and does not discriminate against the commerce, even though the exercise of those powers may materially affect it. Whether we resort to the mechanical test sometimes applied by this Court in determining when interstate commerce begins with respect to a commodity grown or manufactured within a state and then sold and shipped out of it—or whether we consider only the power of the state in the absence of Congressional action to regulate matters of local concern, even though the regulation affects or in some measure restricts the commerce —we think the present regulation is within state power.

In applying the mechanical test to determine when interstate commerce begins and ends (see *Federal Compress Co.* v. *McLean,* 291 U.S. 17, 21 and cases cited; *Minnesota* v. *Blasius,* 290 U.S. 1 and cases cited) this Court has frequently held that for purposes of local taxation or regulation 'manufacture' is not interstate commerce even though the manufacturing process is of slight extent. *Crescent Oil Co.* v. *Mississippi,* 257 U.S. 129; *Oliver Iron Co.* v. *Lord,* 262 U.S. 172; *Utah Power & Light Co.* v. *Pfost,* 286 U.S. 165; *Hope Gas Co.* v. *Hall,* 274 U.S. 284; *Heisler* v. *Thomas Colliery Co.,* 260 U.S. 245; *Champlin Refining Co.* v. *Commission,* 286 U.S. 210; *Bayside Fish Co.* v. *Gentry,* 297 U.S. 422. And such regulations of manufacture have been sustained where, aimed at matters of local concern, they had the effect of preventing commerce in the regulated article. *Kidd* v. *Pearson,* 128 U.S. 1; *Champlin Refining Co.* v. *Commission, supra; Sligh* v. *Kirkwood,* 237 U.S. 52; see *Capital City Dairy Co.* v. *Ohio,* 183 U.S. 238, 245; *Thompson* v. *Consolidated Gas Co.,* 300 U.S. 55, 77; cf. *Bayside Fish Co.* v. *Gentry, supra.* A state is also free to license and tax intrastate buying where the purchaser expects in the usual course of business to resell in interstate commerce. *Chassaniol* v. *Greenwood,* 291 U.S. 584. And no case has gone so far as to hold that a state could not license or otherwise regulate the sale of articles within the state because the buyer, after processing and packing them, will, in the normal course of business, sell and ship them in interstate commerce.

All of these cases proceed on the ground that the taxation or regulation involved, however drastically it may affect interstate commerce, is nevertheless not prohibited by the Commerce Clause where the regulation is imposed before any operation of interstate commerce occurs. Applying that test, the regulation here controls the disposition, including the sale and purchase, of raisins before they are processed and packed preparatory to interstate sale and shipment. The regulation is thus applied to transactions wholly intrastate before the raisins are ready for shipment in interstate commerce.

It is for this reason that the present case is to be distinguished from *Lemke* v. *Farmers Grain Co.,* 258 U.S. 50, and *Shafer* v. *Farmers Grain Co.,* 268 U.S. 189, on which appellee relies. There the state regulation held invalid was of the business of those who purchased grain within the state for immediate shipment out of it. The Court was of opinion that the purchase of the wheat for shipment out of the state without resale or processing was a part of the interstate commerce. Compare *Chassaniol* v. *Greenwood, supra.*

This distinction between local regulation of those who are not engaged in commerce, although the commodity which they produce and sell to local buyers is ultimately destined for interstate commerce, and the regulation of those who engage in the commerce by selling the product interstate, has in general served, and serves here, as a ready means of distinguishing those local activities which, under the Commerce Clause, are the appropriate subject of state regulation despite their effect on interstate commerce. But courts are not confined to so mechanical a test. When Congress has not exerted its power under the Commerce Clause, and state regulation of matters of local concern is so related to interstate commerce that it also operates as a regulation of that commerce, the reconciliation of the power thus granted with that reserved to the state is to be attained by the accommodation of the competing demands of the state and national interests involved. See *Di Santo* v. *Pennsylvania,* 273 U.S. 34, 44 (with which compare *California* v. *Thompson, supra*); *South Carolina Highway Dept.* v. *Barnwell Bros., supra; Milk Control Board* v. *Eisenberg Co.,* 306 U.S. 346; *Illinois Gas Co.* v. *Public Service Co.,* 314 U.S. 498, 504-5.

Such regulations by the state are to be sustained, not because they are 'indirect' rather than 'direct,' see *Di Santo* v. *Pennsylvania, supra;* cf. *Wickard* v. *Filburn, supra* [317 U.S. 111], not because they control interstate activities in such a manner as only to affect the commerce rather than to command its operations. But they are to be upheld because upon a consideration of all the relevant facts and circumstances it appears that the matter is one which may appropriately be regulated in the interest of the safety, health and well-being of local communities, and which, because of its local character, and the practical difficulties involved, may never be adequately dealt with by Congress. Because of its local character also there may be wide scope for local regulation without substantially impairing the national interest in the regulation of commerce by a single authority and without materially obstructing the free flow of commerce, which were the principal objects sought to be secured by the Commerce Clause. See *Minnesota Rate Cases, supra,* 398-412; *California* v. *Thompson, supra,* 113. There may also be, as in the present case, local regulations whose effect upon the national commerce is such as not to conflict but to coincide with a policy which Congress has established with respect to it.

Examination of the evidence in this case and of available data of the raisin industry in California, of which we may take judicial notice, leaves no doubt that the evils attending the production and marketing of raisins in that state present a problem local in character and urgently demanding state action for the economic protection of those engaged in one of its important industries. Between 1914 and 1920 there was a spectacular rise in price of all types of California grapes, including raisin grapes. The price of raisins reached its peak, $235 per ton, in 1921, and was followed by large increase in acreage with accompanying reduction in price. The price of raisins in most years since 1922 has ranged from $40 to $60 per ton but acreage continued to increase until 1926 and production reached its peak, 1,433,000 tons of raisin grapes and 290,000 tons of raisins, in 1938. Since 1920 there has been a substantial carry over of 30 to 50% of each year's crop. The result has been that at least since 1934 the industry, with a large increase in acreage and the at-

tendant fall in price, has been unable to market its product and has been compelled to sell at less than parity prices and in some years at prices regarded by students of the industry as less than the cost of production.

The history of the industry, at least since 1929, is a record of a continuous search for expedients which would stabilize the marketing of the raisin crop and maintain a price standard which would bring fair return to the producers. It is significant of the relation of the local interest in maintaining this program to the national interest in interstate commerce, that throughout the period from 1929 until the adoption of the prorate program for the 1940 raisin crop, the national government has contributed to these efforts either by its establishment of marketing programs pursuant to Act of Congress or by aiding programs sponsored by the state. Local co-operative market stabilization programs for raisins in 1929 and 1930 were approved by the Federal Farm Board which supported them with large loans. In 1934 a marketing agreement for California raisins was put into effect under § 8 (2) of the Agricultural Adjustment Act of 1933, as amended, 48 Stat. 528, which authorized the Secretary of Agriculture, in order to effectuate the Act's declared policy of achieving parity prices, to enter into marketing agreements with processors, producers and others engaged in handling agricultural commodities 'in the current of or in competition with, or so as to burden, obstruct, or in any way affect, interstate or foreign commerce.'

Raisin Proration Zone No. 1 was organized in the latter part of 1937. No proration program was adopted for the 1937 crop, but loans of $1,244,000 were made on raisins of that crop by the Commodity Credit Corporation. In aid of a proration program adopted under the California Act for the 1938 crop, a substantial part of that crop was pledged to the

Commodity Credit Corporation as security for a loan of $2,688,000, and was ultimately sold to the Federal Surplus Commodities Corporation for relief distribution. Substantial purchases of raisins of the 1939 crop were also made by Federal Surplus Commodities Corporation, although no proration program was adopted for that year. In aid of the 1940 program, as we have already noted, the Commodity Credit Corporation made loans in excess of $5,000,000, and 33,000 tons of the raisins pledged to it were sold to the Federal Surplus Marketing Administration.

This history shows clearly enough that the adoption of legislative measures to prevent the demoralization of the industry by stabilizing the marketing of the raisin crop is a matter of state as well as national concern and, in the absence of inconsistent Congressional action, is a problem whose solution is peculiarly within the province of the state. In the exercise of its power the state has adopted a measure appropriate to the end sought. The program was not aimed at nor did it discriminate against interstate commerce, although it undoubtedly affected the commerce by increasing the interstate price of raisins and curtailing interstate shipments to some undetermined extent. The effect on the commerce is not greater, and in some instances was far less, than that which this Court has held not to afford a basis for denying to the states the right to pursue a legitimate state end. . .

In comparing the relative weights of the conflicting local and national interests involved, it is significant that Congress, by its agricultural legislation, has recognized the distressed condition of much of the agricultural production of the United States, and has authorized marketing procedures, substantially like the California prorate program, for stabilizing the marketing of agricultural products. Acting under this legislation the Secretary of Agriculture has established a large num-

ber of market stabilization programs for agricultural commodities moving in interstate commerce in various parts of the country, including seven affecting California crops. All involved attempts in one way or another to prevent over-production of agricultural products and excessive competition in marketing them, with price stabilization as the ultimate objective. Most if not all had a like effect in restricting shipments and raising or maintaining prices of agricultural commodities moving in interstate commerce.

It thus appears that whatever effect the operation of the California program may have on interstate commerce, it is one which it has been the policy of Congress to aid and encourage through federal agencies in conformity to the Agricultural Marketing Agreement Act, and § 302 of the Agricultural Adjustment Act. Nor is the effect on the commerce greater than or substantially different in kind from that contemplated by the stabilization programs authorized by federal statutes. As we have seen, the Agricultural Marketing Agreement Act is applicable to raisins only on the direction of the Secretary of Agriculture who, instead of establishing a federal program has, as the statute authorizes, co-operated in promoting the state program and aided it by substantial federal loans. Hence we cannot say that the effect of the state program on interstate commerce is one which conflicts with Congressional policy or is such as to preclude the state from this exercise of its reserved power to regulate domestic agricultural production.

We conclude that the California prorate program for the 1940 raisin crop is a regulation of state industry of local concern which, in all the circumstances of this case which we have detailed, does not impair national control over the commerce in a manner or to a degree forbidden by the Constitution.

Reversed.

XIV

Agriculture

NOTE

The power of the United States government to institute a program of 'planned economy' has been tested most effectively in the field of agriculture. The Constitution makes no reference to agriculture and farmers are sometimes thought to be leaders in a *laissez-faire* philosophy, yet, since 1789, agriculture has been constantly aided and supervised by Congress. This action has taken a variety of forms and in most cases it has come at the request of a well-organized farm bloc.[1]

As a result of individual initiative, an inheritance of highly productive land much of which was virgin soil, plus the scientific assistance of the federal government, the farmer's problem in the United States by the time of the New Deal was hailed as one of 'over-production.' While this analysis was too simple it did tend to direct the government controls toward a program of marketing regulations and restrictions on production, which were designed to stabilize prices at a higher level.[2] Farmers agreed to reduce acreage planted or marketable commodities in return for cash bounty incentives.[3] The government further eased the marketing problems by export subsidies, a food stamp program for distribution of surpluses among low income families, and the introduction of free school lunches for underprivileged children.

During World War II the government abandoned crop restriction and again turned to a program of increased production. The farmers' long experience with federal controls made the transition from peace to a war economy an easier step than for either labor or capital. The Food Production Administration was authorized to provide for the distribution, storage, and allocation of foods. There was extension of scientific research, the exemption of essential farm labor from Selective Service, priorities, rationing of scarce items, and some price control.

Over a period of years the farmer has received extensive government benefits in credit facilities. In the nineteenth century the Homestead Acts gave the pioneer farmer a special credit extension. During the twentieth century the Federal Land Banks, the Commodity Credit Corporation, the Federal Farm Mortgage Corporation, the Reconstruction Finance Corporation, and other government agencies have sought to relieve the farmers' debt burden. The improvement of rural life has also been sponsored by the federal government through rural electrification,

---

[1] See Gaus, John M., and Wolcott, Leon O., *Public Administration and the United States Department of Agriculture*, Chicago, 1940.

[2] See Blaisdell, Donald C., *Government and Agriculture*, New York, 1940. *Farm Policies under the New Deal*, Public Affairs Pamphlet No. 16, New York, 1938.

[3] This system provided in the Agricultural Adjustment Act of 1933 was declared unconstitutional in *United States* v. *Butler*, 297 U.S. 1 (1936). See Note, *ante*, p. 141.

relief for farm tenants, a medical care program under the Farm Security Administration, the development of model communities known as 'green belt' areas, and the rehabilitation of submarginal lands through resettlement projects and land-use programs.

The 1933 Agricultural Adjustment Act was held unconstitutional on its tax feature. The funds for the cash bounties were to be furnished by an ear-marked tax placed on manufacturers engaged in processing raw products. The Court in its interpretation of the general welfare clause held this expenditure invalid.[4] In order to avoid this criticism the 1938 Agricultural Adjustment Act omitted the tax feature and the cash bounty but secured indirect control over production through the encouragement of soil conservation and control of wheat, cotton, corn, rice, and tobacco through a scheme of marketing quotas established under the commerce clause.

Mulford v. *Smith* was an equity proceeding to prevent the collection of penalties by warehousemen handling flue-cured tobacco that was placed on the market in excess of the quota. The statute provides for a base reserve and if the Secretary of Agriculture upon investigation finds that the supply in a given year is likely to exceed this amount he is authorized to hold a referendum of the tobacco producers on the question of setting a maximum quota. If two-thirds of the tobacco growers favor a quota the amount is to be apportioned among the various states on the basis of production during the past five years with consideration for other relevant factors. Quotas for individual farmers are set by committees of local farmers whose decision is subject to committee review and appeal to the courts. A standard for the quota is set in the statute. Any farmer who sells beyond his quota is subject to a penalty, which is collected by the local warehouseman.

The right of a state government to interfere with individual freedom and property in the interests of the general good was upheld in *Nebbia* v. *New York*[5] insofar as it applied to the price regulation of a vital food, milk. For the national government to place such regulations, however, there must be a direct or indirect connection to some delegated power. That marketing has a direct connection to interstate commerce seems easy to establish and the Court now holds that the control of production is merely incidental to a stable market. The Court went a step further in the case of *Wickard* v. *Filburn*[6] when it upheld a production quota on an individual farmer even though he may use the surplus in home consumption. It was held impossible to make scientific findings on a reserve supply unless home consumption was included in the estimates. Milk produced and sold locally has also been held to have an indirect effect on the whole marketing picture and although it be intrastate in nature it may affect interstate commerce.[7]

This same 'incidental connection' argument was used in upholding the Tennessee Valley Authority, another project directly affecting agriculture. The original Muscle Shoals project was authorized in the National Defense Act of 1916 as an experimental nitrate program needed in the conduct of war. The project

[4] See *United States* v. *Butler, ante,* p. 142.
[5] 291 U.S. 502 (1934).   [6] 317 U.S. 111 (1942).
[7] *United States* v. *Wrightwood Dairy Company,* 315 U.S. 110 (1942).

was extended to provide flood control on the Tennessee River and to promote the conservation of natural resources. The production of electricity was considered only incidental to the exercise of other functions.[8]

The exercise of legislative authority by technical administrators has reached new heights in the field of agriculture and has raised legal questions of delegation.[9] In *United States* v. *Rock Royal Co-Operative*[10] and in *Hood and Sons* v. *United States*,[11] the Agricultural Marketing Agreement Act was upheld permitting the Secretary of Agriculture, after approval of two-thirds of the producers in the area and with the approval of the President, to set prices on milk in the metropolitan districts of New York City and Boston. In *Currin* v. *Wallace*[12] the Court upheld the Tobacco Inspection Act which gave the Secretary of Agriculture the power to establish standards of tobacco and to designate certain markets for government inspection and certification. No market was to be a 'designated market' unless it had the approval of two-thirds of the growers voting in a prescribed referendum. The administration of these agricultural referenda furnishes a significant experiment in democratic procedures.[13]

MULFORD v. SMITH
307 U.S. 38 (1939)

Appeal from a decree of a three-judge District Court which dismissed the bill in a suit brought by tobacco farmers to enjoin warehousemen from deducting, and remitting to the Secretary of Agriculture, the penalties inflicted by the Agricultural Adjustment Act of 1938 on tobacco sold for the plaintiffs in excess of the quotas assigned to their respective farms. The suit was begun in the Superior Court of Georgia. The defendants removed the case to the federal court. The United States intervened, under the Act of August 24, 1937. . .

Mr. Justice Roberts delivered the opinion of the Court.

The appellants, producers of flue-cured tobacco, assert that the Agricultural Adjustment Act of 1938,[1] is unconstitu-

tional as it affects their 1938 crop. . .

Before coming to the merits we inquire whether the court below had jurisdiction as a federal court or as a court of equity. Though no diversity of citizenship is alleged, nor is any amount in controversy asserted so as to confer jurisdiction under subsection (1) of § 24 of the Judicial Code, the case falls within subsection (8) which confers jurisdiction upon District Courts 'of all suits and proceedings arising under any law regulating commerce.' Maintenance of the bill for injunction is not forbidden by R.S. 3224, which applies only to a suit to restrain assessment or collection of a tax. Under the averments of the bill the defendant warehousemen would be wrongdoers if they deducted and paid over the prescribed penalties, but no action at law would be adequate to redress the

---

[8] *Ashwander* v. *Tennessee Valley Authority*, 297 U.S. 288 (1936).

[9] See Appleby, Paul H., *Big Democracy*, New York, 1945. See *Hampton* v. *United States*, 276 U.S. 394 (1928), *ante*, p. 134.   [11] 307 U.S. 588 (1939).

[10] 307 U.S. 533 (1939).   [12] 306 U.S. 1 (1939).

[13] Howard, L. V., 'The Agricultural Referendum,' 2 *Public Administration Rev.* 9 (1942).

[1] 52 Stat. 31, as amended 26 March 1938, 52 Stat. 120, 7 April 1938, 52 Stat. 202, 31 May 1938, 52 Stat. 586, and 20 June 1938, 52 Stat. 775; U.S.C. Supp. IV, Title 7, §§ 1281, *et seq.*

damage thus inflicted. It appears that the total of the penalties involved in this suit is some $374,000. The allegation that the warehousemen would be unable to respond in actions for sums aggregating this amount has, therefore, reasonable basis. Before any such action could be initiated the penal sum would have been paid to the Secretary of Agriculture and by him to the Treasurer of the United States and covered into the general funds of the Treasury. No action could be maintained against the warehousemen or either of these officials for disposing of the penal sums in accordance with the terms of the Act unless prior notice not to do so had been served upon each of them. In the light of the fact that the appellants received notice of their quotas only a few days before the actual marketing season opened, the maintenance of actions based upon collection of the penalties would have been a practical impossibility. We are of opinion, therefore, that a case is stated for the interposition of a court of equity.

The appellants plant themselves upon three propositions: (1) that the Act is a statutory plan to control agricultural production and, therefore, beyond the powers delegated to Congress; (2) that the standard for calculating farm quotas is uncertain, vague, and indefinite, resulting in an unconstitutional delegation of legislative power to the Secretary; (3) that, as applied to appellants' 1938 crop, the Act takes their property without due process of law.

First. The statute does not purport to control production. It sets no limit upon the acreage which may be planted or produced and imposes no penalty for the planting and producing of tobacco in excess of the marketing quota. It purports to be solely a regulation of interstate commerce, which it reaches and affects at the throat where tobacco enters the stream of commerce,—the marketing warehouse.[2] The record discloses that at least two-thirds of all flue-cured tobacco sold at auction warehouses is sold for immediate shipment to an interstate or foreign destination. In Georgia nearly one hundred per cent of the tobacco so sold is purchased by extrastate purchasers. In markets where tobacco is sold to both interstate and intrastate purchasers it is not known, when the grower places his tobacco on the warehouse floor for sale, whether it is destined for interstate or intrastate commerce. Regulation to be effective, must, and therefore may constitutionally, apply to all sales.[3] This court has recently declared that sales of tobacco by growers through warehousemen to purchasers for removal outside the state constitute interstate commerce.[4] Any rule, such as that embodied in the Act, which is intended to foster, protect and conserve that commerce, or to prevent the flow of commerce from working harm to the people of the nation, is within the competence of Congress. Within these limits the exercise of the power, the grant being unlimited in its terms, may lawfully extend to the absolute prohibition of such commerce,[5] and *a fortiori* to limitation of the amount of a given commodity which may be transported in such commerce. The motive of Congress in exerting the power is irrelevant to the validity of the legislation.[6]

[2] *Currin* v. *Wallace*, 306 U.S. 1; compare *Townsend* v. *Yeomans*, 301 U.S. 441.

[3] *The Minnesota Rate Cases*, 230 U.S. 352; *The Shreveport Case*, 234 U.S. 342; *Currin* v. *Wallace*, *supra*.

[4] *Currin* v. *Wallace*, *supra*; and see *Dahnke-Walker Co.* v. *Bondurant*, 257 U.S. 282, 290; *Shafer* v. *Farmers Grain Co.*, 268 U.S. 189, 198. Compare *Lemke* v. *Farmers Grain Co.*, 258 U.S. 50.

[5] *Champion* v. *Ames*, 188 U.S. 321; *Hipolite Egg Co.* v. *United States*, 220 U.S. 45; *Hoke* v. *United States*, 227 U.S. 308; *Brooks* v. *United States*, 267 U.S. 432; *Gooch* v. *United States*, 297 U.S. 124.

[6] Story, *Commentaries on the Constitution* (4th ed.), §§ 965, 1079, 1081, 1089.

The provisions of the Act under review constitute a regulation of interstate and foreign commerce within the competency of Congress under the power delegated to it by the Constitution.

Second. The appellants urge that the standard for allotting farm quotas is so uncertain, vague, and indefinite that it amounts to a delegation of legislative power to an executive officer and thus violates the Constitutional requirement that laws shall be enacted by the Congress.

What has been said in summarizing the provisions of the Act sufficiently discloses that definite standards are laid down for the government of the Secretary, first, in fixing the quota and, second, in its allotment amongst states and farms. He is directed to adjust the allotments so as to allow for specified factors which have abnormally affected the production of the state or the farm in question in the test years. Certainly fairness requires that some such adjustment shall be made. The Congress has indicated in detail the considerations which are to be held in view in making these adjustments, and, in order to protect against arbitrary action, has afforded both administrative and judicial review to correct errors. This is not to confer unrestrained arbitrary power on an executive officer. In this aspect the Act is valid within the decisions of this court respecting delegation to administrative officers.[7]

Third. In support of their contention that the Act, as applied to the crop year 1938, deprives them of their property without due process of law in violation of the Fifth Amendment, the appellants rely on the following undisputed facts.

Tobacco growers in southern Georgia and northern Florida began to arrange for the planting of their 1938 crop in December, 1937, when it was necessary for them to prepare beds for the planting of the seeds. Thereafter it was necessary to cultivate the seed beds, sow and water the seed, cover the beds with cloth, and otherwise care for the plants until they were large enough to be transplanted. At the date of approval of the Act each of the plaintiffs had planted his seed beds and, about the middle of March, began transplanting into the fields, which were prepared and fertilized at large expense. The plants were thereafter cultivated and sprayed, and harvesting began during June and continued during July, followed by the curing and grading of the tobacco.

All of these activities involved labor and expense. The production of flue-cured tobacco requires, at prevailing price levels, a cash outlay of between thirty and forty dollars per acre for fertilizer, plant bed covering, twine, poison, etc. The use of animals and permanent and semi-permanent equipment demands an average expenditure, over a period of years, ranging from twenty to thirty dollars an acre. The labor expended per acre is between three hundred and four hundred man-hours. The total cost per pound varies from ten cents to twenty cents.

The marketing season for flue-cured tobacco in Georgia and Florida commences about August 1st of each year. Each of the appellants was notified of the quota of his farm shortly before the opening of the auction markets. Prior to the receipt of notice each of them had largely, if not wholly, completed planting, cultivating, harvesting, curing and grading his tobacco. Until receipt of notice none knew, or could have known, the exact amount of his quota, although, at the time of filing the bill, each had concluded from available information that he would probably market tobacco in excess of any quota for his farm.

The Act was approved February 16, 1938. The Secretary proclaimed a quota

---

[7] *United States* v. *Grimaud,* 220 U.S. 506; *Avent* v. *United States,* 266 U.S. 127; *Hampton & Co.* v. *United States,* 276 U.S. 394; *New York Central Securities Corp.* v. *United States,* 287 U.S. 12; *Currin* v. *Wallace, supra.*

for flue-cured tobacco on February 18th and, on the same date, issued instructions for holding a referendum on March 12th. March 25th the Secretary proclaimed the result of the referendum which was favorable to the imposition of a national marketing quota. In June he issued regulations governing the fixing of farm quotas within the states. July 22nd he determined the apportionment as between states and issued regulations relative to the records to be kept by warehousemen and others. Shortly before the markets opened each appellant received notice of the allotment to his farm.

On the basis of these facts it is argued that the statute operated retroactively and therefore amounted to a taking of appellants' property without due process. The argument overlooks the circumstance that the statute operates not on farm production, as the appellants insist, but upon the marketing of their tobacco in interstate commerce. The law, enacted in February, affected the marketing which was to take place about August 1st following, and so was prospective in its operation upon the activity it regulated. The Act did not prevent any producer from holding over the excess tobacco produced, or processing and storing it for sale in a later year; and the circumstance that the producers in Georgia and Florida had not provided facilities for these purposes is not of legal significance.

The decree is

Affirmed.

MR. JUSTICE BUTLER, dissenting. . .

The Act declares that, if more than the amount fixed for a farm is marketed, the warehouseman shall pay to the Secretary a penalty equal to one-half the price of the excess, but it authorizes him to retain that amount from the farmer raising and bringing it to market for sale. If, without resort to a warehouseman, the farmer sells directly to one in this country, the purchaser is required to pay the penalty but is authorized to take the amount from the purchase price. If the farmer sells directly to one outside the United States he is required to pay the penalty to the Secretary. Thus, in any event, the penalty is effectively laid upon the farmer. Enforcement of the Act will compulsorily take from plaintiffs an amount of money equal to one-half of the market value of all tobacco raised and sold by them in excess of the prescribed quotas.

In *United States* v. *Butler,* 297 U.S. 1, we held the federal government without power to control farm production. We condemned the statutory plan there sought to be enforced as repugnant to the Tenth Amendment. That scheme was devised and put in effect under the guise of exertion of power to tax. We held it to be in excess of the powers delegated to the federal government; found the tax, the appropriation of the money raised, and the directions for its disbursement, to be but the means to an unconstitutional end; showed that the Constitution confers no power to regulate production and that therefore legislation for that purpose is forbidden; emphasized the principle established by earlier decisions that a prohibited end may not be attained under pretext of exertion of powers which are granted; and finally we declared that, if Congress may use its power to tax and to spend compulsorily to regulate subjects within the reserved power of the States, that power 'would become the instrument for total subversion of the governmental powers reserved to the individual States.'

After failure of that measure, Congress, assuming power under the commerce clause, enacted the provisions authorizing the quotas and penalties the validity of which is questioned in this case. Plaintiffs contend that the Act is a plan to control agricultural production and therefore beyond the powers delegated to Congress. The Court impliedly concedes that such a plan would be beyond congressional power, but says that the provisions do not purport to control production, set no limit upon the acreage which may be planted or produced and impose no penalty upon planting and production in excess of marketing quota. Mere inspection of the statute and Secretary's regulations unmistakably discloses purpose to raise price by lessening production. Whatever may be its declared policy or appearance, the enactment operates to control quantity raised by each farmer. It is wholly fallacious to say that the penalty is not imposed upon production. The farmer raises tobacco only for sale. Punishment for selling is the exact equivalent of punishment for raising the tobacco. The Act is therefore invalid. . .

Assuming that, under *Currin* v. *Wallace,* 306 U.S. 1, plaintiffs' sales in interstate commerce at defendants' auction markets are to be deemed subject to federal power under the commerce clause, the Court now rules that, within suggested limits so vague as to be unascertainable, the exercise of power under that clause, 'the grant being unlimited in its terms, may lawfully extend to the absolute prohibition of such commerce and *a fortiori* to limitation of the amount of a given commodity which may be transported in such commerce.'

That ruling is contrary alike to reason and precedent. To support it, the Court merely cites the following cases:

The Lottery Case, (*Champion* v. *Ames*) 188 U.S. 321, held that an Act of Congress prohibiting transportation of lottery tickets in interstate commerce is not inconsistent with any limitation or restriction imposed upon exercise of the powers granted to Congress. After demonstrating the illicit character of lottery tickets, the Court said (p. 357): 'We should hesitate long before adjudging that an evil of such appalling character, carried on through interstate commerce, cannot be met and crushed by the only power competent to that end. . . [p. 358] It is a

kind of traffic which no one can be entitled to pursue as of right.'

Hipolite Egg Co. v. *United States,* 220 U.S. 45, held within federal power the provisions of the Food and Drug Act forbidding transportation in interstate commerce of food 'debased by adulteration' and authorizing articles so transported to be seized as contraband.

Hoke v. *United States,* 227 U.S. 308, sustained congressional prohibition of interstate transportation of women for immoral purposes.

Brooks v. *United States,* 267 U.S. 432, upheld a statute of the United States making it a crime to transport a stolen automobile in interstate commerce.

Gooch v. *United States,* 297 U.S. 124, construed an Act of Congress making it a crime to transport a kidnapped person in interstate commerce.

Plainly these cases give no support to the view that Congress has power generally to prohibit or limit, as it may choose, transportation in interstate commerce of corn, cotton, rice, tobacco, or wheat. Our decisions establish the contrary:

Wilson v. *New,* 243 U.S. 332, upheld an Act regulating hours of service of employees of interstate carriers by rail. The Court, following the teaching of earlier decisions, said (p. 346): 'The extent of regulation depends on the nature and character of the subject and what is appropriate to its regulation. The powers possessed by government to deal with a subject are neither inordinately enlarged or greatly dwarfed because the power to regulate interstate commerce applies. This is illustrated by the difference between the much greater power of regulation which may be exerted as to liquor and that which may be exercised as to flour, drygoods and other commodities. It is shown by the settled doctrine sustaining the right by regulation absolutely to prohibit lottery tickets and by the obvious consideration that such right to prohibit could not be applied to pig iron, steel rails, or most of the vast body of commodities.'

Hammer v. *Dagenhart*, 247 U.S. 251, held repugnant to the commerce clause and to the Tenth Amendment an Act prohibiting transportation in interstate commerce of articles made at factories in which child labor was employed. The Court said (p. 269): 'In other words, the power [granted by the commerce clause] is one to control the means by which commerce is carried on, which is directly the contrary of the assumed right to forbid commerce from moving and thus destroy it as to particular commodities. But it is insisted that the adjudged cases in this court establish the doctrine that the power to regulate given to Congress incidentally includes the authority to prohibit the movement of ordinary commodities and therefore that the subject is not open for discussion. The cases demonstrate the contrary. They rest upon the character of the particular subjects dealt with and the fact that the scope of governmental authority, state or national, possessed over them is such that the authority to prohibit is as to them but the exertion of the power to regulate. . . [p. 276] In our view the necessary effect of this act is, by means of a prohibition against the movement in interstate commerce of ordinary commercial commodities, to regulate the hours of labor of children in factories and mines within the States, a purely state authority. Thus the act in a twofold sense is repugnant to the Constitution.) It not only transcends the authority delegated to Congress over commerce but also exerts a power as to a purely local matter to which the federal authority does not extend. The far reaching result of upholding the act cannot be more plainly indicated than by pointing out that if Congress can thus regulate matters entrusted to local authority by prohibition of the movement of commodities in interstate commerce, all freedom of commerce will be at an end, and the power of the States over local matters may be eliminated, and thus our system of government be practically destroyed.')

Heretofore, in cases involving the power of Congress to forbid or condition transportation in interstate commerce, this Court has been careful to determine whether, in view of the nature and character of the subject, the measure could be sustained as an appropriate regulation of commerce. If Congress had the absolute power now attributed to it by the decision just announced, the opinions in these cases were unnecessary and utterly beside the mark.

For reasons above suggested, I am of opinion:

The penalty is laid on the farmer to prevent production in excess of his quota. It is therefore invalid.

If the penalty is imposed for marketing in interstate commerce, it is a regulation not authorized by the commerce clause.

To impose penalties for marketing in excess of quotas not disclosed before planting and cultivation is to deprive plaintiffs of their liberty and property without due process of law.

The judgment of the district court should be reversed.

Mr. Justice McReynolds concurs in this opinion.

XV

Government and Labor

NOTE

In *National Labor Relations Board* v. *Jones & Laughlin Steel Corp.*, decided in 1937, the Supreme Court upheld the National Labor Relations Act.[1]

The National Labor Relations Act was enacted for the purpose of diminishing the causes of labor disputes, which burdened or obstructed interstate and foreign commerce, 'by encouraging the practice and procedure of collective bargaining and by protecting the exercise by workers of full freedom of association, self-organization, and designation of representatives of their own choosing, for the purpose of negotiating the terms and conditions of their employment or other mutual aid or protection.' The constitutional basis of the act is the commerce power.

This is a far cry from early English statutes like the Ordinance of Labourers[2] which required that every English man and woman 'not living in merchandize, nor exercising any craft, nor having of his own whereof he may live' might be compelled to work, and at such wages as 'were accustomed to be given in the places where he oweth to serve. . .' And any man or woman 'being so required to serve, will not the same do . . . he shall anon be taken . . . and committed to the next gaol. . .' The concepts that a maximum wage could be fixed by law and that men could be compelled to work led eventually to a charge of criminal conspiracy when workers struck in an effort to increase wages.[3]

The early incorporation of the doctrine of conspiracy into American law made collective action by workers difficult. Early in the 19th century, the journeymen cordwainers of Philadelphia were indicted for conspiring and confederating and unlawfully agreeing not to work for wages below a certain set schedule. The indictment charged that the defendants had conspired and joined together ' "to prevent by threats, menaces, and other unlawful means," other artificers from working in the . . . occupation of a cordwainer, for wages below the fixed schedule of rates.'[4] 'What is the case now before us?', queried Recorder Levy. 'A combination of workmen to raise their wages may be considered in a two fold point of view: one is to benefit themselves . . . the other is to injure those who do not join their society. The rule of law condemns both.' The defendants were found guilty of a combination to increase their wages and each was fined eight dollars and costs.

---

[1] 49 Stat. 449 (1935).

[2] 23 Edward III (1349), in Sayre, Francis Bowes, *A Selection of Cases and Other Authorities on Labor Law,* Cambridge, 1923, p. 3.

[3] *Rex* v. *Hammond,* 2 Espinasse 719 (1799), in Sayre, op. cit. pp. 44-5.

[4] *Case of Philadelphia Cordwainers,* Mayor's Court (1806), in Sayre, op. cit. p. 99.

This harsh rule, with gradual modifications,[5] persisted until 1842 when the Supreme Judicial Court of Massachusetts decided the case of *Commonwealth* v. *Hunt*.[6] In this case the defendants were charged with having formed a society 'and agreed not to work for any person, who should employ any journeyman or other person, not a member of such society,' after notice had been given the employer to discharge such person. On appeal, the conviction was set aside. 'The manifest intent of the association is,' said Chief Justice Shaw, 'to induce all those engaged in the same occupation to become members of it. Such a purpose is not unlawful. It would give them a power which might be exerted for useful and honorable purposes, or for dangerous and pernicious ones. If the latter were the real and actual object . . . it should have been specially charged [in the indictment]. Such an association might be used to afford each other assistance in times of poverty, sickness and distress; or to raise their intellectual, moral and social condition; or to make improvement in their art. . . Or the association might be designed for purposes of oppression and injustice. But in order to charge all those, who become members of an association, with the guilt of a criminal conspiracy, it must be averred and proved that the actual, if not the avowed object of the association, was criminal.' This decision rerpesented a great advance in that 'it permanently arrested the tendency to identify a labor organization as such with a criminal conspiracy. . .'[7] This identification had been real enough; in one case it had been held that whether the defendants had confederated to accomplish either a lawful or an unlawful object, because of their confederation they would be liable to the conspiracy charge.[8]

The first large-scale American labor organization was the Knights of Labor, founded in Philadelphia in 1869. This organization was superseded by the American Federation of Labor. The unions, in time, however, found themselves opposed to large corporations which had at their disposal such protective devices as the injunction,[9] the yellow-dog contract,[10] the blacklist, the lockout, the company union, not to speak of the police, the militia, and other strike-breaking agencies.

The National Industrial Recovery Act[11] was enacted by Congress in 1933 in the face of a national emergency 'productive of widespread unemployment and disorganization of industry, which burdens interstate and foreign commerce.'

---

[5] 'During the next three decades there followed a series of indictments and convictions for criminal conspiracy; but nearly all of them presented elements of coercion and intimidating practices.' Frankfurter, Felix, and Greene, Nathan, *The Labor Injunction*, New York, 1930, p. 3.

[6] 4 Metcalf 111 (1842), in Sayre, op. cit. pp. 104-11.

[7] Frankfurter and Greene, op. cit. p. 4.

[8] *People* v. *Melvin*, 2 Wheeler C.C. (N.Y.) 262, in Sayre, op. cit. pp. 102-4.

[9] *In re Debs*, 158 U.S. 564 (1895). This case relates to the rail strike of 1894. Debs and others had been imprisoned for contempt of court in disobeying an injunction of a Federal court forbidding further obstruction of trains engaged in interstate commerce or in carrying the mails. The Supreme Court decided unanimously that the lower court had power to grant the injunction. The Norris-LaGuardia Act, 47 Stat. 70 (1932), limited the powers of the Federal courts to issue injunctions in labor disputes.

[10] See *Coppage* v. *State of Kansas*, 236 U.S. 1 (1915). Such contracts were made unenforceable in the Federal courts by the Norris-LaGuardia Act of 1932.

[11] 48 Stat. 195.

Among the objectives of the act was the reduction and relief of unemployment and improvement of standards of labor. Section 7-A guaranteed the right of collective bargaining in labor-management relations.

The NIRA was reviewed by the Supreme Court in the case of *A.L.A. Schechter Poultry Corp.* v. *United States.*[12] The act was declared to be, first, an unconstitutional delegation of legislative power, and second, an unconstitutional extension of the power of Congress over intrastate commerce. It was held that the Federal government could not regulate the wages and hours of labor of persons employed in the internal commerce of a state. The Court found no justification for such regulation in the fact that wages and hours affect costs and prices, and so indirectly affect interstate commerce.

On the basis of the commerce power, Congress in 1935 enacted the Bituminous Coal Conservation Act.[13] A Bituminous Coal Code, prepared in pursuance of the act, provided in part that employees be given the right to organize and to bargain collectively through representatives of their own choice, free from any interference, restraint, or coercion by the operators. In *Carter* v. *Carter Coal Company,*[14] the act was declared to be unconstitutional. 'Much stress,' said Mr. Justice Sutherland, 'is put upon the evils which come from the struggle between employers and employees over the matter of wages, working conditions, the right of collective bargaining, et cetera, and the resulting strikes, curtailment and irregularity of production and effect on prices; and it is insisted that interstate commerce is *greatly* affected thereby. But . . . the conclusive answer is that the evils are all local evils over which the federal government has no legislative control. The relation of employer and employee is a local relation. At common law, it is one of the domestic relations. The wages are paid for the doing of local work. Working conditions are obviously local conditions. The employees are not engaged in or about commerce, but exclusively in producing a commodity.'[15]

In 1937, prior to the decision of the Supreme Court in the Jones and Laughlin case, it seemed probable to those who were familiar with the narrow interpretation of the commerce power set forth in the Schechter and Carter cases that the National Labor Relations Act could not survive the scrutiny of the Supreme Court.

NATIONAL LABOR RELATIONS BOARD v. JONES & LAUGHLIN STEEL CORPORATION
301 U.S. 1 (1937)

MR. CHIEF JUSTICE HUGHES delivered the opinion of the Court.

In a proceeding under the National Labor Relations Act of 1935, the National Labor Relations Board found that the respondent, Jones & Laughlin Steel Corporation, had violated the Act by engaging in unfair labor practices affecting commerce. The proceeding was instituted by the Beaver Valley Lodge No. 200, affiliated with the Amalgamated Association of Iron, Steel and Tin Workers of

[12] 295 U.S. 495 (1935).
[13] 49 Stat. 991.
[14] 298 U.S. 238 (1936).
[15] Ibid. 308.

America, a labor organization. The unfair labor practices charged were that the corporation was discriminating against members of the union with regard to hire and tenure of employment, and was coercing and intimidating its employees in order to interfere with their self-organization. The discriminatory and coercive action alleged was the discharge of certain employees.

The National Labor Relations Board, sustaining the charge, ordered the corporation to cease and desist from such discrimination and coercion, to offer reinstatement to ten of the employees named, to make good their losses in pay, and to post for thirty days notices that the corporation would not discharge or discriminate against members, or those desiring to become members, of the labor union. As the corporation failed to comply, the Board petitioned the Circuit Court of Appeals to enforce the order. The court denied the petition, holding that the order lay beyond the range of federal power. 83 F. (2d) 998. We granted certiorari.

The scheme of the National Labor Relations Act—which is too long to be quoted in full—may be briefly stated. The first section sets forth findings with respect to the injury to commerce resulting from the denial by employers of the right of employees to organize and from the refusal of employers to accept the procedure of collective bargaining. There follows a declaration that it is the policy of the United States to eliminate these causes of obstruction to the free flow of commerce. The Act then defines the terms it uses, including the terms 'commerce' and 'affecting commerce.' § 2. It creates the National Labor Relations Board and prescribes its organization. §§ 3-6. It sets forth the right of employees to self-organization and to bargain collectively through representatives of their own choosing. § 7. It defines 'unfair labor practices.' § 8. It lays down rules as to the representation of employees for the purpose of collective bargaining. § 9. The Board is empowered

to prevent the described unfair labor practices affecting commerce and the Act prescribes the procedure to that end. The Board is authorized to petition designated courts to secure the enforcement of its orders. The findings of the Board as to the facts, if supported by evidence, are to be conclusive. If either party on application to the court shows that additional evidence is material and that there were reasonable grounds for the failure to adduce such evidence in the hearings before the Board, the court may order the additional evidence to be taken. Any person aggrieved by a final order of the Board may obtain a review in the designated courts with the same procedure as in the case of an application by the Board for the enforcement of its order. § 10. The Board has broad powers of investigation. § 11. Interference with members of the Board or its agents in the performance of their duties is punishable by fine and imprisonment. § 12. Nothing in the Act is to be construed to interfere with the right to strike. § 13. There is a separability clause to the effect that if any provision of the Act or its application to any person or circumstances shall be held invalid, the remainder of the Act or its application to other persons or circumstances shall not be affected. § 15. The particular provisions which are involved in the instant case will be considered more in detail in the course of the discussion.

The procedure in the instant case followed the statute. The labor union filed with the Board its verified charge. The Board thereupon issued its complaint against the respondent alleging that its action in discharging the employees in question constituted unfair labor practices affecting commerce within the meaning of § 8, subdivisions (1) and (3), and § 2, subdivisions (6) and (7) of the Act. Respondent, appearing specially for the purpose of objecting to the jurisdiction of the Board, filed its answer. Respondent admitted the discharges, but alleged that they were made because of inefficiency or violation of rules or for other good reasons and were not ascribable to union membership or activities. As an affirmative defense respondent challenged the constitutional validity of the statute and its applicability in the instant case. Notice of hearing was given and respondent appeared by counsel. The Board first took up the issue of jurisdiction and evidence was presented by both the Board and the respondent. Respondent then moved to dismiss the complaint for lack of jurisdiction; and, on denial of that motion, respondent in accordance with its special appearance withdrew from further participation in the hearing. The Board received evidence upon the merits and at its close made its findings and order.

Contesting the ruling of the Board, the respondent argues (1) that the Act is in reality a regulation of labor relations and not of interstate commerce; (2) that the Act can have no application to the respondent's relations with its production employees because they are not subject to regulation by the federal government; and (3) that the provisions of the Act violate § 2 of Article III and the Fifth and Seventh Amendments of the Constitution of the United States.

The facts as to the nature and scope of the business of the Jones & Laughlin Steel Corporation have been found by the Labor Board and, so far as they are essential to the determination of this controversy, they are not in dispute. The Labor Board has found: The corporation is organized under the laws of Pennsylvania and has its principal office at Pittsburgh. It is engaged in the business of manufacturing iron and steel in plants situated in Pittsburgh and nearby Aliquippa, Pennsylvania. It manufactures and distributes a widely diversified line of steel and pig iron, being the fourth largest producer of steel in the United States. With its subsidiaries—nineteen in number—it is a completely integrated enterprise, owning and operating

ore, coal and limestone properties, lake and river transportation facilities and terminal railroads located at its manufacturing plants. It owns or controls mines in Michigan and Minnesota. It operates four ore steamships on the Great Lakes, used in the transportation of ore to its factories. It owns coal mines in Pennsylvania. It operates towboats and steam barges used in carrying coal to its factories. It owns limestone properties in various places in Pennsylvania and West Virginia. It owns the Monongahela connecting railroad which connects the plants of the Pittsburgh works and forms an interconnection with the Pennsylvania, New York Central and Baltimore and Ohio Railroad systems. It owns the Aliquippa and Southern Railroad Company which connects the Aliquippa works with the Pittsburgh and Lake Erie, part of the New York Central system. Much of its product is shipped to its warehouses in Chicago, Detroit, Cincinnati and Memphis,—to the last two places by means of its own barges and transportation equipment. In Long Island City, New York, and in New Orleans it operates structural steel fabricating shops in connection with the warehousing of semi-finished materials sent from its works. Through one of its wholly-owned subsidiaries it owns, leases and operates stores, warehouses and yards for the distribution of equipment and supplies for drilling and operating oil and gas wells and for pipe lines, refineries and pumping stations. It has sales offices in twenty cities in the United States and a wholly-owned subsidiary which is devoted exclusively to distributing its product in Canada. Approximately 75 per cent of its product is shipped out of Pennsylvania.

Summarizing these operations, the Labor Board concluded that the works in Pittsburgh and Aliquippa 'might be likened to the heart of a self-contained, highly integrated body. They draw in the raw materials from Michigan, Minnesota, West Virginia, Pennsylvania in part through arteries and by means controlled by the respondent; they transform the materials and then pump them out to all parts of the nation through the vast mechanism which the respondent has elaborated.'

To carry on the activities of the entire steel industry, 33,000 men mine ore, 44,000 men mine coal, 4,000 men quarry limestone, 16,000 men manufacture coke, 343,-000 men manufacture steel, and 83,000 men transport its product. Respondent has about 10,000 employees in its Aliquippa plant, which is located in a community of about 30,000 persons.

Respondent points to evidence that the Aliquippa plant, in which the discharged men were employed, contains complete facilities for the production of finished and semi-finished iron and steel products from raw materials; that its works consist primarily of a by-product coke plant for the production of coke; blast furnaces for the production of pig iron; open hearth furnaces and Bessemer converters for the production of steel; blooming mills for the reduction of steel ingots into smaller shapes; and a number of finishing mills such as structural mills, rod mills, wire mills and the like. In addition there are other buildings, structures and equipment, storage yards, docks and an intra-plant storage system. Respondent's operations at these works are carried on in two distinct stages, the first being the conversion of raw materials into pig iron and the second being the manufacture of semi-finished and finished iron and steel products; and in both cases the operations result in substantially changing the character, utility and value of the materials wrought upon, which is apparent from the nature and extent of the processes to which they are subjected and which respondent fully describes. Respondent also directs attention to the fact that the iron ore which is procured from mines in Minnesota and Michigan and transported to respondent's plant is stored in stock piles for future use,

the amount of ore in storage varying with the season but usually being enough to maintain operations from nine to ten months; that the coal which is procured from the mines of a subsidiary located in Pennsylvania and taken to the plant at Aliquippa is there, like ore, stored for future use, approximately two to three months' supply of coal being always on hand; and that the limestone which is obtained in Pennsylvania and West Virginia is also stored in amounts usually adequate to run the blast furnaces for a few weeks. Various details of operation, transportation, and distribution are also mentioned which for the present purpose it is not necessary to detail.

Practically all the factual evidence in the case, except that which dealt with the nature of respondent's business, concerned its relations with the employees in the Aliquippa plant whose discharge was the subject of the complaint. These employees were active leaders in the labor union. Several were officers and others were leaders of particular groups. Two of the employees were motor inspectors; one was a tractor driver; three were crane operators; one was a washer in the coke plant; and three were laborers. Three other employees were mentioned in the complaint but it was withdrawn as to one of them and no evidence was heard on the action taken with respect to the other two.

While respondent criticizes the evidence and the attitude of the Board, which is described as being hostile toward employers and particularly toward those who insisted upon their constitutional rights, respondent did not take advantage of its opportunity to present evidence to refute that which was offered to show discrimination and coercion. In this situation, the record presents no ground for setting aside the order of the Board so far as the facts pertaining to the circumstances and purpose of the discharge of the employees are concerned. Upon that point it is sufficient to say that the evidence supports the findings of the Board that respondent discharged these men 'because of their union activity and for the purpose of discouraging membership in the union.' We turn to the questions of law which respondent urges in contesting the validity and application of the Act.

First. The scope of the Act.—The Act is challenged in its entirety as an attempt to regulate all industry, thus invading the reserved powers of the States over their local concerns. It is asserted that the references in the Act to interstate and foreign commerce are colorable at best; that the Act is not a true regulation of such commerce or of matters which directly affect it but on the contrary has the fundamental object of placing under the compulsory supervision of the federal government all industrial labor relations within the nation. The argument seeks support in the broad words of the preamble (section one) and in the sweep of the provisions of the Act, and it is further insisted that its legislative history shows an essential universal purpose in the light of which its scope cannot be limited by either construction or by the application of the separability clause.

If this conception of terms, intent and consequent inseparability were sound, the Act would necessarily fall by reason of the limitation upon the federal power which inheres in the constitutional grant, as well as because of the explicit reservation of the Tenth Amendment. *Schechter Corp.* v. *United States,* 295 U.S. 495, 549, 550, 554. The authority of the federal government may not be pushed to such an extreme as to destroy the distinction, which the commerce clause itself establishes, between commerce 'among the several States' and the internal concerns of a State. That distinction between what is national and what is local in the activities of commerce is vital to the maintenance of our federal system. *Id.*

But we are not at liberty to deny effect to specific provisions, which Congress has constitutional power to enact, by superimposing upon them inferences from general legislative declarations of an ambiguous character, even if found in the same statute. The cardinal principle of statutory construction is to save and not to destroy. We have repeatedly held that as between two possible interpretations of a statute, by one of which it would be unconstitutional and by the other valid, our plain duty is to adopt that which will save the act. Even to avoid a serious doubt the rule is the same. . .

We think it clear that the National Labor Relations Act may be construed so as to operate within the sphere of constitutional authority. The jurisdiction conferred upon the Board, and invoked in this instance, is found in § 10 (a), which provides:

'SEC. 10 (a). The Board is empowered, as hereinafter provided, to prevent any person from engaging in any unfair labor practice (listed in section 8) affecting commerce.'

The critical words of this provision, prescribing the limits of the Board's authority in dealing with the labor practices, are 'affecting commerce.' The Act specifically defines the 'commerce' to which it refers (§ 2 (6)):

'The term "commerce" means trade, traffic, commerce, transportation, or communication among the several States, or between the District of Columbia or any Territory of the United States and any State or other Territory, or between any foreign country and any State, Territory, or the District of Columbia, or within the District of Columbia or any Territory, or between points in the same State but through any other State or any Territory or the District of Columbia or any foreign country.'

There can be no question that the commerce thus contemplated by the Act (aside from that within a Territory or the District of Columbia) is interstate and foreign commerce in the constitutional sense. The

Act also defines the term 'affecting commerce' (§ 2 (7)):

'The term "affecting commerce" means in commerce, or burdening or obstructing commerce or the free flow of commerce, or having led or tending to lead to a labor dispute burdening or obstructing commerce or the free flow of commerce.'

This definition is one of exclusion as well as inclusion. The grant of authority to the Board does not purport to extend to the relationship between all industrial employees and employers. Its terms do not impose collective bargaining upon all industry regardless of effects upon interstate or foreign commerce. It purports to reach only what may be deemed to burden or obstruct that commerce and, thus qualified, it must be construed as contemplating the exercise of control within constitutional bounds. It is a familiar principle that acts which directly burden or obstruct interstate or foreign commerce, or its free flow, are within the reach of the congressional power. Acts having that effect are not rendered immune because they grow out of labor disputes. . . It is the effect upon commerce, not the source of the injury, which is the criterion. *Second Employers' Liability Cases,* 223 U.S. 1, 51. Whether or not particular action does affect commerce in such a close and intimate fashion as to be subject to federal control, and hence to lie within the authority conferred upon the Board, is left by the statute to be determined as individual cases arise. We are thus to inquire whether in the instant case the constitutional boundary has been passed.

Second. The unfair labor practices in question.—The unfair labor practices found by the Board are those defined in § 8, subdivisions (1) and (3). These provide:

Sec. 8. It shall be an unfair labor practice for an employer—

'(1) To interfere with, restrain, or coerce employees in the exercise of the rights guaranteed in section 7.'

'(3) By discrimination in regard to hire or tenure of employment or any term or condition of employment to encourage or discourage membership in any labor organization. . .'

Section 8, subdivision (1), refers to § 7, which is as follows:

'Sec. 7. Employees shall have the right to self-organization, to form, join, or assist labor organizations, to bargain collectively through representatives of their own choosing, and to engage in concerted activities, for the purpose of collective bargaining or other mutual aid or protection.'

Thus, in its present application, the statute goes no further than to safeguard the right of employees to self-organization and to select representatives of their own choosing for collective bargaining or other mutual protection without restraint or coercion by their employer.

That is a fundamental right. Employees have as clear a right to organize and select their representatives for lawful purposes as the respondent has to organize its business and select its own officers and agents. Discrimination and coercion to prevent the free exercise of the right of employees to self-organization and representation is a proper subject for condemnation by competent legislative authority. Long ago we stated the reason for labor organizations. We said they were organized out of the necessities of the situation; that a single employee was helpless in dealing with an employer; that he was dependent ordinarily on his daily wage for the maintenance of himself and family; that if the employer refused to pay him the wages that he thought fair, he was nevertheless unable to leave the employ and resist arbitrary and unfair treatment; that union was essential to give laborers opportunity to deal on an equality with their employer. *American Steel Foundries* v. *Tri-City Central Trades Council,* 257 U.S. 184, 209. We reiterated these views when we had under consideration the Railway Labor Act of 1926. Fully recognizing the legality of collective action on the part of employees in order to safeguard their proper interests, we said that Congress was not required to ignore this right but could safeguard it. Congress could seek to make appropriate collective action of employees an instrument of peace rather than of strife. We said that such collective action would be a mockery if representation were made futile by interference with freedom of choice. Hence the prohibition by Congress of interference with the selection of representatives for the purpose of negotiation and conference between employers and employees, 'instead of being an invasion of the constitutional right of either, was based on the recognition of the rights of both.' *Texas & N. O. R. Co.* v. *Railway Clerks* [281 U.S. 548]. We have reasserted the same principle in sustaining the application of the Railway Labor Act as amended in 1934. *Virginian Railway Co.* v. *System Federation, No. 40* [300 U.S. 515].

Third. The application of the Act to employees engaged in production,—The principle involved,—Respondent says that whatever may be said of employees engaged in interstate commerce, the industrial relations and activities in the manufacturing department of respondent's enterprise are not subject to federal regulation. The argument rests upon the proposition that manufacturing in itself is not commerce. . .

The Government distinguishes these cases. The various parts of respondent's enterprise are described as interdependent and as thus involving 'a great movement of iron ore, coal and limestone along well-defined paths to the steel mills, thence through them, and thence in the form of steel products into the consuming centers of the country—a definite and well-understood course of business.' It is urged that these activities constitute a 'stream' or 'flow' of commerce, of which the Aliquippa manufacturing plant is the focal point, and that industrial strife at that point would cripple the entire movement. Reference is made to our decision sustaining the Packers and Stockyards Act. *Stafford* v. *Wallace,* 258 U.S. 495. The Court found that the stockyards were but a 'throat' through which the current of commerce flowed and the transactions which there occurred could not be separated from that movement. Hence the sales at the stockyards were not regarded as merely local transactions, for while they created 'a local change of title' they did not 'stop the flow,' but merely changed the private interests in the subject of the current. Distinguishing the cases which upheld the power of the State to impose a non-discriminatory tax upon property which the owner intended to transport to another State, but which was not in actual transit and was held within the State subject to the disposition of the owner, the Court remarked: 'The question, it should be observed, is not with respect to the extent of the power of Congress to regulate interstate commerce, but whether a particular exercise of state power in view of its nature and operation must be deemed to be in conflict with this paramount authority.' *Id.,* p. 526. See *Minnesota* v. *Blasius,* 290 U.S. 1, 8. Applying the doctrine of *Stafford* v. *Wallace, supra,* the Court sustained the Grain Futures Act of 1922 with respect to transactions on the Chicago Board of Trade, although these transactions were 'not in and of themselves interstate commerce.' Congress had found that they had become 'a constantly recurring burden and obstruction to that commerce.' *Chicago Board of Trade* v. *Olsen,* 262 U.S. 1, 32; compare *Hill* v. *Wallace,* 259 U.S. 44, 69. . .

Respondent contends that the instant case presents material distinctions. Respondent says that the Aliquippa plant is extensive in size and represents a large investment in buildings, machinery, and equipment. The raw materials which are brought to the plant are delayed for long periods and, after being subjected to manufacturing processes 'are changed substantially as to character, utility and value.' The finished products which emerge 'are to a large extent manufactured without reference to pre-existing orders and contracts and are entirely different from the raw materials which enter at the other end.' Hence respondent argues that 'If importation and exportation in interstate commerce do not singly transfer purely local activities into the field of congressional regulation, it should follow that their combination would not alter the local situation.' *Arkadelphia Milling Co.* v. *St. Louis Southwestern Ry. Co.*, 249 U.S. 134, 151; *Oliver Iron Co.* v. *Lord* [262 U.S. 172].

We do not find it necessary to determine whether these features of defendant's business dispose of the asserted analogy to the 'stream of commerce' cases. The instances in which that metaphor has been used are but particular, and not exclusive, illustrations of the protective power which the Government invokes in support of the present Act. The congressional authority to protect interstate commerce from burdens and obstructions is not limited to transactions which can be deemed to be an essential part of a 'flow' of interstate or foreign commerce. Burdens and obstructions may be due to injurious action springing from other sources. The fundamental principle is that the power to regulate commerce is the power to enact 'all appropriate legislation' for 'its protection and advancement' (*The Daniel Ball*, 10 Wall. 557, 564); to adopt measures 'to promote its growth and insure its safety' (*Mobile County* v. *Kimball*, 102 U.S. 691, 696, 697); 'to foster, protect, control, and restrain.' *Second Employers' Liability Cases, supra,* p. 47. See *Texas & N. O. R. Co.* v. *Railway Clerks, supra.* That power is plenary and may be exerted to protect interstate commerce 'no matter what the source of the dangers which threaten it.' *Second Employers' Liability Cases,* p. 51; *Schechter Corp.* v. *United States, supra.*

Although activities may be intrastate in character when separately considered, if they have such a close and substantial relation to interstate commerce that their control is essential or appropriate to protect that commerce from burdens and obstructions, Congress cannot be denied the power to exercise that control. *Schechter Corp.* v. *United States, supra.* Undoubtedly the scope of this power must be considered in the light of our dual system of government and may not be extended so as to embrace effects upon interstate commerce so indirect and remote that to embrace them, in view of our complex society, would effectually obliterate the distinction between what is national and what is local and create a completely centralized government. *Id.* The question is necessarily one of degree. As the Court said in *Chicago Board of Trade* v. *Olsen, supra,* p. 37, repeating what had been said in *Stafford* v. *Wallace, supra:* 'Whatever amounts to more or less constant practice and threatens to obstruct or unduly to burden the freedom of interstate commerce is within the regulatory power of Congress under the commerce clause, and it is primarily for Congress to consider and decide the fact of the danger and meet it.'

That intrastate activities, by reason of close and intimate relation to interstate commerce, may fall within federal control is demonstrated in the case of carriers who are engaged in both interstate and intrastate transportation. There federal control has been found essential to secure the freedom of interstate traffic from interference or unjust discrimination and to promote the efficiency of the interstate service. *Shreveport Case,* 234 U.S. 342, 351, 352; *Wisconsin Railroad Comm'n* v. *Chicago, B. & Q. R. Co.,* 257 U.S. 563, 588. It is manifest that intrastate rates deal *primarily* with a local activity. But in rate-making they bear such a close relation to interstate rates that effective control of the one must embrace some control over the other. *Id*. Under the Transportation Act, 1920, Congress went so far as to authorize the Interstate Commerce Commission to establish a state-wide level of intrastate rates in order to prevent an unjust discrimination against interstate commerce. *Wisconsin Railroad Comm'n* v. *Chicago, B. & Q. R. Co., supra; Florida* v. *United States*, 282 U.S. 194, 210, 211. Other illustrations are found in the broad requirements of the Safety Appliance Act and the Hours of Service Act. *Southern Railway Co.* v. *United States*, 222 U.S. 20; *Baltimore & Ohio R. Co.* v. *Interstate Commerce Comm'n*, 221 U.S. 612. It is said that this exercise of federal power has relation to the maintenance of adequate instrumentalities of interstate commerce. But the agency is not superior to the commerce which uses it. The protective power extends to the former because it exists as to the latter.

The close and intimate effect which brings the subject within the reach of federal power may be due to activities in relation to productive industry although the industry when separately viewed is local. This has been abundantly illustrated in the application of the federal Anti-Trust Act. In the *Standard Oil* and *American Tobacco* cases, 221 U.S. 1, 106, that statute was applied to combinations of employers engaged in productive industry. Counsel for the offending corporations strongly urged that the Sherman Act had no application because the acts complained of were not acts of interstate or foreign commerce, nor direct and immediate in their effect on interstate or foreign commerce, but primarily affected manufacturing and not commerce. 221 U.S. pp. 5, 125. Counsel relied upon the decision in *United States* v. *Knight Co.*, 156 U.S. 1. The Court stated their contention as follows: 'That the act, even if the averments of the bill be true, cannot be constitutionally applied, because to do so would extend the power of Congress to subject *dehors* the reach of its authority to regulate com-

merce, by enabling that body to deal with mere questions of production of commodities within the States.' And the Court summarily dismissed the contention in these words: 'But all the structure upon which this argument proceeds is based upon the decision in *United States* v. *E. C. Knight Co.*, 156 U.S. 1. The view, however, which the argument takes of that case and the arguments based upon that view have been so repeatedly pressed upon this court in connection with the interpretation and enforcement of the Anti-trust Act, and have been so necessarily and expressly decided to be unsound as to cause the contentions to be plainly foreclosed and to require no express notice' (citing cases). 221 U.S. pp. 68, 69.

Upon the same principle, the Anti-Trust Act has been applied to the conduct of employees engaged in production. *Loewe* v. *Lawlor*, 208 U.S. 274; *Coronado Coal Co.* v. *United Mine Workers* [268 U.S. 295]; *Bedford Cut Stone Co.* v. *Stone Cutters' Assn.*, 274 U.S. 37. See, also, *Local 167* v. *United States*, 291 U.S. 293, 397; *Schechter Corp.* v. *United States, supra*. The decisions dealing with the question of that application illustrate both the principle and its limitation. Thus, in the first *Coronado* case, the Court held that mining was not interstate commerce, that the power of Congress did not extend to its regulation as such, and that it had not been shown that the activities there involved—a local strike—brought them within the provisions of the Anti-Trust Act, notwithstanding the broad terms of that statute. . . But in the first *Coronado* case the Court also said that 'if Congress deems certain recurring practices, though not really part of interstate commerce, likely to obstruct, restrain or burden it, it has the power to subject them to national supervision and restraint.' 259 U.S. [344], p. 408. And in the second *Coronado* case the Court ruled that while the mere reduction in the supply of an article to be shipped in interstate commerce by the illegal or tortious prevention of its manufacture or production is ordinarily an indirect and remote obstruction to that commerce, nevertheless when the 'intent of those unlawfully preventing the manufacture or production is shown to be to restrain or control the supply entering and moving in interstate commerce, or the price of it in interstate markets, their action is a direct violation of the Anti-Trust Act.' 268 U.S. p. 310. And the existence of that intent may be a necessary inference from proof of the direct and substantial effect produced by the employees' conduct. *Industrial Association* v. *United States,* 268 U.S. [64], p. 81. What was absent from the evidence in the first *Coronado* case appeared in the second and the Act was accordingly applied to the mining employees.

It is thus apparent that the fact that the employees here concerned were engaged in production is not determinative. The question remains as to the effect upon interstate commerce of the labor practice involved. In the *Schechter* case, *supra,* we found that the effect there was so remote as to be beyond the federal power. To find 'immediacy or directness' there was to find it 'almost everywhere,' a result inconsistent with the maintenance of our federal system. In the *Carter* case, [298 U.S. 238], the Court was of the opinion that the provisions of the statute relating to production were invalid upon several grounds—that there was improper delegation of legislative power, and that the requirements not only went beyond any sustainable measure of protection of interstate commerce but were also inconsistent with due process. These cases are not controlling here.

Fourth. Effects of the unfair labor practice in respondent's enterprise—Giving full weight to respondent's contention with respect to a break in the complete continuity of the 'stream of commerce' by reason of respondent's manufacturing operations, the fact remains that the stoppage of those operations by industrial strife would have a most serious effect upon interstate commerce. In view of respondent's far-flung activities, it is idle to say that the effect would be indirect or remote. It is obvious that it would be immediate and might be catastrophic. We are asked to shut our eyes to the plainest facts of our national life and to deal with the question of direct and indirect effects in an intellectual vacuum. Because there may be but indirect and remote effects upon interstate commerce in connection with a host of local enterprises throughout the country, it does not follow that other industrial activities do not have such a close and intimate relation to interstate commerce as to make the presence of industrial strife a matter of the most urgent national concern. When industries organize themselves on a national scale, making their relation to interstate commerce the dominant factor in their activities, how can it be maintained that their industrial labor relations constitute a forbidden field into which Congress may not enter when it is necessary to protect interstate commerce from the paralyzing consequences of industrial war? We have often said that interstate commerce itself is a practical conception. It is equally true that interferences with that commerce must be appraised by a judgment that does not ignore actual experience.

Experience has abundantly demonstrated that the recognition of the right of employees to self-organization and to have representatives of their own choosing for the purpose of collective bargaining is often an essential condition of industrial peace. Refusal to confer and negotiate has been one of the most prolific causes of strife. This is such an outstanding fact in the history of labor disturbances that it is a proper subject of judicial notice and requires no citation of instances. The opinion in the case of *Virginian Railway Co.* v. *System Federation, No.* 40, *supra,* points out that, in the case of carriers, experience has shown that before the amendment, of 1934, of the Railway Labor Act 'when there was no dispute as to the organizations authorized to represent the employees and when there was a willingness of the employer to meet such representative for a discussion of their grievances, amicable adjustment of differences had generally followed and strikes had been avoided.' That, on the other hand, 'a prolific source of dispute had been the maintenance by the railroad of company unions and the denial by railway management of the authority of representatives chosen by their employees.' The opinion in that case also points to the large measure of success of the labor policy embodied in the Railway Labor Act. But with respect to the appropriateness of the recognition of self-organization and representation in the promotion of peace, the question is not essentially different in the case of employees in industries of such a character that interstate commerce is put in jeopardy from the case of employees of transportation companies. And of what avail is it to protect the facility of transportation, if interstate commerce is throttled with respect to the commodities to be transported!

These questions have frequently engaged the attention of Congress and have been the subject of many inquiries. The steel industry is one of the great basic industries of the United States, with ramifying activities affecting interstate commerce at every point. The Government aptly refers to the steel strike of 1919-20 with its far-reaching consequences. The fact that there appears to have been no major disturbance in that industry in the more recent period did not dispose of the possibilities of future and like dangers to interstate commerce which Congress was entitled to foresee and to exercise its protective power to forestall. It is not necessary again to detail the facts as to respondent's enterprise. Instead of being beyond the pale, we think that it presents in a most striking way the close and intimate relation which a manufacturing industry

may have to interstate commerce, and we have no doubt that Congress had constitutional authority to safeguard the right of respondent's employees to self-organization and freedom in the choice of representatives for collective bargaining.

Fifth. The means which the Act employs—Questions under the due process clause and other constitutional restrictions —Respondent asserts its right to conduct its business in an orderly manner without being subjected to arbitrary restraints. What we have said points to the fallacy in the argument. Employees have their correlative right to organize for the purpose of securing the redress of grievances and to promote agreements with employers relating to rates of pay and conditions of work. *Texas & N. O. R. Co.* v. *Railway Clerks, supra; Virginian Railway Co.* v. *System Federation, No.* 40. Restraint for the purpose of preventing an unjust interference with that right cannot be considered arbitrary or capricious. The provision of § 9 (a) that representatives, for the purpose of collective bargaining, of the majority of the employees in an appropriate unit shall be the exclusive representatives of all the employees in that unit, imposes upon the respondent only the duty of conferring and negotiating with the authorized representatives of its employees for the purpose of settling a labor dispute. This provision has its analogue in § 2, Ninth, of the Railway Labor Act which was under consideration in *Virginian Railway Co.* v. *System Federation, No.* 40, *supra.* The decree which we affirmed in that case required the Railway Company to treat with the representative chosen by the employees and also to refrain from entering into collective labor agreements with anyone other than their true representative as ascertained in accordance with the provisions of the Act. We said that the obligation to treat with the true representative was exclusive and hence imposed the negative duty to treat with no other. We also pointed out that, as conceded by the Government, the injunction against the Company's entering into any contract concerning rules, rates of pay and working conditions except with a chosen representative was 'designed only to prevent collective bargaining with anyone purporting to represent employees' other than the representative they had selected. It was taken 'to prohibit the negotiation of labor contracts generally applicable to employees' in the described unit with any other representative than the one so chosen, 'but not as precluding such individual contracts' as the Company might 'elect to make directly with individual employees.' We think this construction also applies to § 9 (a) of the National Labor Relations Act.

The Act does not compel agreements between employers and employees. It does not compel any agreement whatever. It does not prevent the employer 'from refusing to make a collective contract and hiring individuals on whatever terms' the employer 'may by unilateral action determine.' The Act expressly provides in § 9 (a) that any individual employee or a group of employees shall have the right at any time to present grievances to their employer. The theory of the Act is that free opportunity for negotiation with accredited representatives of employees is likely to promote industrial peace and may bring about the adjustments and agreements which the Act in itself does not attempt to compel. . . The Act does not interfere with the normal exercise of the right of the employer to select its employees or to discharge them. The employer may not, under cover of that right, intimidate or coerce its employees with respect to their self-organization and representation, and, on the other hand, the Board is not entitled to make its authority a pretext for interference with the right of discharge when that right is exercised for other reasons than such intimidation and coercion. The true purpose is the subject of investigation with full opportunity to show the facts. It would seem that when employers freely recognize the right of their employees to their own organizations and their unrestricted right of representation there will be much less occasion for controversy in respect to the free and appropriate exercise of the right of selection and discharge.

The Act has been criticised as one-sided in its application; that it subjects the employer to supervision and restraint and leaves untouched the abuses for which employees may be responsible; that it fails to provide a more comprehensive plan—with better assurances of fairness to both sides and with increased chances of success in bringing about, if not compelling, equitable solutions of industrial disputes affecting interstate commerce. But we are dealing with the power of Congress, not with a particular policy or with the extent to which policy should go. We have frequently said that the legislative authority, exerted within its proper field, need not embrace all the evils within its reach. The Constitution does not forbid 'cautious advance, step by step,' in dealing with the evils which are exhibited in activities within the range of legislative power. . . The question in such cases is whether the legislature, in what it does prescribe, has gone beyond constitutional limits.

The procedural provisions of the Act are assailed. But these provisions, as we construe them, do not offend against the constitutional requirements governing the creation and action of administrative bodies. See *Interstate Commerce Comm'n* v. *Louisville & Nashville R. Co.,* 227 U.S. 88, 91. The Act establishes standards to which the Board must conform. There must be complaint, notice, and hearing. The Board must receive evidence and make findings. The findings as to the facts are to be conclusive, but only if supported by evidence. The order of the Board is subject to review by the designated court, and only when sustained by the court may the order be enforced. Upon that review all questions of the jurisdiction of the Board and the regularity of its proceedings, all questions of constitutional right or statutory authority, are open to examination by the court. We construe the procedural provisions as affording adequate opportunity to secure judicial protection against arbitrary action in accordance with the well-settled rules applicable to administrative agencies set up by Congress to aid in the enforcement of valid legislation. It is not necessary to repeat these rules which have frequently been declared. None of them appears to have been transgressed in the instant case. Respondent was notified and heard. It had opportunity to meet the charge of unfair labor practices upon the merits, and by withdrawing from the hearing it declined to avail itself of that opportunity. The facts found by the Board support its order and the evidence supports the findings. Respondent has no just ground for complaint on this score.

The order of the Board required the reinstatement of the employees who were found to have been discharged because of their 'union activity' and for the purpose of 'discouraging membership in the union.' That requirement was authorized by the Act. § 10 (c). In *Texas & N. O. R. Co.* v. *Railway Clerks, supra,* a similar order for restoration to service was made by the court in contempt proceedings for the violation of an injunction issued by the court to restrain an interference with the right of employees as guaranteed by the Railway Labor Act of 1926. The requirement of restoration to service, of employees discharged in violation of the provisions of that Act, was thus a sanction imposed in the enforcement of a judicial decree. We do not doubt that Congress could impose a like sanction for the enforcement of its valid regulation. The fact that in the one case it was a judicial sanction, and in the other a legislative one, is not an essential difference in determining its propriety.

Respondent complains that the Board not only ordered reinstatement but directed the payment of wages for the time lost by the discharge, less amounts earned by the employee during that period. This part of the order was also authorized by the Act. § 10 (c). It is argued that the requirement is equivalent to a money judgment and hence contravenes the Seventh Amendment with respect to trial by jury. The Seventh Amendment provides that 'In suits at common law, where the value in controversy shall exceed twenty dollars, the right of trial by jury shall be preserved.' The Amendment thus preserves the right which existed under the common law when the Amendment was adopted. *Shields* v. *Thomas,* 18 How. 253, 262; *In re Wood,* 210 U.S. 246, 258; *Dimick* v. *Schiedt,* 293 U.S. 474, 476; *Baltimore & Carolina Line* v. *Redman,* 295 U.S. 654, 657. Thus it has no application to cases where recovery of money damages is an incident to equitable relief even though damages might have been recovered in an action at law. *Clark* v. *Wooster,* 119 U.S. 322, 325; *Pease* v. *Rathbun-Jones Engineering Co.,* 243 U.S. 273, 279. It does not apply where the proceeding is not in the nature of a suit at common law. *Guthrie National Bank* v. *Guthrie,* 173 U.S. 528, 537.

The instant case is not a suit at common law or in the nature of such a suit. The proceeding is one unknown to the common law. It is a statutory proceeding. Reinstatement of the employee and payment for time lost are requirements imposed for violation of the statute and are remedies appropriate to its enforcement. The contention under the Seventh Amendment is without merit.

Our conclusion is that the order of the Board was within its competency and that the Act is valid as here applied. The judgment of the Circuit Court of Appeals is reversed and the cause is remanded for further proceedings in conformity with this opinion.

Reversed.

[JUSTICES MCREYNOLDS, VAN DEVANTER, SUTHERLAND and BUTLER dissented.]

NOTE

The chief provisions of the Fair Labor Standards Act[1] relate to wages, hours of labor, and child labor.

In its findings, the Congress declared 'that the existence, in industries engaged in commerce or in the production of goods for commerce, of labor conditions detrimental to the maintenance of the minimum standard of living necessary for health, efficiency, and general well-being of workers (1) causes commerce and the channels and instrumentalities of commerce to be used to spread and perpetuate such labor conditions among the workers of the several States; (2) burdens commerce and the free flow of goods in commerce; (3) constitutes an unfair method of competition in commerce; (4) leads to labor disputes burdening and obstructing commerce and the free flow of goods in commerce; and (5) interferes with the orderly and fair marketing of goods in commerce.' By virtue of its power to regulate interstate commerce the policy of Congress would be 'to correct and as rapidly as practicable to eliminate the conditions above referred to. . .'

Section 6 contains the minimum wage provisions, that is, it places a 'floor' under wages; section 7 relates to maximum hours; section 12 excludes the products of child labor from interstate commerce. Section 15 provides in part that 'it shall be unlawful for any person—(1) to transport . . . ship, deliver, or sell in commerce . . . any goods in the production of which any employee was employed in violation of section 6 or section 7 . . .' or '(4) to violate any of the provisions of section 12. . .'

In 1914, the Supreme Court of Oregon upheld the State's minimum wage law. Appeal was made to the Supreme Court of the United States which affirmed by an equally divided court the decision of the Oregon court.[2] The validity of minimum wage legislation in general, however, was left in doubt. This uncertainty was removed when the Supreme Court in 1923 declared unconstitutional a minimum wage law of the District of Columbia relating to women and children;[3] the law was held to be contrary to the principle of freedom of contract as established by the 5th Amendment.

The question of minimum wage legislation came before the Supreme Court again in the case of *Morehead* v. *New York ex rel. Tipaldo.*[4] On the authority of the Adkins decision, the Supreme Court by a five to four decision declared the New York minimum wage law to be an arbitrary denial of due process of

---

[1] 52 Stat. 1060 (1938).

[2] *Stettler* v. *O'Hara*, 243 U.S. 629 (1917).

[3] *Adkins* v. *Children's Hospital*, 261 U.S. 525 (1923).

[4] 298 U.S. 587 (1936).

law. Thus, both the Federal government and the state governments were denied the power to enact minimum wage legislation.

By this time, the Supreme Court was the object of severe criticism.[5] The Court was more than criticised, it was threatened by the President's plan for the reorganization of the Federal judiciary.[6] As a possible consequence, the Court proceeded to discard some outworn precedents. When the minimum wage law of the State of Washington came up for review in *West Coast Hotel Co.* v. *Parrish*[7] it was upheld by a five to four decision. In this case, the Supreme Court overruled the Adkins decision.)

(Laws limiting hours of labor for women and children have, in general, been sustained by the courts. Oregon in 1903 limited to ten the number of hours a woman might work in a factory or laundry. This law was attacked as a violation of freedom of contract and a denial of equal protection under the 14th Amendment; but the Supreme Court held the enactment to be a valid exercise of the police power.[8] 'The limitations which this statute places upon her contractual powers,' said Mr. Justice Brewer, '. . . are not imposed solely for her benefit, but also largely for the benefit of all. . .'. The two sexes differ in structure of body, in the functions to be performed by each, in the amount of physical strength, in the capacity for long continued labor, particularly when done standing, the influence of vigorous health upon the future well-being of the race . . . justifies a difference of legislation. . .'[9]

Legislation affecting hours of labor for men has developed slowly. In certain hazardous occupations such as mining, maximum hours legislation has been upheld. For example, a Utah statute limited workers in mines to an eight-hour day. This was challenged as a violation of the 14th Amendment, but the Supreme Court held that the right to freedom of contract was not an absolute right, but a right subject to the police power of the state, particularly when there was reasonable ground to believe that the occupation in question was dangerous or unhealthy.[10]

The Supreme Court in *Lochner* v. *New York*[11] held that a limitation upon hours of labor in a private establishment under non-hazardous conditions was unconstitutional. Finally, in *Bunting* v. *Oregon*,[12] decided in 1917, the Court deemed valid an Oregon ten-hour day law for men employed in factories.

To turn to the case which follows, the Darby Lumber Company was charged with violation of certain sections of the Fair Labor Standards Act. The company demurred to the indictment. The district court sustained the demurrer and quashed the indictment upon 'the broad grounds that the Act, which it interpreted

---

[5] U.S. Congress. Senate. Committee on the Judiciary. *Reorganization of the Federal Judiciary,* Hearings, 75th Cong., 1st sess., 1937.

[6] Ibid. pp. 1-3. See also *Message from the President of the United States transmitting a Recommendation to Reorganize the Judicial Branch of the Federal Government,* 75th Cong., 1st sess., H. Doc. No. 142, 1937.

[7] 300 U.S. 379 (1937).

[8] *Muller* v. *Oregon,* 208 U.S. 412 (1908).

[9] Ibid. 422-3.

[10] *Holden* v. *Hardy,* 169 U.S. 366 (1898).

[11] 198 U.S. 45 (1905).

[12] 243 U.S. 426.

as a regulation of manufacture within the states'[13] was unconstitutional. The district court was of the opinion 'that manufacture is not interstate commerce and that the regulation by the Fair Labor Standards Act of wages and hours of employment of those engaged in the manufacture of goods . . . is not within the congressional power to regulate interstate commerce.'[14] This raised the question of *Hammer* v. *Dagenhart*,[15] decided in 1918.

On the basis of the postal and commerce powers Congress has enacted legislation designed to promote and to protect the safety, morals, and health of the public. Beginning in 1893, Congress enacted a series of safety appliance measures the object of which was the protection of passengers and employees on interstate railroads. Congress also prohibited from interstate commerce such articles as lottery tickets, obscene literature, stolen automobiles, prize-fight films, impure and improperly branded foods and drugs. The White Slave Act makes unlawful the transportation of women across state lines for immoral purposes. More recently, Congress has prohibited the carriage of convict-made goods into any state contrary to the laws of the state.

Encouraged by the trend of Supreme Court decisions, the advocates of child-labor legislation pushed through Congress the first child-labor bill.[16] The products of mine and factory, wholly or in part produced by child-labor, were excluded from interstate commerce. It was expected by many that the Supreme Court would without question uphold the enactment. The law, however, was struck down by a Court divided five to four in the case of *Hammer* v. *Dagenhart*.[17]

Briefly, this case involved a father and two minor sons, all three employees in a cotton mill. The father sought to enjoin enforcement of the act.

The Court invalidated the act first, because it was not a regulation of interstate commerce. Unlike lottery tickets or misbranded food, cotton products were in themselves harmless; and such regulation did not serve to promote the efficiency and safety of interstate commerce. Secondly, the law was deemed a regulation of manufacturing and as such encroached upon the reserved powers of the states contrary to the 10th Amendment.

In this case, Mr. Justice Holmes gave one of his classic dissents. He declared that 'It would not be argued today that the power to regulate does not include the power to prohibit. Regulation means the prohibition of something, and when interstate commerce is the matter to be regulated, I cannot doubt that the regulation may prohibit any part of such commerce that Congress sees fit to forbid.'[18]

Hammer v. *Dagenhart* was not specifically overruled until the Supreme Court's decision in the Darby case; however, in time, the Court began to recognize the validity of Mr. Holmes's view, and the view of Chief Justice Marshall in *Gibbons* v. *Ogden,* namely, that the power of Congress over interstate commerce is plenary, complete, and full.[19]

In conclusion, the Supreme Court in the Darby case overruled a long-standing

13 312 U.S. 100, 111 (1941).
14 Ibid. 111-12.
15 247 U.S. 251.
16 The Keating-Owen Act, 39 Stat. 675 (1916).
17 247 U.S. 251 (1918).
18 Ibid. pp. 277-8.
19 See, for example, *Mulford* v. *Smith*, 307 U.S. 38 (1939).

interpretation of the 10th Amendment which had been given classic form in *Hammer* v. *Dagenhart.* 'The amendment,' says Swisher, 'was read in early decisions as if it meant that the exercise of a power granted to the federal government must stop at the point at which it began encroachment upon matters which had traditionally been regarded as under local jurisdiction.' [20] The Darby decision, continues Swisher, 'makes it clear that the traditional sphere of state activity is immune from federal invasion only to the extent that the right of the invader is limited to the exercise of some power directly given or implied in the Constitution.' [21]

UNITED STATES v. DARBY
312 U.S. 100 (1941)

MR. JUSTICE STONE delivered the opinion of the Court.

The two principal questions raised by the record in this case are, *first,* whether Congress has constitutional power to prohibit the shipment in interstate commerce of lumber manufactured by employees whose wages are less than a prescribed minimum or whose weekly hours of labor at that wage are greater than a prescribed maximum, and, *second,* whether it has power to prohibit the employment of workmen in the production of goods 'for interstate commerce' at other than prescribed wages and hours. A subsidiary question is whether in connection with such prohibitions Congress can require the employer subject to them to keep records showing the hours worked each day and week by each of his employees including those engaged 'in the production and manufacture of goods to-wit, lumber, for "interstate commerce." '

Appellee demurred to an indictment found in the district court for southern Georgia charging him with violation of § 15 (a) (1) (2) and (5) of the Fair Labor Standards Act of 1938; 52 Stat. 1060, 29 U.S.C. § 201, *et seq.* The district court sustained the demurrer and quashed the indictment and the case comes here on direct appeal under § 238 of the Judicial Code as amended, 28 U.S.C. § 345, and

§ 682, Title 18 U.S.C., 34 Stat. 1246, which authorizes an appeal to this Court when the judgment sustaining the demurrer 'is based upon the invalidity or construction of the statute upon which the indictment is founded.'

The Fair Labor Standards Act set up a comprehensive legislative scheme for preventing the shipment in interstate commerce of certain products and commodities produced in the United States under labor conditions as respects wages and hours which fail to conform to standards set up by the Act. Its purpose, as we judicially know from the declaration of policy in § 2 (a) of the Act, and the reports of Congressional committees proposing the legislation, S. Rept. No. 884, 75th Cong. 1st Sess.; H. Rept. No. 1452, 75th Cong. 1st Sess.; H. Rept. No. 2182, 75th Cong. 3d Sess., Conference Report, H. Rept. No. 2738, 75th Cong. 3d Sess., is to exclude from interstate commerce goods produced for the commerce and to prevent their production for interstate commerce, under conditions detrimental to the maintenance of the minimum standards of living necessary for health and general well-being; and to prevent the use of interstate commerce as the means of competition in the distribution of goods so produced, and as the means of spreading and perpetuating such substandard

[20] *The Growth of Constitutional Power in the United States,* Chicago, 1946, p. 34.
[21] Ibid. p. 36.

labor conditions among the workers of the several states. The Act also sets up an administrative procedure whereby those standards may from time to time be modified generally as to industries subject to the Act or within an industry in accordance with specified standards, by an administrator acting in collaboration with 'Industry Committees' appointed by him.

Section 15 of the statute prohibits certain specified acts and § 16 (a) punishes willful violation of it by a fine of not more than $10,000 and punishes each conviction after the first by imprisonment of not more than six months or by the specified fine or both. Section 15 (1) makes unlawful the shipment in interstate commerce of any goods 'in the production of which any employee was employed in violation of section 6 or section 7,' which provide, among other things, that during the first year of operation of the Act a minimum wage of 25 cents per hour shall be paid to employees 'engaged in [interstate] commerce or the production of goods for [interstate] commerce,' § 6, and that the maximum hours of employment for employees 'engaged in commerce or the production of goods for commerce' without increased compensation for overtime, shall be forty-four hours a week. § 7.

Section 15 (a) (2) makes it unlawful to violate the provisions of §§ 6 and 7 including the minimum wage and maximum hour requirements just mentioned for employees engaged in production of goods for commerce. Section 15 (a) (5) makes it unlawful for an employer subject to the Act to violate § 11 (c) which requires him to keep such records of the persons employed by him and of their wages and hours of employment as the administrator shall prescribe by regulation or order.

The indictment charges that appellee is engaged, in the State of Georgia, in the business of acquiring raw materials, which he manufactures into finished lumber with the intent, when manufactured, to ship it in interstate commerce to customers outside the state, and that he does in fact so ship a large part of the lumber so produced. There are numerous counts charging appellee with the shipment in interstate commerce from Georgia to points outside the state of lumber in the production of which, for interstate commerce, appellee has employed workmen at less than the prescribed minimum wage or more than the prescribed maximum hours without payment to them of any wage for overtime. Other counts charge the employment by appellee of workmen in the production of lumber for interstate commerce at wages at less than 25 cents an hour or for more than the maximum hours per week without payment to them of the prescribed overtime wage. Still another count charges appellee with failure to keep records showing the hours worked each day a week by each of his employees as required by § 11 (c) and the regulation of the administrator, Title 29, Ch. 5, Code of Federal Regulations, Part 516, and also that appellee unlawfully failed to keep such records of employees engaged 'in the production and manufacture of goods, to-wit lumber, for interstate commerce.'

The demurrer, so far as now relevant to the appeal, challenged the validity of the Fair Labor Standards Act under the Commerce Clause and the Fifth and Tenth Amendments. The district court quashed the indictment in its entirety upon the broad grounds that the Act, which it interpreted as a regulation of manufacture within the states, is unconstitutional. It declared that manufacture is not interstate commerce and that the regulation by the Fair Labor Standards Act of wages and hours of employment of those engaged in the manufacture of goods which it is intended at the time of production 'may or will be' after production 'sold in interstate commerce in part or in whole' is not within the congressional power to regulate interstate commerce.

The effect of the court's decision and judgment is thus to deny the power of Congress to prohibit shipment in interstate commerce of lumber produced for interstate commerce under the proscribed substandard labor conditions of wages and hours, its power to penalize the employer for his failure to conform to the wage and hour provisions in the case of employees engaged in the production of lumber which he intends thereafter to ship in interstate commerce in part or in whole according to the normal course of his business and its power to compel him to keep records of hours of employment as required by the statute and the regulations of the administrator.

The case comes here on assignments by the Government that the district court erred insofar as it held that Congress was without constitutional power to penalize the acts set forth in the indictment, and appellee seeks to sustain the decision below on the grounds that the prohibition by Congress of those Acts is unauthorized by the Commerce Clause and is prohibited by the Fifth Amendment. The appeal statute limits our jurisdiction on this appeal to a review of the determination of the district court so far only as it is based on the validity or construction of the statute. *United States* v. *Borden Co.,* 308 U.S. 188, 193-195, and cases cited. Hence we accept the district court's interpretation of the indictment and confine our decision to the validity and construction of the statute.

The prohibition of shipment of the proscribed goods in interstate commerce. Section 15 (a) (1) prohibits, and the indictment charges, the shipment in interstate commerce, of goods produced for interstate commerce by employees whose wages and hours of employment do not conform to the requirements of the Act. Since this section is not violated unless the commodity shipped has been produced under labor conditions prohibited by § 6 and

§ 7, the only question arising under the commerce clause with respect to such shipments is whether Congress has the constitutional power to prohibit them.

While manufacture is not of itself interstate commerce, the shipment of manufactured goods interstate is such commerce and the prohibition of such shipment by Congress is indubitably a regulation of the commerce. The power to regulate commerce is the power 'to prescribe the rule by which commerce is governed.' *Gibbons* v. *Ogden,* 9 Wheat. 1, 196. It extends not only to those regulations which aid, foster and protect the commerce, but embraces those which prohibit it. *Reid* v. *Colorado,* 187 U.S. 137; *Lottery Case,* 188 U.S. 321; *United States* v. *Delaware & Hudson Co.,* 213 U.S. 366; *Hoke* v. *United States,* 227 U.S. 308; *Clark Distilling Co.* v. *Western Maryland Ry. Co.,* 242 U.S. 311; *United States* v. *Hill,* 248 U.S. 420; *McCormick & Co.* v. *Brown,* 286 U.S. 131. It is conceded that the power of Congress to prohibit transportation in interstate commerce includes noxious articles, *Lottery Case, supra; Hipolite Egg Co.* v. *United States,* 220 U.S. 45; cf. *Hoke* v. *United States, supra;* stolen articles, *Brooks* v. *United States,* 267 U.S. 432; kidnapped persons, *Gooch* v. *United States,* 297 U.S. 124, and articles such as intoxicating liquor or convict made goods, traffic in which is forbidden or restricted by the laws of the state of destination. *Kentucky Whip & Collar Co.* v. *Illinois Central R. Co.,* 299 U.S. 334.

But it is said that the present prohibition falls within the scope of none of these categories; that while the prohibition is nominally a regulation of the commerce its motive or purpose is regulation of wages and hours of persons engaged in manufacture, the control of which has been reserved to the states and upon which Georgia and some of the states of destination have placed no restriction; that the effect of the present statute is not to exclude the proscribed articles from interstate commerce in aid of state regulation as in *Kentucky Whip & Collar Co.* v. *Illinois Central R. Co., supra,* but instead, under the guise of a regulation of interstate commerce, it undertakes to regulate wages and hours within the state contrary to the policy of the state which has elected to leave them unregulated.

The power of Congress over interstate commerce 'is complete in itself, may be exercised to its utmost extent, and acknowledges no limitations other than are prescribed in the Constitution.' *Gibbons* v. *Ogden, supra,* 196. That power can neither be enlarged nor diminished by the exercise or non-exercise of state power. *Kentucky Whip & Collar Co.* v. *Illinois Central R. Co., supra.* Congress, following its own conception of public policy concerning the restrictions which may appropriately be imposed on interstate commerce, is free to exclude from the commerce articles whose use in the states for which they are destined it may conceive to be injurious to the public health, morals or welfare, even though the state has not sought to regulate their use. . .

Such regulation is not a forbidden invasion of state power merely because either its motive or its consequence is to restrict the use of articles of commerce within the states of destination; and is not prohibited unless by other Constitutional provisions. It is no objection to the assertion of the power to regulate interstate commerce that its exercise is attended by the same incidents which attend the exercise of the police power of the states. . .

The motive and purpose of the present regulation are plainly to make effective the Congressional conception of public policy that interstate commerce should not be made the instrument of competition in the distribution of goods produced under substandard labor conditions, which competition is injurious to the commerce and to the states from and to which the commerce flows. The motive and purpose of a regulation of interstate commerce are

matters for the legislative judgment upon the exercise of which the Constitution places no restriction and over which the courts are given no control. *McCray* v. *United States,* 195 U.S. 27; *Sonzinsky* v. *United States,* 300 U.S. 506, 513 and cases cited. 'The judicial cannot prescribe to the legislative department of the government limitations upon the exercise of its acknowledged power.' *Veazie Bank* v. *Fenno,* 8 Wall. 533. Whatever their motive and purpose, regulations of commerce which do not infringe some constitutional prohibition are within the plenary power conferred on Congress by the Commerce Clause. Subject only to that limitation, presently to be considered, we conclude that the prohibition of the shipment interstate of goods produced under the forbidden substandard labor conditions is within the constitutional authority of Congress.

In the more than a century which has elapsed since the decision of *Gibbons* v. *Ogden,* these principles of constitutional interpretation have been so long and repeatedly recognized by this Court as applicable to the Commerce Clause, that there would be little occasion for repeating them now were it not for the decision of this Court twenty-two years ago in *Hammer* v. *Dagenhart,* 247 U.S. 251. In that case it was held by a bare majority of the Court over the powerful and now classic dissent of Mr. Justice Holmes setting forth the fundamental issues involved, that Congress was without power to exclude the products of child labor from interstate commerce. The reasoning and conclusion of the Court's opinion there cannot be reconciled with the conclusion which we have reached, that the power of Congress under the Commerce Clause is plenary to exclude any article from interstate commerce subject only to the specific prohibitions of the Constitution.

Hammer v. *Dagenhart* has not been followed. The distinction on which the decision was rested that Congressional power to prohibit interstate commerce is limited to articles which in themselves have some harmful or deleterious property—a distinction which was novel when made and unsupported by any provision of the Constitution—has long since been abandoned. *Brooks* v. *United States, supra; Kentucky Whip & Collar Co.* v. *Illinois Central R. Co., supra; Electric Bond & Share Co.* v. *Securities & Exchange Comm'n,* 303 U.S. 419; *Mulford* v. *Smith,* 307 U.S. 38. The thesis of the opinion that the motive of the prohibition or its effect to control in some measure the use or production within the states of the article thus excluded from the commerce can operate to deprive the regulation of its constitutional authority has long since ceased to have force. *Reid* v. *Colorado, supra; Lottery Case, supra; Hipolite Egg Co.* v. *United States, supra; Seven Cases* v. *United States, supra,* 514; *Hamilton* v. *Kentucky Distilleries & Warehouse Co., supra,* 156; *United States* v. *Carolene Products Co., supra,* 147. And finally we have declared 'The authority of the federal government over interstate commerce does not differ in extent or character from that retained by the states over intrastate commerce.' *United States* v. *Rock Royal Co-operative,* 307 U.S. 533, 569.

The conclusion is inescapable that *Hammer* v. *Dagenhart,* was a departure from the principles which have prevailed in the interpretation of the Commerce Clause both before and since the decision and that such vitality, as a precedent, as it then had has long since been exhausted. It should be and now is overruled.

Validity of the wage and hour requirements. Section 15 (a) (2) and §§ 6 and 7 require employers to conform to the wage and hour provisions with respect to all employees engaged in the production of goods for interstate commerce. As appellee's employees are not alleged to be 'engaged in interstate commerce' the validity of the prohibition turns on the question whether the employment, under other than

the prescribed labor standards, of employees engaged in the production of goods for interstate commerce is so related to the commerce and so affects it as to be within the reach of the power of Congress to regulate it.

To answer this question we must at the outset determine whether the particular acts charged in the counts which are laid under § 15 (a) (2) as they were construed below, constitute 'production for commerce' within the meaning of the statute. As the Government seeks to apply the statute in the indictment, and as the court below construed the phrase 'produced for interstate commerce,' it embraces at least the case where an employer engaged, as is appellee, in the manufacture and shipment of goods in filling orders of extrastate customers, manufactures his product with the intent or expectation that according to the normal course of his business all or some part of it will be selected for shipment to those customers.

Without attempting to define the precise limits of the phrase, we think the acts alleged in the indictment are within the sweep of the statute. The obvious purpose of the Act was not only to prevent the interstate transportation of the proscribed product, but to stop the initial step toward transportation, production with the purpose of so transporting it. Congress was not unaware that most manufacturing businesses shipping their product in interstate commerce make it in their shops without reference to its ultimate destination and then after manufacture select some of it for shipment interstate and some intrastate according to the daily demands of their business, and that it would be practically impossible, without disrupting manufacturing businesses, to restrict the prohibited kind of production to the particular pieces of lumber, cloth, furniture or the like which later move in interstate rather than intrastate commerce. Cf. *United States* v. *New York Central R. Co.,* 272 U.S. 457, 464.

The recognized need of drafting a workable statute and the well known circumstances in which it was to be applied are persuasive of the conclusion, which the legislative history supports, S. Rept. No. 884, 75th Cong. 1st Sess., pp. 7 and 8; H. Rept. No. 2738, 75th Cong. 3d Sess., p. 17, that the 'production for commerce' intended includes at least production of goods, which, at the time of production, the employer, according to the normal course of his business, intends or expects to move in interstate commerce although, through the exigencies of the business, all of the goods may not thereafter actually enter interstate commerce.

There remains the question whether such restriction on the production of goods for commerce is a permissible exercise of the commerce power. The power of Congress over interstate commerce is not confined to the regulation of commerce among the states. It extends to those activities intrastate which so affect interstate commerce or the exercise of the power of Congress over it as to make regulation of them appropriate means to the attainment of a legitimate end, the exercise of the granted power of Congress to regulate interstate commerce. See *McCulloch* v. *Maryland,* 4 Wheat. 316, 421. Cf. *United States* v. *Ferger,* 250 U.S. 199.

While this Court has many times found state regulation of interstate commerce, when uniformity of its regulation is of national concern, to be incompatible with the Commerce Clause even though Congress has not legislated on the subject, the Court has never implied such restraint on state control over matters intrastate not deemed to be regulations of interstate commerce or its instrumentalities even though they affect the commerce. *Minnesota Rate Cases,* 230 U.S. 352, 398 *et seq.,* and case cited; 410 *et seq.,* and cases cited. In the absence of Congressional legislation on the subject state laws which are not regulations of the commerce itself or its instrumentalities are not forbidden even though they affect interstate commerce. *Kidd* v. *Pearson,* 128 U.S. 1; *Bacon* v. *Illinois,* 227 U.S. 504; *Heisler* v. *Thomas Colliery Co.,* 260 U.S. 245; *Oliver Iron Co.* v. *Lord,* 262 U.S. 172.

But it does not follow that Congress may not by appropriate legislation regulate intrastate activities where they have a substantial effect on interstate commerce. See *Santa Cruz Fruit Packing Co.* v. *National Labor Relations Board,* 303 U.S. 453, 466. A recent example is the National Labor Relations Act for the regulation of employer and employee relations in industries in which strikes, induced by unfair labor practices named in the Act, tend to disturb or obstruct interstate commerce. See *National Labor Relations Board* v. *Jones & Laughlin Steel Corp.,* 301 U.S. 1, 38, 40; *National Labor Relations Board* v. *Fainblatt,* 306 U.S. 601, 604, and cases cited. But long before the adoption of the National Labor Relations Act this Court had many times held that the power of Congress to regulate interstate commerce extends to the regulation through legislative action of activities intrastate which have a substantial effect on the commerce or the exercise of the Congressional power over it.

In such legislation Congress has sometimes left it to the courts to determine whether the intrastate activities have the prohibited effect on the commerce, as in the Sherman Act. It has sometimes left it to an administrative board or agency to determine whether the activities sought to be regulated or prohibited have such effect, as in the case of the Interstate Commerce Act, and the National Labor Relations Act, or whether they come within the statutory definition of the prohibited Act, as in the Federal Trade Commission Act. And sometimes Congress itself had said that a particular activity affects the commerce, as it did in the present Act, the Safety Appliance Act and the Railway

Labor Act. In passing on the validity of legislation of the class last mentioned the only function of courts is to determine whether the particular activity regulated or prohibited is within the reach of the federal power. See *United States* v. *Ferger, supra; Virginian Ry. Co.* v. *Federation,* 300 U.S. 515, 553.

Congress, having by the present Act adopted the policy of excluding from interstate commerce all goods produced for the commerce which do not conform to the specified labor standards, it may choose the means reasonably adapted to the attainment of the permitted end, even though they involve control of intrastate activities. Such legislation has often been sustained with respect to powers, other than the commerce power granted to the national government, when the means chosen, although not themselves within the granted power, were nevertheless deemed appropriate aids to the accomplishment of some purpose within an admitted power of the national government. See *Jacob Ruppert, Inc.* v. *Caffey,* 251 U.S. 264; *Everard's Breweries* v. *Day,* 265 U.S. 545, 560; *Westfall* v. *United States,* 274 U.S. 256, 259. As to state power under the Fourteenth Amendment, compare *Otis* v. *Parker,* 187 U.S. 606, 609; *St. John* v. *New York,* 201 U.S. 633; *Purity Extract & Tonic Co.* v. *Lynch,* 226 U.S. 192, 201-2. A familiar like exercise of power is the regulation of intrastate transactions which are so commingled with or related to interstate commerce that all must be regulated if the interstate commerce is to be effectively controlled. *Shreveport Case,* 234 U.S. 342; *Railroad Commission of Wisconsin* v. *Chicago, B. & Q. R. Co.,* 257 U.S. 563; *United States* v. *New York Central R. Co., supra,* 464; *Currin* v. *Wallace,* 306 U.S. 1; *Mulford* v. *Smith, supra.* Similarly Congress may require inspection and preventive treatment of all cattle in a disease infected area in order to prevent shipment in interstate commerce of some of the

cattle without the treatment. *Thornton* v. *United States,* 271 U.S. 414. It may prohibit the removal, at destination, of labels required by the Pure Food & Drugs Act to be affixed to articles transported in interstate commerce. *McDermott* v. *Wisconsin,* 228 U.S. 115. And we have recently held that Congress in the exercise of its power to require inspection and grading of tobacco shipped in interstate commerce may compel such inspection and grading of all tobacco sold at local auction rooms from which a substantial part but not all of the tobacco sold is shipped in interstate commerce. *Currin* v. *Wallace, supra,* 11, and see to the like effect *United States* v. *Rock Royal Co-op., supra,* 568, note 37.

We think also that § 15 (a) (2), now under consideration, is sustainable independently of § 15 (a) (1), which prohibits shipment or transportation of the proscribed goods. As we have said the evils aimed at by the Act are the spread of substandard labor conditions through the use of the facilities of interstate commerce for competition by the goods so produced with those produced under the prescribed or better labor conditions; and the consequent dislocation of the commerce itself caused by the impairment or destruction of local businesses by competition made effective through interstate commerce. The Act is thus directed at the suppression of a method or kind of competition in interstate commerce which it has in effect condemned as 'unfair,' as the Clayton Act has condemned other 'unfair methods of competition' made effective through interstate commerce. See *Van Camp & Sons Co.* v. *American Can Co.,* 278 U.S. 245; *Federal Trade Comm'n* v. *Keppel & Bro.,* 291 U.S. 304.

The Sherman Act and the National Labor Relations Act are familiar examples of the exertion of the commerce power to prohibit or control activities wholly intrastate because of their effect on interstate commerce. See as to the Sherman Act,

Northern Securities Co. v. *United States,* 193 U.S. 197; *Swift & Co.* v. *United States,* 196 U.S. 375; *United States* v. *Patten,* 226 U.S. 525; *United Mine Workers* v. *Coronado Coal Co.,* 259 U.S. 344; *Local No. 167* v. *United States,* 291 U.S. 293; *Stevens Co.* v. *Foster & Kleiser Co.,* 311 U.S. 255. As to the National Labor Relations Act, see *National Labor Relations Board* v. *Fainblatt, supra,* and cases cited.

The means adopted by § 15 (a) (2) for the protection of interstate commerce by the suppression of the production of the condemned goods for interstate commerce is so related to the commerce and so affects it as to be within the reach of the commerce power. See *Currin* v. *Wallace, supra,* 11. Congress, to attain its objective in the suppression of nationwide competition in interstate commerce by goods produced under substandard labor conditions, has made no distinction as to the volume or amount of shipments in the commerce or of production for commerce by any particular shipper or producer. It recognized that in present day industry, competition by a small part may affect the whole and that the total effect of the competition of many small producers may be great. See H. Rept. No. 2182, 75th Cong. 1st Sess., p. 7. The legislation aimed at a whole embraces all its parts. Cf. *National Labor Relations Board* v. *Fainblatt, supra,* 606.

So far as *Carter* v. *Carter Coal Co.,* 298 U.S. 238, is inconsistent with this conclusion, its doctrine is limited in principle by the decisions under the Sherman Act and the National Labor Relations Act, which we have cited and which we follow. . .

Our conclusion is unaffected by the Tenth Amendment which provides: 'The powers not delegated to the United States by the Constitution, nor prohibited by it to the States, are reserved to the States respectively, or to the people.' The amendment states but a truism that all is retained which has not been surrendered. There is nothing in the history of its adoption to suggest that it was more than declaratory of the relationship between the national and state governments as it had been established by the Constitution before the amendment or that its purpose was other than to allay fears that the new national government might seek to exercise powers not granted, and that the states might not be able to exercise fully their reserved powers. See e.g., 11 Elliot's Debates, 123, 131; III *id.* 450, 464, 600; IV *id.* 140, 149; 1 Annals of Congress, 432, 761, 767-8; Story, Commentaries on the Constitution, §§ 1907-1908.

From the beginning and for many years the amendment has been construed as not depriving the national government of authority to resort to all means for the exercise of a granted power which are appropriate and plainly adapted to the permitted end. *Martin* v. *Hunter's Lessee,* 1 Wheat. 304, 324, 325; *McCulloch* v. *Maryland, supra,* 405, 406; *Gordon* v. *United States,* 117 U.S. 697, 705; *Lottery Case, supra; Northern Securities Co.* v. *United States, supra,* 344-345; *Everard's Breweries* v. *Day, supra,* 558; *United States* v. *Sprague,* 282 U.S. 716, 733; see *United States* v. *The Brigantine William,* 28 Fed. Cas. No. 16,700, p. 622. Whatever doubts may have arisen of the soundness of that conclusion, they have been put at rest by the decisions under the Sherman Act and the National Labor Relations Act which we have cited. . .

Validity of the requirement of records of wages and hours. § 15 (a) (5) and § 11 (c). These requirements are incidental to those for the prescribed wages and hours, and hence validity of the former turns on validity of the latter. Since, as we have held, Congress may require production for interstate commerce to conform to those conditions, it may require the employer, as a means of enforcing the valid law, to keep a record showing whether he has in fact complied with it. The requirement for records even of the intrastate trans-

238

action is an appropriate means to the legitimate end. See *Baltimore & Ohio R. Co.* v. *Interstate Commerce Comm'n,* 221 U.S. 612; *Interstate Commerce Comm'n* v. *Goodrich Transit Co.,* 224 U.S. 194; *Chicago Board of Trade* v. *Olsen,* 262 U.S. 1, 42.

Validity of the wage and hour provisions under the Fifth Amendment. Both provisions are minimum wage requirements compelling the payment of a minimum standard wage with a prescribed increased wage for overtime of 'not less than one and one-half times the regular rate' at which the worker is employed. Since our decision in *West Coast Hotel Co.* v. *Parrish,* 300 U.S. 379, it is no longer open to question that the fixing of a minimum wage is within the legislative power and that the bare fact of its exercise is not a denial of due process under the Fifth more than under the Fourteenth Amendment.

Nor is it any longer open to question that it is within the legislative power to fix maximum hours. *Holden* v. *Hardy,* 169 U.S. 366; *Muller* v. *Oregon,* 208 U.S. 412; *Bunting* v. *Oregon,* 243 U.S. 426; *Baltimore & Ohio R. Co.* v. *Interstate Commerce Comm'n, supra.* Similarly the statute is not objectionable because applied alike to both men and women. Cf. *Bunting* v. *Oregon,* 243 U.S. 426.

The Act is sufficiently definite to meet constitutional demands. One who employs persons, without conforming to the prescribed wage and hour conditions, to work on goods which he ships or expects to ship across state lines, is warned that he may be subject to the criminal penalties of the Act. No more is required. *Nash* v. *United States,* 229 U.S. 373, 377.

We have considered, but find it unnecessary to discuss other contentions.

Reversed.

XVI

Social Security

NOTE

Three cases concerning the Social Security Act of 1935 were decided by the Supreme Court on 24 May 1937.[1] The Social Security Act was passed in answer to a demand for national assistance to protect individuals against the hazards of sickness, old-age and unemployment. After the 1929 depression it became more obvious that such misfortunes could not be met by either individual or family action or from local taxes. Temporary relief measures of the 1930-35 period were designed for recovery rather than permanent programs of insurance.

President Roosevelt in presenting the social security program to Congress pointed out that 'security was attained in the earlier days through the interdependence of members of families upon each other and of the families within a small community upon each other. The complexities of great communities and of organized industry make less real these simple means of security. Therefore, we are compelled to employ the active interest of the nation as a whole through government in order to encourage a greater security for each individual who composes it.'[2] It was advocated that the program be one of co-operation between the states and the national government. Some congressmen felt that social security measures should provide for the greatest variation in local needs and others doubted the constitutionality of a nation-wide program.

The Act provides for several types of social legislation and incorporates three distinct methods of taxation and administration each expressly separable from the other. By this division it was expected to avoid the criticisms of the AAA in *United States* v. *Butler*.[3] If part of the Act were declared unconstitutional, the remainder would not be invalidated.[4]

1. The Old Age and Survivors Insurance (OASI) is a compulsory insurance plan provided for selected classes of wage-earners and administered directly by the federal government. A pay roll tax is collected from employers and employees, but with specific exemptions, notably agricultural workers, domestic servants, self-employed and those employed by governmental, educational, or charitable institutions. The amount of the tax was to be assessed gradually until it reached a

---

[1] *Steward Machine Company* v. *Davis*, 301 U.S. 548 (1937), *Helvering* v. *Davis*, 301 U.S. 619 (1937), and *Carmichael* v. *Southern Coal and Coke Company*, 301 U.S. 495 (1937), interpreting 49 Stat. 620 (1935).

[2] Message of the President of the United States, *Congressional Record*, 73rd Cong., 2d sess. (8 June 1934), p. 10,770. For further study of the background of social security legislation see Douglas, Paul H., *Social Security in the United States*, New York, 1936, and Meriam, Lewis, *Relief and Social Security*, Washington, 1946.

[3] 297 U.S. 1 (1936). See *ante*, p. 142.

[4] *Pollock* v. *Farmers' Loan and Trust Company*, 158 U.S. 601 (1895).

maximum of three per cent on employers and three per cent on employees in
1949. The tax, however, has been 'frozen' at one per cent.[5] The persons who meet
the qualifications for insurance are given a social security number, and a record
of earnings and payment is kept by the federal government. If the insured
complies with all provisions of the Act, he or certain of his dependents are
entitled to benefits after age 65. This measure was held to be a valid exercise of
the power to spend for the general welfare and the separable tax feature was
held not to be arbitrary or unreasonable.[6]

2. Old Age Assistance, Aid to Dependent Children, Aid to the Blind, Maternal
and Child Welfare Services, Vocational Rehabilitation and Public Health facilities
are provided on a grant-in-aid basis in the Social Security Act. By this process the
federal government, for example in the Old Age Assistance program, has made
available to the states grants to be matched on a fifty-fifty basis up to $40 a month
for men and women over 65 years of age who meet certain minimum qualifications of residence and need. In a similar fashion other grants are provided to
extend services in the other fields under specific regulations. Money for these
services comes from the United States Treasury. The Act is administered by state
and county agencies under federal supervision if the state is willing to match the
grant.

The right of a taxpayer to sue the national government or its agents on an
expenditure coming from the general funds of the Treasury was denied in
Frothingham v. *Mellon*[7] on the ground that there was no real case or controversy.
In that case it was claimed that grants-in-aid for maternal and child welfare under
the Sheppard-Towner Act[8] were not a legal expenditure of the federal government since it did not 'provide for the general welfare.' The Court dismissed the
case for lack of jurisdiction but argued in *obiter dictum* that to provide for
maternal and child welfare might be considered to be for the general good of
the nation. This decision limits the possibility of bringing the grant-in-aid provisions of the Social Security Act to the Court.

3. Unemployment Compensation Plans are encouraged under the Social Security
Act by a system of tax credits or tax offsets extended to the states. Provision is
made for a three per cent federal pay roll tax on all business enterprises employing
eight or more persons.[9] In states where an unemployment compensation law,
which meets the approval of the Social Security Board has been passed, ninety
per cent of this pay roll tax is credited to the state's unemployment compensation
fund. By a grant-in-aid process further money is appropriated for the administration of the fund.

This provision then makes it possible for the state to retain a portion of the

[5] A 1947 amendment to the act 'froze' the tax at 1 per cent through 1949, and requires its increase
to 1½ per cent through 1950 and 1951, and to 2 per cent thereafter. Act of August 10, 1947, Public
Law 379, ch. 510, 80th Cong. 1st. sess.
[6] *Helvering* v. *Davis,* 301 U.S. 619 (1937).
[7] 262 U.S. 447 (1923) decided with *Massachusetts* v. *Mellon.*
[8] 42 Stat. 224 (1921).
[9] Agricultural workers, government officials, and workers for educational and charitable organizations are not covered.

money collected from this federal pay roll tax if the state passes a satisfactory unemployment compensation law. If no law is passed in the state, the national government places the tax proceeds in its general funds. The states, however, pass the law, not the national government. The states' authority in the realm of general welfare is broader, thus better provision for individual state problems can be initiated. In *Carmichael* v. *Southern Coal and Coke Company* [10] the Court held that the Alabama unemployment compensation law did not violate the due process and equal protection clauses of the Fourteenth Amendment nor had the law been adopted as a result of federal coercion amounting to a violation of the Tenth Amendment. The Steward Machine Company case was brought to question the legality of the federal tax.

STEWARD MACHINE CO. v. DAVIS
301 U.S. 548 (1937)

MR. JUSTICE CARDOZO delivered the opinion of the Court.

The validity of the tax imposed by the Social Security Act on employers of eight or more is here to be determined.

Petitioner, an Alabama corporation, paid a tax in accordance with the statute, filed a claim for refund with the Commissioner of Internal Revenue, and sued to recover the payment ($46.14), asserting a conflict between the statute and the Constitution of the United States. Upon demurrer the District Court gave judgment for the defendant dismissing the complaint, and the Circuit Court of Appeals for the Fifth Circuit affirmed. . . An important question of constitutional law being involved, we granted certiorari.

The Social Security Act (Act of August 14, 1935, c. 531, 49 Stat. 620, 42 U.S.C., c. 7 (Supp.)) is divided into eleven separate titles, of which only Titles IX and III are so related to this case as to stand in need of summary.

The caption of Title IX is 'Tax on Employers of Eight or More.' Every employer (with stated exceptions) is to pay for each calendar year 'an excise tax, with respect to having individuals in his employ,' the tax to be measured by prescribed percentages of the total wages payable by the employer during the calendar year with respect to such employment. § 901. One is not, however, an 'employer' within the meaning of the act unless he employs eight persons or more. § 907 (a). There are also other limitations of minor importance. The term 'employment' too has its special definition, excluding agricultural labor, domestic service in a private home and some other smaller classes. § 907 (c). The tax begins with the year 1936, and is payable for the first time on January 31, 1937. During the calendar year 1936 the rate is to be one per cent, during 1937 two per cent, and three per cent thereafter. The proceeds, when collected, go into the Treasury of the United States like internal-revenue collections generally. § 905 (a). They are not earmarked in any way. In certain circumstances, however, credits are allowable. § 902. If the taxpayer has made contributions to an unemployment fund under a state law, he may credit such contributions against the federal tax, provided, however, that the total credit allowed to any taxpayer shall not exceed 90 per centum of the tax against which it is credited, and provided also that the state law shall have been certified to the Secretary of the Treasury by the Social Security Board as satisfying certain minimum cri-

[10] 301 U.S. 495 (1937).

teria. § 902. . . Some of the conditions thus attached to the allowance of a credit are designed to give assurance that the state unemployment compensation law shall be one in substance as well as name. Others are designed to give assurance that the contributions shall be protected against loss after payment to the state. To this last end there are provisions that before a state law shall have the approval of the Board it must direct that the contributions to the state fund be paid over immediately to the Secretary of the Treasury to the credit of the 'Unemployment Trust Fund. . .' For the moment it is enough to say that the Fund is to be held by the Secretary of the Treasury, who is to invest in government securities any portion not required in his judgment to meet current withdrawals. He is authorized and directed to pay out of the Fund to any competent state agency such sums as it may duly requisition from the amount standing to its credit. § 904 (f).

Title III, which is also challenged as invalid, has the caption 'Grants to States for Unemployment Compensation Administration.' Under this title, certain sums of money are 'authorized to be appropriated' for the purpose of assisting the states in the administration of their unemployment compensation laws, the maximum for the fiscal year ending June 30, 1936 to be $4,000,000, and $49,000,000 for each fiscal year thereafter. § 301. No present appropriation is made to the extent of a single dollar. All that the title does is to authorize future appropriations. Actually only $2,250,000 of the $4,000,000 authorized was appropriated for 1936 (Act of Feb. 11, 1936, c. 49, 49 Stat. 1109, 1113) and only $29,000,000 of the $49,000,000 authorized for the following year. Act of June 22, 1936, c. 689, 49 Stat. 1597, 1605. The appropriations when made were not specifically out of the proceeds of the employment tax, but out of any moneys in the Treasury. Other sections of the title prescribe the method by which the pay-

ments are to be made to the state (§ 302) and also certain conditions to be established to the satisfaction of the Social Security Board before certifying the propriety of a payment to the Secretary of the Treasury. § 303. They are designed to give assurance to the Federal Government that the moneys granted by it will not be expended for purposes alien to the grant, and will be used in the administration of genuine unemployment compensation laws.

The assault on the statute proceeds on an extended front. Its assailants take the ground that the tax is not an excise; that it is not uniform throughout the United States as excises are required to be; that its exceptions are so many and arbitrary as to violate the Fifth Amendment; that its purpose was not revenue, but an unlawful invasion of the reserved powers of the states; and that the states in submitting to it have yielded to coercion and have abandoned governmental functions which they are not permitted to surrender.

The objections will be considered seriatim with such further explanation as may be necessary to make their meaning clear.

First. The tax, which is described in the statute as an excise, is laid with uniformity throughout the United States as a duty, an impost or an excise upon the relation of employment.

1. We are told that the relation of employment is one so essential to the pursuit of happiness that it may not be burdened with a tax. Appeal is made to history. From the precedents of colonial days we are supplied with illustrations of excises common in the colonies. They are said to have been bound up with the enjoyment of particular commodities. Appeal is also made to principle or the analysis of concepts. An excise, we are told, imports a tax upon a privilege; employment, it is said, is a right, not a privilege, from which it follows that employment is not subject to an excise. Neither the one appeal nor the other leads to the desired goal.

As to the argument from history: Doubtless there were many excises in colonial days and later that were associated, more or less intimately, with the enjoyment or the use of property. This would not prove, even if no others were then known, that the forms then accepted were not subject to enlargement. . . But in truth other excises *were* known, and known since early times. Thus in 1695 (6 & 7 Wm. III. c. 6), Parliament passed an act which granted 'to His Majesty certain Rates and Duties upon Marriage, Births and Burials,' all for the purpose of 'carrying on the War against France with Vigour.' See *Opinion of the Justices,* 196 Mass. 603, 609, 85 N.E. 545. No commodity was affected there. The industry of counsel has supplied us with an apter illustration where the tax was not different in substance from the one now challenged as invalid. In 1777, before our Constitutional Convention, Parliament laid upon employers an annual 'duty' of 21 shillings for 'every male Servant' employed in stated forms of work. Revenue Act of 1777, 17 George III, c. 39. The point is made as a distinction that a tax upon the use of male servants was thought of as a tax upon a luxury. *Davis* v. *Boston & Maine R. Co., supra.* It did not touch employments in husbandry or business. This is to throw over the argument that historically an excise is a tax upon the enjoyment of commodities. But the attempted distinction, whatever may be thought of its validity, is inapplicable to a statute of Virginia passed in 1780. There a tax of three pounds, six shillings and eight pence was to be paid for every male tithable above the age of twenty-one years (with stated exceptions), and a like tax for 'every white servant whatsoever, except apprentices under the age of twenty-one years.' 10 Hening's Statutes of Virginia, p. 244. Our colonial forbears knew more about ways of taxing than some of their descendants seem to be willing to concede.

The historical prop failing, the prop or fancied prop of principle remains. We learn that employment for lawful gain is a 'natural' or 'inherent' or 'inalienable' right, and not a 'privilege' at all. But natural rights, so called, are as much subject to taxation as rights of less importance. An excise is not limited to vocations or activities that may be prohibited altogether. It is not limited to those that are the outcome of a franchise. It extends to vocations or activities pursued as of common right. What the individual does in the operation of a business is amenable to taxation just as much as what he owns, at all events if the classification is not tyrannical or arbitrary. 'Business is as legitimate an object of the taxing powers as property.' *Newton* v. *Atchison,* 31 Kan. 151, 154 (per Brewer, J.); 1 Pac. 288. Indeed, ownership itself, as we had occasion to point out the other day, is only a bundle of rights and privileges invested with a single name. *Henneford* v. *Silas Mason Co.,* 300 U.S. 577. 'A state is at liberty, if it pleases, to tax them all collectively, or to separate the faggots and lay the charge distributively.' *Ibid.* Employment is a business relation, if not itself a business. It is a relation without which business could seldom be carried on effectively. The power to tax the activities and relations that constitute a calling considered as a unit is the power to tax any of them. The whole includes the parts. *Nashville, C. & St. L. Ry. Co.* v. *Wallace,* 288 U.S. 249, 267, 268.

The subject matter of taxation open to the power of the Congress is as comprehensive as that open to the power of the states, though the method of apportionment may at times be different. 'The Congress shall have power to lay and collect taxes, duties, imposts and excises.' Art. 1, § 8. If the tax is a direct one, it shall be apportioned according to the census or enumeration. If it is a duty, impost, or excise, it shall be uniform throughout the United States. Together, these classes include every form of tax appropriate to

sovereignty. Cf. *Burnet* v. *Brooks,* 288
U.S. 378, 403, 405; *Brushaber* v. *Union
Pacific R. Co.,* 240 U.S. 1, 12. Whether
the tax is to be classified as an 'excise' is
in truth not of critical importance. If not
that, it is an 'impost' (*Pollock* v. *Farmers'
Loan & Trust Co.,* 158 U.S. 601, 622, 625;
Pacific Insurance Co. v. *Soule,* 7 Wall.
433, 445), or a 'duty' (*Veazie Bank* v.
Fenno, 8 Wall. 533, 546, 547; *Pollock* v.
Farmers' Loan & Trust Co., 157 U.S. 429,
570; *Knowlton* v. *Moore,* 178 U.S. 41, 46).
A capitation or other 'direct' tax it certainly is not. 'Although there have been
from time to time intimations that there
might be some tax which was not a direct
tax nor included under the words "duties,
imposts and excises," such a tax for more
than one hundred years of national existence has as yet remained undiscovered,
notwithstanding the stress of particular
circumstances has invited thorough investigation into sources of powers.' *Pollock*
v. *Farmers' Loan & Trust Co.,* 157 U.S.
429, 557. There is no departure from that
thought in later cases, but rather a new
emphasis of it. Thus, in *Thomas* v. *United
States,* 192 U.S. 363, 370, it was said of
the words 'duties, imposts and excises' that
'they were used comprehensively to cover
customs and excise duties imposed on importation, consumption, manufacture and
sale of certain commodities, privileges, particular business transactions, vocations, occupations and the like.' At times taxpayers have contended that the Congress
is without power to lay an excise on the
enjoyment of a privilege created by state
law. The contention has been put aside
as baseless. Congress may tax the transmission of property by inheritance or will,
though the states and not Congress have
created the privilege of succession. *Knowlton* v. *Moore, supra,* p. 58. Congress may
tax the enjoyment of a corporate franchise,
though a state and not Congress has
brought the franchise into being. *Flint* v.
Stone Tracy Co., 220 U.S. 107, 155. The
statute books of the states are strewn with

illustrations of taxes laid on occupations
pursued of common right. We find no
basis for a holding that the power in that
regard which belongs by accepted practice
to the legislatures of the states, has been
denied by the Constitution to the Congress
of the nation.

2. The tax being an excise, its imposition
must conform to the canon of uniformity.
There has been no departure from this
requirement. According to the settled doctrine the uniformity exacted is geographical, not intrinsic. . .

Second. The excise is not invalid under
the provisions of the Fifth Amendment
by force of its exemptions.

The statute does not apply, as we have
seen, to employers of less than eight. It
does not apply to agricultural labor, or
domestic service in a private home or to
some other classes of less importance.
Petitioner contends that the effect of these
restrictions is an arbitrary discrimination
vitiating the tax.

The Fifth Amendment unlike the Fourteenth has no equal protection clause. *La
Belle Iron Works* v. *United States, supra;
Brushaber* v. *Union Pacific R. Co., supra,*
p. 24. But even the states, though subject
to such a clause, are not confined to a
formula of rigid uniformity in framing
measures of taxation. *Swiss Oil Corp.* v.
Shanks, 273 U.S. 407, 413. They may tax
some kinds of property at one rate, and
others at another, and exempt others altogether. . . They may lay an excise on
the operations of a particular kind of business, and exempt some other kind of business closely akin thereto. . . If this lati-
tude of judgment is lawful for the states,
it is lawful, *a fortiori,* in legislation by the
Congress, which is subject to restraints
less narrow and confining. . .

The classifications and exemptions directed by the statute now in controversy
have support in considerations of policy
and practical convenience that cannot be
condemned as arbitrary. The classifications
and exemptions would therefore be upheld

if they had been adopted by a state and the provisions of the Fourteenth Amendment were invoked to annul them. This is held in two cases passed upon today in which precisely the same provisions were the subject of attack, the provisions being contained in the Unemployment Compensation Law of the State of Alabama. *Carmichael* v. *Southern Coal & Coke Co.,* and *Carmichael* v. *Gulf States Paper Corp., ante,* p. 495. The opinion rendered in those cases covers the ground fully. It would be useless to repeat the argument. The act of Congress is therefore valid, so far at least as its system of exemptions is concerned, and this though we assume that discrimination, if gross enough, is equivalent to confiscation and subject under the Fifth Amendment to challenge and annulment.

Third. The excise is not void as involving the coercion of the States in contravention of the Tenth Amendment or of restrictions implicit in our federal form of government.

The proceeds of the excise when collected are paid into the Treasury at Washington, and thereafter are subject to appropriation like public moneys generally. . . No presumption can be indulged that they will be misapplied or wasted. Even if they were collected in the hope or expectation that some other and collateral good would be furthered as an incident, that without more would not make the act invalid. *Sonzinsky* v. *United States,* 300 U.S. 506. This indeed is hardly questioned. The case for the petitioner is built on the contention that here an ulterior aim is wrought into the very structure of the act, and what is even more important that the aim is not only ulterior, but essentially unlawful. In particular, the 90 per cent credit is relied upon as supporting that conclusion. But before the statute succumbs to an assault upon these lines, two propositions must be made out by the assailant. . . There must be a showing in the first place that separated from the credit the revenue provisions are in-

capable of standing by themselves. There must be a showing in the second place that the tax and the credit in combination are weapons of coercion, destroying or impairing the autonomy of the states. The truth of each proposition being essential to the success of the assault, we pass for convenience to a consideration of the second, without pausing to inquire whether there has been a demonstration of the first.

To draw the line intelligently between duress and inducement there is need to remind ourselves of facts as to the problem of unemployment that are now matters of common knowledge. *West Coast Hotel Co.* v. *Parrish,* 300 U.S. 379. The relevant statistics are gathered in the brief of counsel for the Government. Of the many available figures a few only will be mentioned. During the years 1929 to 1936, when the country was passing through a cyclical depression, the number of the unemployed mounted to unprecedented heights. Often the average was more than 10 million; at times a peak was attained of 16 million or more. Disaster to the breadwinner meant disaster to dependents. Accordingly the roll of the unemployed, itself formidable enough, was only a partial roll of the destitute or needy. The fact developed quickly that the states were unable to give the requisite relief. The problem had become national in area and dimensions. There was need of help from the nation if the people were not to starve. It was too late today for the argument to be heard with tolerance that in a crisis so extreme the use of the moneys of the nation to relieve the unemployed and their dependents is a use for any purpose narrower than the promotion of the general welfare. . . The *parens patriae* has many reasons—fiscal and economic as well as social and moral—for planning to mitigate disasters that bring these burdens in their train.

In the presence of this urgent need for some remedial expedient, the question is to be answered whether the expedient adopted has overleapt the bounds of power. The assailants of the statute say that its dominant end and aim is to drive the state legislatures under the whip of economic pressure into the enactment of unemployment compensation laws at the bidding of the central government. Supporters of the statute say that its operation is not constraint, but the creation of a larger freedom, the states and the nation joining in a co-operative endeavor to avert a common evil. Before Congress acted, unemployment compensation insurance was still, for the most part, a project and no more. Wisconsin was the pioneer. Her statute was adopted in 1931. At times bills for such insurance were introduced elsewhere, but they did not reach the stage of law. In 1935, four states (California, Massachusetts, New Hampshire and New York) passed unemployment laws on the eve of the adoption of the Social Security Act, and two others did likewise after the federal act and later in the year. The statutes differed to some extent in type, but were directed to a common end. In 1936, twenty-eight other states fell in line, and eight more the present year. But if states had been holding back before the passage of the federal law, inaction was not owing, for the most part, to the lack of sympathetic interest. Many held back through alarm lest, in laying such a toll upon their industries, they would place themselves in a position of economic disadvantage as compared with neighbors or competitors. . . Two consequences ensued. One was that the freedom of a state to contribute its fair share to the solution of a national problem was paralyzed by fear. The other was that in so far as there was failure by the states to contribute relief according to the measure of their capacity, a disproportionate burden, and a mountainous one, was laid upon the resources of the Government of the nation.

The Social Security Act is an attempt to find a method by which all these public agencies may work together to a common

end. Every dollar of the new taxes will continue in all likelihood to be used and needed by the nation as long as states are unwilling, whether through timidity or for other motives, to do what can be done at home. At least the inference is permissible that Congress so believed, though retaining undiminished freedom to spend the money as it pleased. On the other hand fulfillment of the home duty will be lightened and encouraged by crediting the taxpayer upon his account with the Treasury of the nation to the extent that his contributions under the laws of the locality have simplified or diminished the problem of relief and the probable demand upon the resources of the fisc. Duplicated taxes, or burdens that approach them, are recognized hardships that government, state or national, may properly avoid. . . If Congress believed that the general welfare would better be promoted by relief through local units than by the system then in vogue, the co-operating localities ought not in all fairness to pay a second time.

Who then is coerced through the operation of this statute? Not the taxpayer. He pays in fulfillment of the mandate of the local legislature. Not the state. Even now she does not offer a suggestion that in passing the unemployment law she was affected by duress. . . For all that appears she is satisfied with her choice, and would be sorely disappointed if it were now to be annulled. The difficulty with the petitioner's contention is that it confuses motive with coercion. 'Every tax is in some measure regulatory. To some extent it interposes an economic impediment to the activity taxed as compared with others not taxed.' *Sonzinsky* v. *United States, supra.* In like manner every rebate from a tax when conditioned upon conduct is in some measure a temptation. But to hold that motive or temptation is equivalent to coercion is to plunge the law in endless difficulties. The outcome of such a doctrine is the acceptance of a philosophical determinism by which choice becomes impossible. Till now the law has been guided by a robust common sense which assumes the freedom of the will as a working hypothesis in the solution of its problems. The wisdom of the hypothesis has illustration in this case. Nothing in the case suggests the exertion of a power akin to undue influence, if we assume that such a concept can ever be applied with fitness to the relations between state and nation. Even on that assumption the location of the point at which pressure turns into compulsion, and ceases to be inducement, would be a question of degree,—at times, perhaps, of fact. The point had not been reached when Alabama made her choice. We cannot say that she was acting, not of her unfettered will, but under the strain of a persuasion equivalent to undue influence, when she chose to have relief administered under laws of her own making, by agents of her own selection, instead of under federal laws, administered by federal officers, with all the ensuing evils, at least to many minds, of federal patronage and power. There would be a strange irony, indeed, if her choice were now to be annulled on the basis of an assumed duress in the enactment of a statute which her courts have accepted as a true expression of her will. . . We think the choice must stand.

In ruling as we do, we leave many questions open. We do not say that a tax is valid, when imposed by act of Congress, if it is laid upon the condition that a state may escape its operation through the adoption of a statute unrelated in subject matter to activities fairly within the scope of national policy and power. No such question is before us. In the tender of this credit Congress does not intrude upon fields foreign to its function. The purpose of its intervention, as we have shown, is to safeguard its own treasury and as an incident to that protection to place the states upon a footing of equal opportunity. Drains upon its own resources are to be checked;

obstructions to the freedom of the states are to be leveled. It is one thing to impose a tax dependent upon the conduct of the taxpayers, or of the state in which they live, where the conduct to be stimulated or discouraged is unrelated to the fiscal need subserved by the tax in its normal operation, or to any other end legitimately national. The *Child Labor Tax Case,* 259 U.S. 20, and *Hill* v. *Wallace,* 259 U.S. 44, were decided in the belief that the statutes there condemned were exposed to that reproach. Cf. *United States* v. *Constantine,* 296 U.S. 287. It is quite another thing to say that a tax will be abated upon the doing of an act that will satisfy the fiscal need, the tax and the alternative being approximate equivalents. In such circumstances, if in no others, inducement or persuasion does not go beyond the bounds of power. We do not fix the outermost line. Enough for present purposes that wherever the line may be, this statute is within it. Definition more precise must abide the wisdom of the future.

Florida v. *Mellon,* 273 U.S. 12, supplies us with a precedent, if precedent be needed. What was in controversy there was § 301 of the Revenue Act of 1926, which imposes a tax upon the transfer of a decedent's estate, while at the same time permitting a credit, not exceeding 80 per cent, for 'the amount of any estate, inheritance, legacy, or succession taxes actually paid to any State or Territory.' Florida challenged that provision as unlawful. Florida had no inheritance taxes and alleged that under its constitution it could not levy any. 273 U.S. 12, 15. Indeed, by abolishing inheritance taxes, it had hoped to induce wealthy persons to become its citizens. See 67 Cong. Rec., Part 1, pp. 735, 752. It argued at our bar that 'the Estate Tax provision was not passed for the purpose of raising federal revenue' (273 U.S. 12, 14), but rather 'to coerce States into adopting estate or inheritance tax laws.' 273 U.S. 12, 13. In fact, as a result of the 80 per cent credit, material changes of such laws were made in 36 states. In the face of that attack we upheld the act as valid. Cf. *Massachusetts* v. *Mellon,* 262 U.S. 447, 482; also Act of August 5, 1861, c. 45, 12 Stat. 292; Act of May 13, 1862, c. 66, 12 Stat. 384.

United States v. *Butler, supra,* is cited by petitioner as a decision to the contrary. There a tax was imposed on processors of farm products, the proceeds to be paid to farmers who would reduce their acreage and crops under agreements with the Secretary of Agriculture, the plan of the act being to increase the prices of certain farm products by decreasing the quantities produced. The court held (1) that the so-called tax was not a true one (pp. 56, 61), the proceeds being earmarked for the benefit of farmers complying with the prescribed conditions, (2) that there was an attempt to regulate production without the consent of the state in which production was affected, and (3) that the payments to farmers were coupled with coercive contracts (p. 73), unlawful in their aim and oppressive in their consequences. The decision was by a divided court, a minority taking the view that the objections were untenable. None of them is applicable to the situation here developed.

(a) The proceeds of the tax in controversy are not earmarked for a special group.

(b) The unemployment compensation law which is a condition of the credit has had the approval of the state and could not be a law without it.

(c) The condition is not linked to an irrevocable agreement, for the state at its pleasure may repeal its unemployment law, § 903 (a) (6), terminate the credit, and place itself where it was before the credit was accepted.

(d) The condition is not directed to the attainment of an unlawful end, but to an end, the relief of unemployment, for which nation and state may lawfully co-operate.

Fourth. The statute does not call for a surrender by the states of powers essential to their quasi-sovereign existence.

Argument to the contrary has its source in two sections of the act. One section (903) defines the minimum criteria to which a state compensation system is required to conform if it is to be accepted by the Board as the basis for a credit. The other section (904) rounds out the requirement with complementary rights and duties. Not all the criteria or their incidents are challenged as unlawful. We will speak of them first generally, and then more specifically in so far as they are questioned.

A credit to taxpayers for payments made to a State under a state unemployment law will be manifestly futile in the absence of some assurance that the law leading to the credit is in truth what it professes to be. An unemployment law framed in such a way that the unemployed who look to it will be deprived of reasonable protection is one in name and nothing more. What is basic and essential may be assured by suitable conditions. The terms embodied in these sections are directed to that end. A wide range of judgment is given to the several states as to the particular type of statute to be spread upon their books. For anything to the contrary in the provision of this act they may use the pooled unemployment form, which is in effect with variations in Alabama, California, Michigan, New York, and elsewhere. They may establish a system of merit ratings applicable at once or to go into effect later on the basis of subsequent experience. Cf. §§ 909, 910. They may provide for employee contributions as in Alabama and California, or put the entire burden upon the employer as in New York. They may choose a system of unemployment reserve accounts by which an employer is permitted after his reserve has accumulated to contribute at a reduced rate or even not at all. This is the system which had its origin in Wisconsin. What they may not do, if they would earn the credit, is to depart from those standards which in the judgment of Congress are to be ranked as fundamental. Even if opinion may differ as to the fundamental quality of one or more of the conditions, the difference will not avail to vitiate the statute. In determining essentials Congress must have the benefit of a fair margin of discretion. One cannot say with reason that this margin has been exceeded, or that the basic standards have been determined in any arbitrary fashion. In the event that some particular condition shall be found to be too uncertain to be capable of enforcement, it may be severed from the others, and what is left will still be valid.

We are to keep in mind steadily that the conditions to be approved by the Board as the basis for a credit are not provisions of a contract, but terms of a statute, which may be altered or repealed. § 903 (a) (6). The state does not bind itself to keep the law in force. It does not even bind itself that the moneys paid into the federal fund will be kept there indefinitely or for any stated time. On the contrary, the Secretary of the Treasury will honor a requisition for the whole or any part of the deposit in the fund whenever one is made by the appropriate officials. The only consequence of the repeal or excessive amendment of the statute, or the expenditure of the money, when requisitioned, for other than compensation uses or administrative expenses, is that approval of the law will end, and with it the allowance of a credit, upon notice to the state agency and an opportunity for hearing. § 903 (b) (c).

These basic considerations are in truth a solvent of the problem. Subjected to their test, the several objections on the score of abdication are found to be unreal.

Thus, the argument is made that by force of an agreement the moneys when withdrawn must be 'paid through public employment offices in the State or through such other agencies as the Board may approve.' § 903 (a) (1). But in truth there is no agreement as to the method of dis-

bursement. There is only a condition which the state is free at pleasure to disregard or to fulfill. Moreover, approval is not requisite if public employment offices are made the disbursing instruments. Approval is to be a check upon resort to 'other agencies' that may, perchance, be irresponsible. A state looking for a credit must give assurance that her system has been organized upon a base of rationality.

There is argument again that the moneys when withdrawn are to be devoted to specific uses, the relief of unemployment, and that by agreement for such payment the quasi-sovereign position of the state has been impaired, if not abandoned. But again there is confusion between promise and condition. Alabama is still free, without breach of an agreement, to change her system overnight. No officer or agency of the national Government can force a compensation law upon her or keep it in existence. No officer or agency of that Government, either by suit or other means, can supervise or control the application of the payments.

Finally and chiefly, abdication is supposed to follow from § 904 of the statute and the parts of § 903 that are complementary thereto. § 903 (a) (3). By these the Secretary of the Treasury is authorized and directed to receive and hold in the Unemployment Trust Fund all moneys deposited therein by a state agency for a state unemployment fund and to invest in obligations of the United States such portion of the Fund as is not in his judgment required to meet current withdrawals. We are told that Alabama in consenting to that deposit has renounced the plenitude of power inherent in her statehood.

The same pervasive misconception is in evidence again. All that the state has done is to say in effect through the enactment of a statute that her agents shall be authorized to deposit the unemployment tax receipts in the Treasury at Washington. Alabama Unemployment Act of September 14, 1935, § 10 (i). The statute may be repealed. § 903 (a) (6). The consent may be revoked. The deposits may be withdrawn. The moment the state commission gives notice to the depositary that it would like the moneys back, the Treasurer will return them. To find state destruction there is to find it almost anywhere. With nearly as much reason one might say that a state abdicates its functions when it places the state moneys on deposit in a national bank.

There are very good reasons of fiscal and governmental policy why a State should be willing to make the Secretary of the Treasury the custodian of the fund. His possession of the moneys and his control of investments will be an assurance of stability and safety in times of stress and strain. A report of the Ways and Means Committee of the House of Representatives, quoted in the margin, develops the situation clearly. Nor is there risk of loss or waste. The credit of the Treasury is at all times back of the deposit, with the result that the right of withdrawal will be unaffected by the fate of any intermediate investments, just as if a checking account in the usual form had been opened in a bank.

The inference of abdication thus dissolves in thinnest air when the deposit is conceived of as dependent upon a statutory consent, and not upon a contract effective to create a duty. By this we do not intimate that the conclusion would be different if a contract were discovered. Even sovereigns may contract without derogating from their sovereignty. . . The states are at liberty, upon obtaining the consent of Congress, to make agreements with one another. Constitution Art. 1, § 10, Par. 3. . . We find no room for doubt that they may do the like with Congress if the essence of their statehood is maintained without impairment. Alabama is seeking and obtaining a credit of many millions in favor of her citizens out of the Treasury of the nation. Nowhere in our scheme of government—in the limitations express or implied of our federal constitution—do we find that she is prohibited from assenting to conditions that will assure a fair and just requital for benefits received. But we will not labor the point further. An unreal prohibition directed to an unreal agreement will not vitiate an act of Congress, and cause it to collapse in ruin.

Fifth. Title III of the act is separable from Title IX, and its validity is not at issue.

The essential provisions of that title have been stated in the opinion. As already pointed out, the title does not appropriate a dollar of the public moneys. It does no more than authorize appropriations to be made in the future for the purpose of assisting states in the administration of their laws, if Congress shall decide that appropriations are desirable. The title might be expunged, and Title IX would stand intact. Without a severability clause we should still be led to that conclusion. The presence of such a clause (§ 1103) makes the conclusion even clearer. . .

The judgment is

Affirmed.

[Separate dissenting opinions were filed by Justices McReynolds, Butler and Sutherland. J. Van Devanter concurred with J. Sutherland.]

XVII

Foreign Relations

NOTE

With respect to the control of foreign affairs it is perhaps more appropriate to use the term 'national' rather than 'federal' when describing the central government of the United States; the former term connotes a greater centralization of authority. Since the component parts of the Union are forbidden to enter this field the jurisdiction of the national government is therefore exclusive. At this point the question arises whether this exclusive authority of the national government over external affairs is to be found among those powers delegated to it by the Constitution or whether they are inherent, as 'necessary concomitants of nationality.' The latter alternative has become the accepted doctrine.

Most of the powers of the national government have their immediate source in the Constitution, but not its power to deal with foreign affairs. It has been suggested that this power is simply the arithmetic total of all those enumerated powers dealing directly or indirectly with external matters, but this notion finds no support today. If the power has its source in the Constitution at all, it is only in the sense that, having created a sovereign nation, the Constitution thereby bestowed upon the government of that nation all the powers implicit in sovereignty. Principal among these is the power to conduct its foreign affairs without limitation.

In a case upholding the unlimited power of the national government to exclude aliens, this concept of sovereignty was alluded to by Mr. Justice Field in *Chae Chan Ping* v. *United States* (Chinese Exclusion Case).[1] He said: 'While under our Constitution and form of government the great mass of local matters is controlled by local authorities, the United States, in their relation to foreign countries . . . are one nation, invested with powers which belong to independent nations, the exercise of which can be invoked for the maintenance of its absolute independence and security throughout its entire territory.'[2]

Shortly thereafter, in upholding the correlative power to deport aliens, Mr. Justice Gray said in *Fong Yue Ting* v. *United States*,[3] 'The United States are a sovereign and independent nation, and are vested by the Constitution with the entire control of international relations [*sic*], and with all the powers of government necessary to maintain that control and to make it effective. The only government of this country, which other nations recognize or treat with, is the government of the Union; and the only American flag known throughout the world is the flag of the United States.'[4]

Differentiating between sovereignty over external affairs and sovereignty over

[1] 130 U.S. 581 (1889).   [2] Ibid. 604.   [3] 149 U.S. 698 (1893).   [4] Ibid. 711.

internal affairs, a very early case anticipated the use that was to be made of this distinction in the future. In *Penhallow* v. *Doane*,[5] Mr. Justice Iredell expressed the view that while sovereignty over both external and internal affairs had originally rested with the states, the former had been relinquished and vested in the national government upon the adoption of the Constitution. In the same case, Mr. Justice Paterson contended that at no time had the states possessed external sovereignty; this being the case, they could not have bestowed it upon the national government. Rather, the national government had inherited it directly from the Continental Congress.

It has come to be accepted doctrine in American constitutional law that the power of the national government over the country's foreign relations is necessarily complete and exclusive. It cannot be considered as a mere aggregate of powers enumerated in the Constitution. To the sum of enumerated powers has been added the power implicit in the concept of sovereignty. Professor Corwin has described it as an inherent power 'attributed to the National Government on the ground solely of its belonging to the American People as a sovereign political entity at International Law.'[6] Consequently, 'silence on the part of the Constitution as to the power of the National Government to adopt any particular measure in relation to other nations is not a denial of such power, as it would be if the doctrine of Enumerated Powers applied, but is, on the contrary, an affirmance of power.'[7]

The Supreme Court, speaking through Mr. Justice Sutherland,[8] firmly established this doctrine in *United States* v. *Curtiss-Wright Export Corporation*. Here it will be seen that the line dividing external powers from internal powers cannot be clearly drawn, despite the fact that the doctrine as stated above would seem to imply that there is a distinct difference between the two. Furthermore, the case illustrates the fact that the Court applies criteria of constitutionality in testing the exercise of external power which are considerably different from the criteria used in testing the validity of domestic power.

A joint resolution passed by Congress in 1934 empowered the President to place an embargo upon the sale of arms to certain South American countries when in his opinion, and completely at his discretion, such an embargo would 'contribute to the re-establishment of peace between those countries.' The corporation involved here was convicted of violating the President's proclamation of the embargo by selling machine guns to Bolivia, then at war with Paraguay in the Chaco. Clearly a delegation of legislative power to the President, the joint resolution was upheld despite the lack of a 'standard' by which executive action was to be guided.[9]

[5] 3 Dall. 54 (1795).

[6] Corwin, Edward S., *The Constitution and World Organization*, Princeton, 1944, p. 19.

[7] Ibid.

[8] Three years before he joined the Court, Mr. Sutherland, ex-Senator from Utah, published *Constitutional Power and World Affairs*, New York, 1919. The book in large measure anticipates his opinion in this case.

[9] Compare this case with *Schechter* v. *United States*, 295 U.S. 495 (1935), and *Panama Refining Co.* v. *Ryan*, 293 U.S. 388 (1935), in which sections of the National Industrial Recovery Act were in-

UNITED STATES v. CURTISS-WRIGHT EXPORT CORPORATION
299 U.S. 304 (1936)

Mr. Justice Sutherland delivered the opinion of the Court.

On January 27, 1936, an indictment was returned in the court below, the first count of which charges that appellees, beginning with the 29th day of May, 1934, conspired to sell in the United States certain arms of war, namely fifteen machine guns, to Bolivia, a country then engaged in armed conflict in the Chaco, in violation of the Joint Resolution of Congress approved May 28, 1934, and the provisions of a proclamation issued on the same day by the President of the United States pursuant to authority conferred by § 1 of the resolution. In pursuance of the conspiracy, the commission of certain overt acts was alleged, details of which need not be stated. The Joint Resolution (c. 365, 48 Stat. 811) follows:

'*Resolved by the Senate and House of Representatives of the United States of America in Congress assembled,* That if the President finds that the prohibition of the sale of arms and munitions of war in the United States to those countries now engaged in armed conflict in the Chaco may contribute to the re-establishment of peace between those countries, and if after consultation with the governments of other American Republics and with their co-operation, as well as that of such other governments as he may deem necessary, he makes proclamation to that effect, it shall be unlawful to sell, except under such limitations and exceptions as the President prescribes, any arms or munitions of war in any place in the United States to the countries now engaged in that armed conflict, or to any person, company, or association acting in the interest of either country, until otherwise ordered by the President or by Congress.

'Sec. 2. Whoever sells any arms or munitions of war in violation of section 1 shall, on conviction, be punished by a fine not exceeding $10,000 or by imprisonment not exceeding two years, or both.'

The President's proclamation (48 Stat. 1744), after reciting the terms of the Joint Resolution, declares:

'Now, therefore, I, Franklin D. Roosevelt, President of the United States of America, acting under and by virtue of the authority conferred in me by the said joint resolution of Congress, do hereby declare and proclaim that I have found that the prohibition of the sale of arms and munitions of war in the United States to those countries now engaged in armed conflict in the Chaco may contribute to the re-establishment of peace between those countries, and that I have consulted with the governments of other American Republics and have been assured of the co-operation of such governments as I have deemed necessary as contemplated by the said joint resolution; and I do hereby admonish all citizens of the United States and every person to abstain from every violation of the provisions of the joint resolution above set forth, hereby made applicable to Bolivia and Paraguay, and I do hereby warn them that all violations of such provisions will be rigorously prosecuted.

'And I do hereby enjoin upon all officers of the United States charged with the execution of the laws thereof, the utmost diligence in preventing violations of the said joint resolution and this my proclamation issued thereunder, and in bringing

validated for unconstitutional delegation of legislative authority to the President. Less discretionary power was involved in these cases than in the Curtiss-Wright Case.

to trial and punishment any offenders against the same.

'And I do hereby delegate to the Secretary of State the power of prescribing exceptions and limitations to the application of the said joint resolution of May 28, 1934, as made effective by this my proclamation issued thereunder.'

On November 14, 1935, this proclamation was revoked (49 Stat. 3480), in the following terms:

'Now, therefore, I, Franklin D. Roosevelt, President of the United States of America, do hereby declare and proclaim that I have found that the prohibition of the sale of arms and munitions of war in the United States to Bolivia or Paraguay will no longer be necessary as a contribution to the re-establishment of peace between those countries, and the above-mentioned Proclamation of May 28, 1934, is hereby revoked as to the sale of arms and munitions of war to Bolivia or Paraguay from and after November 29, 1935, provided, however, that this action shall not have the effect of releasing or extinguishing any penalty, forfeiture or liability incurred under the aforesaid Proclamation of May 28, 1934, or the Joint Resolution of Congress approved by the President on the same date; and that the said Proclamation and Joint Resolution shall be treated as remaining in force for the purpose of sustaining any proper action or prosecution for the enforcement of such penalty, forfeiture or liability.'

Appellees severally demurred to the first count of the indictment on the grounds (1) that it did not charge facts sufficient to show the commission by appellees of any offense against any law of the United States; (2) that this count of the indictment charges a conspiracy to violate the joint resolution and the Presidential proclamation, both of which had expired according to the terms of the joint resolution by reason of the revocation contained in the Presidential proclamation of November 14, 1935, and were not in force at the time when the indictment was found. The points urged in support of the demurrers were, first, that the joint resolution effects an invalid delegation of legislative power to the executive; second, that the joint resolution never became effective because of the failure of the President to find essential jurisdictional facts; and third, that the second proclamation operated to put an end to the alleged liability under the joint resolution.

The court below sustained the demurrers upon the first point, but overruled them on the second and third points. 14 F. Supp. 230. The government appealed to this court under the provisions of the Criminal Appeals Act of March 2, 1907, 34 Stat. 1246, as amended, U.S.C. Title 18, § 682. That act authorizes the United States to appeal from a district court direct to this court in criminal cases where, among other things, the decision sustaining a demurrer to the indictment or any count thereof is based upon the invalidity or construction of the statute upon which the indictment is founded.

First. It is contended that by the Joint Resolution, the going into effect and continued operation of the resolution was conditioned (a) upon the President's judgment as to its beneficial effect upon the re-establishment of peace between the countries engaged in armed conflict in the Chaco; (b) upon the making of a proclamation, which was left to his unfettered discretion, thus constituting an attempted substitution of the President's will for that of Congress; (c) upon the making of a proclamation putting an end to the operation of the resolution, which again was left to the President's unfettered discretion; and (d) further, that the extent of its operation in particular cases was subject to limitation and exception by the President, controlled by no standard. In each of these particulars, appellees urge that Congress abdicated its essential functions and delegated them to the Executive.

Whether, if the Joint Resolution had

related solely to internal affairs it would be open to the challenge that it constituted an unlawful delegation of legislative power to the Executive, we find it unnecessary to determine. The whole aim of the resolution is to affect a situation entirely external to the United States, and falling within the category of foreign affairs. The determination which we are called to make, therefore, is whether the Joint Resolution, as applied to that situation, is vulnerable to attack under the rule that forbids a delegation of the law-making power. In other words, assuming (but not deciding) that the challenged delegation, if it were confined to internal affairs, would be invalid, may it nevertheless be sustained on the ground that its exclusive aim is to afford a remedy for a hurtful condition within foreign territory?

It will contribute to the elucidation of the question if we first consider the differences between the powers of the federal government in respect of foreign or external affairs and those in respect of domestic or internal affairs. That there are differences between them, and that these differences are fundamental, may not be doubted.

The two classes of powers are different, both in respect of their origin and their nature. The broad statement that the federal government can exercise no powers except those specifically enumerated in the Constitution, and such implied powers as are necessary and proper to carry into effect the enumerated powers, is categorically true only in respect of our internal affairs. In that field, the primary purpose of the Constitution was to carve from the general mass of legislative powers *then possessed by the states* such portions as it was thought desirable to vest in the federal government, leaving those not included in the enumeration still in the states. *Carter* v. *Carter Coal Co.,* 298 U.S. 238, 294. That this doctrine applies only to powers which the states had, is self

evident. And since the states severally never possessed international powers, such powers could not have been carved from the mass of state powers but obviously were transmitted to the United States from some other source. During the colonial period, those powers were possessed exclusively by and were entirely under the control of the Crown. By the Declaration of Independence, 'the Representatives of the United States of America' declared the United [not the several] Colonies to be free and independent states, and as such to have 'full Power to levy War, conclude Peace, contract Alliances, establish Commerce and to do all other Acts and Things which Independent States may of right do.'

As a result of the separation from Great Britain by the colonies acting as a unit, the powers of external sovereignty passed from the Crown not to the colonies severally, but to the colonies in their collective and corporate capacity as the United States of America. Even before the Declaration, the colonies were a unit in foreign affairs, acting through a common agency—namely the Continental Congress, composed of delegates from the thirteen colonies. That agency exercised the powers of war and peace, raised an army, created a navy, and finally adopted the Declaration of Independence. Rulers come and go; governments end and forms of government change; but sovereignty survives. A political society cannot endure without a supreme will somewhere. Sovereignty is never held in suspense. When, therefore, the external sovereignty of Great Britain in respect of the colonies ceased, it immediately passed to the Union. *See Penhallow* v. *Doane,* 3 Dall. 54, 80-81. That fact was given practical application almost at once. The treaty of peace, made on September 23, 1783, was concluded between his Britannic Majesty and the 'United States of America.' 8 Stat.—European Treaties—80.

The Union existed before the Constitution, which was ordained and established among other things to form 'a more perfect Union.' Prior to that event, it is clear that the Union, declared by the Articles of Confederation to be 'perpetual,' was the sole possessor of external sovereignty and in the Union it remained without change save in so far as the Constitution in express terms qualified its exercise. The Framers' Convention was called and exerted its powers upon the irrefutable postulate that though the states were several their people in respect of foreign affairs were one. Compare *The Chinese Exclusion Case,* 130 U.S. 581, 604, 606. In that convention, the entire absence of state power to deal with those affairs was thus forcefully stated by Rufus King:

'The states were not "sovereigns" in the sense contended for by some. They did not possess the peculiar features of sovereignty,—they could not make war, nor peace, nor alliances, nor treaties. Considering them as political beings, they were dumb, for they could not speak to any foreign sovereign whatever. They were deaf, for they could not hear any propositions from such sovereign. They had not even the organs or faculties of defence or offence, for they could not of themselves raise troops, or equip vessels, for war.' 5 Elliot's Debates 212.

It results that the investment of the federal government with the powers of external sovereignty did not depend upon the affirmative grants of the Constitution. The powers to declare and wage war, to conclude peace, to make treaties, to maintain diplomatic relations with other sovereignties, if they had never been mentioned in the Constitution, would have vested in the federal government as necessary concomitants of nationality. Neither the Constitution nor the laws passed in pursuance of it have any force in foreign territory unless in respect of our own citizens (see *American Banana Co.* v. *United Fruit Co.,* 213 U.S. 347, 356); and operations of the nation in such territory must be governed by treaties, international understandings and compacts, and the principles of international law. As a member of the family of nations, the right and power of the United States in that field are equal to the right and power of the other members of the international family. Otherwise, the United States is not completely sovereign. The power to acquire territory by discovery and occupation (*Jones* v. *United States,* 137 U.S. 202, 212), the power to expel undesirable aliens (*Fong Yue Ting* v. *United States,* 149 U.S. 698, 705 *et seq.*), the power to make such international agreements as do not constitute treaties in the constitutional sense (*Altman & Co.* v. *United States,* 224 U.S. 583, 600-601; Crandall, Treaties, Their Making and Enforcement, 2d ed., p. 102 and note 1), none of which is expressly affirmed by the Constitution, nevertheless exist as inherently inseparable from the conception of nationality. This the court recognized, and in each of the cases cited found the warrant for its conclusions not in the provisions of the Constitution, but in the law of nations.

In *Burnet* v. *Brooks,* 288 U.S. 378, 396, we said, 'As a nation with all the attributes of sovereignty, the United States is vested with all the powers of government necessary to maintain an effective control of international relations.' Cf. *Carter* v. *Carter Coal Co., supra,* p. 295.

Not only, as we have shown, is the federal power over external affairs in origin and essential character different from that over internal affairs, but participation in the exercise of the power is significantly limited. In this vast external realm, with its important, complicated, delicate and manifold problems, the President alone has the power to speak or listen as a representative of the nation. He *makes* treaties with the advice and consent of the Senate; but he alone negotiates. Into the field of negotiation the Senate cannot intrude; and Congress itself is powerless to invade it. As Marshall said in his great argument of March 7, 1800, in the House of Representatives, 'The President is the sole organ of the nation in its external relations, and its sole representative with foreign nations.' Annals, 6th Cong., col. 613. The Senate Committee on Foreign Relations at a very early day in our history (February 15, 1816), reported to the Senate, among other things, as follows:

'The President is the constitutional representative of the United States with regard to foreign nations. He manages our concerns with foreign nations and must necessarily be most competent to determine when, how, and upon what subjects negotiations may be urged with the greatest prospect of success. For his conduct he is responsible to the Constitution. The committee consider this responsibility the surest pledge for the faithful discharge of his duty. They think the interference of the Senate in the direction of foreign negotiations calculated to diminish that responsibility and thereby to impair the best security for the national safety. The nature of transactions with foreign nations, moreover, requires caution and unity of design, and their success frequently depends on secrecy and dispatch.' U.S. Senate, Reports, Committee on Foreign Relations, vol. 8, p. 24.

It is important to bear in mind that we are here dealing not alone with an authority vested in the President by an exertion of legislative power, but with such an authority plus the very delicate, plenary and exclusive power of the President as the sole organ of the federal government in the field of international relations—a power which does not require as a basis for its exercise an act of Congress, but which, of course, like every other governmental power, must be exercised in subordination to the applicable provisions of the Constitution. It is quite apparent that if, in the maintenance of our international relations, embarrassment—perhaps serious embarrassment—is to be avoided and success for our aims achieved, congressional legislation which is to be made effective through negotiation and inquiry within the international field must often accord to the President a degree of discretion and freedom from statutory restriction which would not be admissible were domestic affairs alone involved. Moreover, he, not Congress, has the better opportunity of knowing the conditions which prevail in foreign countries, and especially is this true in time of war. He has his confidential sources of information. He has his agents in the form of diplomatic, consular and other officials. Secrecy in respect of information gathered by them may be highly necessary, and the premature disclosure of it productive of harmful results. Indeed, so clearly is this true that the first President refused to accede to a request to lay before the House of Representatives the instructions, correspondence and documents relating to the negotiation of the Jay Treaty—a refusal the wisdom of which was recognized by the House itself and has never since been doubted. In his reply to the request, President Washington said:

'The nature of foreign negotiations requires caution, and their success must often depend on secrecy; and even when brought to a conclusion a full disclosure of all the measures, demands, or eventual concessions which may have been proposed or contemplated would be extremely impolitic; for this might have a pernicious influence on future negotiations, or produce immediate inconveniences, perhaps danger and mischief, in relation to other powers. The necessity of such caution and secrecy was one cogent reason for vesting the power of making treaties in the President, with the advice and consent of the Senate, the principle on which that body was formed confining it to a small number of members. To admit, then, a right in the House of Representatives to demand and to have as a matter of course all the papers respecting a negotiation with a foreign power would be to establish a dangerous precedent.' 1 *Messages and Papers of the Presidents,* p. 194.

The marked difference between foreign affairs and domestic affairs in this respect is recognized by both houses of Congress in the very form of their requisitions for information from the executive departments. In the case of every department except the Department of State, the resolution *directs* the official to furnish the information. In the case of the State Department, dealing with foreign affairs, the President is *requested* to furnish the information 'if not incompatible with the public interest.' A statement that to furnish the information is not compatible with the public interest rarely, if ever, is questioned.

When the President is to be authorized by legislation to act in respect of a matter intended to affect a situation in foreign territory, the legislator properly bears in mind the important consideration that the form of the President's action—or, indeed, whether he shall act at all—may well depend, among other things, upon the nature of the confidential information which he has or may thereafter receive, or upon the effect which his action may have upon our foreign relations. This consideration, in connection with what we have already said on the subject, discloses the unwisdom of requiring Congress in this field of governmental power to lay down narrowly definite standards by which the President is to be governed. As this court said in *Mackenzie* v. *Hare,* 239 U.S. 299, 311, 'As a government, the United States is invested with all the attributes of sovereignty. As it has the character of nationality it has the powers of nationality, especially those which concern its relations and intercourse with other countries. *We should hesitate long before limiting or embarrassing such powers.*' (Italics supplied.)

In the light of the foregoing observations, it is evident that this court should not be in haste to apply a general rule which will have the effect of condemning legislation like that under review as constituting an unlawful delegation of legislative power. The principles which justify such legislation find overwhelming support in the unbroken legislative practice which has prevailed almost from the inception of the national government to the present day.

Let us examine, in chronological order, the acts of legislation which warrant this conclusion:

The Act of June 4, 1794, authorized the President to lay, regulate and revoke embargoes. He was 'authorized' 'whenever, in his opinion, the public safety shall so require' to lay the embargo upon all ships and vessels in the ports of the United States, including those of foreign nations 'under such regulations as the circumstances of the case may require, and to continue or revoke the same, whenever he shall think proper.' C. 41, 1 Stat. 372. A prior joint resolution of May 7, 1794 (1 Stat. 401), had conferred *unqualified* power on the President to grant clearances, notwithstanding an existing embargo, to ships or vessels belonging to citizens of the United States bound to any port beyond the Cape of Good Hope.

The Act of March 3, 1795 (c. 53, 1 Stat. 444), gave the President authority to permit the exportation of arms, cannon and military stores, the law prohibiting such exports to the contrary notwithstanding, the only prescribed guide for his action being that such exports should be in 'cases connected with the security of the commercial interest of the United States, and for public purposes only.'

By the Act of June 13, 1798 (c. 53, § 5, 1 Stat. 566), it was provided that if the government of France 'shall clearly disavow, and shall be found to refrain from the aggressions, depredations and hostilities' theretofore maintained against vessels and property of the citizens of the United States, 'in violation of the faith of treaties, and the laws of nations, and shall thereby acknowledge the just claims of the United States to be considered as in all respects neutral . . . it shall be lawful for the

President of the United States, being well ascertained of the premises, to remit and discontinue the prohibitions and restraints hereby enacted and declared; and he shall be, and is hereby authorized to make proclamation thereof accordingly.'

By § 4 of the Act of February 9, 1799 (c. 2, 1 Stat. 615), it was made 'lawful' for the President, 'if he shall deem it expedient and consistent with the interest of the United States,' by order to remit certain restraints and prohibitions imposed by the act with respect to the French Republic, and also to revoke any such order 'whenever, in his opinion, the interest of the United States shall require.'

Similar authority, qualified in the same way, was conferred by § 6 of the Act of February 7, 1800, c. 10, 2 Stat. 9.

Section 5 of the Act of March 3, 1805 (c. 41, 2 Stat. 341), made it lawful for the President, whenever an armed vessel entering the harbors or waters within the jurisdiction of the United States and required to depart therefrom should fail to do so, not only to employ the land and naval forces to compel obedience, but 'if he shall think it proper, it shall be lawful for him to forbid, by proclamation, all intercourse with such vessel, and with every armed vessel of the same nation, and the officers and crew thereof; to prohibit all supplies and aid from being furnished them' and to do various other things connected therewith. Violation of the President's proclamation was penalized.

On February 28, 1806, an act was passed (c. 9, 2 Stat. 351) to suspend commercial intercourse between the United States and certain parts of the Island of St. Domingo. A penalty was prescribed for its violation. Notwithstanding the positive provisions of the act, it was by § 5 made 'lawful' for the President to remit and discontinue the restraints and prohibitions imposed by the act at any time 'if he shall deem it expedient and consistent with the interests of the United States' to do so. Likewise in respect of the Non-intercourse Act of

March 1, 1809, (c. 24, 2 Stat. 528); the President was 'authorized' (§ 11, p. 530), in case either of the countries affected should so revoke or modify her edicts 'as that they shall cease to violate the neutral commerce of the United States,' to proclaim the fact, after which the suspended trade might be renewed with the nation so doing.

Practically every volume of the United States Statutes contains one or more acts or joint resolutions of Congress authorizing action by the President in respect of subjects affecting foreign relations, which either leave the exercise of the power to his unrestricted judgment, or provide a standard far more general than that which has always been considered requisite with regard to domestic affairs. . .

It well may be assumed that these legislative precedents were in mind when Congress passed the joint resolutions of April 22, 1898, 30 Stat. 739; March 14, 1912, 37 Stat. 630; and January 31, 1922, 42 Stat. 361, to prohibit the export of coal or other war material. The resolution of 1898 authorized the President 'in his discretion, and with such limitations and exceptions as shall seem to him expedient' to prohibit such exportations. The striking identity of language found in the second resolution mentioned above and in the one now under review will be seen upon comparison. The resolution of March 14, 1912, provides:

'That whenever the President shall find that in any American country conditions of domestic violence exist which are promoted by the use of arms or munitions of war procured from the United States, and shall make proclamation thereof, it shall be unlawful to export except under such limitations and exceptions as the President shall prescribe any arms or munitions of war from any place in the United States to such country until otherwise ordered by the President or by Congress.

'SEC. 2. That any shipment of material hereby declared unlawful after such a proclamation shall be punishable by fine not exceeding ten thousand dollars, or imprisonment not exceeding two years, or both.'

The third resolution is in substantially the same terms, but extends to any country in which the United States exercises extraterritorial jurisdiction, and provides for the President's action not only when conditions of domestic violence exist which *are* promoted, but also when such conditions *may be* promoted, by the use of such arms or munitions of war.

We had occasion to review these embargo and kindred acts in connection with an exhaustive discussion of the general subject of delegation of legislative power in a recent case, *Panama Refining Co.* v. *Ryan,* 293 U.S. 388, 421-2, and in justifying such acts, pointed out that they confided to the President 'an authority which was cognate to the conduct by him of the foreign relations of the government.'

The result of holding that the joint resolution here under attack is void and unenforceable as constituting an unlawful delegation of legislative power would be to stamp this multitude of comparable acts and resolutions as likewise invalid. And while this court may not, and should not, hesitate to declare acts of Congress, however many times repeated, to be unconstitutional if beyond all rational doubt it finds them to be so, an impressive array of legislation such as we have just set forth, enacted by nearly every Congress from the beginning of our national existence to the present day, must be given unusual weight in the process of reaching a correct determination of the problem. A legislative practice such as we have here, evidenced not by only occasional instances, but marked by the movement of a steady stream for a century and a half of time, goes a long way in the direction of proving the presence of unassailable ground for the constitutionality of the practice, to be found in the origin and history of the

power involved, or in its nature, or in both combined.

In *The Laura,* 114 U.S. 411, 416, this court answered a challenge to the constitutionality of a statute authorizing the Secretary of the Treasury to remit or mitigate fines and penalties in certain cases, by repeating the language of a very early case (*Stuart* v. *Laird,* 1 Cranch 299, 309) that the long practice and acquiescence under the statute was a 'practical exposition . . . too strong and obstinate to be shaken or controlled. Of course, the question is at rest, and ought not now to be disturbed.' In *Burrow-Giles Lithographic Co.* v. *Sarony,* 111 U.S. 53, 57, the constitutionality of R. S. § 4952, conferring upon the author, inventor, designer or proprietor of a photograph certain rights, was involved. Mr. Justice Miller, speaking for the court, disposed of the point by saying: 'The construction placed upon the Constitution by the first act of 1790, and the act of 1802, by the men who were contemporary with its formation, many of whom were members of the convention which framed it, is of itself entitled to very great weight, and when it is remembered that the rights thus established have not been disputed during a period of nearly a century, it is almost conclusive.'

In *Field* v. *Clark,* 143 U.S. 649, 691, this court declared that '. . . the practical construction of the Constitution, as given by so many acts of Congress, and embracing almost the entire period of our national existence, should not be overruled, unless upon a conviction that such legislation was clearly incompatible with the supreme law of the land.' The rule is one which has been stated and applied many times by this court. As examples, see *Ames* v. *Kansas,* 111 U.S. 449, 469; *McCulloch* v. *Maryland,* 4 Wheat. 316, 401; *Downes* v. *Bidwell,* 182 U.S. 244, 286.

The uniform, long-continued and undisputed legislative practice just disclosed rests upon an admissible view of the Constitution which, even if the practice found far less support in principle than we think it does, we should not feel at liberty at this late day to disturb.

We deem it unnecessary to consider, *seriatim,* the several clauses which are said to evidence the unconstitutionality of the Joint Resolution as involving an unlawful delegation of legislative power. It is enough to summarize by saying that, both upon principle and in accordance with precedent, we conclude there is sufficient warrant for the broad discretion vested in the President to determine whether the enforcement of the statute will have a beneficial effect upon the re-establishment of peace in the affected countries; whether he shall make proclamation to bring the resolution into operation; whether and when the resolution shall cease to operate and to make proclamation accordingly; and to prescribe limitations and exceptions to which the enforcement of the resolution shall be subject.

Second. The second point raised by the demurrer was that the Joint Resolution never became effective because the President failed to find essential jurisdictional facts; and the third point was that the second proclamation of the President operated to put an end to the alleged liability of appellees under the Joint Resolution. In respect of both points, the court below overruled the demurrer, and thus far sustained the government.

The government contends that upon an appeal by the United States under the Criminal Appeals Act from a decision holding an indictment bad, the jurisdiction of the court does not extend to questions decided in favor of the United States, but that such questions may only be reviewed in the usual way after conviction. We find nothing in the words of the statute or in its purposes which justify this conclusion. The demurrer in the present case challenges the validity of the statute upon three separate and distinct grounds. If the court below had sustained the demurrer without more, an appeal by the govern-

ment necessarily would have brought here for our determination all of these grounds, since in that case the record would not have disclosed whether the court considered the statute invalid upon one particular ground or upon all of the grounds alleged. The judgment of the lower court is that the statute is invalid. Having held that this judgment cannot be sustained upon the particular ground which that court assigned, it is now open to this court to inquire whether or not the judgment can be sustained upon the rejected grounds which also challenge the validity of the statute and, therefore, constitute a proper subject of review by this court under the Criminal Appeals Act. *United States* v. *Hastings,* 296 U.S. 188, 192.

In *Langnes* v. *Green,* 282 U.S. 531, where the decree of a district court had been assailed upon two grounds and the circuit court of appeals had sustained the attack upon one of such grounds only, we held that a respondent in certiorari might nevertheless urge in this court in support of the decree the ground which the intermediate appellate court had rejected. That principle is applicable here.

We proceed, then, to a consideration of the second and third grounds of the demurrers which, as we have said, the court below rejected.

1. The Executive proclamation recites, 'I have found that the prohibition of the sale of arms and munitions of war in the United States to those countries now engaged in armed conflict in the Chaco may contribute to the re-establishment of peace between those countries, and that I have consulted with the governments of other American Republics *and have been assured of the co-operation of such governments as I have deemed necessary as contemplated by the said joint resolution.*' This finding satisfies every requirement of the Joint Resolution. There is no suggestion that the resolution is fatally uncertain or indefinite; and a finding which follows

its language, as this finding does, cannot well be challenged as insufficient.

But appellees, referring to the words which we have italicized above, contend that the finding is insufficient because the President does not declare that the co-operation of such governments as he deemed necessary included any American republic and, therefore, the recital contains no affirmative showing of compliance in this respect with the Joint Resolution. The criticism seems to us wholly wanting in substance. The President recites that he has consulted with the governments of other American republics, and that he has been assured of the co-operation of such governments as he deemed necessary *as contemplated by the joint resolution.* These recitals, construed together, fairly include within their meaning American republics.

2. The second proclamation of the President, revoking the first proclamation, it is urged, had the effect of putting an end to the Joint Resolution, and in accordance with a well-settled rule, no penalty could be enforced or punishment inflicted thereafter for an offense committed during the life of the Joint Resolution in the absence of a provision in the resolution to that effect. There is no doubt as to the general rule or as to the absence of a saving clause in the Joint Resolution. But is the case presented one which makes the rule applicable?

It was not within the power of the President to repeal the Joint Resolution; and his second proclamation did not purport to do so. It 'revoked' the first proclamation; and the question is, did the revocation of the proclamation have the effect of abrogating the resolution or of precluding its enforcement in so far as that involved the prosecution and punishment of offenses committed during the life of the first proclamation? We are of the opinion that it did not.

Prior to the first proclamation, the Joint Resolution was an existing law, but dor-

mant, awaiting the creation of a particular situation to render it active. No action or lack of action on the part of the President could destroy its potentiality. Congress alone could do that. The happening of the designated events—namely, the finding of certain conditions and the proclamation by the President—did not call the law into being. It created the occasion for it to function. The second proclamation did not put an end to the law or affect what had been done in violation of the law. The effect of the proclamation was simply to remove for the future, a condition of affairs which admitted of its exercise.

We should have had a different case if the Joint Resolution had expired by its own terms upon the issue of the second proclamation. Its operative force, it is true, was limited to the period of time covered by the first proclamation. And when the second proclamation was issued, the resolution ceased to be a rule for the future. It did not cease to be the law for the antecedent period of time. The distinction is clearly pointed out by the Superior Court of Judicature of New Hampshire in *Stevens* v. *Dimond,* 6 N.H. 330, 332, 333. There, a town by-law provided that if certain animals should be found going at large between the first day of April and the last day of October, etc., the owner would incur a prescribed penalty. The trial court directed the jury that the by-law, being in force for a year only, had expired so that the defendant could not be called upon to answer for a violation which occurred during the designated period. The state appellate court reversed, saying that when laws 'expire by their own limitation, or are repealed, they cease to be the law in relation to the past, as well as the future, and can no longer be enforced in any case. No case is, however, to be found in which it was ever held before that they thus ceased to be law, unless they expired by express limitation in themselves, or were repealed. It has never been decided that they cease to be law, merely because the time they were intended to regulate had expired. . . A very little consideration of the subject will convince any one that a limitation of the time to which a statute is to apply, is a very different thing from the limitation of the time a statute is to continue in force.'

The first proclamation of the President was in force from the 28th day of May, 1934, to the 14th day of November, 1935. If the Joint Resolution had in no way depended upon Presidential action, but had provided explicitly that, at any time between May 28, 1934, and November 14, 1935, it should be unlawful to sell arms or munitions of war to the countries engaged in armed conflict in the Chaco, it certainly could not be successfully contended that the law would expire with the passing of the time fixed in respect of offenses committed during the period.

The judgment of the court below must be reversed and the cause remanded for further proceedings in accordance with the foregoing opinion.

Reversed.

MR. JUSTICE McREYNOLDS does not agree. He is of opinion that the court below reached the right conclusion and its judgment ought to be affirmed.

MR. JUSTICE STONE took no part in the consideration or decision of this case.

NOTE

Under the American system the Federal government has exclusive jurisdiction over all matters concerning foreign affairs. Though not expressly stated in any particular provision of the written fundamental law, it is clearly deducible from the national character of the Federal government and from many express constitutional provisions.

One of the most important of these express grants of power is that which states that the President 'shall have power, by and with the advice and consent of the Senate, to make treaties, provided two-thirds of the Senators present concur.'[1] Elsewhere the states are forbidden to 'enter into any treaty, alliance, or confederation,'[2] and it is declared that 'This Constitution, and the laws of the United States which shall be made in pursuance thereof, and all treaties made, or which shall be made, under the authority of the United States, shall be the supreme law of the land.'[3]

These three provisions dispose of any doubt regarding the possibility of states rights imposing limitations upon the treaty-making power. But, granted that the power of the Federal government to make treaties is exclusive, is it likewise all inclusive? The fact that no court has ever impugned the constitutionality of a treaty should not be taken to mean that there are absolutely no limits upon the power to make them. Whatever those limits may be, they have thus far never been held to have been passed. Every challenge directed against the validity of a treaty by advocates of the rights of the states has met with failure in the courts; the terms of the Tenth Amendment are in this respect irrelevant.[4] The proposition that a treaty cannot authorize what the Constitution forbids serves more to confuse than to clarify; nor can credibility be given the notion that the President and the Senate may act freely in this sphere providing the matter treated upon is a proper subject of negotiation with a foreign nation. In all likelihood, the decision of whether a particular measure is 'a proper subject of negotiation' is for the President and the Senate to make; but should the question ever reach the Court, it may be assumed that they would either dismiss it summarily as a 'political question' or resolve all doubt in favor of the subject's propriety.

More important than the question of the possible limitations that might be placed upon the treaty-making power is the question of the extent to which Congress may derive legislative authority from it.

Among the specific grants of power given to Congress by the Constitution is

[1] Art. II, sec. 2.   [2] Art. I, sec. 10.   [3] Art. VI, sec. 2.

[4] 'A treaty can totally annihilate any part of the constitution of any of the individual states that is contrary to a treaty . . .' said Mr. Justice Chase in *Ware* v. *Hylton*, 3 Dall. 199, 242-3 (1797). See also *Hauenstein* v. *Lynham*, 100 U.S. 483 (1880), and *DeGeofroy* v. *Riggs*, 133 U.S. 258 (1890).

the power 'to make all laws which shall be necessary and proper for carrying into execution the foregoing powers, and all other powers vested by this Constitution in the government of the United States, or in any department or officer thereof.'[5] Here is ample evidence that Congress possesses not only the power to effectuate the congressional powers enumerated in the preceding seventeen clauses, but also, and more important here, the power to effectuate 'all other powers vested by this Constitution in the government of the United States. . .' Specifically, then, Congress is hereby given authority to pass all laws which in its judgment are necessary and proper to the effective execution of the treaty-making power, a power which Congress itself, of course, does not possess. Hence this derivative authority enables the legislative branch of the government, in the implementation of treaties, to enact laws in spheres otherwise beyond its reach.

In 1913 Congress passed an Act[6] regulating the killing of certain migratory birds within the states. The basis for its passage was presumably the commerce power; it was not a piece of ancillary legislation implementing a treaty. Some doubts as to the constitutionality of the Act were expressed in the Senate soon after its passage, and that body passed a resolution calling for a treaty on the subject.[7] On this occasion Senator Root was quoted as saying with regard to the resolution: 'I think, sir, that that may furnish a pathway along which we can proceed to some practical relief in regard to the very urgent and pressing evil. . . It may be that under the treaty-making power a situation can be created in which the Government of the United States will have constitutional authority to deal with this subject.'[8] Senators Borah and Reed, on the other hand, believed that the treaty-making power could not accomplish ends which were not within the express powers of Congress. Borah said: 'If we cannot ourselves deal with this matter . . . it seems to me inconceivable that we can get any aid by going to a foreign Government and making a treaty with that Government.'[9]

These misgivings as to the Act's validity proved to be well founded and it was soon declared unconstitutional in one state court and two lower Federal courts.[10] Meanwhile, the Department of State had taken notice of the Senate's resolution suggesting a treaty, and had concluded a pact with Great Britain providing for the regulation of migratory bird life. Upon its submittal to the Senate for ratification on 26 August 1916, that body, sitting in executive session, gave its approval in less than half an hour.[11]

Two years later, during debate on a bill to carry out the provisions of the Migratory Bird Treaty, Senator Reed vigorously attacked the measure on the ground that it was unconstitutional, treaty or no treaty. He said: 'The advocates of this bill . . . seem to be obsessed with the idea that Congress can do by treaty an act in violation of the Constitution of the United States which it cannot do by statute—a remarkable kind of logic, which, I think, can only be indulged in by

[5] Art. I, sec. 8.
[6] 37 Stat. 847.
[7] 50 Cong. Rec. 57, 2339-2340 (1913).
[8] 51 Cong. Rec. 8349 (1914).
[9] 51 Cong. Rec. 8354 (1914).
[10] *United States* v. *Shauver*, 214 Fed. 154 (1914); *United States* v. *McCullagh*, 221 Fed. 288 (1915).
[11] 53 Cong. Rec. 13348; 39 Stat. 1702 (1916).

a man who has become thoroughly obsessed with this bird legislation.'[12] Despite
the arguments against its constitutionality expressed by Reed and others in the
Senate, and considerable opposition to it in the House,[13] the bill became law as
the Migratory Bird Treaty Act of 3 July 1918.[14] Its constitutionality was upheld
in 1920 by the Supreme Court in *Missouri* v. *Holland.*

MISSOURI v. HOLLAND
252 U.S. 416 (1920)

MR. JUSTICE HOLMES delivered the opinion of the court.

This is a bill in equity brought by the State of Missouri to prevent a game warden of the United States from attempting to enforce the Migratory Bird Treaty Act of July 3, 1918, c. 128, 40 Stat. 755, and the regulations made by the Secretary of Agriculture in pursuance of the same. The ground of the bill is that the statute is an unconstitutional interference with the rights reserved to the States by the Tenth Amendment, and that the acts of the defendant done and threatened under that authority invade the sovereign right of the State and contravene its will manifested in statutes. The State also alleges a pecuniary interest, as owner of the wild birds within its borders and otherwise, admitted by the Government to be sufficient, but it is enough that the bill is a reasonable and proper means to assert the alleged quasi sovereign rights of a State. *Kansas* v. *Colorado,* 185 U.S. 125, 142. *Georgia* v. *Tennessee Copper Co.,* 206 U.S. 230, 237. *Marshall Dental Manufacturing Co.* v. *Iowa,* 226 U.S. 460, 462. A motion to dismiss was sustained by the District Court on the ground that the act of Congress is constitutional. 258 Fed. Rep. 479. Acc. *United States* v. *Thompson* 258 Fed. Rep. 257; *United States* v. *Rockefeller,* 260 Fed. Rep. 346. The State appeals.

On December 8, 1916, a treaty between the United States and Great Britain was proclaimed by the President. It recited that many species of birds in their annual migrations traversed certain parts of the United States and of Canada, that they were of great value as a source of food and in destroying insects injurious to vegetation, but were in danger of extermination through lack of adequate protection. It therefore provided for specified close seasons and protection in other forms, and agreed that the two powers would take or propose to their lawmaking bodies the necessary measures for carrying the treaty out. 39 Stat. 1702. The above mentioned Act of July 3, 1918, entitled an act to give effect to the convention, prohibited the killing, capturing or selling any of the migratory birds included in the terms of the treaty except as permitted by regulations compatible with those terms, to be made by the Secretary of Agriculture. Regulations were proclaimed on July 31, and October 25, 1918. 40 Stat. 1812; 1863. It is unnecessary to go into any details, because, as we have said, the question raised is the general one whether the treaty and statute are void as an interference with the rights reserved to the States.

To answer this question it is not enough to refer to the Tenth Amendment, reserving the powers not delegated to the United States, because by Article II, § 2, the power to make treaties is delegated expressly, and by Article VI treaties made under the authority of the United States, along with the Constitution and laws of

[12] 55 Cong. Rec. 5547 (1918).
[13] 56 Cong. Rec. 7361, 7363, 7365, 7369, 7446, 7462 (1918).
[14] 40 Stat. 755 (1918).

the United States made in pursuance thereof, are declared the supreme law of the land. If the treaty is valid there can be no dispute about the validity of the statute under Article 1, § 8, as a necessary and proper means to execute the powers of the Government. The language of the Constitution as to the supremacy of treaties being general, the question before us is narrowed to an inquiry into the ground upon which the present supposed exception is placed.

It is said that a treaty cannot be valid if it infringes the Constitution, that there are limits, therefore, to the treaty-making power, and that one such limit is that what an act of Congress could not do unaided, in derogation of the powers reserved to the States, a treaty cannot do. An earlier act of Congress that attempted by itself and not in pursuance of a treaty to regulate the killing of migratory birds within the States had been held bad in the District Court. *United States* v. *Shauver*, 214 Fed. Rep. 154. *United States* v. *McCullagh*, 221 Fed. Rep. 288. Those decisions were supported by arguments that migratory birds were owned by the States in their sovereign capacity for the benefit of their people, and that under cases like *Geer* v. *Connecticut*, 161 U.S. 519, this control was one that Congress had no power to displace. The same argument is supposed to apply now with equal force.

Whether the two cases cited were decided rightly or not they cannot be accepted as a test of the treaty power. Acts of Congress are the supreme law of the land only when made in pursuance of the Constitution, while treaties are declared to be so when made under the authority of the United States. It is open to question whether the authority of the United States means more than the formal acts prescribed to make the convention. We do not mean to imply that there are no qualifications to the treaty-making power; but they must be ascertained in a different way. It is obvious that there may be matters of the sharpest exigency for the national well being that an act of Congress could not deal with but that a treaty followed by such an act could, and it is not lightly to be assumed that, in matters requiring national action, 'a power which must belong to and somewhere reside in every civilized government' is not to be found. *Andrews* v. *Andrews,* 188 U.S. 14, 33. What was said in that case with regard to the powers of the States applies with equal force to the powers of the nation in cases where the States individually are incompetent to act. We are not yet discussing the particular case before us but only are considering the validity of the test proposed. With regard to that we may add that when we are dealing with words that also are a constituent act, like the Constitution of the United States, we must realize that they have called into life a being the development of which could not have been foreseen completely by the most gifted of its begetters. It was enough for them to realize or to hope that they had created an organism; it has taken a century and has cost their successors much sweat and blood to prove that they created a nation. The case before us must be considered in the light of our whole experience and not merely in that of what was said a hundred years ago. The treaty in question does not contravene any prohibitory words to be found in the Constitution. The only question is whether it is forbidden by some invisible radiation from the general terms of the Tenth Amendment. We must consider what this country has become in deciding what that amendment has reserved.

The State as we have intimated founds its claim of exclusive authority upon an assertion of title to migratory birds, an assertion that is embodied in statute. No doubt it is true that as between a State and its inhabitants the State may regulate the killing and sale of such birds, but it does not follow that its authority is exclusive of paramount powers. To put the claim of the State upon title is to lean upon a slender reed. Wild birds are not in the possession of anyone; and possession is the beginning of ownership. The whole foundation of the State's rights is the presence within their jurisdiction of birds that yesterday had not arrived, tomorrow may be in another State and in a week a thousand miles away. If we are to be accurate we cannot put the case of the State upon higher ground than that the treaty deals with creatures that for the moment are within the state borders, that it must be carried out by officers of the United States within the same territory, and that but for the treaty the State would be free to regulate this subject itself.

As most of the laws of the United States are carried out within the States and as many of them deal with matters which in the silence of such laws the State might regulate, such general grounds are not enough to support Missouri's claim. Valid treaties of course 'are as binding within the territorial limits of the States as they are elsewhere throughout the dominion of the United States.' *Baldwin* v. *Franks*, 120 U.S. 678, 683. No doubt the great body of private relations usually fall within the control of the State, but a treaty may override its power. We do not have to invoke the later developments of constitutional law for this proposition; it was recognized as early as *Hopkirk* v. *Bell*, 3 Cranch, 454, with regard to statutes of limitation, and even earlier, as

to confiscation, in *Ware* v. *Hylton*, 3 Dall. 199. It was assumed by Chief Justice Marshall with regard to the escheat of land to the State in *Chirac* v. *Chirac*, 2 Wheat. 259, 275. *Hauenstein* v. *Lynham*, 100 U.S. 483. *Geofroy* v. *Riggs*, 133 U.S. 258. *Blythe* v. *Hinckley*, 180 U.S. 333, 340. So as to a limited jurisdiction of foreign consuls within a State. *Wildenhus' Case*, 120 U.S. 1. See *Ross* v. *McIntyre*, 140 U.S. 453. Further illustration seems unnecessary, and it only remains to consider the application of established rules to the present case.

Here a national interest of very nearly the first magnitude is involved. It can be protected only by national action in concert with that of another power. The subject matter is only transitorily within the State and has no permanent habitat therein. But for the treaty and the statute there soon might be no birds for any powers to deal with. We see nothing in the Constitution that compels the Government to sit by while a food supply is cut off and the protectors of our forests and our crops are destroyed. It is not sufficient to rely upon the States. The reliance is vain, and were it otherwise, the question is whether the United States is forbidden to act. We are of opinion that the treaty and statute must be upheld. *Carey* v. *South Dakota*, 250 U.S. 118.

Decree affirmed.

Mr. Justice Van Devanter and Mr. Justice Pitney dissent.

XVIII

National Defense

NOTE

The provision of the Constitution authorizing Congress 'to raise and support armies'[1] has always been held by the Federal courts to mean that in the further-ance of this power Congress may determine how and under what circumstances such armies shall be raised. Since this grant appears in a clause which is entirely separate from that bestowing upon Congress the power to declare war, it follows that either in the presence or in the absence of a state of war the authority to raise armies is vested in the national legislative body. While the raising of armies is associated in most minds with the existence of hostilities, a state of war is nevertheless not an essential condition to the exercise of this power. This is plainly evident in the enactment by Congress of the Selective Training and Service Act of 13 September 1940[2] almost fifteen months before the United States entered World War II.

Compared with many of the other enumerated powers, the power to raise and support armies has not evoked much doctrinal conflict. What dispute there has been over the proper scope of this power has centered upon the power of Congress to prescribe the *mode* of raising such armies, and it has become established that the enactment of conscription laws is an appropriate mode.

The vividness of wartime experience during the immediate past makes it un-necessary to examine here the constitutional aspects of our most recent legislation in this field; it should be emphasized, however, that the Act of 1940 was the first instance in American history of military conscription in peacetime. The executive and legislative branches relied heavily for guidance at that time upon the conscription legislation of World War I, which, in turn, had been based in large part upon the experiences of the Civil War period. These precedents and a considerable amount of legal opinion supplementing the explicit grants of authority in the Constitution were sufficient to enable the Supreme Court unani-mously to uphold the constitutionality of conscription in the *Selective Draft Law Cases* of 1918.

During the American Revolution some of the states filled their quotas for the Continental Army by conscription, but the Congress embarked upon no such program. In the War of 1812 Congress debated the advisability of raising an army through the draft, but no act of this nature was passed. During the War with Mexico in 1846 the army was recruited entirely by voluntary enlistment.

The Civil War confronted both President and Congress with an urgent need for military forces on a grand scale. President Lincoln promptly called the militia

[1] Art. 1, sec. 8.   [2] 54 Stat. 885.

into the service of the United States and, wholly without Congressional authorization, issued a call for volunteers.[3] As the war continued the pressing need for
more and more troops made it imperative to increase the military forces beyond
the number attainable through the militia and voluntary enlistment. Consequently, steps were taken to augment the existing supply of manpower through
compulsory military conscription. An approximation to a draft was enacted by
Congress on 17 July 1862;[4] the President was therein empowered to regulate the
raising of the states' militia for Federal duty. It proved to be insufficient, however, so in a second Act,[5] passed the following year on March 3rd, Congress
gave authority to the President to conscript men directly into the Union army.[6]

Opposition to this first American draft law quickly came from many quarters
and took varied forms. Constitutional arguments were arrayed against it; 'peace
advocates' attacked it; enterprises appeared for the purpose of establishing mental
or physical disability; draft riots broke out in many cities. The most violent of
the riots took place in New York City and raged unabated for three days during
July, 1863.[7] Less violent, but no less indignant, were the attacks levelled against
the Act's 'three hundred dollar clause'; by paying this commutation sum one
could escape military service.

President Lincoln made no public defense of the Act; he continued to exercise
the power it conferred upon him and confided his defense of the measure to
private papers which were not published for some time thereafter. His position
was that 'The Constitution provides that the Congress shall have power to raise
and support armies; and by this act the Congress has exercised the power to raise
and support armies. . . The Constitution gives Congress the power, but it does not
prescribe the mode, or expressly declare who shall prescribe it. In such case Congress must prescribe the mode, or relinquish the power. There is no alternative. . .
The power is given fully, completely, unconditionally.'[8]

At no time did the Supreme Court of the United States review the constitutionality of this Civil War conscription act, but an exhaustive opinion upholding
it was delivered by the highest court of Pennsylvania in *Kneedler* v. *Lane*[9] which
anticipated most of the subsequent arguments used in behalf of conscription in
the *Selective Draft Law Cases* of 1918. The Pennsylvania court declared: 'That
the United States are a nation, and sovereign in the powers granted to them, is
not denied. . . We cannot conceive of a nation without the inherent power to
carry on war. . . The power to declare war necessarily implies the power to carry
it on, and this implies the means . . . all the means in possession of the nation.

---

[3] An earlier call, that of 15 April 1861, for 75,000 men had been authorized, but this call of 3
May 1861 was made *in anticipation* of Congressional authority, which was given later in a short special
session during the same year.

[4] 12 Stat. 597.

[5] 12 Stat. 731.

[6] See Randall, James G., *Constitutional Problems Under Lincoln*, New York, 1926, ch. XI.

[7] A vivid description of the killing, burning, pillaging, and other assorted forms of violence that
took place on this occasion appears in Sandburg, Carl, *Abraham Lincoln, The War Years*, New York,
1939, II, p. 360 ff.

[8] *Works*, ed. by Nicolay, James G., and Hay, John, New York, 1890, VII, pp. 51-2.

[9] 45 Pa. 238 (1863).

[In war,] as there is no limit to the necessity, there can be no limit to the force to be used to meet it. The power of war, without the essential means, is really no power; it is a solecism. Voluntary enlistment is founded in contract. A power to command differs essentially from a power to contract. The former flows from authority; the latter from assent. . . It is clear, therefore, that the power to make war, without the power to command troops into the field, is no government power, because it lacks the authority to execute itself.' [10]

The Selective Draft Law of 18 May 1917 [11] was tested for its constitutionality in a number of lower Federal courts before it reached the Supreme Court; each time it was upheld.

SELECTIVE DRAFT LAW CASES
245 U.S. 366 (1918)

Mr. Chief Justice White delivered the opinion of the court.

We are here concerned with some of the provisions of the Act of May 18, 1917, c. 15, 40 Stat. 76, entitled, 'An Act to authorize the President to increase temporarily the Military Establishment of the United States.' The law, as its opening sentence declares, was intended to supply temporarily the increased military force which was required by the existing emergency, the war then and now flagrant. The clauses we must pass upon and those which will throw light on their significance are briefly summarized:

The act proposed to raise a national army, first, by increasing the regular force to its maximum strength and there maintaining it; second, by incorporating into such army the members of the National Guard and National Guard Reserve already in the service of the United States (Act of Congress of June 3, 1916, c. 134, 39 Stat. 211) and maintaining their organizations to their full strength; third, by giving the President power in his discretion to organize by volunteer enlistment four divisions of infantry; fourth, by subjecting all male citizens between the ages of twenty-one and thirty to duty in the national army for the period of the existing emergency after the proclamation

of the President announcing the necessity for their service; and fifth, by providing for selecting from the body so called, on the further proclamation of the President, 500,000 enlisted men, and a second body of the same number should the President in his discretion deem it necessary. To carry out its purposes the act made it the duty of those liable to the call to present themselves for registration on the proclamation of the President so as to subject themselves to the terms of the act and provided full federal means for carrying out the selective draft. It gave the President in his discretion power to create local boards to consider claims for exemption for physical disability or otherwise made by those called. The act exempted from subjection to the draft designated United States and state officials as well as those already in the military or naval service of the United States, regular or duly ordained ministers of religion and theological students under the conditions provided for, and, while relieving from military service in the strict sense the members of religious sects as enumerated whose tenets excluded the moral right to engage in war, nevertheless subjected such persons to the performance of service of a non-combatant character to be defined by the President.

The proclamation of the President call-

[10] Ibid. 312.

[11] 40 Stat. 76.

ing the persons designated within the ages described in the statute was made, and the plaintiffs in error, who were in the class and under the statute were obliged to present themselves to the law, failed to do so and were prosecuted under the statute for the penalties for which it provided. They all defended by denying that there had been conferred by the Constitution upon Congress the power to compel military service by a selective draft, and asserted that even if such power had been given by the Constitution to Congress, the terms of the particular act for various reasons caused it to be beyond the power and repugnant to the Constitution. The cases are here for review because of the constitutional questions thus raised, convictions having resulted from instructions of the courts that the legal defences were without merit and that the statute was constitutional.

The possession of authority to enact the statute must be found in the clauses of the Constitution giving Congress power 'to declare war; . . . to raise and support armies, but no appropriation of money to that use shall be for a longer term than two years; . . . to make rules for the government and regulation of the land and naval forces.' Article 1, § 8. And of course the powers conferred by these provisions like all other powers given carry with them as provided by the Constitution the authority 'to make all laws which shall be necessary and proper for carrying into execution the foregoing powers.' Article 1, § 8.

As the mind cannot conceive an army without the men to compose it, on the face of the Constitution the objection that it does not give power to provide for such men would seem to be too frivolous for further notice. It is said, however, that since under the Constitution as originally framed state citizenship was primary and United States citizenship but derivative and dependent thereon, therefore the power conferred upon Congress to raise

armies was only coterminous with United States citizenship and could not be exerted so as to cause that citizenship to lose its dependent character and dominate state citizenship. But the proposition simply denies to Congress the power to raise armies which the Constitution gives. That power by the very terms of the Constitution, being delegated, is supreme. Article vi. In truth the contention simply assails the wisdom of the framers of the Constitution in conferring authority on Congress and in not retaining it as it was under the Confederation in the several States. Further it is said, the right to provide is not denied by calling for volunteer enlistments, but it does not and cannot include the power to exact enforced military duty by the citizen. This however but challenges the existence of all power, for a governmental power which has no sanction to it and which therefore can only be exercised provided the citizen consents to its exertion is in no substantial sense a power. It is argued, however, that although this is absolutely true, it is not concretely so because as compelled military service is repugnant to a free government and in conflict with all the great guarantees of the Constitution as to individual liberty, it must be assumed that the authority to raise armies was intended to be limited to the right to call an army into existence counting alone upon the willingness of the citizen to do his duty in time of public need, that is, in time of war. But the premise of this proposition is so devoid of foundation that it leaves not even a shadow of ground upon which to base the conclusion. Let us see if this is not at once demonstrable. It may not be doubted that the very conception of a just government and its duty to the citizen includes the reciprocal obligation of the citizen to render military service in case of need and the right to compel it. Vattel, *Law of Nations,* Book iii, c. 1 & 2. To do more than state the proposition is absolutely unnecessary in view of the practical illustration afforded by the almost universal legislation to that effect now in force. In England it is certain that before the Norman Conquest the duty of the great militant body of the citizens was recognized and enforceable. Blackstone, Book 1, c. 13. It is unnecessary to follow the long controversy between Crown and Parliament as to the branch of the government in which the power resided, since there never was any doubt that it somewhere resided. So also it is wholly unnecessary to explore the situation for the purpose of fixing the sources whence in England it came to be understood that the citizen or the force organized from the militia as such could not without their consent be compelled to render service in a foreign country, since there is no room to contend that such principle ever rested upon any challenge of the right of Parliament to impose compulsory duty upon the citizen to perform military duty wherever the public exigency exacted, whether at home or abroad. This is exemplified by the present English Service Act.

In the Colonies before the separation from England there cannot be the slightest doubt that the right to enforce military service was unquestioned and that practical effect was given to the power in many cases. Indeed the brief of the Government contains a list of Colonial acts manifesting the power and its enforcement in more than two hundred cases. And this exact situation existed also after the separation. Under the Articles of Confederation it is true Congress had no such power, as its authority was absolutely limited to making calls upon the States for the military forces needed to create and maintain the army, each State being bound for its quota as called. But it is indisputable that the States in response to the calls made upon them met the situation when they deemed it necessary by directing enforced military service on the part of the citizens. In fact the duty of the citizen to render military service and the power to compel

him against his consent to do so was expressly sanctioned by the constitutions of at least nine of the States, an illustration being afforded by the following provision of the Pennsylvania constitution of 1776. 'That every member of society hath a right to be protected in the enjoyment of life, liberty and property, and therefore is bound to contribute his proportion towards the expense of that protection, and yield his personal service when necessary, or an equivalent thereto.' Art. 8, (Thorpe, *American Charters, Constitutions and Organic Laws,* vol. 5, pp. 3081, 3083.) While it is true that the States were sometimes slow in exerting the power in order to fill their quotas—a condition shown by resolutions of Congress calling upon them to comply by exerting their compulsory power to draft and by earnest requests by Washington to Congress that a demand be made upon the States to resort to drafts to fill their quotas—that fact serves to demonstrate instead of to challenge the existence of the authority. A default in exercising a duty may not be resorted to as a reason for denying its existence.

When the Constitution came to be formed it may not be disputed that one of the recognized necessities for its adoption was the want of power in Congress to raise an army and the dependence upon the States for their quotas. In supplying the power it was manifestly intended to give it all and leave none to the States, since besides the delegation to Congress of authority to raise armies the Constitution prohibited the States, without the consent of Congress, from keeping troops in time of peace or engaging in war. Article 1, § 10.

To argue that as the state authority over the militia prior to the Constitution embraced every citizen, the right of Congress to raise an army should not be considered as granting authority to compel the citizen's service in the army, is but to express in a different form the denial of the right to call any citizen to the army.

Nor is this met by saying that it does not exclude the right of Congress to organize an army by voluntary enlistments, that is, by the consent of the citizens, for if the proposition be true, the right of the citizen to give consent would be controlled by the same prohibition which would deprive Congress of the right to compel unless it can be said that although Congress had not the right to call because of state authority, the citizen had a right to obey the call and set aside state authority if he pleased to do so. And a like conclusion demonstrates the want of foundation for the contention that, although it be within the power to call the citizen into the army without his consent, the army into which he enters after the call is to be limited in some respects to services for which the militia it is assumed may only be used, since this admits the appropriateness of the call to military service in the army and the power to make it and yet destroys the purpose for which the call is authorized—the raising of armies to be under the control of the United States.

The fallacy of the argument results from confounding the constitutional provisions concerning the militia with that conferring upon Congress the power to raise armies. It treats them as one while they are different. This is the militia clause:

'The Congress shall have power . . . To provide for calling forth the militia to execute the laws of the Union, suppress insurrections and repel invasions; To provide for organizing, arming, and disciplining the militia, and for governing such part of them as may be employed in the service of the United States, reserving to the States, respectively, the appointment of the officers, and the authority of training the militia according to the discipline prescribed by Congress.' Article 1, § 8.

The line which separates it from the army power is not only inherently plainly marked by the text of the two clauses, but will stand out in bolder relief by considering the condition before the Constitution was adopted and the remedy which it provided for the military situation with which it dealt. The right on the one hand of Congress under the Confederation to call on the States for forces and the duty on the other of the States to furnish when called, embraced the complete power of government over the subject. When the two were combined and were delegated to Congress all governmental power on that subject was conferred, a result manifested not only by the grant made but by the limitation expressly put upon the States on the subject. The army sphere therefore embraces such complete authority. But the duty of exerting the power thus conferred in all its plenitude was not made at once obligatory but wisely left to depend upon the discretion of Congress as to the arising of the exigencies which would call it in part or in whole into play. There was left therefore under the sway of the States undelegated the control of the militia to the extent that such control was not taken away by the exercise by Congress of its power to raise armies. This did not diminish the military power or curb the full potentiality of the right to exert it but left an area of authority requiring to be provided for (the militia area) unless and until by the exertion of the military power of Congress that area had been circumscribed or totally disappeared. This, therefore, is what was dealt with by the militia provision. It diminished the occasion for the exertion by Congress of its military power beyond the strict necessities for its exercise by giving the power to Congress to direct the organization and training of the militia (evidently to prepare such militia in the event of the exercise of the army power) although leaving the carrying out of such command to the States. It further conduced to the same result by delegating to Congress the right to call on occasions which were specified for the militia force, thus again obviating the necessity for exercising the army power to the extent of being ready for every conceivable contingency. This purpose is made manifest by the provision preserving the organization of the militia so far as formed when called for such special purposes although subjecting the militia when so called to the paramount authority of the United States. *Tarble's Case,* 13 Wallace, 397, 408. But because under the express regulations the power was given to call for specified purposes without exerting the army power, it cannot follow that the latter power when exerted was not complete to the extent of its exertion and dominant. Because the power of Congress to raise armies was not required to be exerted to its full limit but only as in the discretion of Congress it was deemed the public interest required, furnishes no ground for supposing that the complete power was lost by its partial exertion. Because, moreover, the power granted to Congress to raise armies in its potentiality was susceptible of narrowing the area over which the militia clause operated, affords no ground for confounding the two areas which were distinct and separate to the end of confusing both the powers and thus weakening or destroying both.

And upon this understanding of the two powers the legislative and executive authority has been exerted from the beginning. From the act of the first session of Congress carrying over the army of the Government under the Confederation to the United States under the Constitution (Act of September 29, 1789, c. 25, 1 Stat. 95) down to 1812 the authority to raise armies was regularly exerted as a distinct and substantive power, the force being raised and recruited by enlistment. Except for one act formulating a plan by which the entire body of citizens (the militia) subject to military duty was to be organized in every State (Act of May 8, 1792, c. 33, 1 Stat. 271) which was never carried into effect, Congress confined itself to providing for the organization of a specified number distributed among the States according to their quota to be trained as directed by Congress and to be called by the President as need might require. When the War of 1812 came the result of these two forces composed the army to be relied upon by Congress to carry on the war. Either because it proved to be weak in numbers or because of insubordination developed among the forces called and manifested by their refusal to cross the border, the Government determined that the exercise of the power to organize an army by compulsory draft was necessary and Mr. Monroe, the Secretary of War, (Mr. Madison being President) in a letter to Congress recommended several plans of legislation on that subject. It suffices to say that by each of them it was proposed that the United States deal directly with the body of citizens subject to military duty and call a designated number out of the population between the ages of 18 and 45 for service in the army. The power which it was recommended be exerted was clearly an unmixed federal power dealing with the subject from the sphere of the authority given to Congress to raise armies and not from the sphere of the right to deal with the militia as such, whether organized or unorganized. A bill was introduced giving effect to the plan. Opposition developed, but we need not stop to consider it because it substantially rested upon the incompatibility of compulsory military service with free government, a subject which from what we have said has been disposed of. Peace came before the bill was enacted.

Down to the Mexican War the legislation exactly portrayed the same condition of mind which we have previously stated. In that war, however, no draft was suggested, because the army created by the United States immediately resulting from the exercise by Congress of its power to raise armies, that organized under its direction from the militia and the volunteer commands which were furnished, proved adequate to carry the war to a successful conclusion.

So the course of legislation from that date to 1861 affords no ground for any other but the same conception of legislative power which we have already stated. In that year when the mutterings of the dread conflict which was to come began to be heard and the Proclamation of the President calling a force into existence was issued it was addressed to the body organized out of the militia and trained by the States in accordance with the previous acts of Congress. (Proclamation of April 15, 1861, 12 Stat. 1258.) That force being inadequate to meet the situation, an act was passed authorizing the acceptance of 500,000 volunteers by the President to be by him organized into a national army. (Act of July 22, 1861, c. 9, 12 Stat. 268.) This was soon followed by another act increasing the force of the militia to be organized by the States for the purpose of being drawn upon when trained under the direction of Congress (Act of July 29, 1861, c. 25, 12 Stat. 281), the two acts when considered together presenting in the clearest possible form the distinction between the power of Congress to raise armies and its authority under the militia clause. But it soon became manifest that more men were required. As a result the Act of March 3, 1863, c. 75, 12 Stat. 731, was adopted entitled 'An Act for enrolling and calling out the National Forces and for other purposes.' By that act which was clearly intended to directly exert upon all the citizens of the United States the national power which it had been proposed to exert in 1814 on the recommendation of the then Secretary of War, Mr. Monroe, every male citizen of the United States between the ages of twenty and forty-five was made subject by the direct action of Congress to be called by compulsory draft to service in a national army at such time and in such numbers as the President in his discretion might find nec-

essary. In that act, as in the one of 1814, and in this one, the means by which the act was to be enforced were directly federal and the force to be raised as a result of the draft was therefore typically national as distinct from the call into active service of the militia as such. And under the power thus exerted four separate calls for draft were made by the President and enforced, that of July, 1863, of February and March, 1864, of July and December, 1864, producing a force of about a quarter of a million men. It is undoubted that the men thus raised by draft were treated as subject to direct national authority and were used either in filling the gaps occasioned by the vicissitudes of war in the ranks of the existing national forces or for the purpose of organizing such new units as were deemed to be required. It would be childish to deny the value of the added strength which was thus afforded. Indeed in the official report of the Provost Marshal General . . . reviewing the whole subject it was stated that it was the efficient aid resulting from the forces created by the draft at a very critical moment of the civil strife which obviated a disaster which seemed impending and carried that struggle to a complete and successful conclusion.

Brevity prevents doing more than to call attention to the fact that the organized body of militia within the States as trained by the States under the direction of Congress became known as the National Guard (Act of January 21, 1903, c. 196, 32 Stat. 775; National Defense Act of June 3, 1916, c. 134, 39 Stat. 211). And to make further preparation from among the great body of the citizens, an additional number to be determined by the President was directed to be organized and trained by the States as the National Guard Reserve. (National Defense Act, *supra.*)

Thus sanctioned as is the act before us by the text of the Constitution, and by its significance as read in the light of the fundamental principles with which the subject is concerned, by the power recognized and carried into effect in many civilized countries, by the authority and practice of the colonies before the Revolution, of the States under the Confederation and of the Government since the formation of the Constitution, the want of merit in the contentions that the act in the particulars which we have been previously called upon to consider was beyond the constitutional power of Congress, is manifest. Cogency, however, if possible, is added to the demonstration by pointing out that in the only case to which we have been referred where the constitutionality of the Act of 1863 was contemporaneously challenged on grounds akin to, if not absolutely identical with, those here urged, the validity of the act was maintained for reasons not different from those which control our judgment. (*Kneedler* v. *Lane,* 45 Pa. St. 238.) And as further evidence that the conclusion we reach is but the inevitable consequence of the provisions of the Constitution as effect follows cause, we briefly recur to events in another environment. The seceding States wrote into the constitution which was adopted to regulate the government which they sought to establish, in identical words the provisions of the Constitution of the United States which we here have under consideration. And when the right to enforce under that instrument a selective draft law which was enacted, not differing in principle from the one here in question, was challenged, its validity was upheld, evidently after great consideration, by the courts of Virginia, of Georgia, of Texas, of Alabama, of Mississippi and of North Carolina, the opinions in some of the cases copiously and critically reviewing the whole grounds which we have stated. . .

In reviewing the subject, we have hitherto considered it as it has been argued, from the point of view of the Constitution as it stood prior to the adoption of the Fourteenth Amendment. But to avoid

all misapprehension we briefly direct attention to that Amendment for the purpose of pointing out, as has been frequently done in the past, how completely it broadened the national scope of the Government under the Constitution by causing citizenship of the United States to be paramount and dominant instead of being subordinate and derivative, and therefore, operating as it does upon all the powers conferred by the Constitution, leaves no possible support for the contentions made, if their want of merit was otherwise not so clearly made manifest.

It remains only to consider contentions which, while not disputing power, challenge the act because of the repugnancy to the Constitution supposed to result from some of its provisions. First, we are of opinion that the contention that the act is void as a delegation of federal power to state officials because of some of its administrative features, is too wanting in merit to require further notice. Second, we think that the contention that the statute is void because vesting administrative officers with legislative discretion has been so completely adversely settled as to require reference only to some of the decided cases. *Field* v. *Clark,* 143 U.S. 649; *Buttfield* v. *Stranahan,* 192 U.S. 470; *Intermountain Rate Cases,* 234 U.S. 476; *First National Bank* v. *Union Trust Co.,* 244 U.S. 416. A like conclusion also adversely disposes of a similar claim concerning the conferring of judicial power. *Buttfield* v. *Stranahan,* 192 U.S. 470, 497; *West* v. *Hitchcock,* 205 U.S. 80; *Oceanic Steam Navigation Co.* v. *Stranahan,* 214 U.S. 320, 338-340; *Zakonaite* v. *Wolf,* 226 U.S. 272, 275. And we pass without anything but statement the proposition that an establishment of a religion or an interference with the free exercise thereof repugnant to the First Amendment resulted from the exemption clauses of the act to which we at the outset referred, because we think its unsoundness is too apparent to require us to do more.

Finally, as we are unable to conceive upon what theory the exaction by government from the citizen of the performance of his supreme and noble duty of contributing to the defense of the rights and honor of the nation, as the result of a war declared by the great representative body of the people, can be said to be the imposition of involuntary servitude in violation of the prohibitions of the Thirteenth Amendment, we are constrained to the conclusion that the contention to that effect is refuted by its mere statement.

Affirmed.

XIX

Military and Civilian Mobilization in Wartime

NOTE

The impact of World War II upon the rights and privileges of American citizens and upon the national defense problem called for a re-examination of the basic principles governing the proper relations between military authority and civilian rights.[1] Under the exigencies of total war, American citizens of Japanese ancestry living in the western states were made subject to curfew regulations,[2] exclusion from the West Coast area, and detention within inland relocation centers.[3] The validity of an exclusion order promulgated by the Commanding General of the Western Defense Command under authority of an executive order and an act of Congress was upheld by the Supreme Court in 1944 in *Korematsu* v. *United States*.

In the past there have been several occasions upon which the courts have sought to reconcile the conflicting interests of national security with the rights of individual citizens guaranteed by the Constitution. Most of the problems encountered in World War I and World War II had likewise to be faced during the Civil War. In a sense the experience of government under President Lincoln served as a model for subsequent wartime administrations. The difference between the position of the citizen in relation to his government in 1942 and his position in 1862 was one of degree, not of kind. President Lincoln and his Congresses had a war to win; they had dissidents to combat and disloyal citizens to restrain; they had also to impose rigid controls upon private property in the interests of national emergency. In some instances the President had pursued a course not authorized by Congress or the Constitution.

Perhaps the most drastic measure taken by the executive at that time was one by which military commanders were empowered to suspend the writ of *habeas corpus*. Inasmuch as the provision that 'The privilege of the writ of *habeas corpus* shall not be suspended, unless when in cases of rebellion or invasion the public safety may require it,'[4] appears in that section of the Constitution devoted entirely to limitations upon Congressional action, it was argued that the President's suspension of the right without Congressional approval was unlawful.

Mr. Chief Justice Taney examined this point in 1861. Sitting as a circuit judge in Baltimore he was petitioned for a writ of *habeas corpus* by a Maryland agi-

[1] See Corwin, Edward S., *Total War and the Constitution,* New York, 1947.
[2] It had been decided in *Hirabayashi* v. *United States,* 320 U.S. 81 (1943) that the discriminatory curfew orders were valid emergency war measures.
[3] In *Ex parte Endo,* 323 U.S. 283 (1944), the Court held that a Japanese American of unquestioned loyalty must be released from a War Relocation Center.
[4] Art. 1, sec. 9.

tator, John Merryman, who had been arrested by military authority and imprisoned in Fort McHenry. A writ was issued directing the fort's commander to appear with his prisoner at the court in Baltimore; the general refused; instead, he submitted a statement outlining the President's authorization for the suspension of the writ. In consequence of the general's ignoring the court's order, Chief Justice Taney issued a writ of contempt and sent a United States marshal to enforce it. When the general ignored this citation the Chief Justice handed down his opinion in *Ex parte Merryman*.[5] He declared that the right of suspension of the writ belonged exclusively to Congress, and then only under circumstances 'when the public safety may require it.' Furthermore, he insisted, a civilian could not be imprisoned and tried by a military court in violation of the Sixth Amendment. Finally, he castigated the President for his dereliction of duty in failing to 'take care that the laws be faithfully executed.' In his view, it was incumbent upon the President to support and enforce the lawful orders of the judiciary as well as the orders of the military. This opinion has since been recognized as a classic defense of civil liberties against military authority.

It should be remembered that prior to this time no case involving these suspensions of the writ had come before the highest court of the land. When that event did take place, as it did during the war in *Ex parte Vallandigham*,[6] the Supreme Court evaded the question by stating that it lacked jurisdiction to review the decision of a military commission,[7] since such a body was not a court within the meaning of laws prescribing the Court's competence. However, shortly after the end of the war the Court squarely faced the issue which it had carefully avoided during the hostilities and denied the power of the President to suspend the writ of *habeas corpus* and to substitute military trial of civilians for trial by the regular courts in areas not immediately in the theatre of war.[8]

Lambdin P. Milligan, a citizen of Indiana, was an active member of the Order of American Knights or Sons of Liberty, a secret society allegedly devoted to the overthrow of the government. Arrested in October, 1864, by order of Brevet Major-General Hovey, commander of the District of Indiana, Milligan was confined in a military prison and tried before a military commission upon charges of conspiracy against the government of the United States, affording aid and comfort to rebels, inciting insurrection, and disloyal practices. The commission sentenced him to be hanged. A short while before sentence was to be executed Milligan petitioned the United States Circuit Court in Indiana for his release; he contended that he had been unlawfully convicted and claimed the constitutional right of a jury trial.

The Habeas Corpus Act of March 3, 1863,[9] had authorized the President to suspend the writ of *habeas corpus* throughout the United States, but further

---

[5] 17 Fed. Cas. No. 9487 (1861).   [6] 1 Wall. 243 (1864).

[7] Soon after the United States entered World War II eight Nazi saboteurs were captured in this country, arrested by the Federal Bureau of Investigation, tried by a military commission and convicted. Six were executed. Their conviction was sustained under the laws of war. *Ex parte Quirin*, 317 U.S. 1 (1942). See also *In re Yamashita*, 327 U.S. 1 (1946), and *Duncan* v. *Kahanamoku*, 327 U.S. 304 (1946).

[8] *Ex parte Milligan*, 4 Wall. 2 (1866).   [9] 12 Stat. 755.

provided that where a grand jury had met and adjourned without taking action against a person charged with violation of national law, it was to be the duty of the court to discharge such person. A grand jury of the United States circuit court for the District of Indiana had in fact met and adjourned without indicting Milligan; accordingly, the circuit court was bound to consider his release. Uncertain of the legality of Milligan's conviction, the judges of the court certified the question to the Supreme Court.

Mr. Justice Davis wrote the opinion of the Court in *Ex parte Milligan*. Noticeably relieved by the cessation of hostilities and the opportunity to decide this pressing question 'without passion or the admixture of any element not required to form a legal judgment,' [10] Mr. Justice Davis declared Milligan to have been convicted unlawfully and ordered his release. He denied the President's authority to establish military commissions for the trial of civilians in such cases and went so far as to imply that even Congress could not authorize the use of such a device outside of the actual theaters of war. He granted, however, that the safety of every government necessitates the 'power somewhere of suspending the writ of *habeas corpus*' [11] on the ground that emergency conditions may not permit recourse to the ordinary legal processes of peacetime.

Concurring in the Court's decision, but disagreeing with its reasoning, Mr. Chief Justice Chase spoke on behalf of four members of the Court in an opinion which has since become the more controlling of the two. He said: 'Congress has the power not only to raise and support and govern armies but to declare war. It has, therefore, the power to provide by law for carrying on war. *This power necessarily extends to all legislation essential to the prosecution of war with vigor and success. . .'* [12] And when the nation is exposed to invasion, 'it is within the power of Congress to determine in what states or districts such great and imminent public danger exists as justifies the authorization of military tribunals for the trial of crimes and offences against the discipline or security of the army or against the public safety.' [13]

Each of these cases arising out of the Civil War involved the commission by citizens of overt acts which were admittedly intended to hamper the successful prosecution of the war by the Union; the insurrectional, treasonable or disloyal character of the acts was unquestioned. In the case below the question of martial law was not involved; Korematsu had not been tried and sentenced by a military commission, nor had his right to a writ of *habeas corpus* been suspended either by Congress or the President. The professed reasons for the regulation which Korematsu had violated were the pressure of time and security and the presence in that vital coastal area of large numbers of Japanese Americans whose loyalty, under the circumstances, could not be deliberately tested. There were no grounds

---

[10] 4 Wall. 2, 109 (1866).   [11] Ibid. 125.

[12] Ibid. 139, italics ours. Addressing the American Bar Association at Saratoga, New York, on 5 September 1917, Charles Evans Hughes discussed the subject, 'War Powers Under the Constitution.' He spoke as a former Justice of the Supreme Court, and his statement: 'The power to wage war is the power to wage it successfully,' has since become a favorite aphorism. *The New York Times,* 6 September 1917, p. 1.   [13] Ibid. 140.

for suspecting him of disloyalty. His conviction in a Federal District Court for remaining in a military area contrary to an exclusion order of a military commander did, however, re-present the basic problem of the compatibility between 'the law of paramount necessity' and the 'inalienable rights of the individual citizen.'

KOREMATSU v. UNITED STATES

323 U.S. 214 (1944)

Certiorari, 321 U.S. 760, to review the affirmance of a judgment of conviction.

MR. JUSTICE BLACK delivered the opinion of the Court.

The petitioner, an American citizen of Japanese descent, was convicted in a federal district court for remaining in San Leandro, California, a 'Military Area,' contrary to Civilian Exclusion Order No. 34 of the Commanding General of the Western Command, U.S. Army, which directed that after May 9, 1942, all persons of Japanese ancestry should be excluded from that area. No question was raised as to petitioner's loyalty to the United States. The Circuit Court of Appeals affirmed, and the importance of the constitutional question involved caused us to grant certiorari.

It should be noted, to begin with, that all legal restrictions which curtail the civil rights of a single racial group are immediately suspect. That is not to say that all such restrictions are unconstitutional. It is to say that courts must subject them to the most rigid scrutiny. Pressing public necessity may sometimes justify the existence of such restrictions; racial antagonism never can.

In the instant case prosecution of the petitioner was begun by information charging violation of an Act of Congress, of March 21, 1942, 56 Stat. 173, which provides that '. . . whoever shall enter, remain in, leave, or commit any act in any military area or military zone prescribed, under the authority of an Executive order of the President, by the Secretary of War, or by any military com-

mander designated by the Secretary of War, contrary to the restrictions applicable to any such area or zone or contrary to the order of the Secretary of War or any such military commander, shall, if it appears that he knew or should have known of the existence and extent of the restrictions or order and that his act was in violation thereof, be guilty of a misdemeanor and upon conviction shall be liable to a fine of not to exceed $5,000 or to imprisonment for not more than one year, or both, for each offense.'

Exclusion Order No. 34, which the petitioner knowingly and admittedly violated, was one of a number of military orders and proclamations, all of which were substantially based upon Executive Order No. 9066, 7 Fed. Reg. 1407. That order, issued after we were at war with Japan, declared that 'the successful prosecution of the war requires every possible protection against espionage and against sabotage to national-defense material, national-defense premises, and national-defense utilities. . .'

One of the series of orders and proclamations, a curfew order, which like the exclusion order here was promulgated pursuant to Executive Order 9066, subjected all persons of Japanese ancestry in prescribed West Coast military areas to remain in their residences from 8 p.m. to 6 a.m. As is the case with the exclusion order here, that prior curfew order was designed as a 'protection against espionage and against sabotage.' In *Hirabayashi* v. *United States,* 320 U.S. 81, we sustained a conviction obtained for violation of the curfew order. The Hirabayashi conviction and this one thus rest on the same 1942 Congressional Act and the same basic executive and military orders, all of which orders were aimed at the twin dangers of espionage and sabotage.

The 1942 Act was attacked in the *Hirabayashi* case as an unconstitutional delegation of power; it was contended that the curfew order and other orders on which it rested were beyond the war powers of the Congress, the military authorities and of the President, as Commander in Chief of the Army; and finally that to apply the curfew order against none but citizens of Japanese ancestry amounted to a constitutionally prohibited discrimination solely on account of race. To these questions, we gave the serious consideration which their importance justified. We upheld the curfew order as an exercise of the power of the government to take steps necessary to prevent espionage and sabotage in an area threatened by Japanese attack.

In the light of the principles we announced in the *Hirabayashi* case, we are unable to conclude that it was beyond the war power of Congress and the Executive to exclude those of Japanese ancestry from the West Coast war area at the time they did. True, exclusion from the area in which one's home is located is a far greater deprivation than constant confinement to the home from 8 p.m. to 6 a.m. Nothing short of apprehension by the proper military authorities of the gravest imminent danger to the public safety can constitutionally justify either. But exclusion from a threatened area, no less than curfew, has a definite and close relationship to the prevention of espionage and sabotage. The military authorities, charged with the primary responsibility of defending our shores, concluded that curfew provided inadequate protection and ordered exclusion. They did so, as pointed out in our *Hirabayashi* opinion, in accordance with Congressional authority to the mili-

tary to say who should, and who should not, remain in the threatened areas.

In this case the petitioner challenges the assumptions upon which we rested our conclusions in the *Hirabayashi* case. He also urges that by May 1942, when Order No. 34 was promulgated, all danger of Japanese invasion of the West Coast had disappeared. After careful consideration of these contentions we are compelled to reject them.

Here, as in the *Hirabayashi* case, *supra,* at p. 99, '. . . we cannot reject as unfounded the judgment of the military authorities and of Congress that there were disloyal members of that population, whose number and strength could not be precisely and quickly ascertained. We cannot say that the war-making branches of the Government did not have ground for believing that in a critical hour such persons could not readily be isolated and separately dealt with, and constituted a menace to the national defense and safety, which demanded that prompt and adequate measures be taken to guard against it.'

Like curfew, exclusion of those of Japanese origin was deemed necessary because of the presence of an unascertained number of disloyal members of the group, most of whom we have no doubt were loyal to this country. It was because we could not reject the finding of the military authorities that it was impossible to bring about an immediate segregation of the disloyal from the loyal that we sustained the validity of the curfew order as applying to the whole group. In the instant case, temporary exclusion of the entire group was rested by the military on the same ground. The judgment that exclusion of the whole group was for the same reason a military imperative answers the contention that the exclusion was in the nature of group punishment based on antagonism to those of Japanese origin. That there were members of the group who retained loyalties to Japan has been confirmed by investigations made subsequent to the exclusion. Approximately five thousand American citizens of Japanese ancestry refused to swear unqualified allegiance to the United States and to renounce allegiance to the Japanese Emperor, and several thousand evacuees requested repatriation to Japan.

We uphold the exclusion order as of the time it was made and when the petitioner violated it. . . In doing so, we are not unmindful of the hardships imposed by it upon a large group of American citizens. Cf. *Ex parte Kawato,* 317 U.S. 69, 73. But hardships are part of war, and war is an aggregation of hardships. All citizens alike, both in and out of uniform, feel the impact of war in greater or lesser measure. Citizenship has its responsibilities as well as its privileges, and in time of war the burden is always heavier. Compulsory exclusion of large groups of citizens from their homes, except under circumstances of direst emergency and peril, is inconsistent with our basic governmental institutions. But when under conditions of modern warfare our shores are threatened by hostile forces, the power to protect must be commensurate with the threatened danger.

It is argued that on May 30, 1942, the date the petitioner was charged with remaining in the prohibited area, there were conflicting orders outstanding, forbidding him both to leave the area and to remain there. Of course, a person cannot be convicted for doing the very thing which it is a crime to fail to do. But the outstanding orders here contained no such contradictory commands.

There was an order issued March 27, 1942, which prohibited petitioner and others of Japanese ancestry from leaving the area, but its effect was specifically limited in time 'until and to the extent that a future proclamation or order should so permit or direct.' 7 Fed. Reg. 2601. That 'future order,' the one for violation of which petitioner was convicted, was issued May 3, 1942, and it did 'direct' ex-

clusion from the area of all persons of Japanese ancestry, before 12 o'clock noon, May 9; furthermore it contained a warning that all such persons found in the prohibited area would be liable to punishment under the March 21, 1942 Act of Congress. Consequently, the only order in effect touching the petitioner's being in the area on May 30, 1942, the date specified in the information against him, was the May 3 order which prohibited his remaining there, and it was that same order, which he stipulated in his trial that he had violated, knowing of its existence. There is therefore no basis for the argument that on May 30, 1942, he was subject to punishment, under the March 27 and May 3 orders, whether he remained in or left the area.

It does appear, however, that on May 9, the effective date of the exclusion order, the military authorities had already determined that the evacuation should be effected by assembling together and placing under guard all those of Japanese ancestry, at central points, designated as 'assembly centers,' in order 'to insure the orderly evacuation and resettlement of Japanese voluntarily migrating from Military Area No. 1, to restrict and regulate such migration.' Public Proclamation No. 4, 7 Fed. Reg. 2601. And on May 19, 1942, eleven days before the time petitioner was charged with unlawfully remaining in the area, Civilian Restrictive Order No. 1, 8 Fed. Reg. 982, provided for detention of those of Japanese ancestry in assembly or relocation centers. It is now argued that the validity of the exclusion order cannot be considered apart from the orders requiring him, after departure from the area, to report and to remain in an assembly or relocation center. The contention is that we must treat these separate orders as one and inseparable; that, for this reason, if detention in the assembly or relocation center would have illegally deprived the petitioner of his liberty, the exclusion order and his conviction under it cannot stand.

We are thus being asked to pass at this time upon the whole subsequent detention program in both assembly and relocation centers, although the only issues framed at the trial related to petitioner's remaining in the prohibited area in violation of the exclusion order. Had petitioner here left the prohibited area and gone to an assembly center we cannot say either as a matter of fact or law that his presence in that center would have resulted in his detention in a relocation center. Some who did report to the assembly center were not sent to relocation centers, but were released upon condition that they remain outside the prohibited zone until the military orders were modified or lifted. This illustrates that they pose different problems and may be governed by different principles. The lawfulness of one does not necessarily determine the lawfulness of the others. This is made clear when we analyze the requirements of the separate provisions of the separate orders. These separate requirements were that those of Japanese ancestry (1) depart from the area; (2) report to and temporarily remain in an assembly center; (3) go under military control to a relocation center there to remain for an indeterminate period until released conditionally or unconditionally by the military authorities. Each of these requirements, it will be noted, imposed distinct duties in connection with the separate steps in a complete evacuation program. Had Congress directly incorporated into one Act the language of these separate orders, and provided sanctions for their violations, disobedience of any one would have constituted a separate offense. Cf. *Blockburger* v. *United States,* 284 U.S. 299, 304. There is no reason why violations of these orders, insofar as they were promulgated pursuant to Congressional enactment, should not be treated as separate offenses.

The *Endo* case . . . graphically illus-trates the difference between the validity of an order to exclude and the validity of a detention order after exclusion has been effected.

Since the petitioner has not been convicted of failing to report or to remain in an assembly or relocation center, we cannot in this case determine the validity of those separate provisions of the order. It is sufficient here for us to pass upon the order which petitioner violated. To do more would be to go beyond the issues raised, and to decide momentous questions not contained within the framework of the pleadings or the evidence in this case. It will be time enough to decide the serious constitutional issues which petitioner seeks to raise when an assembly or relocation order is applied or is certain to be applied to him, and we have its terms before us.

Some of the members of the Court are of the view that evacuation and detention in an Assembly Center were inseparable. After May 3, 1942, the date of Exclusion Order No. 34, Korematsu was under compulsion to leave the area not as he would choose but via an Assembly Center. The Assembly Center was conceived as a part of the machinery for group evacuation. The power to exclude includes the power to do it by force if necessary. And any forcible measure must necessarily entail some degree of detention or restraint whatever method of removal is selected. But whichever view is taken, it results in holding that the order under which petitioner was convicted was valid.

It is said that we are dealing here with the case of imprisonment of a citizen in a concentration camp solely because of his ancestry, without evidence or inquiry concerning his loyalty and good disposition towards the United States. Our task would be simple, our duty clear, were this a case involving the imprisonment of a loyal citizen in a concentration camp because of racial prejudice. Regardless of the true nature of the assembly and relocation centers—and we deem it unjustifiable to call them concentration camps with all the ugly connotations that term implies—we are dealing specifically with nothing but an exclusion order. To cast this case into outlines of racial prejudice, without reference to the real military dangers which were presented, merely confuses the issue. Korematsu was not excluded from the Military Area because of hostility to him or his race. He *was* excluded because we are at war with the Japanese Empire, because the properly constituted military authorities feared an invasion of our West Coast and felt constrained to take proper security measures, because they decided that the military urgency of the situation demanded that all citizens of Japanese ancestry be segregated from the West Coast temporarily, and finally, because Congress, reposing its confidence in this time of war in our military leaders—as inevitably it must—determined that they should have the power to do just this. There was evidence of disloyalty on the part of some, the military authorities considered that the need for action was great, and time was short. We cannot—by availing ourselves of the calm perspective of hindsight—now say that at that time these actions were unjustified.

Affirmed.

MR. JUSTICE FRANKFURTER, concurring. . .
MR. JUSTICE ROBERTS, dissenting. . .
MR. JUSTICE MURPHY, dissenting.
This exclusion of 'all persons of Japanese ancestry, both alien and non-alien,' from the Pacific Coast area on a plea of military necessity in the absence of martial law ought not to be approved. Such exclusion goes over 'the very brink of constitutional power' and falls into the ugly abyss of racism.

In dealing with matters relating to the prosecution and progress of a war, we must accord great respect and consideration to the judgments of the military authorities who are on the scene and who have full knowledge of the military facts. The scope of their discretion must, as a matter of necessity and common sense, be wide. And their judgments ought not to be overruled lightly by those whose training and duties ill-equip them to deal intelligently with matters so vital to the physical security of the nation.

At the same time, however, it is essential that there be definite limits to military discretion, especially where martial law has not been declared. Individuals must not be left impoverished of their constitutional rights on a plea of military necessity that has neither substance nor support. Thus, like other claims conflicting with the asserted constitutional rights of the individual, the military claim must subject itself to the judicial process of having its reasonableness determined and its conflicts with other interests reconciled. 'What are the allowable limits of military discretion, and whether or not they have been overstepped in a particular case, are judicial questions.' *Sterling* v. *Constantin,* 287 U.S. 378, 401.

The judicial test of whether the Government, on a plea of military necessity, can validly deprive an individual of any of his constitutional rights is whether the deprivation is reasonably related to a public danger that is so 'immediate, imminent, and impending' as not to admit of delay and not to permit the intervention of ordinary constitutional processes to alleviate the danger. *United States* v. *Russell,* 13 Wall. 623, 627-8; *Mitchell* v. *Harmony,* 13 How. 115, 134-5; *Raymond* v. *Thomas,* 91 U.S. 712, 716. Civilian Exclusion Order No. 34, banishing from a prescribed area of the Pacific Coast 'all persons of Japanese ancestry, both alien and non-alien,' clearly does not meet that test. Being an obvious racial discrimination, the order deprives all those within its scope of the equal protection of the laws as guaranteed by the Fifth Amendment. It further deprives these individuals of their constitutional rights to live and work where they will, to establish a home where they choose and to move about freely. In excommunicating them without benefit of hearings, this order also deprives them of all their constitutional rights to procedural due process. Yet no reasonable relation to an 'immediate, imminent, and impending' public danger is evident to support this racial restriction which is one of the most sweeping and complete deprivations of constitutional rights in the history of this nation in the absence of martial law.

It must be conceded that the military and naval situation in the spring of 1942 was such as to generate a very real fear of invasion of the Pacific Coast, accompanied by fears of sabotage and espionage in that area. The military command was therefore justified in adopting all reasonable means necessary to combat these dangers. In adjudging the military action taken in light of the then apparent dangers, we must not erect too high or too meticulous standards; it is necessary only that the action have some reasonable relation to the removal of the dangers of invasion, sabotage and espionage. But the exclusion, either temporarily or permanently, of all persons with Japanese blood in their veins has no such reasonable relation. And that relation is lacking because the exclusion order necessarily must rely for its reasonableness upon the assumption that *all* persons of Japanese ancestry may have a dangerous tendency to commit sabotage and espionage and to aid our Japanese enemy in other ways. It is difficult to believe that reason, logic or experience could be marshalled in support of such an assumption.

That this forced exclusion was the result in good measure of this erroneous assumption of racial guilt rather than bona fide military necessity is evidenced by the Commanding General's Final Report on the evacuation from the Pacific Coast area. In it he refers to all individuals of Japanese descent as 'subversive,' as belonging to 'an enemy race' whose 'racial strains are

undiluted,' and as constituting 'over 112,000 potential enemies . . . at large today' along the Pacific Coast. In support of this blanket condemnation of all persons of Japanese descent, however, no reliable evidence is cited to show that such individuals were generally disloyal, or had generally so conducted themselves in this area as to constitute a special menace to defense installations or war industries, or had otherwise by their behavior furnished reasonable ground for their exclusion as a group.

Justification for the exclusion is sought, instead, mainly upon questionable racial and sociological grounds not ordinarily within the realm of expert military judgment, supplemented by certain semi-military conclusions drawn from an unwarranted use of circumstantial evidence. Individuals of Japanese ancestry are condemned because they are said to be 'a large, unassimilated, tightly knit racial group, bound to an enemy nation by strong ties of race, culture, custom and religion.' They are claimed to be given to 'emperor worshipping ceremonies' and to 'dual citizenship.' Japanese language schools and allegedly pro-Japanese organizations are cited as evidence of possible group disloyalty, together with facts as to certain persons being educated and residing at length in Japan. It is intimated that many of these individuals deliberately resided 'adjacent to strategic points,' thus enabling them 'to carry into execution a tremendous program of sabotage on a mass scale should any considerable number of them have been inclined to do so.' The need for protective custody is also asserted. The report refers without identity to 'numerous incidents of violence' as well as to other admittedly unverified or cumulative incidents. From this, plus certain other events not shown to have been connected with the Japanese Americans, it is concluded that the 'situation was fraught with danger to the Japanese population itself' and that the general public 'was ready to take matters into its own hands.' Finally, it is intimated, though not directly charged or proved, that persons of Japanese ancestry were responsible for three minor isolated shellings and bombings of the Pacific Coast area, as well as for unidentified radio transmissions and night signalling.

The main reasons relied upon by those responsible for the forced evacuation, therefore, do not prove a reasonable relation between the group characteristics of Japanese Americans and the dangers of invasion, sabotage and espionage. The reasons appear, instead, to be largely an accumulation of much of the misinformation, half-truths and insinuations that for years have been directed against Japanese Americans by people with racial and economic prejudices—the same people who have been among the foremost advocates of the evacuation. A military judgment based upon such racial and sociological considerations is not entitled to the great weight ordinarily given the judgments based upon strictly military considerations. Especially is this so when every charge relative to race, religion, culture, geographical location, and legal and economic status has been substantially discredited by independent studies made by experts in these matters.

The military necessity which is essential to the validity of the evacuation order thus resolves itself into a few intimations that certain individuals actively aided the enemy, from which it is inferred that the entire group of Japanese Americans could not be trusted to be or remain loyal to the United States. No one denies, of course, that there were some disloyal persons of Japanese descent on the Pacific Coast who did all in their power to aid their ancestral land. Similar disloyal activities have been engaged in by many persons of German, Italian and even more pioneer stock in our country. But to infer that examples of individual disloyalty prove group disloyalty and justify discriminatory action

against the entire group is to deny that under our system of law individual guilt is the sole basis for deprivation of rights. Moreover, this inference, which is at the very heart of the evacuation orders, has been used in support of the abhorrent and despicable treatment of minority groups by the dictatorial tyrannies which this nation is now pledged to destroy. To give constitutional sanction to that inference in this case, however well-intentioned may have been the military command on the Pacific Coast, is to adopt one of the cruelest of the rationales used by our enemies to destroy the dignity of the individual and to encourage and open the door to discriminatory actions against other minority groups in the passions of tomorrow. No adequate reason is given for the failure to treat these Japanese Americans on an individual basis by holding investigations and hearings to separate the loyal from the disloyal, as was done in the case of persons of German and Italian ancestry. See House Report No. 2124 (77th Cong., 2d Sess.) 247-52. It is asserted merely that the loyalties of this group 'were unknown and time was of the essence.' Yet nearly four months elapsed after Pearl Harbor before the first exclusion order was issued; nearly eight months went by until the last order was issued; and the last of these 'subversive' persons was not actually removed until almost eleven months had elapsed. Leisure and deliberation seem to have been more of the essence than speed. And the fact that conditions were not such as to warrant a declaration of martial law adds strength to the belief that the factors of time and military necessity were not as urgent as they have been represented to be.

Moreover, there was no adequate proof that the Federal Bureau of Investigation and the military and naval intelligence services did not have the espionage and sabotage situation well in hand during this long period. Nor is there any denial of the fact that not one person of Japanese ancestry was accused or convicted of espionage or sabotage after Pearl Harbor while they were still free, a fact which is some evidence of the loyalty of the vast majority of these individuals and of the effectiveness of the established methods of combatting these evils. It seems incredible that under these circumstances it would have been impossible to hold loyalty hearings for the mere 112,000 persons involved —or at least for the 70,000 American citizens—especially when a large part of this number represented children and elderly men and women. Any inconvenience that may have accompanied an attempt to conform to procedural due process cannot be said to justify violations of constitutional rights of individuals.

I dissent, therefore, from this legalization of racism. Racial discrimination in any form and in any degree has no justifiable part whatever in our democratic way of life. It is unattractive in any setting but it is utterly revolting among a free people who have embraced the principles set forth in the Constitution of the United States. All residents of this nation are kin in some way by blood or culture to a foreign land. Yet they are primarily and necessarily a part of the new and distinct civilization of the United States. They must accordingly be treated at all times as the heirs of the American experiment and as entitled to all the rights and freedoms guaranteed by the Constitution.

Mr. Justice Jackson, dissenting. . .

XX

Territories and Dependencies

NOTE

In *Balzac* v. *Porto Rico* [1] (1922) the Supreme Court examined the Organic Act of 1917 (Jones Act) and concluded that despite the fact that Congress had therein conferred United States citizenship upon Porto Ricans, the territory had yet not been 'incorporated' into the Union. Consequently, the conviction of a Porto Rican newspaper editor for criminal libel without a jury trial had not violated the Sixth Amendment to the Constitution. It was the Court's opinion that had Congress actually intended to make this island incorporated territory it would have expressly declared so in the Organic Act.

The power of the Federal government to acquire territory has long since come to be recognized as stemming from its powers to admit new states into the Union, to make treaties, and to make war. Indeed, it may be one of the 'necessary concomitants of nationality' of which Mr. Justice Sutherland spoke in the Curtiss-Wright case.

A necessary corollary of this power of territorial acquisition is the power to govern such territories. It is in connection with this latter power, however, that much litigation and public discussion have arisen, making necessary a close examination of the extent to which the recognized power of Congress to legislate for territories is to be conditioned by the several constitutional limitations upon Congressional power.

No particular difficulty was encountered regarding the government of territories and the constitutional rights of their inhabitants until this country, by war with Spain, came into possession of a number of areas geographically remote from the continental limits of the United States and culturally alien to the basically Anglo-Saxon language and legal institutions characteristic thereof. The constitutional problems implicit in the government of these non-contiguous alien lands were carefully examined in a series of cases known as the Insular Cases.

In the first of these, *De Lima* v. *Bidwell*, [2] the Supreme Court was confronted with the question whether Porto Rico had become 'an integral part' of the United States as a result of its annexation. Though answering this question in the negative, the Court proceeded to point out that Porto Rico was nevertheless no longer 'foreign territory' so far as the application of existing United States tariff laws was concerned. By the same token goods imported into Porto Rico from the United States were held to be likewise not dutiable. [3] In *Downes* v. *Bidwell*, [4] however, the Court upheld the constitutionality of the Foraker Act,

---

[1] The correct spelling is Puerto Rico.
[2] 182 U.S. 1 (1901).

[3] *Dooley* v. *United States*, 182 U.S. 222 (1901).
[4] 182 U.S. 244 (1901).

which imposed certain duties on goods imported into the United States from Porto Rico. It was held that the constitutional requirement that 'all duties, imposts, and excises shall be uniform throughout the United States,'[5] was no bar to Congressional action here because Porto Rico was not a part of the United States. The vote was five to four, as in the De Lima case, with Mr. Justice Brown's shifting position explaining the different judgments of the Court. In answer to the persistent and highly controversial question of the day, 'Does the Constitution follow the flag?', the Supreme Court had apparently answered, 'No.' Rather, it was to be left to Congress to determine when, where, and in what respects the provisions of the Constitution were to apply in acquired territory.

Concurring with the majority in *Downes* v. *Bidwell*, Mr. Justice White set forth the doctrine of territorial incorporation which has since become the accepted working principle for the determination of the position of territories in the constitutional law of the United States.[6] He declared that the United States had the undisputed power to acquire new territory by war or by treaty; furthermore, Congress was expressly given power to govern such territory. But the territory did not become a part of the United States, nor did all the provisions of the Constitution apply to it, until Congress had actually 'incorporated' it into the Union. Hence the requirement of uniformity need not be met in the levying of taxes in 'unincorporated' territory. The power of Congress to levy taxes in territories came not from the general power to tax but from the power to govern territories. Mr. Justice White gave no precise definition of what is meant by incorporation, nor any instructions as to the precise mode by which it is to be accomplished. Like many another doctrine in constitutional law its meaning can be discovered only through its application in case after case.

In 1903 the Court held that despite its annexation by joint resolution in 1898 Hawaii had not been incorporated into the United States; the constitutional provision regarding indictment by a grand jury need not, therefore, apply.[7] In 1904 it was decided that since the Philippine Islands had not been incorporated there was no constitutional necessity for providing the citizens of that territory with jury trials.[8] On the other hand, Alaska was declared by the Supreme Court in 1905 to have been incorporated by virtue of the treaty of acquisition and a series of Congressional acts, the latter being held sufficient to indicate inferentially such an intent on the part of Congress. Accordingly, a provision of the Alaska Organic Act of 1900 providing for the trial of misdemeanors by a six-man jury instead of the common law twelve-man jury was held to be an unconstitutional violation of the Sixth Amendment.[9]

In each instance the Court is confronted with the task of determining the intent of Congress with regard to the territory's incorporation. In the absence

[5] Art. 1, sec. 8.
[6] See Coudert, Frederic R., 'The Evolution of the Doctrine of Territorial Incorporation,' 26 *Columbia Law Rev.* 823 (1926).
[7] *Hawaii* v. *Mankichi*, 190 U.S. 197 (1903). Hawaii became incorporated in 1900.
[8] *Dorr* v. *United States*, 195 U.S. 138 (1904).
[9] *Rassmussen* v. *United States*, 197 U.S. 516 (1905).

of an explicit Congressional declaration on the subject the Court's task is not an easy one. Inasmuch as the incorporated or unincorporated status of a territory vitally affects the constitutional rights and immunities of its inhabitants, the determination of that status is clearly of first importance.

BALZAC v. PEOPLE OF PORTO RICO
258 U.S. 298 (1922)

Review of two judgments of the Supreme Court of Porto Rico which affirmed judgments of the District Court for Arecibo imposing sentences to imprisonment based on convictions of criminal libel. . .

MR. CHIEF JUSTICE TAFT delivered the opinion of the court.

These are two prosecutions for criminal libel brought against the same defendant, Jesus M. Balzac, on informations filed in the District Court for Arecibo, Porto Rico, by the District Attorney for that District. Balzac was the editor of a daily paper published in Arecibo, known as 'El Baluarte,' and the articles upon which the charges of libel were based were published on April 16 and April 23, 1918, respectively. In each case the defendant demanded a jury. The code of criminal procedure of Porto Rico grants a jury trial in cases of felony but not in misdemeanors. The defendant, nevertheless, contended that he was entitled to a jury in such a case, under the Sixth Amendment to the Constitution, and that the language of the alleged libels was only fair comment and their publication was protected by the First Amendment. His contentions were overruled, he was tried by the court and was convicted in both cases and sentenced to five months' imprisonment in the district jail in the first, and to four months in the second, and to the payment of the costs in each. The defendant appealed to the Supreme Court of Porto Rico. That court affirmed both judgments. *People* v. *Balzac,* 28 P.R. 139, Second Case, 28 P.R. 141.

The first question in these cases is one of jurisdiction of this court. By § 244 of the Judicial Code, approved March 3, 1911, it was provided that writs of error and appeals from the final judgments and decrees of the Supreme Court of Porto Rico might be prosecuted to this court in any case in which was drawn in question the validity of a treaty or statute of, or authority exercised under, the United States, or wherein the Constitution of the United States, or a treaty thereof, or an act of Congress was brought in question and the right claimed thereunder was denied, and this without regard to the amount involved. By the Act of January 28, 1915, c. 22, 38 Stat. 803, § 244 of the Judicial Code was repealed, but § 246 was amended and made to apply to the appellate jurisdiction of this court in respect to the decisions of the Supreme Court not only of Hawaii, as before, but also Porto Rico, and it was provided that writs of error to those courts from this court could be prosecuted in the same class of cases as those in which this court was authorized under § 237 of the Judicial Code to review decisions of state courts of last resort. Section 237 at that time allowed a writ of error to final decisions in state courts of last resort where was drawn in question the validity of a treaty, or a statute of, or an authority exercised under, the United States, and the decision was against its validity; or where was drawn in question the validity of a statute of, or an authority exercised under any State, on the ground of its being repugnant to the Constitution, treaties, or laws of the United States, and the decision was in favor of its validity; or where any title, right, privilege or immunity was claimed under the Constitution, or any treaty or statute of, or commission held or authority exercised under, the United States, and the decision was against the title, right, privilege or immunity especially set up or claimed by either party under such Constitution, treaty, statute, commission or authority. By Act of January 28, 1915, 38 Stat. 803, 804, amending § 246, this court was given power by certiorari to bring up for review all final judgments or decrees in civil or criminal cases in the supreme courts of Porto Rico and Hawaii, other than those reviewable here by writ of error because in the class similar to that described in § 237 of the Judicial Code. By Act of September 6, 1916, c. 448, 39 Stat. 726, the jurisdiction of this court to review by writ of error, under § 237, final judgments and decrees of state courts of last resort was cut down by omitting cases (other than those involving the validity of a treaty, statute or authority exercised under the United States or any State) wherein a title, right, privilege, or immunity, was claimed under the Constitution, or any treaty or statute of, or commission held, or authority exercised under, the United States, and the decision was against such title, right, privilege or immunity, and such cases, it was provided, could only be examined on review in this court by certiorari.

The question now presented is whether the amendment to § 237 of the Judicial Code by the Act of 1916 applies to, and affects, the appellate jurisdiction of this court in reviewing decisions of the Supreme Court of Porto Rico. We think it does. We think that the manifest purpose of the Act of 1915, amending § 246 of the Code, in its reference to § 237 of the Judicial Code, was to assimilate the appellate jurisdiction of this court over the supreme courts of Porto Rico and Hawaii to that over state courts of last resort, and that the reference in amended § 246 to § 237 may be fairly construed to embrace

subsequent changes in § 237 that are not obviously inapplicable.

This brings us to the question whether there was drawn in question in these cases the validity of a statute of Porto Rico under the Constitution of the United States. The Penal Code of Porto Rico divides crimes into felonies and misdemeanors. (Rev. Stats. and Codes of Porto Rico, 1911, Penal Code, § 13.) A felony is described as a crime punishable by death or by imprisonment in the penitentiary. Every other crime is declared to be a misdemeanor. Penal Code, § 14. Section 178 of the Porto Rican Code of Criminal Procedure provided that issues of fact in cases of felony should be tried by a jury when the defendant so elected, but gave no such right in the case of misdemeanors. This was construed by the Supreme Court to deny such right. *People* v. *Bird,* 5 P.R. 387.

By § 244 (5676) of the Penal Code (as amended by Act of March 9, 1911, p. 71), the publication of a libel is made punishable by a fine not exceeding $5,000, or imprisonment in jail for a term not exceeding two years, or both such fine and imprisonment, and also the costs of the action in the discretion of the court. It is, therefore, plain that libel under the Porto Rican law is a misdemeanor, and a jury trial was not required therein. By the Act of July 22, 1919 (Laws of Porto Rico, 1919, No. 84, p. 684), a jury trial is now given in misdemeanors, but that did not come into force until after these libels were published and these trials had.

When the Penal Code and the Code of Criminal Procedure were first passed in 1901, they both contained the provision that in all cases of libel the jury should determine the law and the fact. It was held, however, by the Supreme Court of Porto Rico in *People* v. *Bird,* 5 P.R. 387, 405, that this did not give a jury trial but only made provision that, if and when a right of jury trial was given in such cases, the jury should have the power to determine the law and the fact. Thereafter the Act of March 10, 1904 (Laws of Porto Rico, 1904, p. 130), expressly repealed all reference to trials for libel in the jury act.

The effect of the Penal Code of Procedure, as construed by the Supreme Court of Porto Rico, and of the Act of March 10th, repealing the jury act as to libel cases, was a statutory denial of the right of jury trial in such cases. A demand for a jury trial in this case, therefore, drew in question the validity of the statutes upon which the court relied in denying the demand. This necessarily leads to the conclusion that these cases are in the same class as those which come to this court by writ of error under § 237, as amended by the Act of 1916, and that jurisdiction by writ of error exists.

Was the issue properly saved in the record by the defendant? We think it was. The demand for a jury trial, the statute to the contrary notwithstanding, was made at the trial. It was renewed in the assignments of error in the Porto Rican Supreme Court and here. Those assignments did not mention the statutes whose validity was involved, but merely averred that the defendant had been denied his right as an American citizen under the Sixth Amendment to the Constitution. While this is informal, we think that it is sufficient when the record discloses the real nature of the controversy and the specification of the assignment leaves no doubt that it is directed to that controversy.

We have now to inquire whether that part of the Sixth Amendment to the Constitution, which requires that, in all criminal prosecutions, the accused shall enjoy the right to a speedy and public trial, by an impartial jury of the State and district wherein the crime shall have been committed, which district shall have been previously ascertained by law, applies to Porto Rico. Another provision on the subject is in Article III of the Constitution providing that the trial of all crimes, except in cases of impeachment, shall be by jury; and

such trial shall be held in the State where the said crimes shall have been committed; but, when not committed within any State, the trial shall be at such place or places as the Congress may by law have directed. The Seventh Amendment of the Constitution provides that in suits at common law, where the value at controversy shall exceed twenty dollars, the right of trial by jury shall be preserved. It is well settled that these provisions for jury trial in criminal and civil cases apply to the Territories of the United States. . . But it is just as clearly settled that they do not apply to territory belonging to the United States which has not been incorporated into the Union. *Hawaii* v. *Mankichi,* 190 U.S. 197; *Dorr* v. *United States,* 195 U.S. 138, 145. It was further settled in *Downes* v. *Bidwell,* 182 U.S. 244, and confirmed by *Dorr* v. *United States,* 195 U.S. 138, that neither the Philippines nor Porto Rico was territory which had been incorporated in the Union or become a part of the United States, as distinguished from merely belonging to it; and that the acts giving temporary governments to the Philippines, 32 Stat. 691, and to Porto Rico, 31 Stat. 77, had no such effect. The *Insular Cases* revealed much diversity of opinion in this court as to the constitutional status of the territory acquired by the Treaty of Paris ending the Spanish War, but the *Dorr Case* shows that the opinion of Mr. Justice White of the majority, in *Downes* v. *Bidwell,* has become the settled law of the court. The conclusion of this court in the *Dorr Case,* p. 149, was as follows:

'We conclude that the power to govern territory, implied in the right to acquire it, and given to Congress in the Constitution in Article IV, § 3, to whatever other limitations it may be subject, the extent of which must be decided as questions arise, does not require that body to enact for ceded territory, not made a part of the United States by Congressional action, a system of laws which shall include the right of trial by jury, and that the Constitution does not, without legislation and of its own force, carry such right to territory so situated.'

The question before us, therefore, is: Has Congress, since the Foraker Act of April 12, 1900, c. 191, 31 Stat. 77, enacted legislation incorporating Porto Rico into the Union? Counsel for the plaintiff in error give, in their brief, an extended list of acts, to which we shall refer later, which they urge as indicating a purpose to make the Island a part of the United States, but they chiefly rely on the Organic Act of Porto Rico of March 2, 1917, c. 145, 39 Stat. 951, known as the Jones Act.

The act is entitled 'An Act To provide a civil government for Porto Rico, and for other purposes.' It does not indicate by its title that it has a purpose to incorporate the Island into the Union. It does not contain any clause which declares such purpose or effect. While this is not conclusive, it strongly tends to show that Congress did not have such an intention. Few questions have been the subject of such discussion and dispute in our country as the status of our territory acquired from Spain in 1899. The division between the political parties in respect to it, the diversity of the views of the members of this court in regard to its constitutional aspects, and the constant recurrence of the subject in the Houses of Congress, fixed the attention of all on the future relation of this acquired territory to the United States. Had Congress intended to take the important step of changing the treaty status of Porto Rico by incorporating it into the Union, it is reasonable to suppose that it would have done so by the plain declaration, and would not have left it to mere inference. Before the question became acute at the close of the Spanish War, the distinction between acquisition and incorporation was not regarded as important, or at least it was not fully understood and had not aroused great controversy. Before that, the purpose of Congress might well be a matter of mere inference from various legis-

lative acts; but in these latter days, incorporation is not to be assumed without express declaration, or an implication so strong as to exclude any other view.

Again, the second section of the act is called a 'Bill of Rights,' and included therein is substantially every one of the guaranties of the Federal Constitution, except those relating to indictment by a grand jury in the case of infamous crimes and the right of trial by jury in civil and criminal cases. If it was intended to incorporate Porto Rico into the Union by this act, which would *ex proprio vigore* make applicable the whole Bill of Rights of the Constitution to the Island, why was it thought necessary to create for it a Bill of Rights and carefully exclude trial by jury? In the very forefront of the act is this substitute for incorporation and application of the Bill of Rights of the Constitution. This seems to us a conclusive argument against the contention of counsel for the plaintiff in error.

The section of the Jones Act which counsel press on us is § 5. This in effect declares that all persons who under the Foraker Act were made citizens of Porto Rico and certain other residents shall become citizens of the United States, unless they prefer not to become such, in which case they are to declare such preference within six months, and thereafter they lose certain political rights under the new government. In the same section the United States District Court is given power separately to naturalize individuals of some other classes of residents. . . Unaffected by the considerations already suggested, perhaps the declaration of § 5 would furnish ground for an inference such as counsel for plaintiff in error contend, but under the circumstances we find it entirely consistent with non-incorporation. When Porto Ricans passed from under the government of Spain, they lost the protection of that government as subjects of the King of Spain, a title by which they had been known for centuries. They had a right to expect, in passing under the domination of the United States, a status entitling them to the protection of their new sovereign. In theory and in law, they had it as citizens of Porto Rico, but it was an anomalous status, or seemed to be so in view of the fact that those who owed and rendered allegiance to the other great world powers were given the same designation and status as those living in their respective home countries so far as protection against foreign injustice went. It became a yearning of the Porto Ricans to be American citizens, therefore, and this act gave them the boon. What additional rights did it give them? It enabled them to move into the continental United States and becoming residents of any State there to enjoy every right of any other citizen of the United States, civil, social and political. A citizen of the Philippines must be naturalized before he can settle and vote in this country. Act of June 29, 1906, c. 3592, § 30, 34 Stat. 606. Not so the Porto Rican under the Organic Act of 1917.

In Porto Rico, however, the Porto Rican can not insist upon the right of trial by jury, except as his own representatives in his legislature shall confer it on him. The citizen of the United States living in Porto Rico can not there enjoy a right of trial by jury under the Federal Constitution, any more than the Porto Rican. It is locality that is determinative of the application of the Constitution, in such matters as judicial procedure, and not the status of the people who live in it.

It is true that, in the absence of other and countervailing evidence, a law of Congress or a provision in a treaty acquiring territory, declaring an intention to confer political and civil rights on the inhabitants of the new lands as American citizens, may be properly interpreted to mean an incorporation of it into the Union, as in the case of Louisiana and Alaska. This was one of the chief grounds upon which this court placed its conclusion that Alaska had been incorporated in the Union, in

Rassmussen v. *United States,* 197 U.S. 516. But Alaska was a very different case from that of Porto Rico. It was an enormous territory, very sparsely settled and offering opportunity for immigration and settlement by American citizens. It was on the American Continent and within easy reach of the then United States. It involved none of the difficulties which incorporation of the Philippines and Porto Rico presents, and one of them is in the very matter of trial by jury. This court refers to the difficulties in *Dorr* v. *United States,* 195 U.S. 138, 148:

'If the right to trial by jury were a fundamental right which goes wherever the jurisdiction of the United States extends, or if Congress, in framing laws for outlying territory belonging to the United States was obliged to establish that system by affirmative legislation, it would follow that, no matter what the needs or capacities of the people, trial by jury, and in no other way, must be forthwith established, although the result may be to work injustice and provoke disturbance rather than to aid the orderly administration of justice. . . Again, if the United States shall acquire by treaty the cession of territory having an established system of jurisprudence, where jury trials are unknown, but a method of fair and orderly trial prevails under an acceptable and long-established code, the preference of the people must be disregarded, their established customs ignored and they themselves coerced to accept, in advance of incorporation into the United States, a system of trial unknown to them and unsuited to their needs. We do not think it was intended, in giving power to Congress to make regulations for the territories, to hamper its exercise with this condition.'

The jury system needs citizens trained to the exercise of the responsibilities of jurors. In common-law countries centuries of tradition have prepared a conception of the impartial attitude jurors must assume. The jury system postulates a conscious duty of participation in the machinery of justice which it is hard for people not brought up in fundamentally popular government at once to acquire. One of its greatest benefits is in the security it gives the people that they, as jurors actual or possible, being part of the judicial system of the country can prevent its arbitrary use or abuse. Congress has thought that a people like the Filipinos or the Porto Ricans, trained to a complete judicial system which knows no juries, living in compact and ancient communities, with definitely formed customs and political conceptions, should be permitted themselves to determine how far they wish to adopt this institution of Anglo-Saxon origin, and when. Hence the care with which from the time when Mr. McKinley wrote his historic letter to Mr. Root in April of 1900, Public Laws, Philippine Commission, pp. 6-9—Act of July 1, 1902, c. 1369, 32 Stat. 691, 692, concerning the character of government to be set up for the Philippines by the Philippine Commission, until the Act of 1917, giving a new Organic Act to Porto Rico, the United States has been liberal in granting to the Islands acquired by the Treaty of Paris most of the American constitutional guaranties, but has been sedulous to avoid forcing a jury system on a Spanish and civil-law country until it desired it. We can not find any intention to depart from this policy in making Porto Ricans American citizens, explained as this is by the desire to put them as individuals on an exact equality with citizens from the American homeland, to secure them more certain protection against the world, and to give them an opportunity, should they desire, to move into the United States proper and there without naturalization to enjoy all political and other rights.

We need not dwell on another consideration which requires us not lightly to infer, from acts thus easily explained on other grounds, an intention to incorporate in the Union these distant ocean communities of a different origin and language from those of our continental people. In-

corporation has always been a step, and an important one, leading to statehood. Without, in the slightest degree, intimating an opinion as to the wisdom of such a policy, for that is not our province, it is reasonable to assume that when such a step is taken it will be begun and taken by Congress deliberately and with a clear declaration of purpose, and not left a matter of mere inference or construction.

Counsel for the plaintiff in error also rely on the organization of a United States District Court in Porto Rico, on the allowance of review of the Porto Rican Supreme Court in cases when the Constitution of the United States is involved, on the statutory permission that Porto Rican youth can attend West Point and Annapolis Academies, on the authorized sale of United States stamps in the Island, on the extension of revenue, navigation, immigration, national banking, bankruptcy, federal employers' liability, safety appliance, extradition, and census laws in one way or another to Porto Rico. With the background of the considerations already stated, none of these nor all of them put together furnish ground for the conclusion pressed on us.

The United States District Court is not a true United States court established under Article III of the Constitution to administer the judicial power of the United States therein conveyed. It is created by virtue of the sovereign congressional faculty, granted under Article IV, § 3, of that instrument, of making all needful rules and regulations respecting the territory belonging to the United States. The resemblance of its jurisdiction to that of true United States courts in offering an opportunity to nonresidents of resorting to a tribunal not subject to local influence, does not change its character as a mere territorial court. Nor does the legislative recognition that federal constitutional questions may arise in litigation in Porto Rico have any weight in this discussion. The Constitution of the United States is in force in Porto Rico as it is wherever and whenever the sovereign power of that government is exerted. This has not only been admitted but emphasized by this court in all its authoritative expressions upon the issues arising in the *Insular Cases,* especially in the *Downes* v. *Bidwell* and the *Dorr Cases.* The Constitution, however, contains grants of power and limitations which in the nature of things are not always and everywhere applicable, and the real issue in the *Insular Cases* was not whether the Constitution extended to the Philippines or Porto Rico when we went there, but which of its provisions were applicable by way of limitation upon the exercise of executive and legislative power in dealing with new conditions and requirements. The guaranties of certain fundamental personal rights declared in the Constitution, as for instance that no person could be deprived of life, liberty or property without due process of law, had from the beginning full application in the Philippines and Porto Rico, and, as this guaranty is one of the most fruitful in causing litigation in our own country, provision was naturally made for similar controversy in Porto Rico. Indeed provision is made for the consideration of constitutional questions coming on appeal and writ of error from the Supreme Court of the Philippines, which are certainly not incorporated in the Union. Judicial Code, § 248.

On the whole, therefore, we find no features in the Organic Act of Porto Rico of 1917 from which we can infer the purpose of Congress to incorporate Porto Rico into the United States with the consequences which would follow.

This court has passed on substantially the same questions presented here in two cases, *Porto Rico* v. *Tapia,* and *Porto Rico* v. *Muratti,* 245 U.S. 639. In the former, the question was whether one who was charged with committing a felonious homicide some twelve days after the passage of the Organic Act in 1917, could be brought to trial without an indictment of a grand jury as required by the Fifth Amendment to the Constitution. The United States District Court of Porto Rico on a writ of habeas corpus held that he could not be held to answer and discharged him. In the other case, the felony charged was alleged to have been committed before the passage of the Organic Act, but prosecution was begun afterwards. In that, the Supreme Court of Porto Rico held that an indictment was rendered necessary by the Organic Act. This court reversed the District Court in the *Tapia Case* and the Supreme Court in the *Muratti Case,* necessarily holding the Organic Act had not incorporated Porto Rico into the United States. These cases were disposed of by a *per curiam.* Counsel have urged us in the cases at the bar to deal with the questions raised more at length in exposition of the effect of the Organic Act of 1917 upon the issue, and we have done so.

A second assignment of error is based on the claim that the alleged libels here did not pass the bounds of legitimate comment on the conduct of the Governor of the Island against whom they were directed, and that their prosecution is a violation of the First Amendment to the Constitution securing free speech and a free press. A reading of the two articles removes the slightest doubt that they go far beyond the 'exuberant expressions of meridional speech,' to use the expression of this court in a similar case in *Gandia* v. *Pettingill,* 222 U.S. 452, 458. Indeed they are so excessive and outrageous in their character that they suggest the query whether their superlative vilification has not overleapt itself and become unconsciously humorous. But this is not a defence.

The judgments of the Supreme Court of Porto Rico are

Affirmed.

Mr. Justice Holmes concurs in the result.

Appendix

Below are listed the persons nominated as Chief Justice and Associate Justice of the United States Supreme Court. Listed also are the state of which the nominee was a resident at the time of appointment, his life span, the President by whom he was appointed, and finally the years of service on the Supreme Court. The first date in the last column refers to the date of confirmation unless the nominee was rejected, withdrawn, or otherwise not acted upon.

Jay, John (Ch. J.)	N. Y.	1745-1829	Washington	1789-1795
Rutledge, John	S. C.	1739-1800	"	1789-1791
Cushing, William	Mass.	1732-1810	"	1789-1810
Harrison, Robert H.	Md.	1745-1790	"	1789 declined
Wilson, James	Pa.	1742-1798	"	1789-1798
Blair, John	Va.	1732-1800	"	1789-1796
Iredell, James	N. C.	1751-1799	"	1790-1799
Johnson, Thomas	Md.	1732-1819	"	1791-1793
Paterson, William	N. J.	1745-1806	"	1793 (Feb.) withdrawn
Paterson, William			"	1793 (Mar.)-1806
Rutledge, John (Ch. J.)	S. C.	1739-1800	"	1795 rejected
Cushing, William (Ch. J.)	Mass.	1732-1810	"	1796 declined
Chase, Samuel	Md.	1741-1811	"	1796-1811
Ellsworth, Oliver (Ch. J.)	Conn.	1745-1807	"	1796-1800
Washington, Bushrod	Va.	1762-1829	Adams, J.	1798-1829
Moore, Alfred	N. C.	1755-1810	"	1799-1804
Jay, John (Ch. J.)	N. Y	1745-1829	"	1800 declined
Marshall, John (Ch. J.)	Va.	1755-1835	"	1801-1835
Johnson, William	S. C.	1771-1834	Jefferson	1804-1834
Livingston, Henry B.	N. Y.	1757-1823	"	1806-1823
Todd, Thomas	Ky.	1765-1826	"	1807-1826
Lincoln, Levi	Mass.	1749-1820	Madison	1811 declined
Wolcott, Alexander	Conn.	1758-1828	"	1811 rejected
Adams, John Quincy	Mass.	1767-1848	"	1811 declined
Story, Joseph	Mass.	1779-1845	"	1811-1845
Duval, Gabriel	Md.	1752-1844	"	1811-1835
Thompson, Smith	N. Y.	1768-1843	Monroe	1823-1843
Trimble, Robert	Ky.	1777-1828	Adams, J. Q.	1826-1828
Crittenden, John J.	Ky.	1787-1863	"	1828 postponed
McLean, John	Ohio	1785-1861	Jackson	1829-1861
Baldwin, Henry	Pa.	1780-1844	"	1830-1844
Wayne, James Moore	Ga.	1790-1867	"	1835-1867
Taney, Roger Brooke	Md.	1777-1864	"	1835 postponed
Taney, Roger Brooke (Ch. J.)			"	1836-1864
Barbour, Philip P.	Va.	1783-1841	"	1836-1841
Smith, William	Ala.	1762-1840	"	1837 declined
Catron, John	Tenn.	1786-1865	"	1837-1865
McKinley, John	Ala.	1780-1852	Van Buren	1837-1852
Daniel, Peter Vivian	Va.	1784-1860	"	1841-1860

Spencer, John Canfield	N. Y.	1788-1855	Tyler	1844 rejected
Walworth, Reuben Hyde	N. Y.	1788-1867	"	1844 withdrawn
King, Edward	Pa.	1794-1873	"	1844 (June) postponed
King, Edward			"	1844 (Dec.) withdrawn
Nelson, Samuel	N. Y.	1792-1873	"	1845-1872
Read, John Meredith	Pa.	1797-1874	"	1845 not acted upon
Woodward, George W.	Pa.	1809-1875	Polk	1845 rejected
Woodbury, Levi	N. H.	1789-1851	"	1846-1851
Grier, Robert Cooper	Pa.	1794-1870	"	1846-1870
Curtis, Benjamin R.	Mass.	1809-1874	Fillmore	1851-1857
Bradford, Edward A.	La.	1813- ?	"	1852 not acted upon
Badger, George E.	N. C.	1795-1866	"	1853 postponed
Micou, William C.	La.	1806- ?	"	1853 not acted upon
Campbell, John A.	Ala.	1811-1889	Pierce	1853-1861
Clifford, Nathan	Me.	1803-1881	Buchanan	1858-1881
Black, Jeremiah S.	Pa.	1810-1883	"	1861 rejected
Swayne, Noah Haynes	Ohio	1804-1884	Lincoln	1862-1881
Miller, Samuel Freeman	Iowa	1816-1890	"	1862-1890
Davis, David	Ill.	1815-1886	"	1862-1877
Field, Stephen J.	Cal.	1816-1899	"	1863-1897
Chase, Salmon P. (Ch. J.)	Ohio	1808-1873	"	1864-1873
Stanbery, Henry	Ohio	1803-1881	Johnson	1866 not acted upon
Hoar, Ebenezer R.	Mass.	1816-1895	Grant	1869 rejected
Stanton, Edwin McM.	Pa.	1814-1869	"	1869 died
Strong, William	Pa.	1808-1895	"	1870-1880
Bradley, Joseph P.	N. J.	1813-1892	"	1870-1892
Hunt, Ward	N. Y.	1810-1886	"	1872-1882
Williams, George H. (Ch. J.)	Ore.	1823-1910	"	1873 withdrawn
Cushing, Caleb	Mass.	1800-1879	"	1874 withdrawn
Waite, Morrison R. (Ch. J.)	Ohio	1816-1888	"	1874-1888
Harlan, John Marshall	Ky.	1833-1911	Hayes	1877-1911
Woods, William B.	Ga.	1824-1887	"	1880-1887
Matthews, Stanley	Ohio	1824-1889	Garfield	1881 not acted upon
Matthews, Stanley			"	1881-1889
Gray, Horace	Mass.	1828-1902	Arthur	1881-1902
Conkling, Roscoe	N. Y.	1829-1888	"	1882 declined
Blatchford, Samuel	N. Y.	1820-1893	"	1882-1893
Lamar, Lucius Q. C.	Miss.	1825-1893	Cleveland	1888-1893
Fuller, Melville W. (Ch. J.)	Ill.	1833-1910	"	1888-1910
Brewer, David J.	Kan.	1837-1910	Harrison, B.	1889-1910
Brown, Henry B.	Mich.	1836-1913	"	1890-1906
Shiras, George, Jr.	Pa.	1832-1924	"	1892-1903
Jackson, Howell E.	Tenn.	1832-1895	"	1893-1895
Hornblower, William B.	N. Y.	1851-1914	Cleveland	1893 rejected
Peckham, Wheeler H.	N. Y.	1833-1905	"	1894 rejected
White, Edward D.	La.	1845-1921	"	1894-1910
Peckham, Rufus W.	N. Y.	1838-1909	"	1895-1909
McKenna, Joseph	Cal.	1843-1926	McKinley	1898-1925
Holmes, Oliver W.	Mass.	1841-1935	Roosevelt, T.	1902-1932
Day, William R.	Ohio	1849-1923	"	1903-1922
Moody, William H.	Mass.	1853-1917	"	1906-1910
Lurton, Horace H.	Tenn.	1844-1914	Taft	1909-1914
White, Edward D. (Ch. J.)	La.	1845-1921	"	1910-1921
Hughes, Charles E.	N. Y.	1862-	"	1910-1916

Van Devanter, Willis	Wyo.	1859-1941	"	1910-1937
Lamar, Joseph R.	Ga.	1857-1916	"	1910-1916
Pitney, Mahlon	N. J.	1858-1924	"	1912-1922
McReynolds, James C.	Tenn.	1862-1946	Wilson	1914-1941
Brandeis, Louis D.	Mass.	1856-1941	"	1916-1939
Clarke, John H.	Ohio	1857-1945	"	1916-1922
Taft, William H. (Ch. J.)	Conn.	1857-1930	Harding	1921-1930
Sutherland, George	Utah	1862-1942	"	1922-1938
Butler, Pierce	Minn.	1866-1939	"	1922-1939
Sanford, Edward T.	Tenn.	1865-1930	"	1923-1930
Stone, Harlan F.	N. Y.	1872-1946	Coolidge	1925-1941
Hughes, Charles E. (Ch. J.)	N. Y.	1862-	Hoover	1930-1941
Parker, John J.	N. C.	1885-	"	1930 rejected
Roberts, Owen J.	Pa.	1875-	"	1930-1945
Cardozo, Benj. N.	N. Y.	1870-1938	"	1932-1938
Black, Hugo L.	Ala.	1886-	Roosevelt, F. D.	1937-
Reed, Stanley F.	Ky.	1884-	"	1938-
Frankfurter, Felix	Mass.	1882-	"	1939-
Douglas, William O.	Conn.	1898-	"	1939-
Murphy, Frank	Mich.	1890-	"	1940-
Stone, Harlan F. (Ch. J.)	N. Y.	1872-1946	"	1941-1946
Byrnes, James F.	S. C.	1879-	"	1941-1942
Jackson, Robert H.	N. Y.	1892-	"	1941-
Rutledge, Wiley B.	Iowa	1894-	"	1943-
Burton, Harold H.	Ohio	1888-	Truman	1945-
Vinson, Frederick M. (Ch. J.)	Ky.	1890-	"	1946-

The Constitution of the United States of America

WE THE PEOPLE of the United States, in Order to form a more perfect Union, establish Justice, insure domestic Tranquility, provide for the common defence, promote the general Welfare, and secure the Blessings of Liberty to ourselves and our Posterity, do ordain and establish this CONSTITUTION for the United States of America.

ARTICLE I.

SECTION 1. All legislative Powers herein granted shall be vested in a Congress of the United States, which shall consist of a Senate and House of Representatives.

SECTION 2. The House of Representatives shall be composed of Members chosen every second Year by the People of the several States, and the Electors in each State shall have the Qualifications requisite for Electors of the most numerous Branch of the State Legislature.

No Person shall be a Representative who shall not have attained to the Age of twenty-five Years, and been seven Years a Citizen of the United States, and who shall not, when elected, be an Inhabitant of that State in which he shall be chosen.

[Representatives and direct Taxes shall be apportioned among the several States which may be included within this Union, according to their respective Numbers, which shall be determined by adding to the whole Number of free Persons, including those bound to Service for a Term of Years, and excluding Indians not taxed, three fifths of all other Persons.] The actual Enumeration shall be made within three Years after the first Meeting of the Congress of the United States, and within every subsequent Term of ten Years, in such Manner as they shall by Law direct. The Number of Representatives shall not exceed one for every thirty Thousand, but each State shall have at Least one Representative; and until such enumeration shall be made, the State of New Hampshire shall

be entitled to chuse three, Massachusetts eight, Rhode-Island and Providence Plantations one, Connecticut five, New-York six, New Jersey four, Pennsylvania eight, Delaware one, Maryland six, Virginia ten, North Carolina five, South Carolina five, and Georgia three.

When vacancies happen in the Representation from any State, the Executive Authority thereof shall issue Writs of Election to fill such Vacancies.

The House of Representatives shall chuse their Speaker and other Officers; and shall have the sole Power of Impeachment.

SECTION 3. The Senate of the United States shall be composed of two Senators from each State, chosen by the Legislature thereof, for six Years; and each Senator shall have one Vote.

Immediately after they shall be assembled in Consequence of the first Election, they shall be divided as equally as may be into three Classes. The Seats of the Senators of the first Class shall be vacated at the Expiration of the second Year, of the second Class at the Expiration of the fourth Year, and of the third Class at the Expiration of the sixth Year, so that one-third may be chosen every second Year; and if Vacancies happen by Resignation, or otherwise, during the Recess of the Legislature of any State, the Executive thereof may make temporary Appointments until the next Meeting of the Legislature, which shall then fill such Vacancies.

No Person shall be a Senator who shall not have attained to the Age of thirty Years, and been nine Years a Citizen of the United States, and who shall not, when elected, be an Inhabitant of that State for which he shall be chosen.

The Vice President of the United States shall be President of the Senate, but shall have no Vote, unless they be equally divided.

The Senate shall chuse their other Officers, and also a President pro tempore, in the absence of the Vice President, or when he shall exercise the Office of President of the United States.

The Senate shall have the sole Power to try all Impeachments. When sitting for that Purpose, they shall be on Oath or Affirmation. When the President of the United States is tried, the Chief Justice shall preside: And no Person shall be convicted without the Concurrence of two thirds of the Members present.

Judgment in Cases of Impeachment shall not extend further than to removal from Office, and disqualification to hold and enjoy any Office of honor, Trust or Profit under the United States: but the Party convicted shall nevertheless be liable and subject to Indictment, Trial, Judgment and Punishment, according to Law.

Section 4. The Times, Places and Manner of holding Elections for Senators and Representatives, shall be prescribed in each State by the Legislature thereof; but the Congress may at any time by Law make or alter such Regulations, except as to the Places of Chusing Senators.

The Congress shall assemble at least once in every Year, and such Meeting shall be on the first Monday in December, unless they shall by Law appoint a different Day.

Section 5. Each House shall be the Judge of the Elections, Returns and Qualifications of its own Members, and a Majority of each shall constitute a Quorum to do Business; but a smaller Number may adjourn from day to day, and may be authorized to compel the Attendance of absent Members, in such Manner, and under such Penalties as each House may provide.

Each House may determine the Rules of its Proceedings, punish its Members for disorderly Behavior, and, with the Concurrence of two thirds, expel a Member.

Each House shall keep a Journal of its Procedings, and from time to time publish the same, excepting such Parts as may in their Judgment require Secrecy; and the Yeas and Nays of the Members of either House on any question shall, at the Desire of one fifth of those Present, be entered on the Journal.

Neither House, during the Session of Congress, shall, without the Consent of the other, adjourn for more than three days, nor to any other Place than that in which the two Houses shall be sitting.

Section 6. The Senators and Representatives shall receive a Compensation for their Services, to be ascertained by Law, and paid out of the Treasury of the United States. They shall in all Cases, except Treason, Felony and Breach of the Peace, be privileged from Arrest during their Attendance at the Session of their respective Houses, and in going to and returning from the same; and for any Speech or Debate in either House, they shall not be questioned in any other Place.

No Senator or Representative shall, during the Time for which he was elected, be appointed to any civil Office under the Authority of the United States, which shall have been created, or the Emoluments whereof shall have been encreased during such time; and no Person holding any Office under the United States, shall be a Member of either House during his Continuance in Office.

Section 7. All Bills for raising Revenue shall originate in the House of Representatives; but the Senate may propose or concur with Amendments as on other Bills.

Every Bill which shall have passed the House of Representatives and the Senate, shall, before it become a Law, be presented to the President of the United States; If he approve he shall sign it, but if not he shall return it, with his Objections to that House in which it shall have originated, who shall enter the Objections at large on their Journal, and proceed to reconsider it. If after such Reconsideration two thirds of that House shall agree to pass the Bill, it shall be sent, together with the Objections, to the other House, by which it shall likewise be reconsidered, and if approved by two thirds of that House, it shall become a Law. But in all such Cases the Votes of both Houses shall be determined by Yeas and Nays, and the Names of the Persons voting for and against the Bill shall be entered on the Journal of each House respectively. If any Bill shall not be returned by the President within ten Days (Sundays excepted) after it shall have been presented to him, the Same shall be a Law, in like Manner as if he had signed it, unless the Congress by their Adjournment prevent its Return, in which Case it shall not be a Law.

Every Order, Resolution, or Vote to which the Concurrence of the Senate and House of

Representatives may be necessary (except on a question of Adjournment) shall be presented to the President of the United States; and before the Same shall take Effect, shall be approved by him, or being disapproved by him, shall be repassed by two thirds of the Senate and House of Representatives, according to the Rules and Limitations prescribed in the Case of a Bill.

SECTION 8. The Congress shall have Power To lay and collect Taxes, Duties, Imposts and Excises, to pay the Debts and provide for the common Defence and general Welfare of the United States; but all Duties, Imposts and Excises shall be uniform throughout the United States;

To borrow money on the credit of the United States;

To regulate Commerce with foreign Nations, and among the several States, and with the Indian Tribes;

To establish an uniform Rule of Naturalization, and uniform Laws on the subject of Bankruptcies throughout the United States;

To coin Money, regulate the Value thereof, and of foreign Coin, and fix the Standard of Weights and Measures;

To provide for the Punishment of counterfeiting the Securities and current Coin of the United States;

To establish Post Offices and post Roads;

To promote the Progress of Science and useful Arts, by securing for limited Times to Authors and Inventors the exclusive Right to their respective Writings and Discoveries;

To constitute Tribunals inferior to the supreme Court;

To define and punish Piracies and Felonies committed on the high Seas, and Offenses against the Law of Nations;

To declare War, grant Letters of Marque and Reprisal, and make Rules concerning Captures on Land and Water;

To raise and support Armies, but no Appropriation of Money to that Use shall be for a longer Term than two Years;

To provide and maintain a Navy;

To make Rules for the Government and Regulation of the land and naval Forces;

To provide for calling forth the Militia to execute the Laws of the Union, suppress Insurrections and repel Invasions;

To provide for organizing, arming, and disciplining the Militia, and for governing such Part of them as may be employed in the Service of the United States, reserving to the States respectively, the Appointment of the Officers, and the Authority of training the Militia according to the discipline prescribed by Congress;

To exercise exclusive Legislation in all Cases whatsoever, over such District (not exceeding ten Miles square) as may, by Cession of particular States, and the acceptance of Congress, become the Seat of the Government of the United States, and to exercise like Authority over all Places purchased by the Consent of the Legislature of the State in which the Same shall be, for the Erection of Forts, Magazines, Arsenals, dock-Yards, and other needful Buildings;—And

To make all Laws which shall be necessary and proper for carrying into Execution the foregoing Powers, and all other Powers vested by this Constitution in the Government of the United States, or in any Department or Officer thereof.

SECTION 9. The Migration or Importation of such Persons as any of the States now existing shall think proper to admit, shall not be prohibited by the Congress prior to the Year one thousand eight hundred and eight, but a tax or duty may be imposed on such Importation, not exceeding ten dollars for each Person.

The privilege of the Writ of Habeas Corpus shall not be suspended, unless when in Cases of Rebellion or Invasion the public Safety may require it.

No Bill of Attainder or ex post facto Law shall be passed.

No capitation, or other direct, Tax shall be laid, unless in Proportion to the Census or Enumeration herein before directed to be taken.

No Tax or Duty shall be laid on Articles exported from any State.

No Preference shall be given by any Regulation of Commerce or Revenue to the Ports of one State over those of another: nor shall Vessels bound to, or from, one State, be obliged to enter, clear, or pay Duties in another.

No Money shall be drawn from the Treasury, but in Consequence of Appropriations made by Law; and a regular Statement and Account of the Receipts and Expenditures of all public Money shall be published from time to time.

No Title of Nobility shall be granted by the United States: And no Person holding any Office of Profit or Trust under them, shall, without the Consent of the Congress, accept of any present, Emolument, Office, or Title, of any kind whatever, from any King, Prince, or foreign State.

SECTION 10. No State shall enter into any Treaty, Alliance, or Confederation; grant Letters of Marque and Reprisal; coin Money; emit Bills of Credit; make any Thing but gold and silver Coin a Tender in Payment of Debts; pass any Bill of Attainder, ex post facto Law, or Law impairing the Obligation of Contracts, or grant any Title of Nobility.

No State shall, without the Consent of the Congress, lay any Imposts or Duties on Imports or Exports, except what may be absolutely necessary for executing it's inspection Laws: and the net Produce of all Duties and Imposts, laid by any State on Imports or Exports, shall be for the Use of the Treasury of the United States; and all such Laws shall be subject to the Revision and Controul of the Congress.

No State shall, without the Consent of Congress, lay any duty of Tonnage, keep Troops, or Ships of War in time of Peace, enter into any Agreement or Compact with another State, or with a foreign Power, or engage in War, unless actually invaded, or in such imminent Danger as will not admit of delay.

ARTICLE II.

SECTION 1. The executive Power shall be vested in a President of the United States of America. He shall hold his Office during the Term of four Years, and, together with the Vice-President, chosen for the same Term, be elected, as follows

Each State shall appoint, in such Manner as the Legislature thereof may direct, a Number of Electors, equal to the whole Number of Senators and Representatives to which the State may be entitled in the Congress: but no Senator or Representative, or Person holding an Office of Trust or Profit under the United States, shall be appointed an Elector.

[The Electors shall meet in their respective States, and vote by Ballot for two persons, of whom one at least shall not be an Inhabitant of the same State with themselves. And they shall make a List of all the Persons voted for, and of the Number of Votes for each; which List they shall sign and certify, and transmit sealed to the Seat of the Government of the United States, directed to the President of the Senate. The President of the Senate shall, in the Presence of the Senate and House of Representatives, open all the Certificates, and the Votes shall then be counted. The Person having the greatest Number of Votes shall be the President, if such Number be a Majority of the whole Number of Electors appointed; and if there be more than one who have such Majority, and have an equal Number of Votes, then the House of Representatives shall immediately chuse by Ballot one of them for President; and if no Person have a Majority, then from the five highest on the List the said House shall in like Manner chuse the President. But in chusing the President, the Votes shall be taken by States, the Representation from each State having one Vote; A quorum for this Purpose shall consist of a Member or Members from two-thirds of the States, and a Majority of all the States shall be necessary to a Choice. In every Case, after the Choice of the President, the Person having the greatest Number of Votes of the Electors shall be the Vice President. But if there should remain two or more who have equal Votes, the Senate shall chuse from them by Ballot the Vice President.]

The Congress may determine the Time of chusing the Electors, and the Day on which they shall give their Votes; which Day shall be the same throughout the United States.

No person except a natural born Citizen, or a Citizen of the United States, at the time of the Adoption of this Constitution, shall be eligible to the Office of President; neither shall any Person be eligible to that Office who shall not have attained to the Age of thirty-five Years, and been fourteen Years a Resident within the United States.

In Case of the Removal of the President from Office, or of his Death, Resignation, or Inability to discharge the Powers and Duties of the said Office, the same shall devolve on the Vice President, and the Congress may by Law provide for the Case of Removal, Death, Resignation or Inability, both of the President and Vice President, declaring what Officer shall then act as President, and such Officer shall act accordingly, until the Disability be removed, or a President shall be elected.

The President shall, at stated Times, receive for his Services, a Compensation, which shall neither be encreased nor diminished during the Period for which he shall have been elected, and he shall not receive within that Period any other Emolument from the United States, or any of them.

Before he enter on the Execution of his Office, he shall take the following Oath or Affirmation:—"I do solemnly swear (or affirm) that I will faithfully execute the Office of President of the United States, and will to the best of my Ability, preserve, protect and defend the Constitution of the United States."

SECTION 2. The President shall be Commander in Chief of the Army and Navy of the United States, and of the Militia of the several States, when called into the actual Service of the United States; he may require the Opinion in writing, of the principal Officer in each of the executive Departments, upon any subject relating to the Duties of their respective Offices, and he shall have Power to Grant Reprieves and Pardons for Offenses against the United States, except in Cases of Impeachment.

He shall have Power, by and with the Advice and Consent of the Senate, to make Treaties, provided two-thirds of the Senators present concur; and he shall nominate, and by and with the Advice and Consent of the Senate, shall appoint Ambassadors, other public Ministers and Consuls, Judges of the supreme Court, and all other Officers of the United States, whose Appointments are not herein otherwise provided for, and which shall be established by Law: but the Congress may by Law vest the Appointment of such inferior Officers, as they think proper, in the President alone, in the Courts of Law, or in the Heads of Departments.

The President shall have Power to fill up all Vacancies that may happen during the Recess of the Senate, by granting Commissions which shall expire at the End of their next Session.

SECTION 3. He shall from time to time give to the Congress Information of the State of the Union, and recommend to their Consideration such Measures as he shall judge necessary and expedient; he may, on ex-

traordinary Occasions, convene both Houses, or either of them, and in Case of Disagreement between them, with Respect to the Time of Adjournment, he may adjourn them to such Time as he shall think proper; he shall receive Ambassadors and other public Ministers; he shall take Care that the Laws be faithfully executed, and shall Commission all the Officers of the United States.

SECTION 4. The President, Vice President and all civil Officers of the United States, shall be removed from Office on Impeachment for, and Conviction of, Treason, Bribery, or other high Crimes and Misdemeanors.

ARTICLE III.

SECTION 1. The judicial Power of the United States, shall be vested in one supreme Court, and in such inferior Courts as the Congress may from time to time ordain and establish. The Judges, both of the supreme and inferior Courts, shall hold their Offices during good Behaviour, and shall, at stated Times, receive for their Services a Compensation which shall not be diminished during their Continuance in Office.

SECTION 2. The judicial Power shall extend to all Cases, in Law and Equity, arising under this Constitution, the Laws of the United States, and Treaties made, or which shall be made, under their Authority;—to all Cases affecting Ambassadors, other public Ministers and Consuls;—to all Cases of admiralty and maritime Jurisdiction;—to Controversies to which the United States shall be a Party;—to Controversies between two or more States;—between a State and Citizens of another State;—between Citizens of different States;—between Citizens of the same State claiming Lands under Grants of different States, and between a State, or the Citizens thereof, and foreign States, Citizens or Subjects.

In all Cases affecting Ambassadors, other public Ministers and Consuls, and those in which a State shall be Party, the supreme Court shall have original Jurisdiction. In all the other Cases before mentioned, the supreme Court shall have appellate Jurisdiction, both as to Law and Fact, with such Exceptions, and under such Regulations as the Congress shall make.

The trial of all Crimes, except in Cases of

Impeachment, shall be by Jury; and such Trial shall be held in the State where the said Crimes shall have been committed; but when not committed within any State, the Trial shall be at such Place or Places as the Congress may by Law have directed.

SECTION 3. Treason against the United States, shall consist only. in levying War against them, or in adhering to their Enemies, giving them Aid and Comfort. No Person shall be convicted of Treason unless on the Testimony of two Witnesses to the same overt Act, or on Confession in open Court.

The Congress shall have power to declare the Punishment of Treason, but no Attainder of Treason shall work Corruption of Blood, or Forfeiture except during the Life of the Person attainted.

ARTICLE IV.

SECTION 1. Full Faith and Credit shall be given in each State to the public Acts, Records, and judicial Proceedings of every other State. And the Congress may by general Laws prescribe the Manner in which such Acts, Records and Proceedings shall be proved, and the Effect thereof.

SECTION 2. The Citizens of each State shall be entitled to all Privileges and Immunities of Citizens in the several States.

A Person charged in any State with Treason, Felony, or other Crime, who shall flee from Justice, and be found in another State, shall on demand of the executive Authority of the State from which he fled, be delivered up, to be removed to the State having Jurisdiction of the Crime.

No Person held to Service or Labour in one State, under the Laws thereof, escaping into another, shall, in Consequence of any Law or Regulation therein, be discharged from such Service or Labour, but shall be delivered up on Claim of the Party to whom such Service or Labour may be due.

SECTION 3. New States may be admitted by the Congress into this Union; but no new State shall be formed or erected within the Jurisdiction of any other State; nor any State be formed by the Junction of two or more States, or parts of States, without the Consent of the Legislatures of the States concerned as well as of the Congress.

The Congress shall have Power to dispose of and make all needful Rules and Regulations respecting the Territory or other Property belonging to the United States; and nothing in this Constitution shall be so construed as to Prejudice any Claims of the United States, or of any particular State.

SECTION 4. The United States shall guarantee to every State in this Union a Republican Form of Government, and shall protect each of them against Invasion; and on Application of the Legislature, or of the Executive (when the Legislature cannot be convened) against domestic Violence.

ARTICLE V.

The Congress, whenever two-thirds of both Houses shall deem it necessary, shall propose Amendments to this Constitution, or, on the Application of the Legislatures of two-thirds of the several States, shall call a Convention for proposing Amendments, which, in either Case, shall be valid to all Intents and Purposes, as part of this Constitution, when ratified by the Legislatures of three-fourths of the several States, or by Conventions in three-fourths thereof, as the one or the other Mode of Ratification may be proposed by the Congress; Provided that no Amendment which may be made prior to the Year One thousand eight hundred and eight shall in any Manner affect the first and fourth Clauses in the Ninth Section of the first Article; and that no State, without its Consent, shall be deprived of it's equal Suffrage in the Senate.

ARTICLE VI.

All Debts contracted and Engagements entered into, before the Adoption of this Constitution, shall be as valid against the United States under this Constitution, as under the Confederation.

This Constitution, and the Laws of the United States which shall be made in Pursuance thereof; and all Treaties made, or which shall be made, under the Authority of the United States, shall be the supreme Law of the Land; and the Judges in every State shall be bound thereby, any Thing in the Constitution or Laws of any State to the Contrary notwithstanding.

The Senators and Representatives before

mentioned, and the Members of the several State Legislatures, and all executive and judicial Officers, both of the United States and of the several States, shall be bound by Oath or Affirmation, to support this Constitution; but no religious Test shall ever be required as a Qualification to any Office or public Trust under the United States.

ARTICLE VII.

The Ratification of the Conventions of nine States shall be sufficient for the Establishment of this Constitution between the States so ratifying the Same.

DONE in Convention by the Unanimous Consent of the States present the Seventeenth Day of September in the Year of our Lord one thousand seven hundred and Eighty seven and of the Independence of the United States of America the Twelfth. In Witness whereof We have hereunto subscribed our Names.

G̲o̲ WASHINGTON
Presidt and deputy from Virginia

New Hampshire.
JOHN LANGDON
NICHOLAS GILMAN

Massachusetts.
NATHANIEL GORHAM
RUFUS KING

Connecticut.
WM SAML JOHNSON
ROGER SHERMAN

New York.
ALEXANDER HAMILTON

New Jersey.
WIL: LIVINGSTON
DAVID BREARLEY.
WM PATERSON
JONA: DAYTON

Pennsylvania.
B. FRANKLIN
ROBT. MORRIS

THOS. FITZSIMONS
JAMES WILSON
THOMAS MIFFLIN
GEO. CLYMER
JARED INGERSOLL
GOUV MORRIS

Delaware.
GEO: READ
JOHN DICKINSON
JACO: BROOM
GUNNING BEDFORD jun
RICHARD BASSETT

Maryland.
JAMES McHENRY
DANL CARROLL
DAN: of ST THOS JENIFER

Virginia.
JOHN BLAIR—
JAMES MADISON Jr.

North Carolina.
WM BLOUNT
HU WILLIAMSON
RICHD DOBBS SPAIGHT,

South Carolina.
J. RUTLEDGE
CHARLES PINCKNEY
CHARLES COTESWORTH PINCKNEY
PIERCE BUTLER

Georgia.
WILLIAM FEW
ABR BALDWIN

Attest:
WILLIAM JACKSON, *Secretary.*

ARTICLES IN ADDITION To, AND AMENDMENT OF, THE CONSTITUTION OF THE UNITED STATES OF AMERICA, PROPOSED BY CONGRESS, AND RATIFIED BY THE LEGISLATURES OF THE SEVERAL STATES, PURSUANT TO THE FIFTH ARTICLE OF THE ORIGINAL CONSTITUTION.

[ARTICLE I.] [1]

Congress shall make no law respecting an establishment of religion, or prohibiting the

---

[1] The first ten Amendments were adopted in 1791.

free exercise thereof; or abridging the freedom of speech, or of the press; or the right of the people peaceably to assemble, and to petition the Government for a redress of grievances.

[ARTICLE II.]

A well regulated Militia, being necessary to the security of a free State, the right of the people to keep and bear Arms, shall not be infringed.

[ARTICLE III.]

No Soldier shall, in time of peace be quartered in any house, without the consent of the Owner, nor in time of war, but in a manner to be prescribed by law.

[ARTICLE IV.]

The right of the people to be secure in their persons, houses, papers, and effects, against unreasonable searches and seizures, shall not be violated, and no Warrants shall issue, but upon probable cause, supported by Oath or affirmation, and particularly describing the place to be searched, and the persons or things to be seized.

[ARTICLE V.]

No person shall be held to answer for a capital, or otherwise infamous crime, unless on a presentment or indictment of a Grand Jury, except in cases arising in the land or naval forces, or in the Militia, when in actual service in time of War or public danger; nor shall any person be subject for the same offence to be twice put in jeopardy of life or limb; nor shall be compelled in any criminal case to be a witness against himself, nor be deprived of life, liberty, or property, without due process of law; nor shall private property be taken for public use, without just compensation.

[ARTICLE VI.]

In all criminal prosecutions, the accused shall enjoy the right to a speedy and public trial, by an impartial jury of the State and district wherein the crime shall have been committed, which district shall have been

previously ascertained by law, and to be informed of the nature and cause of the accusation; to be confronted with the witnesses against him; to have compulsory process for obtaining witnesses in his favor, and to have the Assistance of Counsel for his defence.

[ARTICLE VII.]

In suits at common law, where the value in controversy shall exceed twenty dollars, the right of trial by jury shall be preserved, and no fact tried by a jury, shall be otherwise reexamined in any Court of the United States, than according to the rules of the common law.

[ARTICLE VIII.]

Excessive bail shall not be required, nor excessive fines imposed, nor cruel and unusual punishments inflicted.

[ARTICLE IX.]

The enumeration in the Constitution, of certain rights, shall not be construed to deny or disparage others retained by the people.

[ARTICLE X.]

The powers not delegated to the United States by the Constitution, nor prohibited by it to the States, are reserved to the States respectively, or to the people.

ARTICLE XI.[2]

The Judicial power of the United States shall not be construed to extend to any suit in law or equity, commenced or prosecuted against one of the United States by Citizens of another State, or by Citizens or Subjects of any Foreign State.

ARTICLE XII.[3]

The Electors shall meet in their respective states and vote by ballot for President and Vice-President, one of whom, at least, shall not be an inhabitant of the same state with themselves; they shall name in their ballots the person voted for as President, and in dis-

[2] Adopted, 1798.

[3] Adopted, 1804.

tinct ballots the person voted for as Vice-President, and they shall make distinct lists of all persons voted for as President, and of all persons voted for as Vice-President, and of the number of votes for each, which lists they shall sign and certify, and transmit sealed to the seat of the government of the United States, directed to the President of the Senate;—The President of the Senate shall, in presence of the Senate and House of Representatives, open all the certificates and the votes shall then be counted;—The person having the greatest number of votes for President, shall be the President, if such number be a majority of the whole number of Electors appointed; and if no person have such majority, then from the persons having the highest numbers not exceeding three on the list of those voted for as President, the House of Representatives shall choose immediately, by ballot, the President. But in choosing the President, the votes shall be taken by states, the representation from each state having one vote; a quorum for this purpose shall consist of a member or members from two-thirds of the states, and a majority of all the states shall be necessary to a choice. And if the House of Representatives shall not choose a President whenever the right of choice shall devolve upon them, before the fourth day of March next following, then the Vice-President shall act as President, as in the case of the death or other constitutional disability of the President.—The person having the greatest number of votes as Vice-President, shall be the Vice-President, if such number be a majority of the whole number of Electors appointed, and if no person have a majority, then from the two highest numbers on the list, the Senate shall choose the Vice-President; a quorum for the purpose shall consist of two-thirds of the whole number of Senators, and a majority of the whole number shall be necessary to a choice. But no person constitutionally ineligible to the office of President shall be eligible to that of Vice-President of the United States.

ARTICLE XIII.[4]

SECTION 1. Neither slavery nor involuntary servitude, except as a punishment for crime

[4] Adopted, 1865.

whereof the party shall have been duly convicted, shall exist within the United States, or any place subject to their jurisdiction.

SECTION 2. Congress shall have power to enforce this article by appropriate legislation.

ARTICLE XIV.[5]

SECTION 1. All persons born or naturalized in the United States, and subject to the jurisdiction thereof, are citizens of the United States and of the State wherein they reside. No State shall make or enforce any law which shall abridge the privileges or immunities of citizens of the United States; nor shall any State deprive any person of life, liberty, or property, without due process of law; nor deny to any person within its jurisdiction the equal protection of the laws.

SECTION 2. Representatives shall be apportioned among the several States according to their respective numbers, counting the whole number of persons in each State, excluding Indians not taxed. But when the right to vote at any election for the choice of electors for President and Vice-President of the United States, Representatives in Congress, the Executive and Judicial officers of a State, or the members of the Legislature thereof, is denied to any of the male inhabitants of such State, being twenty-one years of age, and citizens of the United States, or in any way abridged, except for participation in rebellion, or other crime, the basis of representation therein shall be reduced in the proportion which the number of such male citizens shall bear to the whole number of male citizens twenty-one years of age in such State.

SECTION 3. No person shall be a Senator or Representative in Congress, or elector of President and Vice-President, or hold any office, civil or military, under the United States, or under any State, who, having previously taken an oath, as a member of Congress, or as an officer of the United States, or as a member of any State legislature, or as an executive or judicial officer of any State, to support the Constitution of the United States, shall have engaged in insurrection or rebellion against the same, or given aid or comfort to the enemies thereof. But Congress

[5] Adopted, 1868.

may by a vote of two-thirds of each House, remove such disability.

SECTION 4. The validity of the public debt of the United States, authorized by law, including debts incurred for payment of pensions and bounties for services in suppressing insurrection or rebellion, shall not be questioned. But neither the United States nor any State shall assume or pay any debt or obligation incurred in aid of insurrection or rebellion against the United States, or any claim for the loss or emancipation of any slave; but all such debts, obligations and claims shall be held illegal and void.

SECTION 5. The Congress shall have power to enforce, by appropriate legislation, the provisions of this article.

ARTICLE XV.[6]

SECTION I. The right of citizens of the United States to vote shall not be denied or abridged by the United States or by any State on account of race, color, or previous condition of servitude—

SECTION 2. The Congress shall have power to enforce this article by appropriate legislation.

ARTICLE XVI.[7]

The Congress shall have power to lay and collect taxes on incomes, from whatever source derived, without apportionment among the several States, and without regard to any census or enumeration.

ARTICLE XVII.[8]

The Senate of the United States shall be composed of two Senators from each State, elected by the people thereof, for six years; and each Senator shall have one vote. The electors in each State shall have the qualifications requisite for electors of the most numerous branch of the State legislatures.

When vacancies happen in the representation of any State in the Senate, the executive authority of such State shall issue writs of election to fill such vacancies: *Provided,* That the legislature of any State may empower the executive thereof to make temporary appointments until the people fill the vacancies by election as the legislature may direct.

This amendment shall not be so construed as to affect the election or term of any Senator chosen before it becomes valid as part of the Constitution.

ARTICLE XVIII.[9]

SECTION I. After one year from the ratification of this article the manufacture, sale, or transportation of intoxicating liquors within, the importation thereof into, or the exportation thereof from the United States and all territory subject to the jurisdiction thereof for beverage purposes is hereby prohibited.

SECTION 2. The Congress and the several States shall have concurrent power to enforce this article by appropriate legislation.

SECTION 3. This article shall be inoperative unless it shall have been ratified as an amendment to the Constitution by the legislatures of the several States, as provided in the Constitution, within seven years from the date of the submission hereof to the States by the Congress.

ARTICLE XIX.[10]

The right of citizens of the United States to vote shall not be denied or abridged by the United States or by any State on account of sex.

Congress shall have power to enforce this article by appropriate legislation.

ARTICLE XX.[11]

SECTION I. The terms of the President and Vice President shall end at noon on the 20th day of January, and the terms of Senators and Representatives at noon on the 3d day of January, of the years in which such terms would have ended if this article had not been ratified; and the terms of their successors shall then begin.

SECTION 2. The Congress shall assemble at least once in every year, and such meeting shall begin at noon on the 3d day of January, unless they shall by law appoint a different day.

[6] Adopted, 1870.
[7] Adopted, 1913.
[8] Adopted, 1913.
[9] Adopted, 1919.
[10] Adopted, 1920.
[11] Adopted, 1933.

SECTION 3. If, at the time fixed for the beginning of the term of the President, the President elect shall have died, the Vice President elect shall become President. If a President shall not have been chosen before the time fixed for the beginning of his term, or if the President elect shall have failed to qualify, then the Vice President elect shall act as President until a President shall have qualified; and the Congress may by law provide for the case wherein neither a President elect nor a Vice President elect shall have qualified, declaring who shall then act as President, or the manner in which one who is to act shall be selected, and such person shall act accordingly until a President or Vice President shall have qualified.

SECTION 4. The Congress may by law provide for the case of the death of any of the persons from whom the House of Representatives may choose a President whenever the right of choice shall have devolved upon them, and for the case of the death of any of the persons from whom the Senate may choose a Vice President whenever the right of choice shall have devolved upon them.

[12] Adopted, 1933.

SECTION 5. Sections 1 and 2 shall take effect on the 15th day of October following the ratification of this article.

SECTION 6. This article shall be inoperative unless it shall have been ratified as an amendment to the Constitution by the legislatures of three-fourths of the several States within seven years from the date of its submission.

ARTICLE XXI.[12]

SECTION 1. The eighteenth article of amendment to the Constitution of the United States is hereby repealed.

SECTION 2. The transportation or importation into any State, Territory, or possession of the United States for delivery or use therein of intoxicating liquors, in violation of the laws thereof, is hereby prohibited.

SECTION 3. This article shall be inoperative unless it shall have been ratified as an amendment to the Constitution by conventions in the several States, as provided in the Constitution, within seven years from the date of the submission hereof to the States by the Congress.